SOUTH HOLLAND PUBLIC LIBRARY

3 1350 00297 0186

W9-BYH-115

FBI

CAREERS

The Ultimate Guide to Landing a Job as One of America's Finest

Third Edition

Thomas H. Ackerman

JIST
Works
America's Career Publisher®

SOUTH HOLLAND PUBLIC LIBRARY

DISCARD

DISCARD

FBI Careers, Third Edition

© 2010 by Thomas H. Ackerman

Published by JIST Works, an imprint of JIST Publishing
7321 Shadeland Station, Suite 200
Indianapolis, IN 46256-3923
Phone: 800-648-JIST   Fax: 877-454-7839   E-mail: info@jist.com

Visit our Web site at **www.jist.com** for information on JIST, free job search tips, tables of contents, sample pages, and ordering instructions for our many products!

Quantity discounts are available for JIST books. Please call our Sales Department at 800-648-5478 for a free catalog and more information.

Trade Product Manager: Lori Cates Hand
Interior Designer and Page Layout: Aleata Halbig
Cover Designer: Honeymoon Image and Design
Proofreaders: Paula Lowell, Jeanne Clark
Indexer: Jeanne Clark

Printed in the United States of America
14 13 12 11 10 09   9 8 7 6 5 4 3 2 1

Library of Congress Cataloging-in-Publication Data

Ackerman, Thomas H.
  FBI careers : the ultimate guide to landing a job as one of America's finest / Thomas H. Ackerman. -- 3rd ed.
     p. cm.
  Includes index.
  ISBN 978-1-59357-730-8 (alk. paper)
  1. United States. Federal Bureau of Investigation--Vocational guidance. 2. United States. Federal Bureau of Investigation--Officials and employees--Recruiting. I. United States. Federal Bureau of Investigation. II. Title.
  HV8144.F43A25 2010
  363.25023'73--dc22

DISCARD

3 1350 00297 0186

2009038881

All rights reserved. No part of this book may be reproduced in any form or by any means, or stored in a database or retrieval system, without prior written permission of the publisher except in the case of brief quotations embodied in articles or reviews. Making copies of any part of this book for any purpose other than your own personal use is a violation of United States copyright laws. For permission requests, please contact the Copyright Clearance Center at www.copyright.com or (978) 750-8400.

We have been careful to provide accurate information in this book, but it is possible that errors and omissions have been introduced. Please consider this in making any career plans or other important decisions. Trust your own judgment above all else and in all things.

Trademarks: All brand names and product names used in this book are trade names, service marks, trademarks, or registered trademarks of their respective owners.

ISBN 978-1-59357-730-8

ABOUT THIS BOOK

The Federal Bureau of Investigation is one of the most sophisticated and well-respected organizations in the world. Since its formation in 1908, the FBI has protected the American people from enemies both domestic and foreign, while honoring and defending the Constitution and the rule of law. Over the years, "the Bureau" has placed a top priority on fighting threats to America's national security posed by terrorists and spies, while also combating organized crime, drug trafficking, white-collar crime, violent crime, and crimes against children. Although the FBI is known worldwide for being on the cutting edge of law enforcement technology and for using state-of-the-art equipment to fight crime, nothing is more important to the success of the Bureau than its most important resource—its employees. Simply stated, the 32,000 men and women of the FBI who serve as special agents and in professional support positions make the nation a better place for all of us—and there is no higher calling.

If the FBI sounds like the kind of organization you would like to make a career with, this book is for you. The Bureau's special agents and support personnel are given the best training possible and the opportunity to serve with a law enforcement agency that is unlike any other. To land a position with the FBI, you must be armed with accurate and up-to-date information. *FBI Careers* will guide you step by step through the rigorous selection process, including complete details on the positions, how to apply, and what to expect along the way. Whether you're interested in serving as a special agent, biologist, computer specialist, electronics technician, or photographer, or in another area of expertise, this book will provide you with an overview of the positions, the qualification requirements, and the training you can expect to receive. Most importantly, *FBI Careers* presents specific guidance on filling out application forms, improving your test score, making a good impression during interviews, and many other strategies you can use to stand out from the crowd and get hired—even if your goal is to get a foot in the door by serving in an FBI internship.

It is widely known that competition for careers in the FBI is intense, regardless of the position. In order to succeed in your quest to join the ranks of the Bureau, you must carefully identify the steps you will need to take. The first step is to obtain an authoritative source of information that provides expert advice. The next step is to carefully chart a course to success. *FBI Careers* will provide you with the information and expert guidance you'll need to navigate your way to a career as one of America's finest!

Dedication

In memory of Dixie, my mother,
who taught me the meaning of justice
—and to fight for it.

Contents

PART 1

FBI BASICS

CHAPTER 1

The History and Organization of the FBI

"Leadership is the art of accomplishing more than the science of management says is possible."

—Colin Powell

From its roots as the *Bureau of Investigation* in the early 1900s, the FBI has evolved from a force of 34 unarmed detectives to one of the most sophisticated and respected law enforcement organizations in the world. The Bureau now employs more than 32,000 personnel, including almost 14,000 special agents, and serves as the principal investigative arm of the United States Department of Justice. In addition to conducting investigations, the Bureau offers cooperative services such as fingerprint identification, laboratory examination, police training, and the National Crime Information Center to duly authorized law enforcement agencies. Today's FBI is headed by a director, who is appointed by the president and confirmed by the senate for a term not to exceed 10 years. The Bureau has an annual budget of more than $5 billion.

The mission of the FBI is "to protect and defend the United States against terrorist and foreign intelligence threats; to uphold and enforce the criminal laws of the United States; and to provide leadership and criminal justice services to federal, state, municipal, and international agencies and partners."

Fulfillment of this mission requires a professional, skilled, and highly trained workforce to address a wide variety of challenges in an ever-changing environment.

The History of the FBI

The FBI originated from a force of special agents created in 1908 by Attorney General Charles Bonaparte during the presidency of Theodore Roosevelt. The two men first met years earlier, in 1892, when they spoke at a meeting of the Baltimore Civil Service Reform Association. Roosevelt, then United States Civil Service Commissioner, boasted of his reforms in federal law enforcement and his efforts to eliminate conflicts of interest in civil service hiring processes.

Roosevelt spoke with pride of his insistence that Border Patrol applicants pass marksmanship tests, with the most accurate getting the jobs. Following Roosevelt on the program, Bonaparte responded, tongue in cheek, that target shooting was not the way to select the best-qualified people, and announced an alternative plan: "Roosevelt should have had the men shoot at each other, and given the jobs to the survivors," he declared.

Roosevelt and Bonaparte did share the conviction that competence, not political connections, should determine who could best serve in government. Roosevelt became President of the United States in 1901 and appointed Bonaparte as Attorney General in 1905. Three years later, on July 26, 1908, Stanley W. Finch was hired to manage an investigative unit of 34 special agents within the Justice Department. Finch's new investigative team consisted of former United States Secret Service agents and detectives. Both Bonaparte and Roosevelt, who completed their terms in March 1909, recommended that the agents become a permanent part of the Department of Justice. Attorney General George Wickersham, Bonaparte's successor, named the force the Bureau of Investigation on March 16, 1909.

Early Expansion of the Bureau

When the Bureau was established, there were few federal crimes on the books. The Bureau of Investigation primarily investigated violations of laws involving national banking, bankruptcy, naturalization, antitrust, peonage, and land fraud. Because the early Bureau provided no formal training, previous law enforcement experience or a background in the law was quite beneficial.

The first major expansion of the Bureau's jurisdiction occurred in June 1910, when the Mann Act was passed. Known also as the "White Slavery Act," this law made it a crime to transport women over state lines for immoral purposes. It also provided a tool by which the federal government could investigate criminals who evaded state laws but committed no other federal violations. Finch became Commissioner of White Slavery Act Violations in 1912, and former Special Examiner A. Bruce Bielaski became the new Bureau of Investigation Chief.

Over the next few years, the number of special agents grew to more than 300, complemented by another 300 support employees. Field offices existed from the Bureau's inception. Each field operation was controlled by a special agent in charge, who was responsible to Washington. Most field offices were located in major cities. However, several were located near the Mexican border, where they concentrated on smuggling, neutrality violations, and intelligence collection, often in connection with the Mexican Revolution.

During World War I, the Bureau's mission was broadened as the agency acquired responsibility for the Espionage, Selective Service, and Sabotage Acts, and assisted the Department of Labor by investigating enemy aliens. During these years, special agents with general investigative experience and proficiency in certain languages augmented the Bureau. In July 1919, William J. Flynn, former head of the Secret Service, became director of the Bureau and was the first to use that title. Three months later, the National Motor Vehicle Theft Act provided a means to prosecute criminals who previously evaded the law by crossing state lines.

Gangsters and the Prohibition Era

The period from 1920 to 1933 was characterized by gangsterism and the public disregard for Prohibition, the legislation that made it illegal to sell or import alcoholic beverages. This period, sometimes referred to as "the lawless years," created a new federal medium for fighting crime. However, the Department of the Treasury—not the Department of Justice—had jurisdiction over federal alcohol violations. The Bureau had limited success using its narrow jurisdiction to investigate gangsters during this period because its Agents had neither arrest privileges nor the authority to carry firearms. Nonetheless, as a result of investigations involving the Ku Klux Klan, neutrality violations, and antitrust violations, the Bureau of Investigation gained stature.

William J. Burns was appointed director of the Bureau in August 1921. Later that year, Burns appointed 26-year-old J. Edgar Hoover as assistant director. Hoover had served the Department of Justice since 1917 and led the Department's General Intelligence Division, where he investigated suspected anarchists and communists. Hoover was appointed as head of the Bureau in May 1924. At that time, the agency had about 650 employees, including 441 special agents who worked in field offices in nine cities. Over the following six years, the number of field offices grew to 30, with divisional headquarters in New York, Baltimore, Atlanta, Cincinnati, Chicago, Kansas City, San Antonio, San Francisco, and Portland.

In an effort to professionalize the agency, Hoover immediately fired agents he considered unqualified, abolished the seniority rule of promotion, and introduced uniform performance appraisals. He also scheduled regular inspections of the operations in all field offices. In 1928, Hoover established the requirement that applicants for special agent positions had to be between the ages of 25 and 35. He also reaffirmed the Bureau's earlier preference for special agents with law or accounting experience, and established a formal training course for new agents. The following year, 27-year-old Edwin Shanahan became the first FBI Agent to be killed in the line of duty when a car thief in Chicago murdered him.

During the early days of his directorship, Hoover also established the Identification Division in an effort to track criminals by matching their fingerprints. Although many large cities had already started their own fingerprint collections, law enforcement agencies across the country began contributing fingerprint cards to the Bureau in 1926. By the end of the decade, special agent training was institutionalized, the field office inspection system was solidly in place, and the National Division of Identification and Information was collecting and compiling crime statistics for the entire United States. In 1929, after the St. Valentine's Day Massacre occurred in Chicago, the Bureau conducted ballistics tests in the case, leading to the creation of the agency's Technical Laboratory, which would eventually become the FBI Laboratory. Originally, the small laboratory operated only as a research facility, although it eventually added specialized microscopes and extensive reference collections of guns, watermarks, typefaces, and automobile tire designs. These and other advancements gave the Bureau the tools it needed to end the "lawless years."

The Gangster Era Ends and the FBI Is Born

The stock market crash of 1929 and the Great Depression brought widespread unemployment, the collapse of many businesses and financial institutions, and an increase in crime. In response to the crime wave, President Franklin D. Roosevelt influenced Congress to expand federal law enforcement jurisdiction, and his Attorney General fought an unrelenting campaign against rampant crime. At the same time, Hoover utilized the media to publicize the work of the Bureau to the American people. The Bureau of Investigation was renamed the United States Bureau of Investigation in July 1932.

The passage of several pieces of legislation during the early- and mid-1930s significantly enhanced the Bureau's jurisdiction. Responding to the kidnapping of Charles Lindbergh's son in 1932, Congress passed a federal kidnapping statute. Between September 1933 and July 1934, John Dillinger and his violent gang terrorized the Midwest—robbing 11 banks, killing 10 men, and staging three jailbreaks—which earned him the title of "Public Enemy Number One." With gangsters such as Dillinger evading capture by crossing over state lines, Congress made robbery of a federally insured bank and interstate flight federal crimes, and also granted FBI agents statutory authority to carry firearms and make arrests. In July 1934, Bureau agents shot and killed Dillinger during a stakeout on Chicago's near-west side.

In March 1935, the agency changed its name to the Federal Bureau of Investigation. Four months later, the FBI National Academy was established to train police officers in modern investigative methods because at that time only a few states and localities provided formal training to their officers. The National Academy taught investigative techniques to police officials throughout the United States, and starting in the 1940s, to people from all over the world.

The legal tools Congress gave the FBI, as well as Bureau initiatives to upgrade its own professionalism, resulted in the arrest or demise of all major gangsters by 1936. By that time, however, Fascism in Hitler's Germany and Mussolini's Italy and Communism in Stalin's Soviet Union threatened American democratic principles. With war on the horizon, the FBI faced a new set of challenges.

The World War II Period

During the late 1930s, Germany, Italy, and Japan embarked on an unchecked series of invasions. In September 1939, Germany and Soviet Russia seized Poland, and Russia overran the Baltic States a short time later. Great Britain and France declared war on Germany, and World War II began. The United States, however, continued to adhere to the neutrality acts it had passed in the mid-1930s.

Meanwhile, the American depression continued, providing as fertile an environment for radicalism in the United States as it did in Europe. European Fascists had their counterparts and supporters in the United States in the German-American Bund, the Silver Shirts, and similar groups. At the same time, labor unrest, racial disturbances, and sympathy for the Spanish Loyalists presented an unparalleled opportunity for the American Communist Party to recruit supporters. The FBI was alert to these Fascist and Communist groups as threats to American security. Authority to investigate these organizations came in 1936 with President Roosevelt's authorization through Secretary of State Cordell Hull. A 1939 presidential directive further strengthened the FBI's authority to investigate subversives in the United States, and Congress reinforced it by passing the Smith Act in 1940, outlawing advocacy of violent overthrow of the government.

With the outbreak of World War II, the FBI's responsibilities escalated. Subversion, sabotage, and espionage became major concerns in the United States. The FBI responded by placing at least one agent in each of its 42 field offices who was trained in defense plant protection. In addition, the FBI also developed a network of informational sources, often using members of fraternal or veterans' organizations, to investigate potential threats to national security.

After France fell to the Germans in 1940, Great Britain stood virtually alone against the Axis powers. An Axis victory in Europe and Asia would threaten democracy in North America. Because of the Nazi-Soviet Pact, the American Communist Party and its sympathizers posed a double-edged threat to American interests. Under the direction of Russia, the American Communist Party vigorously advocated continued neutrality for the United States. In 1940 and 1941, the United States actively aided the Allies. In late 1940, Congress reestablished the draft, and the FBI was responsible for locating draft evaders and deserters.

After the Germans attacked Russia in June 1941, the FBI focused its internal security efforts on potentially dangerous German, Italian, and Japanese nationals as well as native-born Americans whose beliefs and activities aided the Axis powers. The FBI also participated in intelligence collection, with the Technical Laboratory playing a pioneering role. Lab staff cooperated with engineers, scientists, and cryptographers in other agencies to enable the United States to penetrate and sometimes control the flow of information from the belligerents in the Western Hemisphere.

Prior to the U.S. entry into the war, the FBI uncovered a major espionage ring. This group, the Frederick Duquesne spy ring, was the largest one discovered up to that time. The FBI was assisted by a loyal American with German relatives who acted as a double agent. For 16 months, the FBI ran a short-wave radio station on Long Island for him, learning what Germany was sending to its spies in the United States while controlling the information that was being transmitted to Germany. The investigation led to the arrest and conviction of 33 spies.

The FBI also engaged in sabotage investigations. In June 1942, two German submarines dropped off four saboteurs each in New York and Florida, all of whom had been trained in explosives, chemistry, secret writing, and how to blend into American surroundings. The FBI arrested the saboteurs, which helped to alleviate fear of Axis subversion and bolstered America's faith in the FBI.

On December 7, 1941, immediately after the Japanese attacked Pearl Harbor, Hawaii, the United States declared war on Japan. On that day, the FBI shifted into wartime mode and placed its Headquarters and all field offices on 24-hour schedules. The FBI immediately arrested previously identified aliens who threatened national security and turned them over to military or immigration authorities. On December 8, Germany and Italy declared war on the United States.

The FBI expanded substantially during the war, increasing its agent force from 896 in 1940 to about 4,000 by the end of 1943, and to 4,370 in 1945. During this period, the FBI's focus shifted from apprehending gangsters to investigating saboteurs and spies. In April 1945, Vice President Harry Truman took office as president after the death of President Roosevelt. Before the end of the month, Hitler committed suicide and the German commander in Italy surrendered. Although the May 1945 surrender of Germany ended the war in Europe, war continued in the Pacific until August 14, 1945. Although the war had ended and the world was once more at peace, hanging over the euphoria was a newly realized threat: atomic weaponry.

The Postwar Era

The threat of Communism continued after the war. In 1946, Joseph Stalin gave a public address in which he implied that future wars were inevitable until Communism replaced capitalism worldwide. Events in Europe and North America convinced Congress that Stalin was well on his way to achieving his goal, and Americans feared Communist expansion was not limited to Europe. In June 1945, the FBI raided the offices of *Amerasia,* a magazine concerned with Far Eastern affairs, where agents discovered copies of classified State Department and Navy documents, including some that were labeled "Top Secret." Several months later, Canadian officials arrested 22 people for trying to steal atomic secrets. By 1947, evidence existed that pro-Soviet individuals had infiltrated the American government. Previously, Americans felt secure behind their monopoly of the atomic bomb. Fear of a Russian bomb now came to dominate American thinking. The Soviets detonated their own bomb in 1949.

Counteracting the Communist threat became a paramount focus of government at all levels, as well as the private sector. Any public or private agency or individual with information about subversive activities was urged to report it to the FBI, and a poster to that effect was distributed to police departments nationwide. The FBI's authority to conduct background investigations on present and prospective government employees also expanded dramatically in the postwar years. The 1946 Atomic Energy Act gave the FBI "responsibility for determining the loyalty of individuals having access to restricted Atomic Energy data." Later, executive orders from Presidents Truman and Eisenhower gave the FBI responsibility for investigating allegations of disloyalty among federal employees. Considering that many suspected and convicted spies, such as Julius and Ethel Rosenberg, had been federal employees, background investigations were viewed to be just as vital as cracking major espionage cases. Despite the FBI's focus on subversion and espionage, and the time-consuming nature of background investigations, the Bureau's workforce did not expand until the Korean War in the early 1950s. After the end of the Korean War in 1953, the number of agents stabilized at about 6,200.

The FBI expanded its crime-fighting role in the postwar period through its assistance to state and local law enforcement agencies and increased jurisdictional responsibility. In March 1950, the FBI began its "Ten Most Wanted Fugitives" program to increase law enforcement's ability to capture dangerous fugitives. In addition, advances in forensic science and technical development enabled the FBI to devote a significant proportion of its resources to assisting state and local law enforcement agencies. For example, in the aftermath of the midair explosion of a plane over Colorado in 1955, the FBI Laboratory examined hundreds of airplane parts, pieces of cargo, and the personal effects

SOUTH HOLLAND
PUBLIC LIBRARY
16250 Wausau Avenue
South Holland, IL 60473
(708) 527-3150
www.shlibrary.org
Renew by Phone or Online!

outh Holland Public
ibrary
itle: FBI careers [2002 to
: the ultimate guide
tem ID: 31350002970186
ate due: 7/6/2021,23:59

otal amount saved by
sing your library today:
20.00

of passengers. It pieced together evidence of a bomb explosion from passenger luggage, and then investigated the backgrounds of the 44 victims. Ultimately, agents identified the perpetrator and secured his confession and then turned the case over to Colorado authorities, who successfully prosecuted it in a state court.

Civil-Rights Investigations of the 1960s

In the 1960s, Congress enacted new federal laws that provided the FBI with new tools to fight civil-rights violations, racketeering, gambling, and other offenses. These included the Civil Rights Acts of 1960 and 1964, the Crimes Aboard Aircraft Act of 1961, an expanded Federal Fugitive Act, and the Sports Bribery Act of 1964. Until the 1960s, the FBI had been reluctant to pursue civil-rights violations.

The turning point in federal civil-rights actions occurred in the summer of 1964, after the murders of three voting registration workers in Mississippi who allegedly were killed by members of the Ku Klux Klan. The Department of Justice ordered the FBI to investigate the incident, and the case against the perpetrators took years to proceed through the courts. The FBI arrested 19 suspects in December 1964, and all were indicted on federal civil-rights violations one month later. After a trial was held in 1967, seven of the suspects were found guilty, including both a Klan leader and a Neshoba County sheriff's deputy. The investigation was dramatized in the 1988 movie, *Mississippi Burning.*

Other high-profile civil-rights investigations in the 1960s focused on the 1963 murder of Medger Evers, who served as Mississippi Field Secretary of the NAACP, and the 1968 assassination of Martin Luther King, Jr. The FBI also investigated members of the Ku Klux Klan for the 1965 murder of Viola Liuzzo, a white civil-rights worker from Detroit who was transporting African Americans from Montgomery to Selma, Alabama, after a four-day civil-rights march. After four Klansmen were acquitted on state murder charges, federal prosecutors pursued civil-rights charges against the suspects and three of them were convicted.

The FBI and Organized Crime

Involvement of the FBI in organized crime investigations also was hampered by the lack of federal laws covering crimes perpetrated by racketeers. After Prohibition, many mob activities were carried out locally, or if interstate, they did not constitute major violations within the Bureau's jurisdiction. An impetus for federal legislation occurred in 1957 with the New York State Police's discovery that many of the nation's best-known mobsters had met in upstate New York. The FBI collected information on the individuals who attended the meeting, confirming the existence of a national organized-crime network. Later the FBI persuaded mob insider Joseph Valachi to testify against the mob before a Senate subcommittee. Valachi's testimony provided the public with a firsthand account of *La Cosa Nostra,* the American "Mafia."

On the heels of Valachi's disclosures, Congress passed two new laws to strengthen federal racketeering and gambling statutes to aid the Bureau's fight against mob influence. The Omnibus Crime Control and Safe Streets Act of 1968 provided for the use of court-ordered electronic surveillance in the investigation of certain violations. The Racketeer Influenced and Corrupt Organizations (RICO) statute of 1970 allowed organized groups to be prosecuted for all of their diverse criminal activities, without the crimes being linked by a perpetrator or all-encompassing conspiracy. Along with greater use of agents for undercover work in the 1970s and 1980s, these laws helped the FBI develop cases that put almost all of the leaders of major organized crime families in prison.

By the end of the 1960s, the Bureau employed 6,703 special agents and 9,320 support personnel in 58 field offices and 12 legal attaché offices. A national tragedy produced another expansion of FBI jurisdiction when President Kennedy was assassinated. This crime was considered a local homicide because no federal law addressed the murder of a president. Nevertheless, President Lyndon Johnson tasked the FBI with conducting the investigation, and Congress then passed a new law to ensure that any such act in the future would be a federal crime.

The Vietnam War Era

President Kennedy's assassination introduced a violent aspect of the era of the 1960s, known commonly as the Vietnam War Era. This period, which actually lasted into the mid-1970s, was characterized by idealism, but also by increased urban crime and a propensity for some groups to resort to violence in challenging the "establishment." Many Americans who objected to involvement in Vietnam or to other policies wrote to Congress or carried peace signs in orderly demonstrations. Nevertheless, others resorted to violent means and, in 1970 alone, an estimated 3,000 bombings and 50,000 bomb threats occurred in the United States. The emergence of anti-establishment groups who opposed the Vietnam War—coupled with the convergence of crime, violence, civil-rights issues, and potential national security issues—ensured that the FBI played a significant role during this troubled period.

In May 1970, the FBI investigated the violent events at Kent State University, after the U.S. Army Reserve Officers Training Corps building was destroyed by fire and four students were killed by National Guardsmen during a Vietnam War protest. Four months later, a powerful bomb killed one student and injured others when it exploded at the Army Math Research Center at the University of Wisconsin. By 1971, with few exceptions, the most extreme members of the antiwar movement concentrated on more peaceable yet still radical tactics, such as the clandestine publication of *The Pentagon Papers*. However, the violent Weathermen and its successor groups continued to challenge the FBI into the 1980s.

The Watergate Scandal

FBI Director J. Edgar Hoover died in May 1972, just shy of 48 years as the FBI director. The next day his body lie in state in the rotunda of the capitol, an honor accorded only 21 other Americans. President Nixon appointed L. Patrick Gray as acting director the day after Hoover's death. Six weeks later, five men were arrested photographing documents at the Democratic National Headquarters in the Watergate office building in Washington, D.C., during a break-in that was authorized by Republican Party officials. Within hours, the White House began its effort to cover up its role. The investigation disclosed that the burglars and two conspirators, G. Gordon Liddy and E. Howard Hunt, were linked to Nixon's reelection committee, and that five of the men had ties to the CIA. More than 300 FBI agents undertook an investigation.

In the midst of the Watergate investigation, the Senate Judiciary Committee held hearings for the confirmation of L. Patrick Gray as the permanent FBI director. During the hearings, Gray admitted to providing copies of files relating to the Watergate investigation to John Dean, who served as Nixon's legal counsel, and also to destroying documents related to the break-in that he received from White House staff. The controversy caused Gray to withdraw from consideration as FBI director, and he was replaced hours later by William Ruckleshaus, a former congressman and the first head of the Environmental Protection Agency. Ruckleshaus served as acting director for less than three months, until Clarence Kelley was appointed director in July 1973. Kelley was serving as chief of the Kansas City Police Department when he received the appointment, and had been an FBI agent from 1940 to 1961.

Three days after Kelley's appointment, top aides in the Nixon Administration resigned amid charges of White House efforts to obstruct justice in the Watergate case. Days later, two former members of Nixon's cabinet were indicted by a federal grand jury on charges related to the Watergate cover-up. Vice President Spiro Agnew resigned in October 1973, following charges of tax evasion. Then, following impeachment hearings that were televised to the American public, President Nixon resigned in August 1974. One month after Vice President Gerald Ford was sworn in as president, he granted an unconditional pardon to Nixon and vowed to heal the nation.

The Aftermath of Watergate

Director Kelley also sought to restore public trust in the FBI, and instituted many policy changes that targeted the selection and training of FBI personnel, the procedures of investigative intelligence collection, and the prioritization of investigative programs. Kelley also responded to scrutiny by Congress and the media on whether FBI methods of collecting intelligence in domestic security and counterintelligence investigations abridged Constitutional rights. Kelley's most significant management innovation, however, was implementing the concept of "Quality over Quantity" investigations. He directed each field office to set priorities based on the types of cases most important in its territory, and to concentrate resources on those matters. Under J. Edgar Hoover, the Bureau had followed a quota system for the assignment of investigations in each office. Strengthening Kelley's concept, the FBI also established three national priorities, including foreign counterintelligence, organized crime, and white-collar crime. To address these priorities, the Bureau intensified its recruitment of accountants and expanded its use of undercover operations in major cases.

During Kelley's tenure as director, the FBI made a strong effort to develop an agent force with more women and one that was more reflective of the ethnic composition of the United States. By the late 1970s, nearly 8,000 special agents and 11,000 support employees worked in 59 field offices and 13 legal attaché offices. Kelley resigned in 1978 and was replaced by William Webster, who was serving as judge of the United States Court of Appeals for the Eighth Circuit.

Drugs, Corruption, and Terrorism in the 1980s

Webster's tenure as director was marked by efforts to modernize the FBI. Following a rash of terrorist incidents worldwide, he made counterterrorism a fourth national priority in 1982, and expanded FBI initiatives in the areas of foreign counterintelligence, organized crime, and white-collar crime. Part of this expansion was the creation of the National Center for the Analysis of

Violent Crime at the FBI National Academy in 1984. The FBI solved so many espionage cases during the mid-1980s that the media dubbed 1985 "the year of the spy." The most serious espionage damage uncovered by the Bureau was committed by the John Walker spy ring, and by former National Security Agency employee William Pelton.

The illegal drug trade severely challenged the resources of American law enforcement throughout the 1980s. To ease this challenge, in 1982 the attorney general gave the FBI concurrent jurisdiction with the Drug Enforcement Administration over narcotics violations in the United States. The expanded Department of Justice attention to drug crimes resulted in the seizure of millions of dollars in controlled substances, the arrests of major narcotics figures, and the dismantling of important drug rings. One of the most publicized, dubbed the "Pizza Connection" case, involved the heroin trade in the United States and Italy. It resulted in 18 convictions, including a former leader of the Sicilian Mafia. Then Assistant United States Attorney Louis Freeh, who was to be appointed FBI director in 1993, was key to successful prosecution of the case.

Webster also strengthened the FBI's response to white-collar crime, with particular emphasis on public corruption. From 1978 to early 1980, the Bureau conducted Operation ABSCAM to expose bribery and conspiracy by members of Congress. An FBI investigation undertaken throughout the 1980s focused on bribery within the Cook County Circuit Court in Chicago, resulting in the conviction of more than 90 corrupt judges, attorneys, police officers, and court employees. In 1986, following an FBI investigation that unveiled corruption in government procurement activities, dozens of Defense Department officials and contractors were indicted on charges of fraud, bribery, and other crimes. Between 1981 and 1987, the FBI also uncovered fraud surrounding the failure of almost 300 savings and loan institutions.

In 1984, the FBI acted as lead agency for security of the Los Angeles Olympics, and unveiled its Hostage Rescue Team as a force capable of responding to situations such as the tragedy that occurred in Munich at the 1972 games. In 1986, Congress expanded FBI jurisdiction to cover terrorist acts against United States citizens outside the United States. Three years later, the Department of Justice authorized the FBI to arrest terrorists, drug traffickers, and other fugitives abroad without the consent of the foreign country in which they resided.

In May 1987, Webster left the FBI to become director of the Central Intelligence Agency, and Executive Assistant Director John Otto became acting director. During his six-month tenure, Otto designated drug investigations as the FBI's fifth national priority. In November 1987, former Federal Judge William Sessions was sworn in as FBI director. Prior to his appointment as FBI director, Sessions had served as the chief judge of the United States District Court for the Western District of Texas, and also as a United States attorney for that district.

Under Director Sessions, crime-prevention efforts were expanded to include a drug demand–reduction program, and FBI offices nationwide began working closely with local school and civic groups to educate young people about the dangers of drugs. By 1988, the FBI employed 9,663 special agents and 13,651 support employees in 58 field offices and 15 legal attachés. In response to a 40 percent increase in violent crime over the previous 10 years, Director Sessions designated the investigation of violent crime as the FBI's sixth national priority program in 1989.

The Post–Cold War Era

The dismantling of the Berlin Wall in November 1989 brought down the Iron Curtain—the final act in the Cold War—and the Soviet Union was dissolved in December 1991. The FBI reassessed its strategies in defending national security, now no longer defined as the containment of Communism and the prevention of nuclear war. It reassigned 300 special agents from foreign counterintelligence duties to violent crime investigations in January 1992. By creating the National Security Threat List, the Bureau changed its approach from defending against hostile intelligence agencies to protecting U.S. information and technologies. It also defined expanded threat issues, including the proliferation of chemical, biological, and nuclear weapons; the loss of critical technologies; and the improper collection of trade secrets and proprietary information. As President Clinton was to note in 1994, with the dramatic expansion of the global economy, "national security now means economic security."

Two events occurred in late 1992 and early 1993 that were to have a major impact on FBI policies and operations. In August 1992, the FBI responded to the shooting death of Deputy U.S. Marshal William Degan, who was killed at Ruby Ridge, Idaho, while participating in a surveillance of federal fugitive Randall Weaver. In the course of the standoff, Weaver's wife was accidentally shot and killed by an FBI sniper. Eight months later, at a remote compound outside Waco, Texas, FBI agents sought to end a 51-day standoff with members of a heavily armed religious sect who had killed four officers of the Bureau of Alcohol, Tobacco, and Firearms. Instead, the compound burned to the ground from fires lit by members of the sect. Eighty people, including children, died in the blaze. These two events set the stage for public and congressional inquiries into the FBI's ability to respond to crisis situations. In July 1993, following allegations of ethics violations committed by Director Sessions, President Clinton removed him from office and appointed Deputy Director Floyd Clarke as acting FBI director.

Reorganization and International Cooperation

Louis Freeh was sworn in as director of the FBI in September 1993. He had served as an FBI Agent from 1975 to 1981 in the New York City field office and at FBI Headquarters before leaving to join the United States Attorney's Office for the Southern District of New York. Freeh prosecuted many major FBI cases, including the notorious Pizza Connection case and the "VANPAC" mail-bomb case. He had been appointed as a United States District Court judge for the Southern District of New York in 1991.

Freeh moved quickly to reorganize and streamline Headquarters operations. Selected divisions and offices were merged, reorganized, or abolished. He then ordered the transfer of 600 special agents serving in administrative positions to investigative positions in field offices. Freeh also emphasized law enforcement cooperation as a necessary way to combat domestic and international crime, and in 1999 the FBI placed Osama Bin Laden on their "Ten Most Wanted" list for his alleged involvement in the 1999 bombings of United States embassies in Africa. In 1994, Freeh led a delegation of high-level diplomatic and federal law enforcement officials to meet with senior officials of 11 European nations on international crime issues, and also announced the opening of an FBI legal attaché office in Moscow. By the end of 2000, the Bureau established Legal Attaché offices in Hungary, Ukraine, Poland, and Romania.

FBI investigations during the early- to mid-1990s included the Archer Daniels Midland international price-fixing conspiracies, and the attempted theft of Schering-Plough and Merck pharmaceutical trade secrets. At the time, the United States Department of Justice characterized the Archer Daniels Midland investigation as the largest criminal antitrust case in U.S. history. In 1996, Congress passed the Economic Espionage Act, enabling the FBI to significantly strengthen its investigations involving the theft of trade secrets and intellectual property.

In December 1988, an explosion on board Pan Am flight 103 above Lockerbie, Scotland, caused the deaths of 259 passengers and 11 people on the ground. The FBI investigated the incident along with Scottish authorities. The investigation, which involved the U.S. Intelligence Community and numerous foreign law enforcement agencies, was one of the most extensive international investigations ever conducted by the Bureau. In January 2001, three Scottish judges convicted a Libyan national of murder for planting a bomb in a suitcase on the New York–bound flight.

Director Freeh initiated many changes to prepare for evolving criminal challenges, including formation of the Critical Incident Response Group in 1994, and the groundbreaking for its new state-of-the-art FBI forensic laboratory in 1999. He also initiated a comprehensive and integrated FBI response to nuclear, biological, and chemical crisis incidents.

Fighting Domestic Terrorism: America's "New War"

As the 20th century came to a close, terrorism on U.S. soil shocked the nation and the world. In 1995, the bombing of the Alfred P. Murrah Federal Building in Oklahoma City was the worst terrorist attack ever to occur in the United States, killing 168 people and wounding nearly 700 more. The FBI initiated one of the most intensive investigations in its history, which led to the arrests and convictions of Timothy McVeigh and Terry Nichols. McVeigh was later sentenced to death and executed, and Nichols received a sentence of life in prison.

Between 1994 and 1997, six Muslim fundamentalists were convicted for the bombing of a parking garage at the World Trade Center complex in New York City. Six people were killed and more than 1,100 were injured. The FBI led a coordinated law enforcement effort to determine who was responsible for the terrorist incident.

Over the years following the Oklahoma City and World Trade Center bombings, funding in support of FBI counterterrorism programs tripled from $97 million in fiscal year 1996 to $301 million in 1999. To consolidate FBI counterterrorism initiatives, Director Freeh established the FBI Counterterrorism Division in 1999, and assigned the National Infrastructure Protection Center and the National Domestic Preparedness Office to the Division.

In February 2001, veteran FBI Special Agent Robert Hanssen was arrested and charged with committing espionage by providing highly classified national security information to Russia and the former Soviet Union. At the time of his arrest, Hanssen was surreptitiously delivering classified information to a prearranged "drop site," where it was to be retrieved by Russian intelligence operatives. It was in this fashion that Hanssen provided more than 6,000 pages of top-secret material to the Russians over a period of more than 20 years, for which he was paid substantial sums of money. Louis Freeh retired from the FBI four months after Hanssen's arrest, in June 2001. He was replaced by Thomas Pickard, who served as acting director for three months.

Robert Mueller III, a former deputy attorney general for the United States Department of Justice, took over as FBI director on September 4, 2001. In doing so, he pledged to make drastic changes to the Bureau's information technology infrastructure, to improve the agency's records management system, and to strengthen FBI foreign counterintelligence analysis and security.

Seven days after Mueller's appointment, on September 11, the FBI responded to the worst terrorist attacks the world had ever witnessed. On that morning, terrorists hijacked four commercial jets and crashed them into the World Trade Center in New York City, the Pentagon in Washington, D.C., and a field southeast of Pittsburgh. Almost 3,000 people were killed in the attacks, including 343 firefighters and 71 law enforcement officers who gave their lives in the rescue attempts at the World Trade Center. The investigative response by the FBI included more than 7,000 agents and support personnel—about one in four of the Bureau's workforce—who worked around the clock. The FBI soon released photographs of 19 individuals believed to be hijackers of the four airliners—all of whom were killed in the attacks—and cautioned Americans to prepare for additional terrorist incidents within the United States and against U.S. interests overseas. Within three weeks, the Bureau also launched an investigation relating to anthrax exposures in Florida, New York, and Washington, D.C.

One month after the attacks, President George W. Bush signed an executive order establishing the Office of Homeland Security, to coordinate national strategy and strengthen protections against terrorist threats or attacks in the United States. Two days later, President Bush unveiled the Most Wanted Terrorists List, a new initiative similar to the FBI's Ten Most Wanted Fugitives Program, to spotlight the names and faces of terrorists who might be living, working, or hiding in the United States or overseas. The list combines the power of the media with the eyes and ears of millions of citizens around the world to fight against terrorism. Today, in the aftermath of terrorist incidents in the United States and around the world, the FBI has an enhanced capability to track the activities of foreign terrorist organizations maintaining a presence in the United States.

Reengineering the FBI: A Change of Priorities and Strategies

On June 6, 2002, Director Mueller testified before the United States Senate Committee on the Judiciary concerning the FBI's reorganization plan and refocusing of the Bureau's mission and priorities. Director Mueller made it clear to the Committee, the American public, law enforcement agencies, and FBI personnel that changes were necessary as a result of the terrorist attacks of 9/11. Mueller then announced that prevention of terrorist attacks had become the Bureau's top priority. He also explained that protecting the United States against foreign intelligence operations and espionage was the FBI's second priority, followed by the prevention of cybercrime attacks and other high-technology crimes. At the same time, Mueller reassured the Committee that the FBI remained dedicated to protecting civil rights and combating public corruption, organized crime, white-collar crime, and major acts of violent crime. In furtherance of these goals, the Bureau launched an effort to strengthen its relationship with federal, county, municipal, and international law enforcement agencies, and also to upgrade its technological infrastructure.

Reengineering the FBI since 9/11 has focused primarily on six core processes, including intelligence, information management, investigative programs, human resources, strategic planning and execution, and security management. Changes have occurred at every level, from reassigning personnel to counterterrorism duties, to examining recruiting and hiring practices, to modifying the manner in which information is shared internally and with other organizations.

In September 2001, the FBI had temporarily diverted more than 4,000 field agents to investigate the 9/11 attacks or the subsequent anthrax incidents. By April 2004, the number of agents permanently assigned to counterterrorism matters had increased from 1,351 to 2,398. During the same period, 460 intelligence analysts were added to support the counterterrorism mission, and nearly 700 translators were hired into Language Specialist or Contract Linguist positions. The FBI also created the National Joint Terrorism Task Force (NJTTF) and local JTTFs throughout the United States to manage interagency intelligence-gathering initiatives. These task force operations are coordinated with components of the Department of Homeland Security, the Defense Department, Railroad Police Departments, and agencies such as the U.S. Capitol Police, U.S. Department of Agriculture Office of Inspector General, Nuclear Regulatory Commission, Drug Enforcement Administration, Treasury Inspector General for Tax Administration, and the New York City Police Department.

The FBI's mission has become increasingly complex in recent years. In response, recruiting methods and hiring goals have been reevaluated, and the Bureau has developed a needs-forecasting system to identify the skills necessary of special agents and professional support personnel. The agency also has developed a marketing plan to promote FBI employment in critical skill areas, and has expanded training programs for new employees and career-development opportunities for all personnel.

In recent years, the FBI has carried out substantial upgrades to its information technology infrastructure and security operations. These have included creation of a standalone Security Division to improve security practices and standards, and establishment of a Records Management Division to modernize recordkeeping systems and policies. A new Cyber Division also was formed to prevent and respond to high-tech and computer crimes that terrorists and other criminals around the world are exploiting. Significant improvements to the FBI's fingerprint identification and criminal history systems also are underway, and the new FBI Laboratory provides state-of-the-art forensic resources for the Bureau and international, federal, state, and local law enforcement agencies.

Beginning in 2007, the FBI initiated an aggressive effort to accelerate and strengthen its intelligence capabilities by creating standard structures and processes for its intelligence functions in the field. The Bureau's counterintelligence program focuses on international terrorism threats, weapons of mass destruction threats, and attacks on the nation's critical infrastructures (such as communications, banking systems, and transportation systems), among other matters.

Today, each of the Bureau's 56 field offices are staffed with a Field Intelligence Group. These components, which consist of FBI special agents, intelligence analysts, language specialists, and surveillance specialists, obtain and process raw intelligence information to fill in gaps in national investigations and "connect the dots." Field Intelligence Groups also share their findings with local and tribal police departments, other federal and state law enforcement agencies, the CIA, and police agencies worldwide.

To further strengthen its investigative and intelligence operations, the FBI also created a Counterespionage Section at FBI Headquarters to consolidate and oversee all of the Bureau's espionage efforts, including economic espionage. This section also evaluates and prioritizes all espionage cases to ensure effective allocation of financial and human resources and expertise to these critical investigations. Supported by other U.S. and foreign agencies, the FBI conducts espionage investigations anywhere in the world when the subject of the investigation is a U.S. citizen. Counterespionage has become one of the FBI's highest priorities, because foreign espionage strikes at the heart of America's national security and impacts our political, military, and economic strengths. Within the Counterespionage Section, the FBI has also established a Penetration Unit, which seeks to uncover "moles" within the FBI.

In other words, the attacks of September 11, 2001, have forever changed America, and the FBI has responded by refocusing its priorities and making comprehensive changes to its structure and practices in order to protect and serve America.

Preparing for the Future

Since its formation as a small group of investigators in 1908, the FBI has undergone myriad changes in technology, jurisdiction, and mission. To address the challenges it will face in the future, the Bureau must adapt to the ever-changing face of crime and strive to achieve even greater excellence. This can be accomplished through positive relationships with other law enforcement agencies, new scientific techniques to identify dangerous criminals who would otherwise evade law enforcement, and laws that enable the FBI to protect the civil rights of the nation's citizens. Perhaps the most critical resources the FBI will need to accomplish its mission in the future, however, will be its human resources: the special agents and support personnel it selects and trains to promote justice, act with fairness and compassion, protect the public, and uphold the Constitution.

The Organization of the FBI

The following sections present an overview of how the FBI is organized, including its jurisdiction and authority, its field offices, and its operational divisions.

Jurisdiction and Authority

The FBI serves as the principal criminal investigative arm of the United States Department of Justice. The Bureau is charged with protecting and defending the United States against terrorist and foreign intelligence threats, and investigating all violations of federal law except those that have been assigned to other federal agencies. Its jurisdiction includes a wide range of responsibilities in the criminal, civil, and security fields. Priority is given to investigations that affect society the most, including domestic and international terrorism, foreign counterintelligence and espionage, cyber-based attacks and high-technology crimes, public corruption, organized crime and drugs, white-collar crime, violent crime and major offenses, and civil-rights violations. The work that FBI special agents and support personnel perform has a daily impact on the nation's security and the quality of life for all United States citizens. Other law enforcement agencies of the Department of Justice include the Office of Inspector General (OIG); Drug Enforcement Administration (DEA); Bureau of Prisons (BOP); Bureau of Alcohol, Tobacco, Firearms, and Explosives (ATF); and United States Marshals Service (USMS). Department of Justice components also include the U.S. National Central Bureau, which facilitates international law enforcement cooperation as the United States representative with the International Criminal Police Organization (INTERPOL), on behalf of the Attorney General.

Title 28 of the United States Code, Section 533, authorizes the attorney general to "...appoint officials to detect and prosecute crimes against the United States," and also to "...conduct investigations regarding official matters under the control of the Department of Justice...as may be directed by the Attorney General." This statute designated the FBI as the lead U.S. law enforcement agency for the investigation of terrorism. Various statutes also give the FBI authority to investigate terrorist crimes committed overseas. Among these are the Comprehensive Crime Control Act of 1984, which created a new section in the United States Code for hostage taking, and the Omnibus Diplomatic Security and Anti-terrorism Act of 1986, which created a new statute pertaining to terrorist acts conducted abroad against U.S. nationals or U.S. interests. Other federal statutes give the FBI the authority and responsibility to investigate specific crimes. The Bureau presently has investigative jurisdiction over violations of more than 200 categories of federal offenses. Throughout the 1980s, the illegal drug trade severely challenged the resources of American law enforcement. To ease this challenge, in 1982 the attorney general gave the FBI concurrent jurisdiction with the Drug Enforcement Administration over narcotics violations in the United States.

FBI special agents enforce more than 260 federal statutes, including those relating to organized crime, financial fraud, bank robbery, kidnapping, fugitive matters, and many other violations of federal laws. Information obtained through FBI investigations is presented to the appropriate United States Attorney or Department of Justice official, who decides whether prosecution or other action is warranted.

The FBI routinely cooperates with other federal, state, and local law enforcement agencies on joint investigations and through formal task force operations. These investigations focus on domestic and international terrorism, organized crime, bank robbery, kidnapping, motor vehicle theft, and other offenses. The Bureau also offers cooperative services such as fingerprint identification, laboratory examination, police training, and the National Crime Information Center to federal, state, and local law enforcement agencies. FBI Headquarters is located in Washington, D.C.

FBI Field Offices and Resident Agencies

The rubber meets the road within the FBI's 56 field offices and 400 satellite offices, known as resident agencies (RAs). FBI special agents based "in the field" locate witnesses; conduct interviews; track down leads; meet with informants; work with federal, state, and local law enforcement agencies; execute search warrants and make arrests; and otherwise compile evidence in cases involving federal jurisdiction. The FBI's field offices are located in major cities throughout the United States and in San Juan, Puerto Rico, while resident agencies are staffed in smaller cities across the country. (See appendix J for a listing of FBI field offices.) The locations of these offices are determined according to population density, crime trends, and available resources, leaving some field offices with jurisdiction in surrounding states and others with jurisdiction over smaller geographic areas. For example, the Boston field office investigates criminal activity in Massachusetts, Maine, New Hampshire, and Rhode Island, whereas the Detroit field office has jurisdiction over Michigan only.

All but three field offices are headed by a special agent in charge (SAC), who manages the operations of the office. At the next level of supervision, SACs are supported by one or more assistants, each known as assistant special agent in charge (ASAC). Below the ASAC, supervisory special agents manage investigative squads, and relief supervisors take over in their absence. Due to their large size, the Los Angeles, New York, and Washington, D.C., field offices are managed by an assistant director in charge (ADIC). In these offices, the ADICs are assisted by SACs.

Field offices conduct investigations from their facilities and through resident agencies. The number of RAs under each field office varies, as does the territory they cover. For example, 11 RAs throughout Michigan report to the Detroit field office, and the number of counties served by these RAs ranges from 1 (for the Oakland County RA) to 21 (for the Bay City RA).

Special agents assigned to field offices and RAs are organized into work groups known as *squads*. The responsibilities and focus of each squad depend on a number of variables, such as office size and the nature of investigations that are emphasized within the office. For example, various squads nationwide specialize in foreign counterintelligence, counterterrorism, violent crime, drug trafficking, organized crime, homicide, computer crime, financial institution fraud, white-collar crime, healthcare fraud, interstate property crimes, and other offenses.

Legal Attaché Offices

The growth of international criminal activity and the authority granted by Congress has expanded the FBI's role in international investigations. Given the increasing international occurrences of illegal drug trafficking, organized crime, espionage, terrorism, and white-collar crimes that affect U.S. citizens, the FBI establishes and maintains liaisons with principal law enforcement and intelligence organizations in many foreign countries.

The primary element of the FBI's international law enforcement initiative is the Legal Attaché (Legat) program. Special agents assigned to Legats work closely with foreign law enforcement agencies on investigations conducted overseas, while also facilitating resolution of the Bureau's domestic investigations that have international leads. Among its top priorities, Legal Attaché offices cooperate with U.S. State Department and Central Intelligence Agency personnel to prevent and investigate terrorist attacks on United States interests worldwide. Whether the FBI's efforts focus on foreign or domestic criminal activity, terrorism, or fugitive investigations, Legat personnel collectively handle tens of thousands of leads each year. Legats provide the FBI with a solid presence overseas, where the agents assigned to foreign posts of duty know the cultures, the legal and criminal justice systems, and the law enforcement officials in a given country. These agents also present a variety of training programs to foreign law enforcement officers.

The Bureau has been assigning personnel abroad since World War II, and presently has Legal Attaché staff stationed at 75 American embassies and consulates around the world, providing coverage for more than 200 countries. Special agents serving overseas are among the Bureau's most experienced investigators, and carry the titles of Legal Attaché, Deputy Legal Attaché, or Assistant Legal Attaché. With few exceptions, these agents are fluent in the language of the country to which they are posted. Legal Attachés are overseen by the Office of International Operations at FBI Headquarters (see p. 26).

Headquarters Operational Divisions

The FBI is headed by a director, who is supported by a deputy director. Public Law 94-503, Section 203, provides for the appointment of the FBI director by the president with the advice and consent of the Senate. The FBI director's term is limited to 10 years.

In December 2001, only three months after the terrorist attacks of 9/11, Director Mueller announced a restructuring of FBI Headquarters in an effort to improve the Bureau's analytical capabilities and prevent terrorist attacks. This strategy has resulted in new leadership, priorities, technology, and resources. The restructuring established six new Executive Assistant Director positions to oversee the Intelligence Branch, Counterterrorism and Counterintelligence Branch, Criminal Investigations Branch, Law Enforcement Services Branch, and Administration Branch.

The new Headquarters structure established the Office of Intelligence, which was created to advance the FBI's strategic analysis efforts and improve the exchange of critical national security information with other agencies, and the Investigative Technologies Division, which was created to support and upgrade the FBI's technological capabilities. The Bureau's new Cyber Division is charged with preventing and responding to computer crimes, and protecting the nation's electronic infrastructure. The reorganization also created a new Security Division to improve security practices, a Records Management Division to modernize recordkeeping systems and procedures, and the Office of Law Enforcement Coordination to improve relationships and intelligence sharing with other law enforcement agencies.

An assistant director heads each of the Bureau's Headquarters divisions (see figure 1.1), as well as the Office of Professional Responsibility, the Office of Public Affairs, and the Office of Congressional Affairs. The Office of General Counsel is headed by the FBI's General Counsel, and the Office of Equal Employment Opportunity is administered by the Equal Employment Officer. Assistant directors of each division are supported by deputy assistant directors. FBI Headquarters divisions and offices usually are arranged along broad functional lines into sections, and then into smaller, more specialized work groups known as units.

The following sections provide an overview of the functions carried out by FBI divisions. An organizational chart showing these divisions and other operational sections is shown in figure 1.1.

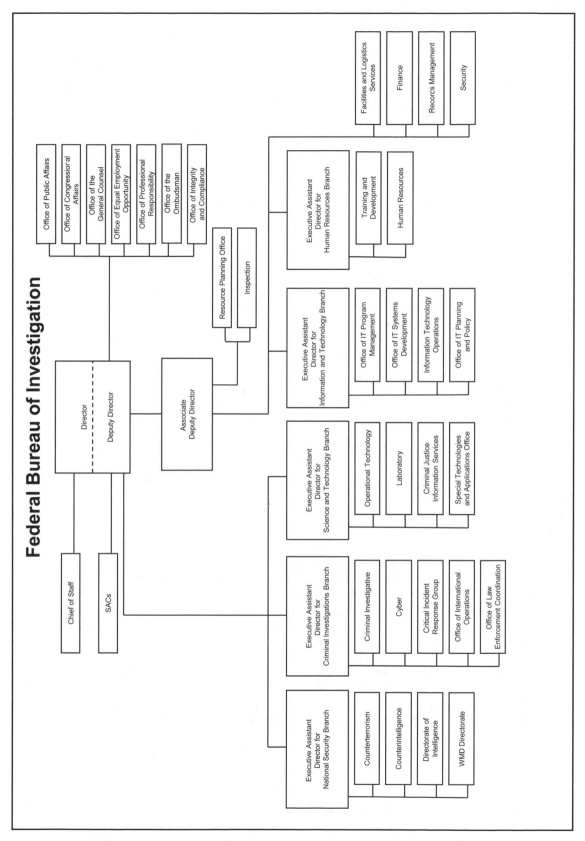

Figure 1.1: FBI organization chart.

National Security Branch

As the lead counterintelligence and counterterrorism agency in the United States, the FBI is responsible for identifying and neutralizing ongoing threats to national security. This FBI branch is responsible for national security initiatives such as the collection and analysis of terrorist threat data and intelligence, responses to threats and attacks against the critical infrastructure, counterterrorism and counterintelligence investigations, and coordination of federal intelligence and investigative efforts to assist state and local first responders. The Executive Assistant Director for National Security manages the Counterterrorism and Counterintelligence Divisions under this branch, as well as the Directorate of Intelligence, Weapons of Mass Destruction Directorate, and Terrorist Screening Center. Intelligence data generated by these components is used to brief the President nearly every morning.

Counterterrorism Division

In response to the terrorist attacks of September 11, 2001, the FBI initiated a complete reorganization of the agency and established new investigative priorities. As a result of this initiative, the FBI placed "protection of the United States from terrorist attack" as its top priority. A significant restructuring and expansion of the Counterterrorism Division also was initiated to improve investigative strategies, operational support to FBI field offices, and collaboration with other law enforcement agencies and members of the Intelligence Community. These changes were designed to result in a more proactive approach to preventing terrorism and denying terrorists the ability to raise funds.

The Counterterrorism Division provides a centralized, comprehensive, and intelligence-driven approach to address both international and domestic terrorism. The division is staffed with intelligence analysts, technical information specialists, financial analysts, and other subject-matter experts who work closely with special agents in the field. Some functions of the division include providing analysis of terrorist threat data and other information within the Bureau and to outside organizations, detecting terrorist sleeper cells in the United States before they act, and dismantling terrorist support networks. The division also disseminates intelligence bulletins to law enforcement agencies nationwide that are used primarily by patrol officers and detectives who encounter situations or obtain information through direct contact with the public, and oversees multi-agency Joint Terrorism Task Force operations nationwide.

The division is divided into various branches, sections, and units, with each focusing on a different aspect of terrorism. These components support investigations relating to al Qaeda, Hizballah, Hamas, and the Palestinian Islamic Jihad, as well other groups and state sponsors of terrorism. They also lend support to field offices engaged in counterterrorism operations for events such as the Super Bowl and Olympic Games, provide support to field office–based Rapid Deployment Teams, and work closely with the Counterintelligence Division and other FBI components.

Counterintelligence Division

As a critical element in the FBI's mission to identify and neutralize national security threats, the Counterintelligence Division provides centralized management and oversight for all foreign counterintelligence investigations. The

Division's primary function is to protect the United States against foreign intelligence operations and espionage. Its personnel coordinate investigations with other components of the U.S. Intelligence Community, and also integrate law enforcement with intelligence efforts to investigate espionage.

Other investigative priorities of the Division include misuse of classified data, attacks on the nation's critical infrastructures (for example, communications, banking systems, and transportation systems), theft of intellectual property and technology by foreign parties or governments, and infiltration of the U.S. Intelligence Community and government agencies or contractors. This Division conducts a wide range of investigations and operations focusing on nations that constitute the most significant threat to U.S. strategic interests and other threats to national security.

Directorate of Intelligence

The Directorate of Intelligence (DI) was established in 2005 as a dedicated national workforce with responsibility for all FBI intelligence functions. This component carries out its mission through intelligence elements at FBI headquarters and in each field division through the Bureau's Field Intelligence Groups. DI personnel address current and emerging national security and criminal threats by focusing proactive intelligence efforts toward threats to U.S. interests; building and sustaining intelligence policies and capabilities; and providing useful and timely information and analysis to the national security, homeland security, and law enforcement communities. The DI also is responsible for establishing and executing standards for recruiting, hiring, and training the Bureau's intelligence analysts and language specialists.

Weapons of Mass Destruction Directorate

In 2006, the FBI consolidated all Weapons of Mass Destruction (WMD) operations into a new WMD Directorate (WMDD) within the National Security Branch. This component identifies and disrupts WMD operations and threats primarily through countermeasures, preparedness programs, and managing all WMD investigations and intelligences functions. The WMDD uses a wide array of intelligence and investigative resources to detect and prevent the acquisition and use of WMD by terrorists and other adversaries. WMDD staff also direct the U.S. government WMD Threat Credibility Assessment process and coordinate operations with the FBI's Counterterrorism, Counterintelligence, Criminal Investigation, and Laboratory Divisions. Each of the Bureau's 56 field offices has a highly trained WMD Coordinator who manages the assessment of and response to incidents involving the use or threatened use of WMDs.

In an effort to address the threat of agroterrorism, WMD coordinators and other WMDD personnel work closely with agriculture industry partners, U.S. Department of Agriculture (USDA) Office of Inspector General special agents, other USDA agencies, and the U.S. Food and Drug Administration (FDA) to gather intelligence, increase awareness of potential threats, and facilitate reporting of information with potential intelligence value. WMDD staff also participate with first responders, law enforcement, and health agencies nationwide in mock training exercises to improve the Bureau's capability to investigate and respond to the threat or use of WMD.

Terrorist Screening Center

The FBI's Terrorist Screening Center (TSC) maintains the federal government's consolidated Terrorist Watchlist, a database of information about those known or reasonably suspected of being involved in terrorist activity. The Watchlist is an effective counterterrorism tool that is used by various frontline agencies to positively identify known or suspected terrorists trying to obtain visas, enter the country, board aircraft, or engage in other activity.

The TSC supports federal, state, local, territorial, and tribal law enforcement agencies and some foreign governments that conduct terrorist screening by making TSC database information available to them. For example, the TSC supports terrorism screening relating to the processing of passport and visa applications by the U.S. State Department, international border crossings monitored by the Bureau of Customs and Border Protection, immigration and citizenship applications processed by the Bureau of Citizenship and Immigration Services, and domestic flights under the jurisdiction of the Transportation Security Administration. TSC data also is accessible through the FBI's National Crime Information Center (NCIC) database, a tool used by more than one million U.S. law enforcement agency personnel nationwide.

Criminal Investigations Branch

The Criminal Investigations Branch incorporates the Cyber Division and the Criminal Investigation Division, which together account for a substantial proportion of the FBI's investigative activities. This branch is managed by the Executive Assistant Director for Criminal Investigations.

Cyber Division

Investigations conducted by the Cyber Division focus on federal violations in which computer systems, computer networks, the Internet, online services, or other information technology are used as the primary means for carrying out criminal activity. For example, the division investigates computer hacking and intrusion cases, intellectual property rights crimes involving theft of trade secrets and signals, copyright infringement involving computer software, online child pornography and child sexual exploitation crimes, and a variety of other offenses. Support also is provided to the Counterterrorism and Counterintelligence Divisions with investigations concerning national security matters.

The Cyber Division coordinates activities with the National Infrastructure Protection Center, and also maintains a partnership with the National White-Collar Crime Center to operate the Internet Fraud Complaint Center. In addition, the Division assists the FBI Operational Technology Division with the Computer Analysis Response Team program and deployment of Regional Computer Forensic Laboratories. The Division also supports FBI Cyber Crime Squads and task forces working with U.S. Department of Justice Computer Hacking and Intellectual Property units nationwide.

Criminal Investigation Division

The FBI's investigative mandate is the broadest of all federal law enforcement agencies. This division coordinates investigations into organized crime, including drug matters, racketeering, and money laundering; investigations of violent crimes, including fugitives, escaped federal prisoners (in some instances), unlawful flight to avoid prosecution, violent gangs, serial murders, kidnapping, bank robberies, crime of an interstate nature, crime on Indian reservations, theft of government property, and crimes against U.S. citizens overseas; investigations of white-collar crime, fraud against the government, corruption of public officials, healthcare fraud, election law violations, business and economic frauds and corruption crimes; and investigations of civil-rights violations.

Congress provides the FBI with the broadest investigative mandate of all U.S. federal law enforcement agencies. As a result, the Criminal Investigation Division conducts a wide range of investigations. For example, the Division's Financial Crimes Section investigates "white-collar" offenses such as healthcare fraud, public corruption, fraud against the government, environmental crimes, bankruptcy fraud, securities and commodities fraud, fraud involving financial institutions, antitrust violations, insurance fraud, telemarketing fraud, and money laundering. Collectively, these and other white-collar offenses cost American citizens, businesses, and the government billions of dollars annually.

The Criminal Investigation Division also conducts investigations relating to fugitives, corruption of public officials, election law violations, theft of government property, organized crime, racketeering, drug trafficking, serial murders, kidnapping, bank robberies, violent gangs, unlawful flight to avoid prosecution, crime of an interstate nature, crime on Indian reservations, and crimes against U.S. citizens overseas. The investigation of civil-rights violations also falls under the jurisdiction of this Division, including offenses involving hate crimes, church arson and damage to other religious property, slavery, police misconduct, Criminal Interference with Right to Fair Housing, prevention of access to health clinics, and violence against healthcare providers.

Law Enforcement Services Branch

Many of the FBI's most important functions are carried out by the multifaceted Law Enforcement Services Branch. This branch offers a wide range of services in support of the FBI Training Academy, the Laboratory Division, international operations, and a variety of criminal justice information services. Law enforcement agencies throughout the United States and overseas rely on the Law Enforcement Services Branch for assistance ranging from forensic laboratory services to fingerprint identification, crime statistics, information on wanted persons, training courses, response to crisis situations, and tactical support. The components of this branch are described next.

Office of Law Enforcement Coordination

In recognition of the need to strengthen relationships and coordinate activities more effectively with the nation's federal, state, and local law enforcement agencies, in December 2001 the FBI established the Office of Law Enforcement Coordination (OLEC). The office facilitates collaboration and communication with law enforcement agencies to protect the United States from criminal and terrorist activities, and also provides guidance to FBI management concerning the use of state and local law enforcement resources in criminal, cyber, and counterterrorism investigations.

The OLEC coordinates the Director's Law Enforcement Advisory Group and the FBI Police Executive Fellowship Program, and also supports the Bureau's intelligence-sharing and technological efforts with state and local law enforcement. The FBI sends an unclassified weekly *Intelligence Bulletin* to more than 17,000 U.S. law enforcement agencies, and has granted clearances to many police chiefs and other law enforcement officials to increase information sharing. The office also is responsible for liaison with the Department of Justice's

Office of Justice Programs and Office of Community Oriented Policing Services, as well as the Department of Homeland Security and other federal agencies.

In addition to carrying out liaison activities with law enforcement agencies, the OLEC works closely with groups such as the International Association of Chiefs of Police (IACP) and the Fraternal Order of Police (FOP). In coordinating efforts with the OLEC, associations such as the IACP and FOP have input when the FBI is developing law enforcement and crime prevention strategies.

Office of International Operations

The Office of International Operations (OIO) promotes relations with foreign law enforcement agencies and security services in furtherance of reciprocal cooperation and more effective joint international investigations. The office is responsible for managing the FBI Legal Attaché program, in which experienced agents are assigned to dozens of critically located U.S. embassies and consulates around the world, and for contacts with the International Criminal Police Organization (INTERPOL) and foreign law enforcement officers based in Washington, D.C.

Prior to the terrorist attacks of September 11, 2001, the FBI's overseas investigations focused primarily on cases to be prosecuted in the United States. The Bureau's focus has since changed to providing foreign agencies with investigative, analytical, forensic, and technical support to prevent and disrupt terrorist attacks. The efforts carried out by FBI Legal Attaché offices and other initiatives of the OIO play a critical role in the Bureau's international operations.

Critical Incident Response Group

Crisis incidents requiring immediate response are managed by the Critical Incident Response Group (CIRG), whether the incidents are investigated by the FBI or other law enforcement agencies. The CIRG was created in 1994 to incorporate investigative expertise, tactical resources, and rapid deployment in response to a variety of critical incidents. The CIRG is divided into three functional areas, including the Operations Support Branch, the Tactical Support Branch, and the National Center for the Analysis of Violent Crime. Within these areas of expertise, CIRG personnel respond to matters such as bombing incidents, aviation accidents, train crashes, natural disasters, prison riots, terrorist activities, hostage situations, child abductions, and other circumstances. CIRG personnel are trained and prepared to respond to crisis situations 24 hours a day, 365 days a year. In addition to providing operational assistance, the CIRG also conducts training for FBI personnel and other federal, state, local, and foreign law enforcement agencies.

Operational Technology Division

The FBI's recent change in priorities places particular emphasis on proactive and preventive counterterrorism, counterintelligence, and cyber activities requiring state-of-the-art intelligence collection and analysis strategies. One of the most effective tools in the investigation of terrorists, foreign government intelligence services, and sophisticated criminal enterprises has been electronic surveillance (ELSUR), especially in recent years. In recognition of the value of ELSUR to FBI operations and its change in mission, the agency established the Operational Technology Division (OTD) in June 2002 to consolidate technical investigative activities and to increase the emphasis on future investigative technologies.

This division concentrates on technical and tactical services in support of investigators and the Intelligence Community, including electronic surveillance, physical surveillance, cyber technology, and wireless and radio communications. OTD provides support related to the collection and processing of computer, audio, and visual media. OTD's services support the counterterrorism, counterintelligence, cyber, and criminal programs of the FBI, the intelligence community, and the law enforcement community. This division also is engaged in the development of new investigative technologies and techniques, and the training of technical agents and personnel. Some of the staff assigned to this division include Central Intelligence Agency personnel who are detailed to the FBI.

Training and Development Division

Located at the FBI Academy in Quantico, Virginia, the Training and Development Division manages the FBI Academy, trains FBI special agents and support staff, and also offers courses to local, state, federal, and international law enforcement agencies. This division operates the 21-week New Agent Training program, the 11-week FBI National Academy for veteran state and local law enforcement managers, a broad range of in-service courses for FBI agents and support staff, and many other specialized courses designed for all levels of personnel serving law enforcement agencies worldwide. In addition to teaching responsibilities, FBI Academy faculty members conduct research and provide assistance to federal, state, and local law enforcement agencies on many topics and investigative techniques.

Laboratory Division

The FBI Laboratory is one of the largest and most comprehensive crime laboratories in the world. It provides leadership and service in scientific solution and prosecution of crimes nationwide, and is the only full-service federal forensic laboratory in the United States. Laboratory Division activities include crime-scene searches, special surveillance photography, latent-fingerprint examinations, forensic examinations of evidence, DNA testing, court testimony, and other scientific and technical services. The FBI offers these services free of charge to all law enforcement agencies in the United States, and also provides training to other state and local crime laboratory and law enforcement personnel.

Located in Quantico, Virginia, the FBI Laboratory is responsible for the collection, processing, and analysis of evidence in support of criminal investigations and disaster responses carried out by the FBI and other law enforcement agencies worldwide. As one of the largest and most comprehensive crime laboratories in the world, and the only full-service federal forensic laboratory in the United States, the FBI Laboratory analyzes evidence ranging from blood and other biological materials to fingerprints, explosives, drugs, firearms, questioned documents, audio and video recordings, and many other items and substances. The Laboratory conducts more than one million examinations each year. The Laboratory also provides training to other state and local crime laboratory and law enforcement personnel on subjects such as DNA analysis, latent fingerprint identification, document examination, hair and fiber examination, firearm and tool-mark identification, bomb disposal, shoe print and tire tread analysis, polygraph testing, and artist sketching.

Criminal Justice Information Services Division

The centerpiece of the FBI's information technology operations is located on a 986-acre parcel in Clarksburg, West Virginia, home of the Criminal Justice Information Services (CJIS) Division. CJIS Division operations feature the latest technology to deliver criminal identification and information services to federal, state, local, and international law enforcement agencies.

A key CJIS component is the National Crime Information Center, which provides law enforcement agencies with information concerning wanted persons, convicted sexual offenders, persons on probation or parole, fingerprint identification, mug shots, vehicle and watercraft identification numbers, and stolen property. The CJIS Division also operates the National Instant Criminal Background Check System, which is used to determine whether individuals qualify to purchase or receive firearms. Other components of the CJIS Division include the Fingerprint Identification Program, the Uniform Crime Reporting Program, and the Integrated Automated Fingerprint Identification System. The CJIS Division is the largest division within the FBI.

Administration Branch

Many services that provide vital support to the director and day-to-day management of the FBI are the responsibility of the Administration Branch. These range from personnel matters to the management of information resources, technology upgrades, forecast processes, records systems, budgetary and fiscal matters, and internal security. This branch, which is managed by the Executive Assistant Director for Administration, also works closely with offices that provide direct support to the deputy director, and offers comprehensive support to all FBI branches. An overview of Administration Branch components is provided in the following sections.

Security Division

The FBI's Security Division works to ensure a safe and secure work environment for FBI personnel and others with access to FBI facilities, and to prevent the compromise of national security and FBI information. This division also is responsible for preventing espionage and protecting personnel, facilities, and information from external and internal threats. The division uses the results of personnel security investigations to determine whether FBI employees should have access to sensitive or classified information. In addition, the division performs polygraph examinations to help determine trustworthiness of FBI personnel, contractors, and job applicants, and to support criminal investigations.

Programs relating to facility access control, force protection, incident reporting and management, and continuity of operations planning are managed by this division as well. Security Division personnel also conduct training to prepare staff and contract personnel to execute various security tasks. Responsibilities of the division are carried out by security specialists and technical experts from all security disciplines, including personnel security, physical security, and training, as well as information assurance and information systems security.

Finance Division

The Finance Division manages FBI budget and accounting matters, voucher and payroll functions, the procurement process, forfeiture and seized property processes, property management, automotive management, competition advocacy, relocation and transportation services, and Chief Financial Officers Act requirements. This division also is responsible for the Bureau's financial planning. The Assistant Director of the Finance Division serves as the FBI's Chief Financial Officer and is Chairperson of the Contract Review Board.

Records Management Division

In conjunction with the reorganization of FBI Headquarters in 2002, the Records Management Division was established to update and modernize all of the agency's records management control systems. The Division is charged with oversight of FBI records policy and functions, as well as consolidating all records operations to ensure consistency, thoroughness, and accountability. A total of three components carry out these functions, including the Records Maintenance and Disposition Section, the Records Review and Dissemination Section, and the Freedom of Information/Privacy Acts Section. The Division also maintains the FBI Reading Room at Headquarters and the Electronic Reading Room maintained by the FBI on the Internet.

Among the leading priorities of the division is to make the transition from paper-based to electronic recordkeeping systems. So far, the FBI Document Conversion Laboratory (DocLab) has scanned millions of pages of material into readable text and images, uploading them into electronic applications. This process results in digital files and information that can be exchanged easily, rapidly, and inexpensively among Bureau field offices, joint task forces, and FBI Headquarters.

Administrative Services Division

The Administrative Services Division is responsible for managing and providing executive direction in all aspects of FBI personnel management matters, such as personnel assistance, personnel benefits, and personnel selection. This division also manages all personnel recruitment programs and selection systems, and oversees background investigations of applicants for FBI employment and employment with other agencies. Other functions carried out by this division focus on internal placement of employees, performance management, executive development and selection, health and safety matters, printing and supply services, office space and facilities management, and employee assistance programs.

Information and Technology Branch

The Information and Technology Branch (ITB) oversees the development and management of information technology (IT) projects and systems throughout the FBI. The ITB is organized into four components, including the IT Operations Division, Office of IT Policy and Planning, Office of IT Program Management, and Office of IT Systems Development. This structure results in end-to-end management of IT projects within the agency and incorporates best practices for governing a large IT organization.

Some of the tasks carried out by ITB staff include development of IT policies and procedures; determining IT priorities for the FBI Strategic Plan; maintaining the FBI's technology assets, such as IT systems, applications, networks, and databases; identifying the Bureau's future IT needs; and providing technical direction for the reengineering of FBI business processes. The ITB also ensures that FBI information technology assets are compatible with IT systems throughout the Intelligence Community. To accomplish this objective, ITB personnel work closely with the chief information officers of the Department of Defense, the Department of Homeland Security, the FBI's Criminal Justice Information Services Division, and Intelligence Community agencies to develop technology interoperability and upgrades, as well as an IT infrastructure that provides for secure communication with Intelligence Community partners.

The following components are under the Bureau's ITB umbrella.

Information Technology Operations Division

The Information Technology Operations Division (ITOD) impacts a broad range of the Bureau's IT operations, such as policy and planning, systems analysis, applications software, operating systems, network services, data management, Internet and intranet operations, systems administration, and customer support. This includes ensuring compliance with policies and standards, the management of all IT programs, strategic planning, information security management, and performing needs analyses. ITOD staff also develop cost estimates for new or modified IT systems; ensure the integration of IT components; maintain databases; develop software; install and maintain hardware, networks, and operating systems; troubleshoot and diagnose technical problems; develop Web sites; and provide technical support to IT users, among many other tasks.

Office of Information Technology Policy and Planning

The Office of IT Policy and Planning is responsible for optimizing FBI IT resources through policy and planning, providing guidance for integrating FBI IT strategies and solutions, and ensuring compliance with various governance frameworks. For example, IT Policy and Planning staff facilitated completion of the FBI Intelligence Information Report Dissemination System, a Web-based software application that allows FBI personnel to create and disseminate standardized intelligence reports quickly and efficiently. IT Policy and Planning personnel also provided oversight for the development of the Bureau's Public Key Infrastructure program, which provides enhanced encryption and other security safeguards within the Bureau's IT systems.

Office of Information Technology Program Management

The primary mission of the Office of Information Technology Program Management (OIPM) is to coordinate program development and control functions across all of the Bureau's major information technology projects. The staff of this office is broken down into subunits that provide guidance and assistance in IT program management, program oversight, contract and acquisition management, and administrative support systems. Some tasks carried out by OIPM staff include tracking project progress, risk management, applying quality-assurance controls, developing technical requirements for IT projects, performing contract review and negotiations, conducting research, conducting inventory of computers and other equipment, providing program management training to FBI employees, and identifying security issues affecting IT programs.

Office of Information Technology Systems Development

Enterprise-level IT capabilities are created by the FBI Office of IT Systems Development (ITSD). This component is responsible for managing various IT programs from the concept stage in the Research and Development Section, to prototype in the Prototype Section, to program deployment in the Data Engineering and Systems Development Section. ITSD staff also are responsible for technology exploration, managing a variety of technical resources, developing new knowledge management capabilities to support FBI special agents and intelligence analysts, and strengthening engineering for the Bureau's IT projects.

Direct Support to the Director and Deputy Director

Several offices provide skilled support to the FBI director and deputy director, including the Chief of Staff, Inspection Division, Office of Public Affairs, Congressional Affairs Office, Office of the Ombudsman, Office of General Counsel, Chief Information Officer, Office of Equal Employment Opportunity, and Office of Professional Responsibility. Personnel assigned to these offices are skilled, highly educated, and well trained. The functions they perform ensure that the FBI carries out its mission and responsibilities in a professional, ethical, and efficient manner, while also within legal limits and through best business practices. In accordance with the FBI's organizational structure, these offices report directly to the deputy director.

Director's Resource Planning Office

The Director's Resource Planning Office (RPO) carries out a variety of functions to provide unified, coordinated, and efficient use of FBI resources. The RPO was established in 2006 to implement a corporate approach to maximizing efficiency and effectiveness by managing and aligning strategic planning with financial and human resources, performance measurement, and the management of FBI policies. RPO personnel are engaged in matters related to strategy and resource management, business process reengineering, corporate information, policy coordination, and security services. For example, the RPO sets and communicates strategic priorities, monitors FBI effectiveness, provides FBI decision makers with standardized management reporting processes, and identifies technology solutions to facilitate improved business processes. The RPO also is responsible for providing guidance relating to oversight of the FBI's personnel security, industrial security, physical security, information security, and information systems security.

Inspection Division

The Inspection Division provides independent oversight of the FBI's investigative, financial, and administrative operations to ensure their compliance with FBI objectives, policies, governing laws, rules, and regulations. These examinations ensure that FBI personnel conduct themselves in a proper and professional manner. The Inspection Division also conducts organizational streamlining studies, process reengineering and improvement projects, and program evaluations, and makes recommendations for improved organizational efficiency and effectiveness.

Office of Public Affairs

In August 2003, FBI Director Robert Mueller reorganized the Bureau's Office of Public and Congressional Affairs into two offices with separate leadership. According to Mueller, the change was initiated to improve communication with Congress and the public during a time of change for the FBI and heightened concern for national security. The Office of Public Affairs (OPA) was first established in 1997 to replace the External Affairs Division.

Today, the OPA ensures that the public and media are informed about the Bureau's activities, priorities, and policies. The Office serves as the primary point of contact for the national and international news media, and advises the director and other FBI staff on all aspects of media relations and communications issues. Other OPA responsibilities include the preparation and issuance of news releases and statements, responding to inquiries from reporters, arranging interviews, conducting news conferences, and providing information to the public about the FBI and programs operated by the Bureau that benefit the public. The office also ensures that laws, regulations, and policies involving the release of information to the public are followed so that maximum disclosure is made without jeopardizing investigations and prosecutions, violating rights of individuals, or compromising national security interests.

Office of Congressional Affairs

The Office of Congressional Affairs (OCA) serves as the principal point of contact for members of Congress and their staff. Some of the activities carried out by the office include sharing information on the FBI's programs and operations, delivering intelligence information to the Senate and House Intelligence Committees, providing the Bureau's weekly *Law Enforcement Bulletin* to the oversight committees and Congressional leaders, arranging tours of FBI facilities in the Washington area and field offices nationwide, and coordinating courtesy visits between the FBI director and lawmakers. With the assistance of OCA staff, each year FBI officials testify at dozens of Congressional hearings, provide hundreds of briefings to members of Congress and their staff, and respond to thousands of inquiries from members of Congress.

Office of the Ombudsman

Since 1981, the FBI has had an Ombudsman on staff to assist with the informal resolution of workplace problems in a manner that is fair and equitable to all involved parties. The Office of the Ombudsman provides neutral, impartial, and confidential assistance to FBI employees who encounter difficult workplace problems so that formal grievance processes can be avoided. The office offers coaching, advice, referrals, and options for resolution to personnel throughout the Bureau, and works to achieve balance and harmony in the workplace by encouraging good communication at all levels.

Office of General Counsel

Legal counsel to the FBI director and other Bureau officials is provided by the Office of General Counsel (OGC). OGC attorneys provide legal advice to the Director, other FBI officials and divisions, and field offices on all aspects of law, particularly in the areas of national security, the Foreign Intelligence Surveillance Act, criminal investigation, Title III wiretap affidavits, asset forfeiture, information law and policy, procurement and contracting, fiscal law and policy, and all areas of litigation in which the FBI is involved.

OGC is comprised of four components, including the Legal Advice and Training Branch, the Litigation Branch, the Investigative Law Branch, and the National Security Law Branch. Collectively, these branches provide legal advice to the director and other FBI officials, defend the FBI in civil and administrative actions, respond to subpoenas and civil discovery requests, provide legal support to the FBI's asset forfeiture program, and present legal instruction at the FBI Academy, among a multitude of other tasks. OGC personnel also maintain liaison relationships with the Intelligence Community, the Department of Homeland Security, the Defense Department, and other government agencies to share information on legal issues and operational requirements relating to national security.

Office of Equal Employment Opportunity Affairs

The Office of Equal Employment Opportunity (EEO) Affairs ensures equality of opportunity for all FBI employees and applicants, and prohibits discrimination in employment based on race, color, religion, age, sex, national origin, disabled status, or reprisal for previous involvement in a protected activity. This office handles EEO-complaint processing, training, and monitoring of employment practices and policies. Additional responsibilities include the operation of special-emphasis programs relating to American Indians, Alaskan Natives, Asian Americans, Pacific Islanders, Black Affairs, Federal Women, Hispanic Employment, Selective Placement of individuals with disabilities (including disabled veterans), and Upward Mobility.

Office of Professional Responsibility

The Office of Professional Responsibility (OPR) was established in 1976 to ensure that FBI personnel conduct themselves with the highest level of integrity and professionalism, and to address allegations of serious employee misconduct or criminality. The activities of this Office ensure that allegations of wrongdoing are thoroughly investigated and that discipline is appropriate and fair regardless of the assignment or seniority of the employee involved. OPR is responsible for the adjudication of cases of administrative discipline based on its investigation, determining whether the allegations have been substantiated, and making written findings and recommendations regarding what (if any) disciplinary action is appropriate.

OPR also is responsible for establishing policies and procedures regarding the disciplinary process, and for monitoring its effectiveness to ensure that the ability of the FBI to perform its law enforcement and national security functions is not impaired.

SOUTH HOLLAND PUBLIC LIBRARY DISCARD

DISCARD

CHAPTER 2

Salary and Benefits

"A wise man will make more opportunities than he finds."

—*Francis Bacon*

FBI employees enjoy competitive salaries and a wide range of fringe benefits that are superior to those provided by many state and municipal government agencies and firms in the private sector. All full-time Bureau personnel receive health and life insurance coverage, paid holidays, vacation and sick leave, travel allowances, and injury-compensation benefits. In addition, FBI special agents are also covered under special salary and benefit programs. This chapter provides an overview of salary structures and the primary benefits available to FBI special agents and professional support staff.

Salary Structure and Rates

This section presents an overview of the pay system and salary progression procedures the FBI follows for its special agents and support personnel, including locality adjustments for those who serve in certain geographic areas.

The General Schedule Pay System

Although FBI personnel serve in *Excepted Service* appointments—meaning that they are part of an independent personnel system that is excluded from competitive civil-service procedures—the Bureau follows the General Schedule (GS) pay system for most of its employees, as do the vast majority of federal agencies. Most FBI jobs allow employees to advance from an entry-level pay grade to higher grades over a period of time.

Advancement to Higher Grades

The General Schedule consists of 15 grades, ranging from GS-1 to GS-15. Advancement to higher grades varies from one position to another. FBI personnel employed in professional and administrative occupations progress by two-grade increments beginning at GS-5 and advancing to GS-11, and then in single-grade intervals from GS-12 to GS-15. For example, the document analyst position covers a pay range from GS-7 through GS-13 and also provides for advancement to the next higher grade level in one-year increments. Therefore, document analysts who are hired at the GS-7 level can advance to GS-9 after one year, then to GS-11 one year later, to GS-12 after another year, and finally to GS-13 after another year. On the other hand, FBI employees whose work is clerical and technical in nature progress by single-grade increments. For example, FBI Electronic Surveillance Operations Technicians advance from GS-6 to GS-7 after one year, to GS-8 after another year, and to GS-9 one year later. Regardless of the position, employees must demonstrate work at an acceptable level of competence to qualify for advancement to the next higher grade. Of course, some positions allow for advancement to higher grades than others.

Within-Grade Increases

As shown in the following schedules, a salary range of 10 steps is provided within each grade, with employees normally starting at step 1 within a particular grade at entry level. Within-grade increases to the next step normally occur after 52 weeks of service in the first three steps in a grade, after 104 weeks in steps 4 through 6, and after 156 weeks in steps 7 and above. Employees who reach the highest possible grade in their position continue to receive within-grade increases until they "top-out" at step 10.

Special Agent Salaries

FBI special agents are hired at the GS-10 level and can advance to the GS-11, GS-12, and GS-13 grade levels in non-supervisory assignments. Advancement from GS-10 to GS-13 is based on satisfactory performance and is noncompetitive. In order to obtain promotions to supervisory, management, and executive positions, special agents must compete with other candidates in formal application processes. Promotions are available to grades GS-14 and GS-15, and also to Senior Executive Service positions. Like most other federal criminal investigators, FBI special agents receive Law Enforcement Availability Pay (LEAP), which is an additional salary premium for unscheduled duty fixed at 25 percent of base pay.

Table 2.1 provides an overview of salaries for FBI special agents, including LEAP, based on 2009 General Schedule salary rates.

Table 2.1: Annual Salary for FBI Special Agents, Including Locality Pay for "Rest of United States" Geographic Areas (Based on 2009 General Schedule Salary Rates)

	Step 1	Step 2	Step 3	Step 4	Step 5	Step 6	Step 7	Step 8	Step 9	Step 10
GS-10	64,181	66,320	68,460	70,599	72,738	74,878	77,016	79,155	81,295	83,434
GS-11	70,514	72,864	75,213	77,563	79,913	82,263	84,613	86,963	89,311	91,661
GS-12	84,516	87,334	90,150	92,966	95,784	98,600	101,416	104,234	107,050	109,866
GS-13	100,503	103,854	107,204	110,554	113,904	117,255	120,605	123,955	127,305	130,656
GS-14	118,763	122,723	126,683	130,641	134,601	138,560	142,520	146,480	150,439	154,399
GS-15	139,700	144,358	149,014	153,671	158,328	162,985	167,641	172,299	176,955	181,613

Professional Support Personnel Salaries

Most FBI professional support employees are paid under the General Schedule pay system, at levels ranging from GS-5 to GS-15. Advancement to non-supervisory, supervisory, and management positions varies from one position to another, depending on salary structures for each position. Professional support personnel are not eligible for LEAP because only federal criminal investigators are authorized to receive this premium pay. FBI blue-collar personnel, such as automotive workers and aircraft mechanics, are paid under the Federal Wage System, which includes the Wage Grade Schedule.

Table 2.2 provides an overview of salaries for FBI professional support personnel.

Table 2.2: Annual Salary for FBI Professional Support Personnel, Including Locality Pay for "Rest of United States" Geographic Areas (Based on 2009 General Schedule Salary Rates)										
	Step 1	Step 2	Step 3	Step 4	Step 5	Step 6	Step 7	Step 8	Step 9	Step 10
GS-5	30,772	31,798	32,824	33,849	34,875	35,901	36,927	37,953	38,979	40,005
GS-6	34,300	35,443	36,587	37,730	38,873	40,016	41,159	42,302	43,446	44,589
GS-7	38,117	39,388	40,658	41,929	43,200	44,470	45,741	47,012	48,282	49,553
GS-8	42,214	43,621	45,028	46,436	47,843	49,250	50,657	52,065	53,472	54,879
GS-9	46,625	48,179	49,733	51,287	52,841	54,395	55,950	57,504	59,058	60,612
GS-10	51,345	53,056	54,768	56,479	58,190	59,902	61,613	63,324	65,036	66,747
GS-11	56,411	58,291	60,170	62,050	63,930	65,810	67,690	69,570	71,449	73,329
GS-12	67,613	69,867	72,120	74,373	76,627	78,880	81,133	83,387	85,640	87,893
GS-13	80,402	83,083	85,763	88,443	91,123	93,804	96,484	99,164	101,844	104,525
GS-14	95,010	98,178	101,346	104,513	107,681	110,848	114,016	117,184	120,351	123,519
GS-15	111,760	115,486	119,211	122,937	126,662	130,388	134,113	137,839	141,564	145,290

Locality Payments

FBI personnel receive locality-based comparability payments, known as *locality pay*, for the difference between prevailing federal and private-sector salaries in the geographic location where they are employed. More than 30 metropolitan areas in the United States are designated as qualifying for locality pay. Personnel employed in all other areas receive locality pay according to the rate established for the "Rest of United States" (RUS) category. Locality pay rates are adjusted annually.

Salary schedules shown in tables 2.1 and 2.2 include Rest of U.S. locality pay rates for calendar year 2009. Table 2.3 provides an overview of locality pay for personnel not employed in "Rest of U.S." areas. In other words, employees in these areas receive locality pay in addition to the Rest of U.S. rate, as shown.

Table 2.3: Locality Pay Adjustments for 2009. Rates in Metropolitan Areas in Addition to the "Rest of U.S." Rate	
Metropolitan Area	**Percentage Adjustment**
Atlanta–Sandy Springs–Gainesville, GA-AL	4.69%
Boston–Worcester–Manchester, MA-NH-ME-RI	10.12%
Buffalo–Niagara–Cattaraugus, NY	2.53%
Chicago–Naperville–Michigan City, IL-IN-WI	10.61%
Cincinnati–Middletown–Wilmington, OH-KY-IN	4.42%
Cleveland–Akron–Elyria, OH	4.30%
Columbus–Marion–Chillicothe, OH	2.76%
Dallas–Fort Worth, TX	6.09%
Dayton–Springfield–Greenville, OH	2.04%
Denver–Aurora–Boulder, CO	8.17%
Detroit–Warren–Flint, MI	9.70%
Hartford–West Hartford–Willimantic, CT-MA	11.22%
Houston–Baytown–Huntsville, TX	14.42%
Huntsville–Decatur, AL	1.60%
Indianapolis–Anderson–Columbus, IN	0.37%
Los Angeles–Long Beach–Riverside, CA	12.65%
Miami–Fort Lauderdale–Pompano Beach, FL	6.35%
Milwaukee–Racine–Waukesha, WI	3.79%
Minneapolis–St. Paul–St. Cloud, MN-WI	6.50%
New York–Newark–Bridgeport, NY-NJ-CT-PA	14.10%
Philadelphia–Camden–Vineland, PA-NJ-DE-MD	7.39%
Phoenix–Mesa–Scottsdale, AZ	2.22%
Pittsburgh–New Castle, PA	2.00%
Portland–Vancouver–Beaverton, OR-WA	5.85%
Raleigh–Durham–Cary, NC	3.52%
Richmond, VA	2.24%
Sacramento–Arden–Arcade–Yuba City, CA-NV	7.67%
San Diego–Carlsbad–San Marcos, CA	9.58%
San Jose–San Francisco–Oakland, CA	20.49%
Seattle–Tacoma–Olympia, WA	7.20%
Washington–Baltimore–Northern VA, DC-MD-VA-WV-PA	9.24%

Paid Leave

All FBI personnel receive time off for vacations, sickness and medical care, maternity and paternity leave, holidays, and other purposes. The following sections provide details on the FBI's paid leave policies.

Annual Leave

The Bureau's full-time employees accumulate paid annual leave for vacations or other purposes based on their years of federal service. Annual leave accrues at the rate of 13 days per year (4 hours per pay period) for employees with fewer than 3 years of service, at 20 days per year (6 hours per pay period) for those with 3 to 15 years of service, and at 26 days per year (8 hours per pay period) for personnel with more than 15 years of service. Employees normally are prohibited from carrying forward more than 240 hours of annual leave from year to year.

Paid Holidays

Full-time FBI employees receive paid leave for 10 holidays annually, including the following: New Year's Day, Martin Luther King's Birthday, Washington's Birthday, Memorial Day, Independence Day, Labor Day, Columbus Day, Veterans Day, Thanksgiving Day, and Christmas Day. If a holiday falls on Saturday, the preceding Friday is observed as the legal holiday for employees whose basic workweek is Monday through Friday. Similarly, holidays that fall on Sunday are observed on the following Monday. In the case of employees whose basic workweek is other than Monday through Friday, when a holiday falls on a non-workday, these personnel receive paid leave on the first workday before the holiday. If an employee is required to work on a holiday because of an emergency or special need, the employee receives holiday pay.

Sick Leave

All full-time FBI personnel earn 13 days of paid sick leave per year, in four-hour increments each biweekly pay period. Sick leave can be used for the following:

- Medical, dental, or optical examination or treatment
- Incapacitation
- To prevent the exposure of communicable diseases
- To conduct adoption-related activities
- To provide care for ill family members
- To make arrangements necessitated by the death of a family member or to attend the funeral of a family member

Family and Medical Leave

Under provisions of the Family and Medical Leave Act of 1993, FBI employees can take up to 12 weeks of unpaid leave per year for the following occurrences:

- The birth of or care for a child
- The placement of a child with the employee for adoption or foster care

- The care of a spouse, son, daughter, or parent of the employee who suffers from a serious health condition
- A serious health condition of the employee that makes him or her unable to perform the essential functions of the position

Family and medical leave is available only to those who have served as federal employees for at least one year.

Maternity Leave

Women who want to take time off for maternity purposes—and then return to their positions—can be granted up to six months' leave of absence. During the time the employee is physically incapacitated from duty, she is charged with sick leave. Annual leave and leave without pay can be used after a doctor has determined that the employee is able to return to duty.

Paternity Leave

Male employees can take up to five days of paternity leave to assist or care for their newborn or minor children while the mother is incapacitated for maternity reasons. This leave of absence is charged to the employee's sick leave balance. Up to an additional eight days of paternity leave may be allowed in certain circumstances.

Family-Friendly Leave

Under Family-Friendly Leave provisions, FBI employees can use up to 40 hours of sick leave per year to care for a family member or to arrange or attend an immediate family member's funeral. In certain circumstances, employees can use an additional 64 hours for these purposes.

Additional Leave Benefits

FBI employees are also eligible for leave to attend court either as a witness or a member of a jury, for bone-marrow or organ donations, to serve military obligations, or to vote in elections.

Health Care and Wellness Benefits

The FBI provides a comprehensive package of health benefits to ensure the physical and emotional well-being of its personnel. This section provides an overview of health insurance programs, on-site clinic services, counseling programs, and child-care services that are available to FBI personnel.

Federal Employees Health Benefits Program

Group healthcare insurance is available to all permanent FBI employees through the Federal Employees Health Benefits Program (FEHBP), which is the largest employer-sponsored health insurance program in the world. The FEHBP offers the widest selection of health plans in the nation, including managed fee-for-service plans, point of service (POS) plans, and health maintenance organization (HMO) programs. Enrollees are granted coverage without medical examinations or restrictions relating to age or medical condition, and can elect self-only or self-and-family protection. The government contributes between 60 and 75 percent toward the total cost of premiums, depending on the plan. Employees pay their share of premiums through a payroll deduction.

Federal Long Term Care Insurance

Comprehensive insurance coverage through the Federal Long Term Care Insurance Program is available to all FBI employees. This optional insurance plan pays for chronic care needed in the event of ongoing illness or disability, whether the care is received in the home or at a nursing home, hospice, adult daycare center, or other assisted-living facility. The plan pays for the services of licensed healthcare practitioners, such as assistance with bathing, dressing, or eating, or aid getting in and out of bed, chairs, or a wheelchair. FBI employees and their spouses, children, parents, parents-in-law, and stepparents can obtain insurance coverage under the program.

Federal Flexible Spending Account Program

All FBI personnel are eligible to participate in the Federal Flexible Spending Account (FSA) program, a tax-favored program that allows employees to pay for eligible out-of-pocket healthcare and dependent care expenses with pre-tax dollars. Using pre-tax dollars to pay for healthcare and dependent care expenses provides an immediate discount on these expenses equal to the income taxes that would have been paid. In other words, FSA program participants can both reduce their taxes and save from 20 percent to more than 40 percent on out-of-pocket healthcare and dependent care expenses. Employees can set aside up to $5,000 per year for healthcare expenses and up to an additional $5,000 for dependent care expenses. However, the money in these accounts must be spent in full each year for qualifying expenses incurred that year, and cannot be carried over to future years.

Health Care Programs Unit

The FBI offers a variety of occupational health services to its employees at the J. Edgar Hoover Headquarters Building, the FBI Academy, and the Bureau's 56 field offices. At FBI Headquarters, the Bureau's Health Care Programs Unit (HCPU) provides assessment and treatment of work-related injuries and illnesses, health counseling, referral service to physicians or hospitals, and emergency response in the clinic and throughout the building. The HCPU provides travel immunizations to employees, immunization injections to at-risk personnel, and health screenings for cholesterol, hypertension, and diabetes. The unit also offers educational classes on health and safety issues, such as basic cardiac support and first aid, weight reduction, smoking cessation, back care, safety in the workplace, health issues concerning men and women, proper nutrition, and other areas. Employees assigned to the FBI Academy and the Bureau's field offices are offered similar facilities that are staffed with experienced healthcare professionals and specialty support staff.

Employee Assistance Program

The FBI Employee Assistance Program (EAP) is a service that is available to employees and their immediate families. The EAP is designed to address problems such as alcohol and drug abuse, marital difficulties, legal and financial concerns, and job stress that can adversely affect job performance, reliability, and personal health. The program is staffed by professional counselors who discuss and assess problems and provide short-term counseling. If needed, EAP counselors also provide referrals to other professional services and resources.

The EAP is a confidential program that is protected by strict confidentiality laws and regulations, and by professional ethical standards for counselors. Details of discussions with counselors cannot be released without the written consent of the employee, and EAP records do not become part of any employee security or personnel record. There are no fees for EAP services.

Child-Care Services

The availability of child care for FBI employees varies from one duty station to another. Personnel who serve at FBI Headquarters—which amounts to almost one-third of the Bureau's workforce—have access to "Just Us Kids," a child-development center operated by the United States Department of Justice. This center is located approximately two blocks from the J. Edgar Hoover FBI Building. It accommodates up to 68 children, ages three months to five years, and offers a tuition-assistance program for low-income families. Employees assigned to the Criminal Justice Information Services Division in Clarksburg, West Virginia, have access to a child-development center known as "Lasting Impressions" that operates at the FBI Complex. In addition, many FBI field offices are located in federal office buildings that provide child-care services to federal employees. The Bureau also addresses the need for child care by maintaining listings of resources throughout the country.

Life Insurance

FBI employees can protect themselves and their families with life insurance, disability insurance, and professional liability insurance through a variety of programs. Insurance coverage is available to all FBI personnel, and participation is optional.

Federal Employees' Group Life Insurance

FBI special agents and professional support personnel are eligible to participate in the Federal Employees' Group Life Insurance (FEGLI) Program, a plan that offers both life insurance and accidental death and dismemberment coverage. Premiums are based on the employee's age and are paid through regular payroll deductions. FEGLI policies build no cash or loan value, and participants are not permitted to borrow against life insurance benefits. Participants can purchase additional life insurance to cover eligible family members, although accidental death and dismemberment coverage is not included. The amount of basic life insurance coverage is equal to an employee's annual basic pay, rounded up to the next even $1,000, plus an additional $2,000, although employees can purchase additional insurance equal to as much as five times their annual basic pay. The government pays approximately one-third of the premium for basic life insurance; the remaining two-thirds is withheld from the employee's pay by payroll deduction.

Other Sources of Insurance Coverage

FBI personnel can also purchase life insurance, accidental death and dismemberment insurance, disability insurance, and professional liability insurance through the Special Agents Mutual Benefit Association and the Special Agents Trust for Insurance. In addition, FBI employees can join the Employee Benevolent Fund, which pays their survivors $17,500 within one workday if they die while employed by the FBI. The fund pays an additional $100,000 if the employee dies due to a terrorist-related incident. The Special Agents Insurance Fund pays a $30,000 benefit for the death of an agent, whether job-related or not.

Travel and Commuting Allowances

FBI special agents and many professional support employees must travel on official business from time to time. The Bureau provides full reimbursement for airfare, lodging, rental cars, parking, taxis, and other expenses for travel throughout the United States and worldwide. FBI employees can also receive subsidies to help pay the costs of traveling to and from work.

Reimbursement of Travel Expenses

FBI employees who travel on official business normally receive reimbursement for their transportation and lodging expenses, plus a daily allowance for meals and incidental expenses (M&IE). This allowance applies to travel undertaken during the course of investigative assignments, attendance in training programs, and other activities in furtherance of the Bureau's mission. Most hotel chains and many independent establishments offer discounted lodging rates for FBI employees and other government travelers. M&IE allowances are paid at a government-wide flat daily rate, which varies from one locality to another depending on prevailing costs in the area visited.

Public Transportation Subsidies

The FBI offers public transportation subsidies to its personnel to encourage the use of mass transit and to defray the costs of commuting. Employees are eligible to receive the Justice Employees' Transit Subsidy if they travel to and from work via subway, bus, train, commuter vehicles occupied by six or more adults (such as van pools), or other qualifying transportation modes.

Death and Disability Benefits for Special Agents

The United States Congress enacted the Public Safety Officers' Benefits Act and the Federal Law Enforcement Dependents Assistance Act to provide benefits to the families of law enforcement officers whose deaths or disabilities are the result of injuries sustained in the line of duty. Congress has also enacted provisions to allow federal officers to attend funerals for fellow law enforcement personnel during duty hours.

Public Safety Officers' Benefits Program

The families of federal law enforcement officers, including FBI special agents, are eligible to receive death and disability benefits under the Public Safety Officers' Benefits (PSOB) Act, which was enacted to assist in the recruitment and retention of law enforcement officers and firefighters. The act was designed to offer peace of mind to men and women seeking careers in public safety and to make a strong statement about the value American society places on the contributions of those who serve their communities in potentially dangerous circumstances.

The PSOB program provides a one-time financial payment to the eligible survivors of public safety officers whose deaths are the direct and proximate result of a traumatic injury sustained in the line of duty. The program provides the same benefit to those who have been permanently and totally disabled by a catastrophic personal injury sustained in the line of duty if that injury permanently prevents them from performing any gainful work. Since 1988, the benefit has been adjusted annually to reflect the percentage of change in the Consumer Price Index. In fiscal year 2009, the benefit was adjusted to $315,746.

Law enforcement officers eligible for PSOB program benefits include, but are not limited to, police, corrections, probation, parole, judicial, and other law enforcement officers of federal, state, county, and local public agencies, as well as the District of Columbia, the Commonwealth of Puerto Rico, and any U.S. territory or possession.

Federal Law Enforcement Dependents Assistance Program

Congress enacted the Federal Law Enforcement Dependents Assistance (FLEDA) Act of 1996 to provide financial assistance for higher education to the spouses and children of federal law enforcement officers killed or disabled in the line of duty. FLEDA benefits are intended for the sole purpose of paying for educational expenses, including tuition, room and board, books, supplies, and fees for dependents who attend a qualifying program of education at an eligible institution. Assistance under the program is available for a period of 45 months of full-time education or training, or for a proportional period for a part-time program.

Funeral Leave for Law Enforcement Officers

FBI special agents and other federal law enforcement officers may be excused from duty, without loss of pay or leave, to attend the funeral of a fellow federal law enforcement officer who was killed in the line of duty. Attendance at such a service is considered to be an official duty, and employing agencies are authorized under the United States Code to pay the costs of travel and subsistence for those who attend (Title 5, U.S. Code, Section 6328).

Retirement Benefits

Most federal civilian employees, including FBI professional support staff, are eligible to receive an unreduced retirement annuity at age 60 with 20 years of service, and at age 62 with five years of service. With 30 years of service, those who are covered under the Federal Employees Retirement System (FERS), which includes most employees hired after December 31, 1983, can retire at age 55 to 57, depending on their year of birth. Employees who are covered under the Civil Service Retirement System (CSRS), the predecessor to FERS, can retire at age 55 with 30 years of service. There is no mandatory retirement age for FBI professional support employees. Special agents, however, must retire by age 57 because they are covered under special retirement provisions for law enforcement officers.

FERS is a three-tiered plan consisting of a Basic Annuity Benefit, the Thrift Savings Plan, and Social Security. Upon completion of five years of civilian service, prior military service can be counted toward the service requirements under certain circumstances.

Basic Annuity Benefit

Retired FBI employees receive a basic annuity benefit based on the length of their federal service and their earnings history. If an employee reaches the minimum retirement age and has at least 20 years of creditable service, he can retire and begin receiving the basic annuity benefit immediately. This benefit is reduced if the employee retires under the age of 62, unless he retires under one of the following conditions:

- With 20 years of service at age 60
- With 30 years of service at the minimum retirement age
- Following an involuntary separation through no fault of the employee after completing 25 years of service (or 20 years if at least age 50)

An employee is also entitled to a basic annuity benefit at any age if approved for disability retirement, although some restrictions apply.

Thrift Savings Plan

The federal Thrift Savings Plan (TSP) is a retirement savings and investment plan for federal personnel that offers the same type of savings and tax benefits that many private firms provide under 401(k) plans. The TSP offers tax-deferred investment earnings, a choice of investment funds, a loan program, portable benefits on leaving government service, and a choice of withdrawal options.

Employees may contribute up to 15 percent of their basic pay each pay period to a TSP account, although contributions are restricted by annual limits prescribed by the Internal Revenue Code. The FBI matches each employee contribution dollar for dollar on the first 3 percent contributed, and 50 cents on the dollar for the next 2 percent. All contributions to an employee's TSP account earn interest and can be divided among six funds, including government securities investments (the "G Fund"), fixed income investments (the "F Fund"), common stock investments (the "C Fund"), small capitalization stock investments (the "S Fund"), international stock investments (the "I Fund"), and Lifecycle investments (the "L Fund"). Employees also have the opportunity to borrow against their TSP contributions.

An employee who leaves the government prior to retirement can either obtain a refund of their contributions or leave the contributions in his or her account and allow the account to earn interest. Employee contributions, agency matching funds, and earnings on all TSP accounts are deferred from income taxes until funds are withdrawn.

Social Security

All new FBI personnel are automatically covered under the Social Security system. An employee can apply for regular Social Security benefits as early as age 62. Disability Social Security benefits are conditionally available at any age.

Special Retirement Provisions for Special Agents

The majority of fully commissioned federal law enforcement officers are covered under special provisions that provide for voluntary and mandatory retirement at an earlier age than other government employees. These provisions apply not only to FBI special agents, but also to other law enforcement officers who serve in certain "covered" positions, including most criminal investigators, police officers, correctional officers, field personnel assigned to federal correctional institutions and military detention or rehabilitation facilities, and certain other law enforcement officers and security specialists. FBI special agents can receive an unreduced retirement annuity at age 50 with 20 years of federal law enforcement service, or at any age with 25 years of such service. Retirement is mandatory for FBI special agents at the end of the month in which they turn 57, provided that they have at least 20 years of law enforcement service.

PART 2

GETTING INTO
THE FBI

CHAPTER 3

FBI Special Agent Career Opportunities

"Courage is its own reward."

—Plautus

FBI special agents are recruited from a broad range of educational disciplines and professions, and receive outstanding basic and in-service training to prepare them for unique challenges. In addition to conducting investigations and protecting the United States from foreign intelligence and terrorist threats, FBI special agents also provide leadership and assistance to law enforcement agencies nationwide and throughout the world. The Bureau has the largest force of criminal investigators of all federal law enforcement agencies, with almost one-half of its 32,000 personnel serving as special agents.

Investigative responsibilities of FBI special agents include more than 260 federal statutes, such as those relating to bank robbery, bank fraud, credit card fraud, money laundering, wire fraud, computer crimes, mail fraud, organized crime, and bankruptcy fraud. Among the greatest challenges FBI special agents face is involvement with high-profile cases, such as investigations relating to public corruption, bribery, kidnapping, air piracy, terrorism, and civil-rights violations. These investigations demand skill, tact, and undaunted perseverance, and frequently require sensitive investigative methods, undercover operations, court-ordered electronic surveillance, and interaction with informants. The investigative techniques and strategies special agents use are subject to rigorous review and approval procedures.

Many investigations are conducted through task force or joint operations with other law enforcement agencies, through cooperation with law enforcement agencies in foreign countries, and with the assistance of assistant United States Attorneys. Cases are prosecuted by United States Attorney's offices located within the jurisdiction of the investigation.

This chapter provides insight into what it takes to become one of America's finest, as well as the types of investigative and special assignments that FBI special agents can expect throughout their careers.

Investigative Priorities

The FBI focuses its investigative efforts primarily on complex cases that have a major impact on the security and quality of life for U.S. citizens. The FBI's strategic plan enumerates 10 priorities to articulate the manner in which the FBI will address its responsibilities, each of which is detailed in the following sections.

1. Protect the United States from Terrorist Attacks

Terrorism is the most significant threat to national security our nation faces. Congress has designated the FBI as the lead federal law enforcement agency for the investigation of incidents involving terrorism in the United States, as well as terrorist acts against U.S. citizens overseas. Since the terrorist attacks of 9/11, the FBI has shifted its counterterrorism culture from a reactive approach to a proactive, "threat-based" strategy. The FBI's Counterterrorism Program is responsible for the investigation of incidents involving weapons of mass destruction, threats against atomic energy, sabotage, hostage-taking, civil unrest, and other threats and attacks. The program's mission to combat terrorism is carried out through the Bureau's Counterterrorism Division, which includes the National Infrastructure Protection Center and the National Domestic Preparedness Office, as well as Joint Terrorism Task Force (JTTF) operations nationwide. The FBI coordinates intelligence-gathering and other counterterrorism activities with various Defense Department agencies, the Department of Homeland Security, the Central Intelligence Agency, and dozens of other federal agencies. Counterterrorism is the FBI's top priority in the allocation of funding, personnel, physical space, resources, hiring, and training.

2. Protect the United States Against Foreign Intelligence Operations and Espionage

As the remaining world superpower, the United States is targeted by nations and terrorist groups from nearly every corner of the globe. The Bureau plays a vital role in America's counterintelligence efforts, and is responsible for producing domestic foreign intelligence in support of other members of the Intelligence Community. The FBI's foreign counterintelligence responsibilities revolve around preventing and investigating foreign espionage; economic espionage; international terrorism threats; weapons of mass destruction threats; and attacks on the nation's critical infrastructures, including communications, transportation, and banking systems. The Counterintelligence Program focuses on preventing hostile groups from acquiring technology to produce weapons of mass destruction; preventing the compromise of personnel, information, technology, and economic interests vital to national security; and producing intelligence on the strategies and plans of terrorists. The FBI is the lead agency within the U.S. intelligence community for the investigation and prevention of foreign counterintelligence and espionage.

3. Protect the United States Against Cyber-Based Attacks and High-Technology Crimes

The cybercrime threat confronting the United States is rapidly increasing as the number of people with the ability to use computers is rising. Cyber threats fall into categories such as computer intrusions, theft of sensitive data and intellectual property, illicit file sharing, online sexual exploitation of children, and Internet fraud. The FBI Cyber Program supports crucial counterterrorism, counterintelligence, and criminal investigations to identify and neutralize those who unlawfully access computer systems, spread malicious code, support terrorists, or otherwise pose a threat to the nation's high-technology infrastructure or national security. The FBI is uniquely positioned with its investigative jurisdiction, technical resources, personnel, and network relationships to address the threat from multi-jurisdictional cyber crimes and cyber terrorism.

4. Combat Public Corruption at All Levels

Investigations of public officials are among the most sensitive operations carried out by the FBI. A wide range of federal statutes and investigative techniques are utilized in corruption investigations. These cases focus on personnel serving in federal, state, and municipal agencies, whether in the executive, legislative, or judicial branches of government. The Bureau's public corruption investigations have focused on a variety of officials and circumstances, such as law enforcement officers who assisted drug-trafficking enterprises, members of Congress who supported legislation for a fee, judges who accepted bribes to rule on court cases, school board members who received kickbacks, and city officials who accepted bribes in exchange for granting lucrative government construction contracts. In an effort to prevent the illegal entry of terrorists into the United States, the FBI places particular emphasis on anti-corruption strategies along the nation's borders.

5. Protect Civil Rights

The FBI is the primary federal agency responsible for investigating violations of civil-rights laws focusing on hate crimes, discrimination in housing programs, slavery, church arson, and other offenses. Violations of the Civil Rights Act of 1964, Voting Rights Act of 1965, Fair Housing Act, Equal Credit Opportunity Act, Freedom of Access to Clinic Entrances Act, and other statutes are the responsibility of the FBI's Civil Rights Program. Investigations pertaining to excessive use of force by federal, state, and local law enforcement officers also fall under the civil-rights umbrella.

6. Combat Transnational and National Criminal Organizations and Enterprises

The FBI's Organized Crime Program consists of strategies and initiatives that target complex national and international criminal enterprises engaged in activities such as loan sharking, drug trafficking, money laundering, cargo theft, art and cultural antiquity theft, weapons trafficking, and homicide by violent gang members.

With the investigation of international organized crime established as a leading priority, the FBI Organized Crime Section includes special units dedicated to the investigation of African, Asian, Italian, and Eastern European organized crime enterprises. To combat drug trafficking, the Bureau combines forces with the Drug Enforcement Administration and other law enforcement agencies through nationwide joint task forces, including the Organized Crime and Drug Enforcement Task Force (OCDETF) and High Intensity Drug Trafficking Area (HIDTA) initiatives. Investigations involving labor racketeering often target violations under the Racketeer Influenced and Corrupt Organizations (RICO) statute. The Organized Crime Program relies largely upon sophisticated investigative techniques, informants, and extensive criminal intelligence.

7. Combat Major White-Collar Crime

Economic crime investigations are among the Bureau's highest priorities. These investigations are managed primarily by the FBI's Financial Crimes Section, which is a component of the Criminal Investigations Division. Offenses investigated under the White-Collar Crime Program focus on fraud against the government, healthcare fraud, financial institution fraud, money laundering, government procurement fraud, corruption of public officials, environmental crimes, election law violations, insurance fraud, telemarketing fraud, identity theft, and other offenses. The White-Collar Crime Program is the largest of the FBI's criminal investigation programs. Much of its success in the white-collar crime arena is a result of the strong relationships the Bureau maintains with federal law enforcement and regulatory agencies.

8. Combat Major Thefts and Significant Violent Crime

The FBI plays a significant role in the investigation of major thefts and violent crimes through its investigative proficiency, technical expertise, national and international response capabilities, crisis management and command post operations, crime scene processing, forensic analysis, and other resources. Under the Violent Crime and Major Offenders Program, the FBI investigates offenses such as kidnapping, assaults, crimes against children, extortion, bank robbery, consumer product tampering, crimes on Indian reservations, and unlawful flight to avoid prosecution. Investigations relating to assaults on the president, vice president, members of Congress, and federal officers also are targeted, as are crimes aboard aircraft, murder for hire, and criminal activity of street gangs. Many of the FBI's violent crime and major theft investigations are managed through joint task force operations in partnership with other federal, state, and local law enforcement agencies.

9. Support Federal, State, Municipal, and International Partners

A critical component of the FBI's mission is to provide leadership and support to federal, state, local, and international law enforcement agencies. In furtherance of this goal, the FBI created the Office of Law Enforcement Coordination within months of the 9/11 attacks to improve cooperation and the flow of information to and from other law enforcement and intelligence agencies. The FBI is planning to expand its Legal Attaché program to better assist federal, state, and local agencies with investigative leads crossing international boundaries, while also assisting foreign agencies with technical and investigative expertise. The FBI Laboratory offers substantial support to U.S. and international law enforcement agencies by conducting scientific analyses of physical evidence; providing expert testimony in court cases; and offering forensic science courses, technical assistance, and crime scene training to all levels of laboratory personnel and law enforcement officers. The Bureau also has increased its level of support to other agencies through technical, tactical, and intelligence services, including cyber technology, electronic surveillance, radio communications, and criminal justice information services.

10. Upgrade Technology to Successfully Perform the FBI's Mission

Following the terrorist attacks of 9/11, the FBI launched an aggressive effort to upgrade the tools that are fundamental to achieving its mission. These encompass a wide range of investigative technology, forensics, information technology, communications technology, and records management systems. As a result, upgrades now underway are focusing on the Bureau's electronic surveillance devices; communications equipment; intelligence-gathering tools; forensic laboratory equipment and services; computer equipment, software, and databases; security programs to protect its personnel, facilities, data, and other assets; information-sharing and reporting technologies; and recordkeeping systems. These investments directly support the FBI's investigations; collection, analysis, and dissemination of intelligence and other information; administrative processes; and other operations that empower the FBI and its law enforcement partners in the United States and worldwide.

Qualifications for the Special Agent Position

Special agent applicants must meet a number of qualifications to be eligible for employment, including standards relating to citizenship, entry age, education, eyesight, hearing, and physical fitness, among others. These qualifications represent the first hurdle applicants must clear on the road to becoming an FBI special agent.

Basic Qualifications

The work of FBI special agents is rigorous and demanding—and sometimes dangerous. Special agents must be mentally and physically fit in order to perform surveillance and undercover work, conduct interviews and interrogations, execute search warrants, make arrests, and respond to critical incidents. The position demands alertness, intelligence, and good judgment, whether special agents are involved in fact-finding tasks, working with informants, using sophisticated electronic investigative equipment, advising assistant United States Attorneys, or testifying in court. To ensure that the FBI recruits qualified personnel who can face these challenges successfully, special agent applicants must meet the following qualifications to be considered for the position.

United States Citizenship

All applicants for special agent positions must be citizens of the United States or of the Northern Mariana Islands. Resident aliens of the U.S. and other non-citizens do not qualify for FBI employment.

U.S. citizens who possess dual citizenship may or may not qualify for appointment to FBI jobs, depending on each applicant's particular circumstances.
Although U.S. laws and FBI policies do not prevent the Bureau from hiring
dual citizens, the manner in which an applicant has held or exercised his
or her dual citizenship status may be relevant when considering them for
employment. In addition, dual citizenship may be incorporated as one of
many factors to be considered in decisions to grant or withhold a security
clearance. The FBI follows government-wide Executive Orders and adjudicative
standards in evaluating dual-citizenship issues, and decisions are made on a
case-by-case basis.

Some circumstances relating to dual citizenship that could be of particular
concern and may result in disqualification from the hiring process include the
following:

- Possession or use of a foreign passport

- Military service or a willingness to bear arms for a foreign country

- Accepting educational, medical, or other benefits, such as retirement and
  social welfare, from a foreign country

- Residence in a foreign country to meet citizenship requirements

- Using foreign citizenship to protect financial or business interests in
  another country

- Seeking or holding political office in a foreign country

- Voting in foreign elections

- Performing or attempting to perform duties to serve the interests of
  another government in preference to the interests of the United States

Security concerns could be alleviated if the dual citizenship is based solely on
parents' citizenship or birth in a foreign country, or if an applicant's previous
foreign preference (such as foreign military service) occurred before obtaining
U.S. citizenship. An applicant's willingness to renounce his or her foreign citizenship also could be a consideration.

Minimum and Maximum Age

Special agent candidates must be at least 23 years of age, and must not have
reached their 37th birthday at the time of appointment. The maximum entry
age of 37 ensures that special agents will be able to complete 20 years of service by age 57, which is the mandatory retirement age. (Special agents must
serve for at least 20 years to qualify for retirement.) The FBI advises anyone
over the age of 36½ not to apply for a special agent position, considering the
length of time it takes to test, process, and hire new agents.

Education Requirements

Applicants must possess a bachelor's degree from a four-year resident program
at a college or university accredited by one of the regional or national institutional associations recognized by the United States Secretary of Education. No
particular major is required, unless an applicant wants to qualify under the
Accounting Program (see "Entrance Programs," later in this chapter).

Driver's License

Special agent candidates must have a driver's license to be eligible for appointment to the special agent position. Accordingly, a question on the FBI Online Application for employment asks applicants whether they possess a valid U.S. driver's license.

Eyesight Requirements

Eyesight requirements include uncorrected vision not worse than 20/200 (on the Snellen scale) and corrected vision not worse than 20/20 in one eye and 20/40 in the other eye. However, the FBI may grant a waiver to applicants with uncorrected vision worse than 20/200 if (a) soft contact lenses are worn and have been worn for a period of more than one year, (b) the minimum corrected vision requirement (shown above) has been met, and (c) there are no indications of corneal change that might require discontinuation of contact lenses in the future. Applicants seeking a waiver are evaluated on a case-by-case basis, and no formal Snellen scale limit has been established. Applicants who have undergone surgical vision correction also are evaluated on a case-by-case basis by the FBI's Health Care Programs Unit. The Bureau has accepted applicants who have had LASIK laser vision correction in the past, although these candidates must wait six months from the time of surgery to be considered as a special agent. All candidates must also pass a color-vision test. Those who fail initial color-vision screening—presently the Ishihara color plates test—will be permitted to continue with applicant processing upon successfully completing the Farnsworth D-15 color-vision test.

Hearing Requirements

An audiometer test is used to determine whether special agent candidates meet minimum hearing requirements. Hearing loss must not exceed: (a) average hearing loss of 25 decibels (ANSI) at 1000, 2000, and 3000 Hertz; (b) a single reading of 35 decibels at 1000, 2000, and 3000 Hertz; (c) a single reading of 35 decibels at 500 Hertz; and (d) a single reading of 45 decibels at 4000 Hertz.

Medical Examination

An extensive physical examination is required during the final screening phase of the application process. Prior to appointment, each candidate's medical history is reviewed, and a determination is made about whether any medical issue or condition could possibly affect the applicant's ability to perform the basic functions of the position. Additional information concerning the medical examination and preexisting conditions is provided in chapter 4, "The Special Agent Hiring Process."

Physical Fitness

FBI special agents must have the strength and endurance necessary to successfully deal with strenuous and dangerous situations. Therefore, applicants must be in excellent physical condition and deemed by the FBI's chief medical officer to be physically able to use firearms, participate in raids, execute defensive tactics, and perform other essential functions of the job. Applicants must pass a Physical Fitness Test (PFT) toward the end of the hiring process. The PFT consists of four events, including a 300-meter timed sprint, push-ups, sit-ups, and a 1.5-mile timed run. Additional details regarding the PFT, including scoring scales, are provided in chapter 4, "The Special Agent Hiring Process."

Entrance Programs

The FBI fulfills its mission by employing a diverse workforce with a variety of talents. To this end, the Bureau requires special agent candidates to qualify under at least one of five entry programs, including Law, Accounting, Language, Computer Science/Information Technology, and Diversified. The following sections provide an overview of the entry requirements under each program.

Law

Applicants must have a law degree (Juris Doctorate) from an accredited resident law school to qualify under the Law Entry Program.

Accounting

Applicants can qualify under the Accounting Entry Program through Certified Public Accountant certification or a combination of education and experience. Those who have not attained CPA certification must have a four-year college degree with a major in accounting, or a related business degree that included or was supplemented by 24 hours of accounting courses and an additional six semester hours of business law or other elective business courses. An applicant who is not a CPA also must have three years of progressively responsible accounting work in a professional accounting firm or comparable public setting, such as a state comptroller or the Government Accountability Office. (An applicant who is not a CPA and has earned a master's degree must have only two years of accounting experience as just described.) These applicants also must have experience either in management, as a team leader, or in a position that provided experience in areas such as banking, insurance, or problem solving.

Language

Applicants must have a bachelor's degree in any discipline and be proficient in a language that meets the needs of the FBI to qualify under the Language Entry Program. Candidates must pass both the listening and reading portions of the Defense Language Proficiency Test and demonstrate a proficiency of three or higher on the Speaking Proficiency Test in a critical foreign language. Applicants who want to qualify under the Language Program are required to answer questions about their language proficiency in the Online Application for the Special Agent Position (see appendix E for the Language Proficiency Self-Assessment Chart).

Computer Science/Information Technology

To qualify under the Computer Science/Information Technology Entry Program, applicants must have a bachelor's degree related to computer science or information technology, or have a bachelor's degree in electrical engineering, or have earned certification as either a Cisco Certified Network Professional (CCNP) or Cisco Certified Internetworking Expert (CCIE). Applicants who qualify by virtue of CCNP or CCIE certification can qualify with a bachelor's degree in any discipline.

Diversified

Applicants who qualify under the Diversified Entry Program must have a bachelor's degree in any discipline and three years of full-time work experience, or an advanced degree and two years of full-time work experience. The FBI does not consider internships, co-op positions, summer employment, or temporary employment as full-time work experience.

Critical Skills

In addition to requiring applicants to meet basic entry requirements, the FBI may give priority to applicants who possess certain "critical skills," depending on the needs of the Bureau at any given time. Although the list of critical skills varies periodically, applicants with experience in the following areas were deemed most competitive during a recent recruiting drive:

- Accounting

- Finance

- Computer science or other information technology

- Engineering

- Foreign language proficiency (especially Arabic, Farsi, Hebrew, Hindi, Pashtu, Punjabi, Urdu, Chinese, Japanese, Korean, Russian, Spanish, and Vietnamese)

- Intelligence (also includes candidates who possess a degree in international studies, international finance, or other closely related disciplines)

- Law

- Law enforcement or investigations

- Military

- Physical sciences (such as physics, chemistry, biology, forensics, mathematics, medical specialties, or nursing)

- Tactical operations and special forces (law enforcement or military)

Keep in mind that the needs of the FBI are constantly changing, and that applicants who possess knowledge, skills, and abilities in areas other than those on the "critical skills list" also may qualify to apply. For example, during the period in which the FBI had given priority to candidates with any of the skills just listed, applicants with experience in business, education, and other fields also were encouraged to apply.

Automatic Disqualifiers

The FBI will automatically disqualify applicants from consideration for the special agent position under certain circumstances. Automatic disqualifiers include the following:

- Conviction of a felony

- Use or sale of illegal drugs in violation of the FBI Employment Drug Policy (see chapter 4), or an applicant's misrepresentation of his or her drug history during the hiring process

- Refusal to submit to FBI urinalysis drug testing

- Failure of a urinalysis drug test

- Default of a student loan that was insured by the U.S. Government

- Refusal to submit to an FBI polygraph examination

- Failure to register with the Selective Service System, if required

- Omitting, misstating, or falsifying any information—in writing or orally—to the FBI during the hiring process (If the omission, misstatement, or falsification is discovered after hiring, the person may be subject to administrative or disciplinary action, or dismissal.)

- Unwillingness to be available for employment within 90 days of phase II testing or to report for New Agent Training within two weeks of completion of the application process

- Unwillingness to accept a permanent or temporary assignment anywhere worldwide according to the needs of the Bureau

- Unwillingness to undergo a comprehensive background investigation

- Membership in any foreign or domestic organization, association, movement, group, or combination of persons that is totalitarian, fascist, communist, or subversive; or that has adopted, or shows a policy of advocating or approving the commission of acts of force or violence to deny other persons their rights under the Constitution of the United States; or that seeks to alter the form of government of the U.S. by unconstitutional means

Additional Requirements

Additional requirements for the special agent position include a willingness to carry firearms, a willingness to relocate, the ability to report for duty within 90 days of phase II testing, availability for duty at all times, and completion of basic training. The following sections give details on these additional requirements.

Willingness to Carry Firearms

Applicants must be willing to carry firearms and use them in training and life-threatening situations if they are hired as a special agent. All newly hired special agents are trained in the use and maintenance of firearms during the New Agent Training Program at the FBI Academy in Quantico, Virginia. Prior experience or proficiency with firearms is not required. Special agents must also agree to be armed or have immediate access to a firearm at all times when on official duty unless good judgment dictates otherwise, and to utilize deadly force should circumstances dictate.

Willingness to Relocate

Anyone appointed to the special agent position must be willing to relocate anywhere in the FBI's geographic jurisdiction. Although newly hired special agents normally are not assigned to permanent posts of duty outside the United States, they must be available for duty anywhere in the world.

Therefore, as a condition of employment, new special agents must sign a Worldwide Mobility Agreement (FD-918) indicating their willingness to accept a permanent or temporary duty (TDY) assignment anywhere worldwide according to the needs of the Bureau (see appendix C for a copy of this agreement). Applicants must also attest to their willingness to accept assignments anywhere in the FBI's geographic jurisdiction when completing the Online Application for employment early in the hiring process (see appendix A for a copy of the application questions). Normally, the FBI seeks qualified volunteers for assignments overseas.

Reporting for Duty

Applicants must be available for employment within 90 days of phase II testing, and to accept no more than two weeks' notice to report for New Agent Training upon successful completion of the application process. Applicants must attest to their willingness to report for duty, as specified in the preceding section, in the Online Application.

Availability for Duty at All Times

Applicants must indicate their willingness to be available for duty around the clock, 365 days per year, according to the needs of the Bureau. Availability for duty may include weekends, holidays, overtime, or an irregular schedule. Special agents must work an average of 10 hours per day.

Completion of Basic Training

Newly hired special agents must successfully complete the 21-week New Agent Training Program at the FBI Academy in Quantico, Virginia, before being assigned to a post of duty. (See chapter 8 for additional details about initial and in-service training.)

Assignment of New Special Agents

Although new hires who land jobs with private companies—as well as with most federal law enforcement agencies—have the luxury of knowing in advance where they will be assigned, FBI special agents could end up almost anyplace in the United States upon completing basic training. After reporting for duty, new agents are assigned to offices and investigative squads where they apply what they learned at the FBI Academy under the guidance of experienced agents. This section provides some insight into the assignment and work life of new FBI special agents.

Location of Initial Assignment

At the beginning of the New Agent Training Program, all special agent trainees are provided with a list of the FBI's 56 nationwide field offices. New agent trainees are asked to review the list and indicate where they would like to be assigned, in order of their preference from 1 through 56. Office assignments are based on the current staffing and critical specialty needs of the Bureau at the time. The Bureau notifies trainees of their office assignments around the sixth week of training, and about 70 percent receive one of their top 10 choices. Initial assignment to the trainee's hometown, however, is unusual.

Although trainees are allowed to rank-order the 56 field offices on their "wish list," assignments can also include any of the FBI's resident agencies. For example, if the Bureau were to honor a trainee's preference for the Detroit field office, the trainee could be assigned to a resident agency in Lansing, Grand Rapids, Bay City, or any other resident agency under the jurisdiction of the Detroit field office. New special agents normally remain at their first office of assignment for a minimum of four years.

Probationary Period

Newly hired special agents are required to serve a two-year probationary period. Preference-eligible veterans, however, are required to serve only a one-year probationary period. In either case, much of a special agent's first two years on the job are spent under the watchful eye of veteran special agents and supervisory personnel, who provide advice and guidance.

A Special Agent's Work Life

One of the most interesting aspects of an FBI special agent's work life is that their job is anything but routine. Whether they are reviewing business records at an FBI field office, conducting interviews at a local bank, executing a search warrant, or conducting surveillance throughout the night, the daily activities, work environments, dress code, and work hours of special agents can vary widely from one day to another.

Office Environment

Office and workspace in FBI field offices and resident agencies vary widely from one location to another. Many FBI offices are located in federal office buildings along with an assortment of other agencies. Being co-located with other federal offices in the same building has its advantages, as taking the elevator to another floor makes quick work of conducting interviews, reviewing files, or obtaining information from other federal agencies. Many Bureau offices occupy space in federal courthouses or post office facilities. Others rent office space within private buildings, and some have their own buildings. Special agents assigned to task-force operations often share offsite office space with personnel from other law enforcement agencies.

Personal workspace arrangements also vary from office to office. Some field offices provide desks in open "bullpen" areas, whereas others offer semi-private cubicles or private offices.

Dress Code

The dress code in FBI offices varies, although this is more dependent on agents' activities than office location. When J. Edgar Hoover was FBI Director, special agents were required to wear suits along with white shirts, and neckties that matched the color of their suit lining. It wasn't until 1972, when L. Patrick Gray was appointed Director, that special agents were permitted to wear colored shirts. Today, agents are allowed to dress according to their day-to-day activities and assignments. For example, an agent who is conducting mobile surveillance is permitted to "dress down," and casual attire would be appropriate. Similarly, the execution of search or arrest warrants could call for either casual or tactical attire and equipment—such as raid pants, jackets with FBI markings, leather gear, and body armor—depending on the situation and environment. Agents are expected to wear business attire—such as a suit, dress, or pantsuit for females, and a suit or coat and tie for males—while in the office or working in a business atmosphere outside the office.

Work Hours

In consideration of rules relating to Law Enforcement Availability Pay, Congress requires FBI special agents and most other federal agents to average a 10-hour workday. Most FBI special agents work 50 to 55 hours per week, although this can vary considerably during weeks in which surveillance or special operations are undertaken, or when preparing for a criminal trial or execution of a search warrant. Special agents often begin or end their workday away from the office. For example, if an agent is scheduled to meet with an assistant United States Attorney or other law enforcement officer at 8:00 a.m., the agent probably could drive to the meeting site directly from home. In this case, time associated with the agent's commute to the meeting would count toward his or her 10-hour workday. The same holds true when returning home from activities in the field.

Equipment

Most special agents are issued a cellular telephone, a car that is equipped with law enforcement communications equipment, and a credit card to cover travel expenses. Many are also issued a laptop computer. Presently, new agents are issued a .40 caliber semiautomatic pistol and soft body armor, as well as equipment such as holsters, ammunition pouches, eye and hearing protection for the firearms range, and handcuffs. FBI field offices are equipped with shotguns and submachine guns, so that there is one shoulder weapon per field agent nationwide. Members of special response teams are issued additional equipment according to their responsibilities.

Squad Assignments

FBI field office personnel are organized into various investigative "squads" that specialize in certain crimes, ranging from bank robbery to healthcare fraud, public corruption, counterterrorism, and white-collar crime, among others. The variety of squads and number of assigned members varies from one office to another, depending largely on the size of the office, the nature of crime in the area, the existence of task force operations, or investigative priorities established by the FBI or United States Attorney's offices. In addition, many offices combine the investigative responsibilities of various squads. For example, some offices combine organized crime and drug squads because these offenses often are committed by the same groups. Other offices have squads that combine the investigation of economic and environmental crimes, property crime with violent crime, or public corruption with government fraud. To provide its personnel with a broad range of investigative responsibilities and experiences, the Bureau tends to rotate special agents periodically from one squad to another throughout their careers.

Although not all-inclusive, the following sections provide examples of the functions carried out by many of the primary FBI squads presently operating at the Bureau's field offices.

Applicant Squads

FBI applicant squads are responsible for the recruitment and processing of candidates for employment with the Bureau, including special agents and professional support personnel. Among their primary responsibilities, applicant squads conduct background investigations for all FBI candidates who have been issued a conditional letter of appointment—from mail clerks to the FBI director. These squads also conduct background investigations for appointees to presidential cabinet posts, other presidential appointees, White House staff, and applicants for positions with the Department of Energy, Nuclear Regulatory Commission, Department of Justice, and United States Courts. Some applicant squads are also responsible for training, media relations, security programs, and other tasks.

Civil-Rights Squads

The FBI is the primary federal agency responsible for investigating violations of federal civil-rights laws. Investigations carried out by civil-rights squads focus on hate crimes and discrimination cases that, based on their severity, cannot be addressed appropriately on local or state levels. Special agents assigned to civil-rights squads maintain liaisons with local, state, and federal law enforcement agencies and community and civic organizations to identify, detect, and deter all forms of discrimination, as well as acts of hatred and violence. Guidelines relating to federal civil-rights investigations have been established by the FBI and the United States Attorney General.

Civil-rights squads investigate crimes involving racial and religious discrimination, and other violations under the Civil Rights Act of 1964; Color of Law violations, which focus most often on excessive force by law enforcement officers; and violations of the Church Arson Prevention Act. Investigations also focus on violations of the Freedom of Access to Clinic Entrances Act violations, which involves use of force, threats, or physical obstruction of persons seeking to obtain or provide reproductive health services; involuntary servitude and slavery cases; and discrimination in housing under the Fair Housing Act. Civil-rights squads also investigate violations of the Voting Rights Act of 1965, the Equal Credit Opportunity Act, and the Civil Rights of Institutionalized Persons Act.

Computer Crime Squads

Illegal electronic intrusion into computer networks is a rapidly escalating crime and security risk. Businesses and government agencies are vulnerable to attacks that are designed to alter, steal, or destroy information in their computer systems. Such attacks could be devastating if launched on critical systems constituting the national critical infrastructures, including telecommunications, transportation, government operations, and emergency services. Computer crimes also include attempts to illegally transfer funds from financial institutions; financial crimes perpetrated on the Internet, such as investment and pyramid schemes; sales of illegally reproduced computer software; and fraudulent sales of other goods.

To address the problem, FBI computer crime squads investigate computer intrusions, attacks on computer systems and networks, data loss or data manipulations, and software copyright violations. These investigations may focus on white-collar criminals, terrorists, economic espionage agents, organized crime groups, and foreign intelligence agents—all of whom have been identified as "electronic intruders" responsible for penetrations of American computer systems and networks. Computer crime squads also are responsible for the forensic examination and analysis of computers and systems.

Counterterrorism Squads

The FBI is the lead federal law enforcement agency in the United States Government's fight against international and domestic terrorism. FBI counterterrorism squads conduct sensitive intelligence and investigations to prevent terrorism before it occurs, and to effectively and swiftly respond to terrorist acts. Crimes of terrorism can include bombings or other acts of violence, weapons of mass destruction, hostage taking, overseas homicide of U.S. citizens, sabotage, nuclear extortion, sedition, and crimes directed at federally designated special events such as the Olympic Games and presidential inaugurations.

FBI counterterrorism squads frequently participate in task-force operations with federal law enforcement agencies such as the Secret Service; the State Department Bureau of Diplomatic Security; the USDA Office of Inspector General; the Federal Protective Service; the Naval Criminal Investigative Service; the Internal Revenue Service; and the Bureau of Alcohol, Tobacco, Firearms, and Explosives. Investigations and task-force operations also are conducted with other federal, state, and local law enforcement agencies, as well as firms in the private sector. Each of the Bureau's 56 field offices is staffed with a Weapons of Mass Destruction (WMD) Coordinator who manages the assessment of and response to incidents involving the use or threatened use of WMDs.

Drug Squads

In 1982, the attorney general assigned concurrent jurisdiction for enforcement of the Controlled Substances Act to the FBI and the Drug Enforcement Administration. FBI drug squads are responsible for the investigation of domestic and international trafficking, the laundering of illegal proceeds from drug trafficking, and acts of violence associated with drug trafficking. As tools of the trade, these squads utilize sophisticated investigative techniques and equipment, extensive criminal intelligence, and cooperation from other law enforcement agencies to disrupt and dismantle drug organizations and enterprises. In addition to seeking criminal prosecution of drug traffickers, FBI drug squads also concentrate on the seizure and forfeiture of assets used in or derived from criminal activity. These squads also coordinate investigative activities with agencies such as the Drug Enforcement Administration, U.S. Immigration and Customs Enforcement, Coast Guard Investigative Service, USDA Forest Service, and other federal, state, and local law enforcement agencies.

Economic Crime Squads

Economic crime squads investigate a variety of financial crimes that significantly affect the community. These offenses range from telemarketing fraud to securities and commodities fraud, wire-transfer fraud, bankruptcy fraud, insurance fraud, investment fraud, lottery schemes, copyright and trademark violations, industrial and economic espionage, and pyramid schemes. Particular emphasis is given to the investigation of "con artists" who prey on unsuspecting victims using elaborate schemes. These schemes include get-rich-quick and prize scams; high-yield investment opportunities; and the issuance of bogus guaranties, performance bonds, and other financial obligations. Many FBI economic crime squads also investigate intellectual-property offenses, including copyright and trademark infringement. These include crimes such as the manufacture and sale of counterfeit designer apparel or computer chips, and piracy of computer software, videos, compact discs, tapes, or DVD recordings. Economic crimes may be investigated not only with the assistance of other law enforcement agencies, but also with cooperation from representatives of the securities industry, financial institutions, insurance companies and other private firms, and government regulatory agencies.

Environmental Crime Squads

The Bureau has authority to investigate a full range of environmental crimes, including offenses that involve discharge of toxic substances into the air, water, or soil that pose a significant threat of harm to people, property, or the environment. Investigative priorities of FBI environmental crime squads include air and water pollution violations, discharges from industrial users, wetlands violations, spills of hazardous substances, illegal dumping, and the illegal importation and use of Freon. These investigations focus on violations of the Clean Air Act, Clean Water Act, Resource Conservation and Recovery Act, Toxic Substances Control Act, and other environmental statutes. FBI environmental crime squads also conduct investigations jointly with special agents of the Criminal Investigation Division of the Environmental Protection Agency.

Financial Institution Fraud Squads

Federal crimes involving federally insured banks, savings and loan firms, and credit unions are investigated by the Bureau's financial institution fraud squads. These investigations often focus on bank embezzlement, bribery of bank officials, check-kiting schemes, fraud involving checks and other negotiable instruments, counterfeit and stolen-check schemes, organized check rings, wire-transfer frauds, and loan and mortgage frauds. Organized groups involved in check-fraud and loan-fraud schemes often are involved in illegal money-laundering activities in an effort to conceal the proceeds of their crimes. The successful prosecution of bank failure cases is largely the result of task forces that have combined the efforts of FBI financial institution fraud squads and the resources of other federal law enforcement and regulatory agencies. Inasmuch as financial institution fraud cases periodically are tied to fraud in government programs, these investigations may be conducted jointly with special agents representing various Office of Inspector General agencies.

Government Fraud Squads

Fraud against the federal government is costly not only for the government but for all taxpayers, and certain forms of fraud can pose grave risks to public safety. The FBI's government fraud squads investigate a wide range of fraud against the federal government, including offenses involving bribery of public officials in connection with contracts or procurement processes, collusion among government contractors, bid rigging, false or double billing, false certification of the quality of parts or of test results, substitution of bogus or otherwise inferior parts, antitrust matters, false claims, conflict of interest, and fraud in various public benefits programs. Government fraud cases are often investigated jointly with special agents representing various Office of Inspector General agencies.

Healthcare Fraud Squad

The Bureau has statutory authority to investigate all forms of fraud affecting government-sponsored healthcare programs, including Medicare and Medicaid, as well as private insured health benefit programs. FBI healthcare fraud squad investigations focus primarily on bribery, kickbacks, billing for services not rendered, false claims, managed-care abuses, and diversion of controlled substances, among other crimes. These offenses may be committed by physicians, hospitals, nursing homes, home healthcare providers, medical equipment companies, laboratories, clinics, and others who provide goods and services to the healthcare industry. FBI healthcare squads often cooperate with other law enforcement agencies and private organizations to combat healthcare fraud, including the Department of Defense—Defense Criminal Investigative Service, the Department of Health and Human Services—Office of Inspector General, the Drug Enforcement Administration, the Food and Drug Administration, the Internal Revenue Service, the Department of Veterans Affairs—Office of Inspector General, various state agencies, private insurance companies, and healthcare industry associations.

Homicide Squads

In joining forces and combining investigative expertise with state and local police departments, FBI homicide squads focus on heinous and unsolved murders. These squads are staffed by agents with a solid background in violent crime investigations and a thorough knowledge of the Bureau's resources and capabilities, and police detectives who have extensive experience in investigating homicide cases. Homicides investigated by this squad frequently target drug-trafficking organizations and urban gangs. These investigations employ a combination of scientific techniques, confidential informants, cooperative witnesses, and expert legal guidance from prosecutors and assistant United States Attorneys to solve crimes.

Organized Crime Squads

The FBI's organized crime squads investigate sophisticated groups who conspire to violate federal laws for personal gain, including La Cosa Nostra (more commonly known as "the Mafia" or "the mob"); and Italian, Russian, Eastern European, African, and Asian criminal enterprises, as well as gangs and other organizations. Special agents who investigate organized crime utilize a broad range of investigative techniques, but emphasize the use of informants, intelligence gathering, undercover operations, and obtaining evidence through court-authorized electronic surveillance. Investigations focus on criminal enterprises that engage in drug trafficking, money laundering, labor racketeering, and both traditional and nontraditional organized-crime activities. FBI organized crime squads cooperate with agencies such as the Drug Enforcement Administration, Internal Revenue Service, USDA Office of Inspector General, and other law enforcement agencies in conjunction with Organized Crime and Drug Enforcement Task Force (OCDETF) and High Intensity Drug Trafficking Area (HIDTA) operations.

Property Crime Squads

Major thefts that affect interstate commerce are investigated by FBI property crime squads. These investigations often revolve around the interstate or worldwide transportation of stolen property by organized groups. Many of these groups steal high-value merchandise—such as art, jewelry, and motor vehicles—and market the goods nationally and internationally. During the course of these investigations, FBI special agents frequently come in contact with representatives of various manufacturers, distribution centers, warehouse facilities, trucking companies and terminals, airlines and air cargo firms, and railroad yards. The Bureau's property crime squads often conduct investigations jointly with U.S. Immigration and Customs Enforcement; other federal, state, and local law enforcement agencies; and the National Insurance Crime Bureau, a private-sector organization that works with law enforcement agencies on behalf of insurance companies. Many of the Bureau's property crime squads also investigate theft or destruction of U.S. Government property, and crimes that occur on property owned by the government.

Public Corruption Squads

Public corruption investigations are among the most sensitive investigations the FBI handles. Investigations carried out by public corruption squads focus on the corruption of elected or appointed public officials on the federal, state, and local levels, including law enforcement officers, judiciary and executive department employees, and others in positions of trust. Generally speaking, public corruption occurs when a government official asks, demands, solicits, seeks, accepts, receives, or agrees to receive anything of value in return for being influenced in the performance of his or her official duties. Corruption schemes are secretive and characterized by unwritten agreements sealed with whispered conversations, handshakes, and under-the-table payments. These crimes often lack physical evidence, such as fingerprints or a "smoking gun," and rarely involve violent acts. Public corruption destroys public confidence in government and casts a cloud over the majority of public officials who are honest and hardworking.

Violent Crime Squads

The Bureau's violent crime squads investigate a wide variety of criminal offenses, including bank robbery, armed robbery of commercial establishments, armored car robbery, burglary, extortion, kidnapping, homicide, assault on federal officers, sexual exploitation of children, interstate transportation of child pornography, and child abduction. In addition, many of the Bureau's violent crime squads locate and arrest fugitives, and investigate crimes committed by violent street gangs. These squads frequently participate in task force operations with special agents and detectives of other federal, state, and local law enforcement agencies. The FBI also provides assistance to other law enforcement agencies with the behavioral profiling of violent felons and the investigation of serial murders.

Beyond the Initial Assignment

After gaining experience, FBI special agents can be assigned to a variety of special response teams, promoted to supervisory positions, or transferred to other field offices or Headquarters. In some cases, agents can work part-time to meet family obligations and other personal needs. This section provides an overview of opportunities that are available to veteran agents, as well as a discussion of the Special Agent Transfer Policy and opportunities for part-time employment.

The Special Agent Transfer Policy

As a condition of their employment, FBI special agents must be willing to be transferred to other offices according to the needs of the Bureau. By signing both the Worldwide Mobility Agreement and the Application Checklist for the Special Agent Position during the hiring process, applicants indicate their acceptance of the FBI's transfer policy. In 1996, the Bureau made significant modifications to the Special Agent Transfer Policy which, over the following two years, allowed more than 3,200 agents to transfer to offices where they preferred to work. As a result of the policy modifications, since 1996 the transfer of special agents who did not want to move has been significantly limited.

Presently, special agents who have worked in their first office of assignment for at least four years can be considered for a nonvoluntary rotational transfer to another office, depending on the Bureau's staffing needs at the time. However, those who remain in their first office of assignment for more than 10 years generally will not be considered for a nonvoluntary transfer. The FBI pays for personal moving expenses associated with promotions and nonvoluntary transfers.

Special Response Teams

Experienced and highly motivated special agents may have the opportunity to join special operational and enforcement response teams. Unlike squads, whose role is to investigate particular types of crimes, the FBI's response teams are geared to deploy to crime scenes and critical incidents to locate and collect evidence or intervene in dangerous situations. Special agents normally participate on response teams as collateral duty, meaning their involvement is undertaken in addition to investigative responsibilities. Response team assignments require particular skills and abilities, and offer ongoing advanced training opportunities. The following sections provide examples of special teams that special agents may join.

Underwater Search and Evidence Response Team

The FBI Underwater Search and Evidence Response Team consists of highly trained and experienced special agents who fulfill a variety of functions, although their primary responsibilities revolve around evidence recovery. Its members must be skilled enough to accomplish recovery missions in hazardous conditions and hostile underwater environments, under ice, in varying degrees of current, and along silted bottoms. The team was formed in 1981, under the FBI's chief of special operations, with an elite group of divers that included former Navy Seals. Using inflatable boats, metal detectors, sonar units, dive computers, underwater scooters, and other high-tech equipment, the team has participated in a number of high-profile operations. For example, its dive operations played a key role in search-and-recovery operations following the explosions of Pan Am 103 over Lockerbie, Scotland in 1988, and of TWA Flight 800 over Long Island Sound in 1996. They also worked around the clock in support of the 1996 Summer Olympics in Atlanta, and performed search-and-recovery tasks following the I-35 bridge collapse in Minneapolis in 2007. In 2009, the team helped pinpoint the location of an aircraft engine after US Airways flight 1549 ditched in the Hudson River shortly after takeoff from New York La Guardia Airport. The team supports missions throughout the United States and anywhere in the world where the FBI has an interest.

Evidence Response Teams

Each of the FBI's 56 field offices has an evidence response team (ERT) that specializes in organizing and conducting major evidence-recovery operations. These teams identify, collect, and preserve evidence during the execution of search warrants, and at crime scenes involving bank robberies, kidnappings, bombing incidents, and other offenses. ERTs are staffed not only with special agents, but also with support personnel such as forensic anthropologists, evidence collection specialists, paralegals, language specialists, fingerprint specialists, and photographers. These specialists have responded to countless high-profile crime scenes, including the World Trade Center bombings in 1993 and 2001, the Alfred P. Murrah Federal Building bombing in Oklahoma City, Atlanta's 1996 Olympic Park bombing, and the Montana cabin used by Theodore Kaczynski—the "Unabomber." In 2005, ERT members assisted with the identification of tsunami victims in Thailand. In 2007, the Minneapolis ERT recovered evidence alongside the Underwater Search and Evidence Response Team after a bridge on Interstate 35 collapsed over the Mississippi River. These teams undergo continuous training to develop and maintain their organizational and forensic skills.

Hazardous Materials Response Unit

A key component of the Bureau's efforts to prevent terrorists from using nuclear, biological, or chemical weapons in the United States is the Hazardous Materials (HAZMAT) Response Unit, which is based at the FBI Laboratory. Special agents and support personnel assigned to this unit respond to criminal acts and incidents involving the use of weapons of mass destruction and other hazardous materials. For example, in the wake of the terrorist attacks on the World Trade Center and the Pentagon on September 11, 2001, the HAZMAT unit participated in the investigation and recovery of a letter containing anthrax spores that was mailed to U.S. Senator Patrick Leahy in Washington, D.C. Since the unit's formation in 1996, its personnel have also responded to a variety of special events, such as Pope John Paul II's visit to the United States, the World Alpine Games, and the Super Bowl. In 2005, the HAZMAT unit traveled to Thailand and worked with FBI evidence response team members to assist in the identification of tsunami victims. Although the HAZMAT unit is based at the FBI Academy in Quantico, Virginia, it also trains, equips, and certifies FBI field office personnel for hazardous materials operations.

Hostage Rescue Team

The FBI's Hostage Rescue Team (HRT) is a full-time tactical force that conducts high-threat rescue operations involving persons who are being held illegally by terrorists or other criminals. With headquarters at the FBI Academy in Quantico, Virginia, the HRT's special agents are prepared to deploy to any location within four hours of notification. Since being activated in 1983, its members have deployed on more than 200 occasions in support of incidents involving terrorism, violent crimes, foreign counterintelligence, and other matters. The team has performed missions involving hostage rescue, barricaded subjects, high-risk arrest and search-warrant operations, and dive-search operations. The HRT also has performed traditional law enforcement roles during hurricane-relief operations, dignitary-protection missions, tactical surveys, and special events such as the Olympic Games, presidential inaugurations, and political conventions. Assignment to the HRT is open to all FBI special agents, and selection is based on their background and experience, as well as their performance during a rigorous two-week selection course. Once selected, team members undergo a four-month initial training program. Ongoing in-service training includes instruction in maritime operations from the U.S. Navy Seals, sniper tactics, explosives, nonlethal weapons, communications, and other subjects.

Crisis Negotiation Unit

The Crisis Negotiation Unit (CNU) responds to significant crisis events worldwide. The FBI has approximately 340 crisis negotiators in the Bureau's 56 field offices who are trained to deploy to kidnapping and hostage situations, barricaded suspect incidents, suicide threat incidents, and other crisis situations. The CNU is responsible for the initial training of all FBI negotiators, which includes a two-week national negotiation course conducted at the FBI Academy. Its members also conduct research projects and case studies to expand the Bureau's capabilities to assess, manage, and successfully resolve critical events. The unit is based with all other critical incident response group units at the FBI Academy in Quantico, Virginia.

Special Weapons and Tactics Teams

Each FBI field office has a special weapons and tactics (SWAT) team, although the size of each team varies from one office to another depending on the geographical area covered, population density, and the potential for violent crime in the area. SWAT teams are well trained and specially equipped to conduct dangerous raids, rescues, and other missions. These operations could include drug raids, the execution of other high-risk search or arrest warrants, barricaded suspect situations, dignitary protection, and other specialized operations or critical incidents. The FBI also has nine technically advanced district SWAT teams that are configured to provide technical and operational support to field offices during major or protracted crisis situations. About 1,100 special agents are members of the Bureau's SWAT teams.

Canine Teams

The FBI has canine (K-9) teams that specialize in locating fleeing criminals, missing persons, explosives, and narcotics. The Bureau's K-9 teams are based at FBI Headquarters and field offices in cities such as New York, Philadelphia, Los Angeles, and Dallas, although they are prepared to respond to any FBI field office nationwide. Each K-9 team consists of a dog handler and a specially trained dog. The Bureau's dog handlers serve as special agents, special agent bomb technicians, or police officers.

Chemical explosives detection dogs are trained to detect odors from a wide range of explosives, explosives residues, and firearms. Narcotics detection dogs search for drugs such as marijuana, hashish, cocaine, methamphetamine, and heroin. Search and rescue dogs are trained to track fleeing criminals and locate missing persons and cadavers over many forms of terrain, under rubble or snow, and in a variety of climatic conditions. The teams train year-round, and must be certified annually in their areas of expertise by organizations such as the North American Police Work Dog Association and the United States Police Canine Association. Certification is valuable not only for its affirmation that K-9 teams are performing up to standards, but also in the event that a dog handler is required to testify in court. Canine teams have provided support to many investigations, including the crash of TWA Flight 800 over Long Island Sound, as well as special events such as the Super Bowl and the Goodwill Games.

Promotion

Newly hired special agents advance from grade GS-10 to GS-11 after two years of service, from GS-11 to GS-12 after one additional year, and from GS-12 to GS-13 after two additional years. Promotion from GS-10 to GS-13 is contingent on agents successfully meeting performance standards and other criteria. Those who want to remain in nonsupervisory field investigative positions for the remainder of their careers will then climb the GS-13 step structure, "topping out" at GS-13 step 10.

On the other hand, agents who aspire to advance to supervisory and management positions typically serve as a relief supervisor before taking on full-time responsibilities as a squad supervisor. This allows special agents on the management track to obtain supervisory experience on an occasional basis while the squad supervisor is out of the office. Relief supervisor responsibilities are a collateral duty, meaning that an agent serving in this position must also maintain investigative assignments. Promotions to supervisory and management ranks are available at the GS-14 and GS-15 levels, and in the Senior Executive Service. Promotions often require a stint at FBI Headquarters.

Part-Time Special Agents

Since 1990, special agents who meet certain criteria have been able to convert to part-time employment status in order to address personal needs and family obligations. For example, a female agent could request a part-time schedule after returning from maternity leave, and work three eight-hour days per week for a period of months or years. Presently, the FBI special agent part-time program permits agents to remain in part-time status for up to 10 years, while still maintaining active caseloads, squad assignments, and participation in training programs. The program allows the FBI to retain skilled agents who might otherwise have resigned.

Organizations for FBI Personnel

FBI employees can join a number of associations that provide a collective voice in employment issues, scholarships, financial assistance, insurance, legal counsel, recreation, and camaraderie. These organizations allow FBI personnel to address common concerns and needs that are unique to past and present members of the "FBI family."

FBI Agents Association

The FBI Agents Association (FBIAA) was founded in 1981 to protect and advance the interests of FBI special agents both within and outside the FBI. The association has promoted issues benefiting agents on matters such as Law Enforcement Availability Pay, due process during administrative inquiries, passage of the Federal Employees Pay Comparability Act, pay grade raises, and relocation benefits. FBIAA also maintains a college scholarship fund for the children and spouses of deceased agents. Member benefits include legal representation for administrative actions. The association's quarterly newsletter, *FBI Agent,* includes articles on current matters affecting FBI personnel, including legislative issues, legal representation, employee rights, and other topics. Membership is open to current and former FBI agents, including supervisors and managers. Approximately 70 percent of active FBI special agents are members of the FBIAA.

Special Agents Mutual Benefits Association

The Special Agents Mutual Benefits Association (SAMBA) provides group insurance coverage to active and retired employees of the FBI and other federal law enforcement agencies. SAMBA insurance products include a health plan, dental and vision coverage, personal accident insurance, life insurance, disability income protection, long-term care insurance, terrorism coverage, and legal insurance. The association also offers a legal services plan. The SAMBA Health Benefit Plan is part of the Federal Employees Health Benefits Program.

FBI Recreation Association

The FBI Recreation Association (FBIRA) is a nonprofit organization that encourages athletics, recreation, and overall fitness activities among FBI employees and the communities they serve. FBI special agents and support personnel are eligible to participate in FBIRA recreation and athletic programs—including softball, volleyball, and basketball leagues—and other activities. The association provides sponsorship funds to community athletic leagues, as well as other school and community activities. FBIRA also hosts an annual 5K run in memory of FBI Special Agent Jerry Dove, who was killed in the line of duty in 1986 during a shootout with bank robbery suspects in Miami.

Society of Former Special Agents of the FBI

The Society of Former Special Agents of the FBI was formed in 1937 to offer assistance to fellow agents and to support activities of the FBI. The society provides social opportunities for its members, hosts regional and national conventions around the United States, offers scholarships, and performs charitable activities. Since 1946, the organization's job-placement program has served as a clearinghouse for members seeking employment. Through a permanent trust fund and continued contributions, the society funds a variety of charitable programs, including college scholarships for the children and grandchildren of former agents, financial assistance to former FBI special agents and their families, and a program that provides gifts and pays travel expenses for terminally ill children. Other charitable activities include grants to other organizations that have performed services for the benefit of the society, a disaster relief program, and humanitarian service awards. The society publishes *The Grapevine,* a monthly journal that includes information on chapter meetings and activities, conventions, member achievements, awards, and other matters of interest to its members.

Society of FBI Alumni

In 1973, the Society of FBI Alumni was originally organized as the *Society of Former FBI Women,* to promote fellowship and support law enforcement causes on the local, state, and national levels. In 1992, the society modified its bylaws and allowed men to join, and changed its name two years later. Through its 8,000 members in 28 chapters nationwide, the society provides temporary financial assistance to members in need, and scholarships for the children and grandchildren of members. This organization maintains liaison with FBI Headquarters and field offices, and the Society of Former Special Agents of the FBI. Its quarterly newsletter, *The Informant,* provides information on its annual convention, meetings, chapter news, society business, and other items of interest. Membership is open to special agents and support personnel who served with the FBI for at least one year.

Federal Law Enforcement Officers Association

The Federal Law Enforcement Officers Association (FLEOA) is a nonpartisan organization that represents more than 25,000 federal law enforcement officers from about 70 agencies of the federal government. FLEOA provides its members with immediate expert legal advice and representation following critical incidents or other legal matters, and also works on legislative action and issues affecting federal law enforcement officers. FLEOA publishes *The Eighteen-Eleven,* a monthly newsletter that includes up-to-date information on legislative matters, member awards and accomplishments, articles of interest to the federal law enforcement community, and news relating to events and meetings held by various FLEOA chapters. The organization also funds grants to the survivors of federal law enforcement officers killed in the line of duty, financial assistance to disabled officers, educational scholarships, and charitable contributions. Membership is open to current full-time federal law enforcement officers, as well as certain former officers, retirees, and others who have an interest in promoting the objectives of FLEOA.

CHAPTER 4

The Special Agent Hiring Process

"A journey of a thousand miles must begin with a single step."

—*Chinese Proverb*

The application process for FBI special agent positions is rigorous and time-consuming. It's also very different from hiring processes followed in private industry, by police departments, or even by other federal law enforcement agencies. This chapter provides a step-by-step overview of the components in the hiring process, including the forms applicants encounter along the way. Additional information and specific strategies for carrying out a successful campaign for FBI employment are provided in chapter 7, "Standing Out from the Crowd." In addition, copies of FBI application forms are exhibited in the appendixes. Minimum qualifications for the special agent position—as well as automatic disqualifiers—are discussed in chapter 3, "FBI Special Agent Career Opportunities."

FBI Hiring Policies

The FBI application process is guided by a number of written policies to ensure not only that the Bureau hires the best and brightest to carry out its mission, but also to comply with employment laws and ensure that hiring decisions are based on merit principles. These policies address drug use, false statements, Veterans' Preference, equal employment opportunity, and applicants with disabilities, among other issues. The following sections discuss each of these topics in more detail.

FBI Employment Drug Policy

All applicants for FBI positions must meet the Bureau's Drug Policy Criteria in order to be considered for employment:

- An applicant who has used any illegal drug while employed in any law enforcement or prosecutorial position, or while employed in a position that carries with it a high level of responsibility or public trust, will be found unsuitable for employment.

- An applicant who is discovered to have misrepresented their drug history in completing the application will be found unsuitable for employment.

- An applicant who has sold any illegal drug for profit at any time will be found unsuitable for employment.

- An applicant who has used any illegal drug (including anabolic steroids after February 27, 1991), other than marijuana, within the last 10 years or more than minimal experimentation will be found unsuitable for employment. In determining an applicant's suitability for employment, the FBI considers all relevant facts, including the frequency of drug use.

- An applicant who has used marijuana within the past three years will be found unsuitable for employment.

Failure to meet the preceding criteria will result in disqualification. In an effort to allow prospective candidates to provide a self-assessment of their eligibility under the FBI's drug policy, applicants are asked to answer the following questions:

1. Have you used marijuana at all within the last three years?

2. Have you used any other illegal drug (including anabolic steroids after February 27, 1991) at all in the past 10 years?

3. Have you ever sold any illegal drug for profit?

4. Have you ever used an illegal drug (no matter how many times or how long ago) while in a law enforcement or prosecutorial position, or in a position that carries with it a high level of responsibility or public trust?

Anyone who answers "Yes" to any of these questions would be disqualified and should not apply for employment with the FBI. All Bureau personnel are subject to random drug screening throughout their careers.

False Statements

It is critical for applicants to be truthful throughout the application process. Any intentional false statement or willful misrepresentation will result in disqualification for FBI employment, and could result in prosecution in accordance with Title 18, United States Code, Section 1001. In addition, if the misrepresentation is discovered after hiring, the agent may be subject to inquiry and administrative or disciplinary action up to and including dismissal.

Veterans' Preference

Certain applicants may be entitled to preference in the hiring process based on their service in the armed forces. To receive Veterans' Preference, applicants must have done all of the following:

- Served on active duty

- Been honorably discharged from active duty in the U.S. Army, Navy, Air Force, Marine Corps, or Coast Guard

- Performed service that meets certain criteria

To be considered for Veterans' Preference, applicants must present a DD-214 (Report of Separation from Active Duty) issued by the armed forces, the Department of Veterans Affairs (DVA), or the National Personnel Records Center of the National Archives and Records Administration. For additional information about the rights of veterans in the hiring process, including how and when Veterans' Preference is applied, contact either the DVA or the applicant coordinator at any FBI field office.

Applicants who want to receive Veterans' Preference must clearly identify their claim on application forms and other materials, including dates of service and campaign badges. Veterans entitled to preference who meet minimum qualifications will be contacted and asked to submit a copy of their DD-214 or a statement specifying the type of discharge, dates of service, campaign badges received and, if applicable, an SF-15 (Application for 10-Point Veteran Preference), together with the required proof outlined on the form.

Applicants with Disabilities

The FBI is committed to satisfying its affirmative obligations under the Rehabilitation Act of 1973, to ensure that persons with disabilities have every opportunity to be hired and advanced on the basis of merit within the Department of Justice. The Bureau welcomes and encourages applications from persons with physical and mental disabilities and will reasonably accommodate their needs. Any applicant with a disability who requires an accommodation to complete the application process should notify the applicant coordinator of the nearest FBI field office. Notification should be in writing, including the need for the accommodation and medical documentation concerning the disability. Although the Bureau will make reasonable accommodations, applicants must be physically and mentally able to perform the essential functions of a special agent position in order to be hired.

Equal Employment Opportunity

Except where otherwise provided by law, the FBI cannot discriminate because of an applicant's color, race, religion, national origin, political affiliation, marital status, disability, age, gender, sexual orientation, or membership or non-membership in an employee organization; or on the basis of personal favoritism.

An Overview of Applicant Processing

It is important for special agent applicants to be aware of the hiring process sequence, application and testing procedures, factors that could exclude them from employment consideration, how final screening is carried out, and the application time frame. This section provides a snapshot of applicant processing. The remainder of the chapter covers each step of the process in greater detail.

Application, Testing, and Final Screening

The FBI special agent application process requires candidates to submit various application materials in a specific sequence. Those who meet minimum qualifications are administered a battery of written examinations in the first phase of the selection process. Candidates who pass the tests may be eligible for an interview based on their overall qualifications, their competitiveness with other candidates, and the needs of the FBI. The interview and written exercise are conducted in phase II of the process. To complete the process, final screening includes a physical fitness test, security interview, background investigation, physical examination, drug screening, and polygraph examination.

Automatic Disqualifiers

Certain factors disqualify a candidate from selection as a special agent. Competitive candidates will be physically fit to participate in the demanding physical training conducted at the FBI Academy, and able to execute the duties of a law enforcement officer. All candidates must also meet either a standardized weight-to-height ratio or body fat requirement to be qualified for appointment, although they are not required to meet both standards. In other words, those who fall outside of the weight-to-height ratio can qualify by meeting the body fat standard, and vice versa. (Appendix D is a chart of the desirable weight ranges and body fat requirements.) Candidates must also pass a physical examination to ensure that they are physically suited for the special agent position. Additional details relating to automatic disqualifiers are provided in chapter 3, "FBI Special Agent Career Opportunities."

Application Time Frame

The road from the preliminary application stage to completion of final screening takes at least nine months—although it often lasts more than a year—depending on a variety of factors, such as the number of applicants being processed and issues that arise during the background investigation or physical examination. Figure 4.1 is a flow chart showing the step-by-step progression of the process.

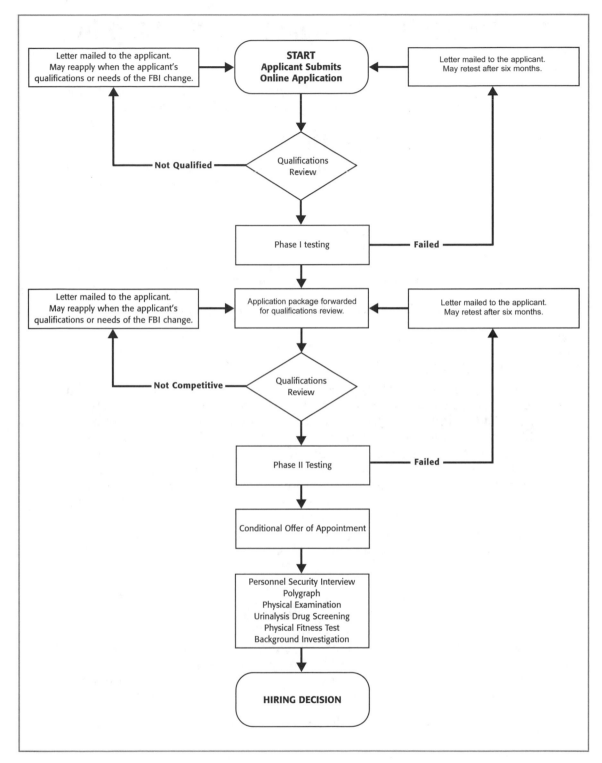

Figure 4:1: The special agent application and selection process.

From Application to Appointment, Step by Step

The following sections provide a detailed explanation of each step in the journey from initial application to appointment as an FBI special agent.

Step One: The Online Application

To begin the application process, applicants must submit to the FBI biographical details and information relating to their qualifications and background. Applications are no longer accepted by mail. Instead, candidates must access application materials online at both the FBI and U.S. Office of Personnel Management (OPM) Web sites to apply for FBI employment. The FBI reviews data submitted to OPM and responses to job-specific questions submitted to the Bureau to determine the eligibility and competitiveness of applicants. A list of Online Application questions is provided in appendix A.

This section offers an overview of the variety of information requested in the Online Application process.

Application Processing

Candidates for FBI special agent positions initiate the application process on the FBI Web site at www.fbijobs.gov. To facilitate processing of applications, the Bureau first identifies the FBI field office through which each application will be handled. Applications are processed by the field office that is covered by the applicant's residence, place of employment, or school (if presently enrolled). Applicants must first visit the FBI Web site and enter their ZIP code to identify the appropriate FBI field office. If the locations of an applicant's residence, employment, or school are different, processing will be handled by the field office that is most convenient for the applicant. After the local field office has been identified, applicants are automatically directed to www.usajobs.gov to apply for FBI employment. The USAJOBS Web site is operated by OPM.

USAJOBS Registration and Processing

To begin the online application process, candidates must create an account on the USAJOBS Web site and build an online resume. The USAJOBS Resume Builder allows users to create and store up to five separate resumes. Applicants also can use the resumes when applying for employment with other federal agencies.

The following information is collected at this stage in the process.

Applicant Personal Data

The USAJOBS Resume Builder begins with personal data questions. In this section, you must provide basic biographical information, including your name, Social Security number, home address, phone number, and e-mail address. Questions relating to citizenship, registration for Selective Service, and Veterans' Preference also are asked.

Federal Employment Information

This section requires applicants to indicate whether they have served as a federal civilian employee, as well as the pay plan involved, the occupation series and grade of the position(s), and the dates of service. Applicants for FBI employment are not required to have served in a federal civilian position.

Employment Experience

The Employment Experience section requests information relating to the nature of employment held, locations of employment, starting and ending dates, salaries, and the number of hours worked per week. This section also includes space that applicants can use to describe their employment duties, accomplishments, and related skills.

Education

Information relating to schools attended is entered in this section, including completion dates, major and minor fields of study, grade-point averages, credits earned, degrees received, and honors awarded. Information relating to licenses held and certificates earned also is requested in this section.

Job-Related Training

In this section, applicants should enter information concerning all training courses, seminars, or conferences attended that are relevant to the position. Each entry should include the dates attended, title and location of training, name of the organization presenting the training, and length of training.

References

Personal and professional references are listed in this section. Although the USAJOBS Web site does not limit the number of references applicants can submit, there is no need to list more than three references in this section because the FBI will request additional information concerning references later in the application process.

Foreign-Language Skills

In this section, applicants are asked to identify their ability to speak, write, and read foreign languages. Applicants must provide a self-assessment of their proficiency with each foreign language, whether novice, intermediate, or advanced in each functional area.

Professional Publications

This section requests information relating to published materials, such as magazine or newspaper articles, academic journal articles, or books. Entries should include the title, publication, date, volume and issue number, publisher, ISBN, or other pertinent data.

Additional Information

Applicants can enter a variety of information in this section, such as details concerning job-related honors and awards, leadership activities, proficiency with computer hardware or software, and other special skills or accomplishments. Applicants also can use this section to provide details relating to other information requested in the vacancy announcement.

FBI Online Questionnaire

After an online resume has been created on the USAJOBS Web site, an applicant can continue the process on the FBI Web site. At this stage, applicants are again asked to provide biographical details and information concerning citizenship, military service, Veterans' Preference, previous federal employment, and other issues. The following information is requested in the FBI online questionnaire.

Applicant Demographic Survey

The applicant demographic survey is the only optional component of the Online Application process. In this section, the FBI asks applicants to identify their race, ethnicity, gender, and disabilities. This data is used only for planning and monitoring of the Bureau's Equal Employment Opportunity and recruitment programs, and does not have an effect on application processing or selection for employment.

Job Requirements

Questions pertaining to job requirements focus on your understanding of conditions concerning FBI employment, as well as difficult aspects of the FBI special agent position. These questions are concerned with matters such as two-week notice from time of appointment to reporting for duty, starting salary, successful completion of New Agent Training, willingness to accept assignment anywhere within the FBI's jurisdiction, the two-year probationary period, carrying firearms and making arrests, maintaining physical conditioning, and availability for work on weekends and holidays. Questions concerning your age focus on completion of the application process prior to reaching age 37, and retirement prior to age 57.

Employment Suitability and Disqualifiers

Several automatic employment disqualifiers are addressed in this section, which includes questions concerning criminal convictions, drug use, registering for the Selective Service, default on federally insured student loans, and membership in subversive or extremist groups. Applicants must also attest to their willingness to undergo a background investigation, polygraph examination, physical examination, and urinalysis drug test.

Federal Employment and Security Clearances Held

Questions in this section are concerned with current or prior federal employment, including agencies worked for, duty stations served, salary grades attained, security clearances held, and retirement information. You must also indicate whether you have participated in an FBI Honors Internship.

Minimum Education and Experience Requirements

There are several ways in which applicants can qualify for the special agent position. Accordingly, this segment of the application is used to determine whether applicants have the appropriate combination of education and experience to meet basic eligibility requirements. These general questions are concerned with the nature of four-year and graduate degrees earned, full-time employment experience, professional certifications, and fluency in foreign languages.

Special Skills, Education, and Experience

In this section, applicants are asked to indicate any special skills, experience, education, certifications, or licenses they possess. Some of the special skills identified include pilot's licenses, accounting or finance degrees, Certified Public Accountant (CPA) certification, experience as an attorney or in the physical sciences, computer science degrees or certifications, foreign counter-intelligence or counterterrorism experience, and law enforcement or military experience. For each area, applicants are asked to provide relevant dates and a brief explanation of their expertise. Indicating special skills automatically generates additional questions relating to the area chosen.

Foreign-Language Proficiency

Applicants with proficiency in foreign languages have been given particular attention since the terrorist attacks of September 11, 2001. The list of foreign languages of interest to the FBI changes from time to time. Questions in this section are used to identify foreign languages you can speak, read, and write. Indicating foreign language proficiency automatically leads to additional questions that afford a preliminary assessment of your speaking, reading, writing, and listening proficiency.

Further Processing

After the FBI reviews Online Applications, candidates who are considered competitive for further processing are notified by the applicant coordinator from the nearest FBI field office and may be scheduled for phase I testing. The applicant coordinator serves as the point of contact through the remainder of the hiring process. Applicants who are not considered competitive are sent a letter indicating that their applications will not be considered further.

Step Two: Phase I Testing

The first phase of the testing process consists of a battery of written tests, including a Biodata Inventory, a three-part Logical Reasoning Test, and a Situational Judgment Test. These are paper-and-pencil exams that are scored on a "pass or fail" basis. Applicants are not told their numeric scores. Applicants normally are notified in writing within 30 days whether they passed or failed the phase I test. Applicants who fail the exam may be eligible for a one-time retest. (See "Phase I Retest Policy," later in this section.) For additional details relating to these tests—as well as specific test-taking strategies—see chapter 7, "Standing Out from the Crowd."

Phase I Procedures and Rules

Rules and procedures for phase I testing are explained in the following sections, including details on test location and scheduling, test materials and prohibited items, basic ground rules, and nondisclosure of testing information.

Test Location and Scheduling

Phase I testing is administered at various locations throughout the United States. Applicant coordinators or staffing assistants at each FBI field office coordinate the testing and inform applicants of the date, time, and location of their testing sessions. Test processing normally takes place in the office that covers the applicant's residence, place of education, or place of employment.

Exceptions to this policy must be approved by FBI Headquarters officials. Candidates usually have a 30-day notice of scheduled testing dates, times, and locations. Applicants who are tardy will not be permitted to participate in the testing process because testing is conducted on a strict time schedule. The phase I test takes approximately four hours to complete.

Test Materials and Prohibited Items

Applicants must bring a driver's license to phase I and phase II testing for identification purposes. If an applicant does not have a photo on their driver's license, they must provide an additional form of photo identification. The FBI will not allow anyone to participate in the testing process without proper identification.

Candidates are not permitted to bring certain items to phase I or phase II testing sessions, such as reference materials, dictionaries, pens or pencils, books, magazines, newspapers, briefcases, resumes, blank paper, pagers, cellular phones, tape recorders, cassettes, compact disc players, radios, calculators, cameras, and firearms.

Basic Ground Rules

Eating and drinking are not permitted during testing, but will be allowed during breaks. Smoking and chewing tobacco are not allowed. Candidates are permitted to use restroom facilities and telephones during breaks, but not during administration of the tests. Rules against cheating are strictly enforced.

Nondisclosure of Testing Information

To reduce the likelihood of giving other applicants an unfair advantage or disadvantage in the selection process, the FBI prohibits candidates from discussing any part of the tests and interview questions with anyone during or after tests. Applicants are required to sign a nondisclosure form at phase I and phase II testing. The FBI will disqualify anyone who violates the nondisclosure agreement. If this misrepresentation is discovered after hiring, the employee may be subject to inquiry and suitable disciplinary action, including dismissal.

Components of the Test

Phase I testing consists of three components:

- The Biodata Inventory
- The Logical Reasoning Test
- The Situational Judgment Test

The following sections provide more details on each of these components.

The Biodata Inventory

The Biodata Inventory measures the following critical skills and abilities:

- Ability to organize, plan, and prioritize
- Ability to maintain a positive image
- Ability to evaluate information and make judgment decisions
- Initiative and motivation

- Ability to adapt to changing situations
- Ability to relate effectively with others

This component includes 40 questions that the applicant must complete within 30 minutes, which allows most candidates to finish without being rushed. Answers are recorded on machine-readable answer sheets.

The Logical Reasoning Test

The Logical Reasoning Test measures the following critical skills and abilities that are relevant to the special agent position:

- Ability to evaluate information
- Ability to make judgments and decisions
- Attention to detail

Each of the questions in the Logical Reasoning Test contains a reading passage followed by a lead-in phrase that introduces five response choices. The questions do not require job knowledge of the special agent position. Candidates are given 90 minutes to complete this portion of the phase I test.

The Situational Judgment Test

The 45-minute Situational Judgment Test measures a variety of critical skills and abilities, such as the following:

- Ability to organize, plan, and prioritize
- Ability to relate effectively with others
- Ability to maintain a positive image
- Attention to evaluate information and make appropriate decisions
- Attention to adapt to changing situations
- Integrity

Many of these traits are also measured in the Biodata Inventory. Although the focus is similar in both tests, the Situational Judgment Test explores what applicants would do in hypothetical situations, whereas the Biodata Inventory examines applicants' behavior in actual situations in the past. In this test, candidates are faced with descriptions of problem situations and a list of actions that could be taken. The questions require candidates to rate the effectiveness of each action using a 1–7 rating scale, where 7 is highly effective and 1 is completely ineffective. In other words, you must imagine that you are involved in the situation and weigh the effectiveness or ineffectiveness of each action listed.

Scoring of Phase I Testing

The phase I test is scored on a "pass or fail" basis. The FBI has established a passing score that will be applied uniformly to all applicants taking the test. For security purposes, the FBI does not release the passing score.

Candidates normally are notified within two weeks of the test as to whether they passed or failed, although the FBI does not disseminate actual test scores.

Those who pass the phase I tests may be eligible to participate in phase II testing, depending on their competitiveness and the needs of the FBI at the time.

Phase I Retest Policy

Those who fail phase I testing may be eligible for one retest at least six months after their initial test date. The FBI does not allow applicants who have passed their 37th birthday (or who cannot be processed prior to their 37th birthday) to be retested. Due to the overwhelming volume of special agent applications, the FBI is able to offer retest opportunities only to those who are found to meet minimum qualifications and are the most competitive. An updated Online Application must be submitted before the applicant retakes the test, after the six-month waiting period has elapsed. Applicants who want to retake the phase I test must contact their applicant coordinator.

Step Three: Phase II Testing

The phase II testing process consists of a structured interview and a written exercise. Candidates who successfully complete this segment of the hiring process receive a conditional offer of employment and must be available for employment within 90 days of the testing.

Phase II Procedures and Rules

Testing procedures are similar to those followed in phase I testing. Arrangements for phase II testing are coordinated by either applicant coordinators or other staff. These personnel notify applicants of the date, time, and location of phase II testing sessions. Candidates usually are given 30 days' notice prior to testing. The phase II test takes approximately three hours to complete. As with phase I testing, applicants must bring a driver's license to the phase II test. If an applicant does not have a photo on his or her driver's license, he or she must provide an additional form of photo identification. Applicants are prohibited from discussing any part of the Structured Interview or Written Exercise with anyone, and must sign a Nondisclosure Form prior to taking the test.

The Structured Interview

The Structured Interview measures skills and abilities that are critical to the performance of FBI special agents. These include many of the skills and abilities that are also measured during phase I testing, although in a different format and setting. The Structured Interview focuses on the following abilities and characteristics:

- Ability to communicate orally
- Ability to organize, plan, and prioritize
- Ability to relate effectively with others
- Ability to maintain a positive image
- Ability to evaluate information and make appropriate decisions
- Initiative and motivation
- Ability to adapt to changing situations
- Honesty and integrity

The interview is administered by specially trained FBI special agents who serve as evaluators. Interestingly enough, however, the evaluators receive no application or background information on the applicants prior to the interviews. Because the evaluators know nothing about the applicants, each applicant is on an equal footing and the evaluators can be completely objective. The evaluators rate each candidate's performance using standardized scoring criteria. All interviews are audiotaped and the recordings are stored at FBI Headquarters in Washington, D.C.

To begin the interview, a panel member reads the following instructions to the applicant:

We'd like to spend the next hour getting to know more about you. During the interview, we will ask you to tell us how you've dealt with various kinds of situations in the past. In answering our questions, we strongly encourage you to draw on experiences from work or school; however, you may use experiences from social situations that may apply. We would like you to describe the situation, tell us what you did in that situation, and how things turned out.

We will be asking you 13 questions. Feel free to take a few moments to think about the answer you would like to give for each question. If you would like a question repeated, please ask. You'll be doing most of the talking during the interview. We will be taking notes while you talk to document the interview. The interview is being tape recorded.

Remember, be as specific and detailed as possible in describing the situation, YOUR actions, and the outcome of your actions.

After instructions have been given, the panel members ask a series of 13 situational response questions over a one-hour period. If a candidate cannot answer a question, the interview continues with the next question on the list. Panel members return to unanswered questions at the end of the interview and the candidate is not penalized for this. Failure to answer any questions during the interview, however, might adversely affect a candidate's score.

The Written Exercise

Phase II testing includes a written exercise that measures the following:

- Ability to communicate in writing
- Attention to detail
- Ability to evaluate and make judgments and decisions

For the written exercise, applicants are asked to evaluate a problem or situation and compose a written response that addresses the issues at hand. For example, candidates who recently completed the exercise were asked to write a report as if it were being sent to the editor of a newspaper. Fact situations or theme can change from one written exercise to the next. The written exercise is assessed by FBI special agents who serve as evaluators. This segment takes 90 minutes to complete.

Scoring of Phase II Testing

Phase II testing is scored on a "pass or fail" basis, using a passing score that is applied uniformly to all candidates. The Structured Interview is weighted as 75 percent of the total score, whereas the Written Exercise is weighted at 25 percent. As with phase I testing, the FBI does not release the passing score and cannot provide individual feedback regarding test performance.

Candidates are notified in writing as to whether they passed or failed. Applicants who pass the exam receive a conditional offer of an employment from the FBI, although a final employment decision is contingent upon successful completion of the final screening process.

Phase II Retest Policy

Applicants who fail phase II testing may be eligible to retest at least six months from the test date. Any applicant who has reached the age of 37—or cannot be processed prior to their 37th birthday—is not eligible to be retested. Only those who are most competitive will be offered an opportunity to retest. The FBI determines eligibility for retesting based on qualifications, skills, experience, the needs of the Bureau at the time, and information provided within a newly submitted Online Application. Applicants who want to retake the phase II test must contact their applicant coordinator.

Step Four: Conditional Letter of Appointment

Candidates who pass phase II testing are eligible to receive a Conditional Letter of Appointment as a special agent, contingent upon budgetary limitations, authorized positions, and successful completion of final screening. In this letter, candidates are provided with information concerning the remainder of the hiring process, including details relating to the nature of the background investigation and issues that might surface in it.

Step Five: Physical Fitness Test

The Physical Fitness Test (PFT) is given at this point in the application process to provide the FBI with some assurance that new agent trainees are in good shape and likely to succeed in physical fitness activities at the Academy. The PFT consists of four events, including push-ups, sit-ups, a 300-meter timed sprint, and a 1.5-mile timed run. These events were selected by the FBI because they provide an appropriate measure of overall physical fitness relative to the essential tasks performed by FBI special agents. Each candidate completes the PFT near the field office that is processing their application. The test also is given to new agent trainees at the Academy, although pull-ups are added (but not scored for pass/fail purposes) during New Agent Training.

Components of the Test

The following is a breakdown of the protocol for each event:

- **Sit-ups** begin with the candidate lying on his or her back with the tops of the shoulder blades touching the floor. The hands are placed behind the head with fingers interlaced. The knees are bent at a 90-degree angle with the feet placed flat on the floor. The feet are held in place by a partner, with the partner's hands at the tongue of the candidate's shoes and their knees on the candidate's toes. The torso is raised until the base of the neck is in line with the base of the spine. At this point, the back is perpendicular to the floor. The candidate then returns to the starting position, with the tops of both shoulder blades touching the floor. Candidates are given one minute to complete as many sit-ups as possible in a continuous motion.

- **Push-ups** begin with the hands on the floor, one to two hand widths beyond shoulder width, and the arms fully extended. The body is held straight, with the feet no more than three inches apart and the toes touching the floor. As the arms are flexed, the body is lowered toward the floor until the upper arms are parallel to the floor. One push-up is credited after the candidate returns to the starting position. Candidates are scored on the number of pushups completed. Although this event is not timed, it is a continuous-motion exercise and candidates are not permitted to rest.

- The **300-meter timed sprint** is held on a standard one-quarter-mile oval track, such as those used for high school and college track meets. Candidates start from a standing position and run 300 meters, which is three-quarters of one lap.

- The **1.5-mile timed run** also takes place on a standard one-quarter-mile oval track. Candidates start from a standing position and run six laps around the track.

PFT Scoring Scales

To pass the PFT, you must score at least one point in each event and achieve a minimum cumulative score of 12 points. Scoring scales for each event are provided in tables 4.1 through 4.4.

Table 4.1: Physical Fitness Test Scoring for Number of Push-Ups		
Males	**Females**	**Points**
71 or more	45 or more	10
65–70	42–44	9
61–64	39–41	8
57–60	36–38	7
54–56	33–35	6
50–53	30–32	5
44–49	27–29	4
40–43	22–26	3
33–39	19–21	2
30–32	14–18	1
20–29	5–13	0
19 or fewer	4 or fewer	–2

Table 4.2: Physical Fitness Test Scoring for Number of Sit-Ups in One Minute

Males	Females	Points
58 or more	57 or more	10
56–57	55–56	9
54–55	53–54	8
52–53	51–52	7
50–51	49–50	6
48–49	47–48	5
45–47	43–46	4
43–44	41–42	3
39–42	37–40	2
38	35–36	1
32–37	30–34	0
31 or fewer	29 or fewer	–2

Table 4.3: Physical Fitness Test Scoring for 300-Meter Timed Sprint (in Seconds)

Males	Females	Points
40.9 or fewer	49.9 or fewer	10
41.0–41.9	50.0–50.9	9
42.0–42.9	51.0–51.9	8
43.0–43.9	52.0–52.9	7
44.0–44.9	53.0–53.9	6
45.0–46.0	54.0–55.9	5
46.1–47.9	56.0–57.4	4
48.0–49.4	57.5–59.9	3
49.5–51.0	60.0–62.4	2
51.1–52.4	62.5–64.9	1
52.5–55.0	65.0–67.4	0
55.1 or more	67.5 or more	–2

Table 4.4: Physical Fitness Test Scoring for 1.5-Mile Timed Run (in Minutes and Seconds)		
Males	**Females**	**Points**
08:59 and below	10:34 and below	10
09:00–09:19	10:35–10:44	9
09:20–09:34	10:45–11:05	8
09:35–09:54	11:06–11:14	7
09:55–10:14	11:15–11:34	6
10:15–10:34	11:35–11:56	5
10:35–11:09	11:57–12:29	4
11:10–11:34	12:30–12:59	3
11:35–12:14	13:00–13:34	2
12:15–12:24	13:35–13:59	1
12:25–13:29	14:00–14:59	0
13:30 and over	15:00 and over	−2

Physical Fitness Test Retest Policy

The Conditional Letter of Appointment is rescinded if a passing score is not achieved during the PFT. Once the Conditional Letter of Appointment has been rescinded, you must wait a minimum of 60 days prior to notifying your applicant coordinator of your readiness to retake the PFT.

Step Six: Background Investigation and Polygraph Examination

All FBI applicants are subject to a thorough background investigation and polygraph examination prior to appointment. The FBI's applicant program administers these processes to all applicants for FBI employment. The Bureau also conducts background investigations for certain other government entities, such as the White House, Department of Justice, Department of Energy, Nuclear Regulatory Commission, Administrative Office of the United States Courts, and certain Senate and House committees.

The Background Investigation

Background investigations of applicants for FBI special agent positions typically are conducted by special investigators under contract with the FBI. Most of these investigators are retired FBI special agents. They are responsible only for gathering information and reporting their findings in accordance with a standard format, and not for making any determinations regarding suitability for employment or granting of a security clearance. Occasionally, current FBI special agents conduct applicants' background investigations, depending on the workload of special investigators, budget considerations, or other issues.

Background Investigation Forms

Prior to the background investigation, applicants are required to submit several forms, including the SF-86 Questionnaire for National Security Positions, the FD-979 Personnel Consent to Release Information, and the DOJ-555 Disclosure and Authorization Pertaining to Consumer Reports. Copies of these forms are in the appendixes.

The SF-86 is a 21-page form that requests information relating to birth and citizenship, places of residence, educational background, employment history, military service, references and social acquaintances, foreign contacts, passport information, association membership, civil and criminal court record, financial status, relatives, roommates, alcohol and drug use, and security clearances previously held. The SF-86 also includes an Authorization for Release of Medical Information that permits the Bureau to obtain information from healthcare practitioners.

The FD-979 authorizes the FBI to obtain information pertaining to your academic record, credit history, employment, criminal convictions, traffic violations, military service, and professional licenses, among other issues. Similarly, the DOJ-555 provides authorization for the release of credit bureau records.

Personnel Security Interview

The background investigation includes a Personnel Security Interview (PSI), which consists of a one-on-one discussion at an FBI field office, most often with either an FBI applicant coordinator or another special agent. In this meeting, the FBI reviews and discusses with each candidate the information provided in the employment application and Questionnaire for National Security Positions (SF-86), including issues surrounding foreign travel and contacts, the extent of alcohol and drug usage, employment history, financial obligations, and legal matters. This is done to ensure the accuracy of details supplied on these forms, and to give applicants an opportunity to update, clarify, and explain information more completely. Information obtained from the forms and during the PSI is used as the basis for both the polygraph examination and background investigation.

Applicants may be asked to bring important documents to the interview, such as a passport in the case of applicants with significant international travel experience. The PSI usually takes place about three to six weeks after the completion of phase II testing.

Scope and Coverage

FBI special agents must hold a Top Secret security clearance as a condition of employment. Security clearance determinations are governed by Presidential Executive Orders and Director of Central Intelligence Directives that are extensive and detailed. There are two primary purposes for the background investigation. First, information gathered during the investigation allows the FBI to assess whether applicants are suitable for Bureau employment. This includes an evaluation of character, integrity, and professional skills. In addition, a separate determination is made regarding national security issues, including access to classified or Top Secret information.

The background investigation routinely encompasses activity beginning at the age of 18, and earlier years if necessary to fully resolve issues that arise. The investigation typically includes credit history and criminal record checks; driving record and license inquiries; verification of employment history, licenses, credentials, and certifications; interviews of associates, personal and business references, past and present employers, and neighbors; verification of educational achievements and medical history; and verification of birth, citizenship, residency, and medical and military records. Interviews conducted by FBI special investigators almost always are performed in person, although in rare circumstances may take place by telephone.

In conducting interviews and reviewing records, background investigators place particular emphasis on the following areas in determining the suitability of applicants for FBI employment:

- **Character,** including attributes such as honesty, trustworthiness, judgment, reliability, attitude, discretion, diplomacy, dependability, punctuality, stability, and temperament

- **Associates,** with emphasis on the types of people, groups, or organizations with which the applicant has been involved or affiliated, and whether any of these associations has been of a disreputable or disloyal nature

- **Reputation,** relating to the applicant's standing in the community and in their profession or field of work

- **Loyalty,** in terms of their allegiance toward the United States, employers, and others

- **Ability,** as far as their level of competency and capacity to perform well in their occupation

- **Financial responsibility,** meaning the applicant maintains a satisfactory relationship with creditors and has spending habits that are consistent with their means

- **Biases or prejudice,** which concerns actions and attitude toward people of various racial, ethnic, gender, or religious groups

- **Alcohol abuse,** which focuses on excessive use of alcoholic beverages and related behavioral issues

- **Drug abuse,** including the use of any illegal drugs or abuse of prescription medications

Derogatory Information

It is not unusual for background investigations to uncover derogatory information about applicants. In these instances, FBI special investigators ask follow-up questions and otherwise explore details to elicit all available information. These inquiries often focus on the following:

- The nature, extent, and seriousness of the conduct

- The motivation for and circumstances surrounding the conduct

- The frequency and recentness of the conduct

- The applicant's age and maturity at the time of the conduct

- Whether the conduct was voluntary or whether there was pressure, coercion, or exploitation leading to the conduct

- Whether the applicant has been rehabilitated or has exhibited other pertinent behavioral changes since the conduct

In other words, derogatory information is not necessarily the kiss of death. Special investigators attempt to determine not only the nature and seriousness of the conduct, but whether the applicant has made positive changes in behavior. Inquiries concerning derogatory information also explore whether there may be personal animosity or bias toward the applicant on the part of the person providing derogatory information. Finally, information of a derogatory nature is forwarded to FBI Headquarters in Washington, D.C., for adjudication. The complete background investigation is assessed before a final decision on employment is rendered.

Lack of Candor

Without question, lack of candor is one of the most likely pathways to disqualification from the FBI hiring process. Lack of candor occurs when an applicant fails to disclose or conceals derogatory information, misrepresents facts, or otherwise provides untruthful information on application forms, during the personnel security interview or polygraph examination, or at any other point along the way. Interestingly enough, a common and fatal mistake applicants make is failure to be forthright about something that would not have resulted in disqualification if only they had been upfront and truthful about a particular matter.

It is important to be mindful of the fact that FBI background investigations are performed by experienced investigators who know exactly how to get to the bottom of things. Therefore, with this and basic ethics principles in mind, your best bet is to disclose and thoroughly discuss during the application process any information you think could come back to haunt you. In other words, "when in doubt, get it out."

Length of the Background Investigation

The background investigation normally is completed in one to four months, although in some cases it takes much longer. The length of the investigation depends on a number of variables, such as the following:

- Accuracy and completeness of application materials
- Issues that arise requiring further investigation
- The extent of foreign travel, or whether the applicant has resided in another country
- The number of residences or employers the applicant has had
- Ability to locate and interview employers, references, or other persons
- Availability of records
- The number of applicants being processed at any given time
- The workload of background investigators

Background Investigation Results

All applicants are informed of the outcome of their background investigation in writing. Applicants can obtain a copy of their background investigation report in accordance with the Freedom of Information Act (FOIA) and the Privacy Act (PA). Written requests should be mailed to the Bureau's Freedom of Information/Privacy Act (FOI/PA) Section at FBI Headquarters in Washington, D.C. The Bureau might black out certain portions of the report, however, in accordance with FOIA and PA laws.

The Polygraph Examination

Candidates must clear another significant hurdle prior to reporting to the FBI Academy for New Agent Training. A polygraph examination is administered to every FBI applicant who receives a conditional offer of appointment. This examination focuses on national security and counterintelligence issues, whether the applicant has ever sold illegal drugs for profit or violated the FBI guidelines pertaining to the use of illegal drugs, and the veracity of information provided in the Online Application for employment. All FBI polygraph activities—including criminal and personnel matters—are coordinated by the Bureau's Polygraph Unit, which is a component of the FBI's Security Division.

The Functions of the Polygraph

The polygraph examination is used to determine whether someone shows the physiological and psychological reactions that are believed to accompany deception. The examination allows the polygraph examiner to render a diagnostic opinion regarding the honesty or dishonesty of an individual. The basic function of the polygraph is to record signs of internal stress that people are believed to experience when they respond to questions in a deceptive manner.

The polygraph instrument consists of three or more components, including the following:

- A cardiograph, which monitors pulse and changes in blood pressure

- A pneumograph, which records respiration rate by measuring chest expansions and contractions

- A galvanometer that is normally attached to the hand to measure electrical conductivity through perspiration

Some polygraph instruments measure gross muscular movements, also. The polygraph measures changes in cardiovascular activity, respiratory rate, and skin chemistry while the applicant is asked a series of questions. These changes are recorded in graphic form.

The Phases of the Polygraph Examination

The polygraph examination typically is conducted in three phases, including a pretest, data collection, and data analysis. The examination typically begins with a face-to-face interview between the polygraph examiner and the applicant, during which the instrument and the examination are explained. The pretest interview allows the examiner to secure the confidence and cooperation of the applicant, and to evaluate the applicant's idiosyncrasies that might affect the examination results.

During the data-collection phase, the examiner asks a series of control questions—typically of the "true or false" and "yes or no" variety. Many of the control questions are simple and straightforward. These questions might focus on the applicant's name, place of birth, residence, and other biographical details. The examiner uses the responses to control questions to establish a baseline to which to compare the applicant's reactions to essential questions later. Control questions are followed by specific questions that explore national security and counterintelligence issues, experience with illegal drugs, and other information provided in application materials.

In the third phase of the polygraph, the examiner analyzes the results to determine whether they are indicative of truthfulness or deception. If any responses appear to be deceptive, the examiner might ask the applicant additional questions or ask them to explain these responses. The expertise of the examiner is very important in assessing truthfulness or deception.

Polygraph Examination Results

Results of the polygraph examination are sent to FBI Headquarters in Washington, D.C. Applicants who do not fall within acceptable parameters for the polygraph examination are disqualified. Polygraph results are not official until they are approved by FBI Headquarters personnel. Applicants are not notified in writing as to whether they passed or failed the examination.

Step Seven: Medical Examination and Drug Screening

All special agent applicants must undergo a thorough physical examination and drug screening that is coordinated and paid for by the FBI. Once on board, special agents under age 33 undergo a physical exam every three years, while those 33 years of age and older are given a physical exam annually. After age 40, special agents also complete a cardiac stress test every two years.

The Medical Examination

Prior to appointment, each candidate's medical history is reviewed and the FBI's Chief Medical Officer determines whether any medical issue or condition could possibly affect the applicant's ability to perform the basic functions of the position.

Pre-existing Medical Conditions

Each candidate's medical history is reviewed thoroughly and a determination is made whether any medical issue or condition could potentially affect their ability to perform the basic functions of the special agent position. A history of certain surgical procedures (for example, radial keratotomy) or preexisting medical conditions (for example, hypertension) are evaluated on a case-by-case basis.

Additional Examination

Occasionally, issues or conditions of concern require candidates to undergo additional examination by a medical specialist, normally at the candidate's expense. In these instances, the specialist performs an examination and sends a report of the findings to the FBI. Although a candidate's doctor also may provide information about a medical condition, the final decision concerning a candidate's physical ability to perform the duties of an FBI special agent rests solely with the Bureau's Chief Medical Officer. Medical issues and preexisting conditions requiring additional examination often result in delay of both application processing and placement in a New Agent Training class.

Drug Testing

The FBI is committed to maintaining a drug-free workforce. During the medical examination, all applicants are required to submit to a urinalysis test, which screens for illegal drug use.

A candidate who successfully completes the final step in the application process is appointed as an FBI special agent and reports for basic training at the FBI Academy soon thereafter.

CHAPTER 5

Professional Support Career Opportunities

"No amount of ability is of the slightest avail without honor."

—Andrew Carnegie

The FBI offers a broad range of rewarding career opportunities—including more than 300 types of jobs—for those who are interested in non-agent positions that contribute significantly to the Bureau's mission. More than one-half of the FBI workforce is employed in professional support positions, including intelligence analysts, fingerprint specialists, biologists, security specialists, document analysts, evidence technicians, electronics engineers, and many others. These personnel carry out a variety of tasks within their particular areas of expertise, whether analyzing blood samples, taking surveillance photographs, gathering intelligence information, examining handwriting samples or counterfeit documents, maintaining computer systems, or carrying out other vital functions.

As a member of the Bureau's administrative, technical, scientific, or clerical staff, FBI professional support personnel have a ringside seat to events that make news headlines around the world every day. In addition, although the vast majority of professional support employees are content to remain in non-agent positions, many have used their experience with the Bureau as a stepping stone to becoming an FBI special agent.

Requirements and Qualifications for Professional Support Positions

To be eligible for FBI professional support positions, you must be able to show that your background has prepared you for FBI employment. This section provides an overview of education requirements, experience requirements, and other minimum qualifications that you must address in the hiring process to be considered for appointment to professional support positions.

Minimum Qualifications

Each professional support position has a prescribed set of minimum qualifications that applicants must meet. All applicants must be United States citizens, and most jobs require a particular level of education or experience, depending on the nature of the position. Job vacancy announcements issued by the FBI describe minimum qualifications for each position. Candidates for positions that involve exposure to hazardous situations—such as electronics technician and investigative specialist—must pass a physical examination prior to appointment, and FBI police officer applicants must also meet standards relating to eyesight and hearing. Candidates for most positions also are required to submit a resume and answer several questions presented on the FBI's Web site in order to apply for employment. Additional details concerning the online application process are discussed later in this chapter.

Experience Requirements

Qualification standards for professional support positions often require applicants to possess experience that is either general or specialized in nature. Qualifying general and specialized experience varies widely in its degree of specialty from one position to another, and also between salary grades of the same position. For example, whereas some positions might not require knowledge of law enforcement or investigative techniques, others might call for varying levels of knowledge in these areas, with higher salary grades requiring the most. In addition, qualification standards often specify that a certain amount of the experience must be at a level of difficulty and responsibility equivalent to the next lower grade level in the federal service. In other words, a candidate who wants to qualify for appointment to a position at the GS-12 level might need experience equivalent to a GS-11 position to qualify. Job vacancy announcements normally provide descriptions of qualifying general and specialized experience.

General Experience

General experience is usually required at grade levels where the specific knowledge and skills needed to perform the duties of a position are not prerequisites, but where applicants must have demonstrated the *ability* to acquire the particular knowledge and skills. For some occupations, any progressively responsible work experience should qualify. Others require experience that provided a familiarity with the subject matter or processes of the occupation, or of the equipment used on the job, although not to the extent required of specialized experience.

Specialized Experience

In contrast to general experience, specialized experience is that which has equipped an applicant with the particular knowledge, skills, and abilities to successfully perform the duties of the position, and which is in or directly related to the line of work of the position. For example, qualifying specialized experience for the FBI police officer position is defined as follows:

> *Experience that provided knowledge of a body of basic laws and regulations, law enforcement operations, practices, and techniques and involved responsibility for maintaining order and protecting life and property. Creditable*

specialized experience may have been gained in work on a police force; through service as a military police officer; in work providing visitor protection and law enforcement in parks, forests, or other natural resource or recreational environments; in performing criminal investigative duties; or in other work that provided the required knowledge and skills.

For many positions, candidates who possess a bachelor's degree but no specialized experience in the career field of the position sought may be eligible for appointment at the GS-5 level. Positions at or above the GS-7 level typically require one year of specialized experience equivalent to the next lower grade level. This means, for example, that in order to qualify for a position at GS-12, an applicant must have had at least one year of specialized experience equivalent to at least GS-11.

Many positions allow applicants to substitute graduate-level education for specialized experience in order to qualify for careers at the GS-7 level and above. In lieu of specialized experience, one year of graduate study is normally qualifying for appointment to GS-7. Similarly, a master's degree or two years of graduate study can be substituted for specialized experience when applying for positions at the GS-9 level, and a Ph.D. or three years of graduate-level education can be substituted for specialized experience for positions at the GS-11 level. In addition, applicants without specialized experience who achieved high academic standing during undergraduate studies—also known as Superior Academic Achievement—may qualify for many FBI jobs at the GS-7 level (see "Education Requirements," in the following section).

Education Requirements

Generally speaking, qualifying education for FBI employment includes study at institutions that have been accredited by one of the regional or national accrediting associations recognized by the United States Secretary of Education. However, education completed at foreign colleges or universities can be used to meet educational requirements if the applicant can show that the foreign education is comparable to that received in an accredited educational institution in the United States.

Applicants who achieved high academic standing during undergraduate study may qualify for appointment at the GS-7 level for many FBI jobs under Superior Academic Achievement provisions, even if they lack job-related experience. Qualification is based on class standing, grade-point average, or honor society membership, as follows:

- **Class standing.** Applicants must be in the upper third of their graduating class in the college, university, or major subdivision (such as the College of Liberal Arts or School of Criminal Justice) based on completed courses.

- **Grade-point average.** Applicants must have a grade-point average of 2.95 or higher out of a possible 4.0 for all courses completed at the time of application or during the last two years of the curriculum; or a 3.45 or higher out of a possible 4.0 for all courses completed in the major field of study at the time of application or during the last two years of the curriculum.

- **Honor society membership.** Applies to applicants who have membership in one of the national honor societies (other than freshman or sophomore societies) recognized by the Association of College Honor Societies. Dozens of honor societies are qualifying, such as Phi Beta Kappa, Mortar Board, Alpha Phi Sigma Criminal Justice Honor Society, and Order of the Coif.

For some positions, coursework must have been related to the field of the position applied for in order to be qualifying under Superior Academic Achievement provisions. For example, qualification standards for the Biologist position specify that undergraduate coursework must have been related to biochemistry, biological sciences, or biotechnology to be acceptable.

Qualifying for Salary Grade Levels

Qualification standards for each position also give specific criteria for salary grade levels for which candidates can qualify. Not surprisingly, positions filled at higher grade levels call for a higher level of education or more experience than those filled at lower salary levels. Criteria for each salary level normally are described in vacancy announcements.

Temporary Duty Assignments and Permanent Transfers

Candidates for many FBI jobs, such as financial analyst and police officer, must be willing to accept temporary duty (TDY) assignments in areas that are located away from their permanent duty station. These assignments may last anywhere from a few weeks to several months—or longer under certain circumstances. Other personnel, such as investigative specialists and language specialists, must also be willing to accept permanent transfer to other areas. The majority of professional support employees, however, are in positions that do not require TDY assignments or permanent transfers.

Profiles of Key Professional Support Positions

The remainder of this chapter provides profiles of two dozen key professional support positions, including an overview of the responsibilities, minimum qualifications, and requirements for salary grade levels of each position.

Auditor

FBI auditors provide skilled support to the FBI agency-wide by auditing a broad range of programs and functions. These personnel are based at FBI Headquarters and field offices nationwide. Audit assignments vary depending on the office served and experience of the auditor.

Overview of the Position

The work of FBI auditors involves the application of professional accounting and auditing practices, methods, and techniques to evaluate the Bureau's programs and functions. Typically, the audit process begins with a review of background materials and guidelines to gain knowledge of the program or function to be audited, as well as appropriate planning tasks. Auditors then examine accounts and records pertaining to various programs and functions, such as the FBI Financial Management System, funding of undercover operations, evidence control, property inventory, procurement activities, and the Bureau's payroll to determine whether transactions were properly documented and supported. This often includes examining items such as invoices, purchase orders, vouchers, cash receipts, contracts and agreements, third-party drafts, and various forms. Audits also involve interviewing appropriate personnel and examining organizational plans, policies, procedures, and documentation relating to previous audits.

FBI auditors are responsible for evaluating internal controls, validating year-end account balances, assisting in the formulation of budgets for undercover operations, preparing audit reports and financial statements, and conducting meetings with other FBI personnel to discuss audit findings, problems identified, and recommendations. In addition, the audit process involves reviewing operating practices of programs or functions to ensure that the FBI is in compliance with applicable laws, regulations, and Bureau policies, and to determine the economy, efficiency, and effectiveness of various FBI operations. Auditors also develop, test, evaluate, and apply basic and advanced techniques and methodologies used in auditing or accounting, such as cost principles, cost accounting standards, statistical sampling, regression analysis, decision theory, and other quantitative and qualitative auditing methods.

Minimum Qualifications and Salary Requirements

Basic eligibility requirements for the auditor position include a bachelor's degree in accounting, or a degree in a related field (such as business administration, finance, or public administration) that included at least 24 semester hours in accounting. Applicants also can qualify with a combination of education and experience that included at least four years of experience in accounting, or an equivalent combination of accounting education, training, and experience that provided professional accounting knowledge.

Evaluation Criteria Examples

Applicants for auditor positions must respond to online application questions and submit details in a resume to address elements such as the following:

- Ability to prepare audits in accordance with federal audit requirements
- Experience developing and documenting audit findings
- Ability to prepare audit-related correspondence
- Skill analyzing financial records, reports, or data to ensure compliance with laws and regulations
- Knowledge of federal acquisition regulations
- Experience relating to applying audit techniques and providing advice and guidance on audit problems

Salary Grade Requirements

GS-7   One full year of graduate-level education, or superior academic achievement during undergraduate studies; or a bachelor's degree and one year of specialized experience

GS-9   A master's degree or two years of graduate-level education; or a bachelor's degree and one year of specialized experience equivalent to at least GS-7

GS-11   A Ph.D. or equivalent doctoral degree, or three years of graduate-level education; or a bachelor's degree and one year of specialized experience equivalent to at least GS-9

GS-12   A bachelor's degree and one year of specialized experience equivalent to GS-11

GS-13   A bachelor's degree and one year of specialized experience equivalent to GS-12

Aviation Investigative Specialist

The Bureau's Aviation Program provides important investigative resources and other support services to FBI Headquarters and field offices, and also to other federal, state, and local law enforcement agencies nationwide. Aviation Program personnel support all investigative programs in all FBI divisions, and also provide transportation of critical personnel, equipment, and evidence in crisis situations. Serving under the Aviation and Surveillance Operations Section of the Critical Incident Response Group, aviation investigative specialists conduct aerial surveillance in investigations that focus on terrorism, counterintelligence, kidnapping, extortion, organized crime, drug trafficking, and many other crimes. The FBI's fleet includes more than 100 aircraft, including single- and multi-engine planes, as well as helicopters. The vast majority of the Bureau's aviation assets—about 90 percent—are dedicated to surveillance.

Overview of the Position

Aviation investigative specialists operate sophisticated cameras and other technical equipment as members of aerial surveillance teams that provide discreet coverage in support of ground surveillance. These surveillance missions involve observing and photographing vehicles, watercraft, and persons in a variety of situations, and communicating with FBI personnel on the ground. Aviation investigative specialists operate a wide range of cameras, video recording equipment, phones, radar devices, sensors, thermal imaging systems, and other technical surveillance equipment. They also monitor electronic listening devices that have been surreptitiously placed in vehicles or buildings, along roadways, or in other locations. Surveillance operations are carried out around the clock, seven days a week.

The work of aviation investigative specialists is highly technical and requires extended periods of intense concentration. Their responsibilities include deciding which equipment is appropriate for each surveillance mission, preparing the equipment for use, adjusting the equipment as necessary, troubleshooting any problems encountered, analyzing and interpreting data obtained, and preparing documentation that provides a record of the equipment used and results obtained. Aviation investigative specialists also present briefings to FBI personnel or representatives of other law enforcement agencies to discuss surveillance results and make recommendations for future operations. Their responsibilities also include conducting training sessions concerning aerial surveillance capabilities and other aspects of flight surveillance operations.

Minimum Qualifications and Salary Requirements

Unlike most professional support positions, aviation investigative specialists are required to be available for permanent transfers or temporary duty assignments wherever the needs of the FBI dictate. Applicants are required to sign an agreement in which they commit to remaining in the position for at least two years. They must also pass a physical examination, and must not be susceptible to motion sickness. A fitness-for-duty examination also may be required periodically.

Evaluation Criteria Examples

When applying for aviation investigative specialist positions, candidates must respond to online application questions and submit details in a resume to address elements such as the following:

- Knowledge of aerial surveillance equipment properties and characteristics
- Ability to correlate, evaluate, and analyze unrelated facts and events in order to anticipate the actions of suspects and victims during fast-breaking surveillance
- Ability to operate sensor, radar, video recording, tracking, and related support equipment used to locate and track suspects
- Knowledge of intelligence gathering methods

Salary Grade Requirements

GS-7   One full year of graduate-level education, or superior academic achievement during undergraduate studies; or a bachelor's degree and one year of specialized experience

GS-9   A master's degree or two years of graduate-level education; or a bachelor's degree and one year of specialized experience equivalent to at least GS-7

GS-11   A Ph.D. or equivalent doctoral degree, or three years of graduate-level education; or a bachelor's degree and one year of specialized experience equivalent to at least GS-9

GS-12   A bachelor's degree and one year of specialized experience equivalent to GS-11

GS-13   A bachelor's degree and one year of specialized experience equivalent to GS-12

Biologist (Forensic Examiner)

FBI biologists provide critical support to criminal investigations conducted by the FBI and other federal, state, and local law enforcement agencies. These personnel are assigned to the FBI Laboratory, which is one of the largest and most comprehensive forensic science facilities in the world, and the only full-service federal forensic laboratory.

Overview of the Position

Biologists plan, coordinate, direct, and perform a wide variety of examinations and comprehensive technical analyses. Their primary responsibilities revolve around the examination and analysis of body tissues, body fluids, and stains recovered as evidence in violent crimes. In doing so, they apply a full range of scientific theories and principles, serological techniques, and biochemical analysis to identify and characterize hair, bones, blood, teeth, semen, saliva, urine, and other body fluids and substances.

On the cutting edge of forensics, FBI biologists perform mitochondrial DNA analysis (mtDNA), a powerful analytical tool that was implemented at the FBI Laboratory in 1996. MtDNA is applied to forensic specimens such as human hair, bone, teeth, blood, and other tissues, and is the most sensitive of all forensic DNA techniques. MtDNA analysis can be used to associate body fluids or a single hair from a crime scene to a suspect, or to identify the skeletal remains of unidentified crime victims. Once a sample is obtained, it is characterized by protein analysis or DNA analysis, and the results are compared to known blood or saliva samples submitted from victims or suspects. Biologists determine whether DNA is present in a variety of samples. For example, cigarette butts, postage stamps, hat bands, shirt collars, and other items that have been in close contact with a person can often yield a genetic profile.

Biologists also analyze samples for use in the Bureau's Federal Convicted Offender Program. Under the program, samples are taken from federal offenders who have been convicted of violent crimes, and the results are entered into a database for potential comparison to unknown DNA samples collected from crime scenes. At the FBI Laboratory's Forensic Science Research and Training Center, biologists also conduct research to improve and develop the methodology of forensic analyses.

In support of criminal investigations and prosecutions, FBI biologists prepare and present oral briefings and detailed written reports to case agents and supervisory personnel, Assistant United States Attorneys, and grand juries. Biologists also play a crucial role in the courtroom because they must occasionally provide expert testimony in evidentiary hearings and criminal trials in support of their findings. Their testimony could relate not only to scientific procedures and analytical findings, but also to the preservation and inventory of evidence obtained at crime scenes and turned over to the FBI Laboratory for examination. In order to prevail in the face of scrutiny surrounding the integrity of evidence, biologists must maintain a detailed inventory of items submitted to the laboratory to establish the so-called "chain of evidence."

Minimum Qualifications and Salary Requirements

Basic eligibility requirements for the biologist position include a bachelor's degree in biochemistry, biological sciences, biotechnology, or a related field with at least 24 semester hours in biochemistry or the biological sciences.

Evaluation Criteria Examples

Biologist applicants must respond to online application questions and submit details in a resume to address elements such as the following:

- Knowledge of biological principles and practices
- Skill in interpreting test results and evaluating data
- Skill in oral and written communication
- Ability to operate various scientific instruments
- Ability to organize, plan, and prioritize testing and analysis activities

Salary Grade Requirements

GS-7   One full year of graduate-level education, or superior academic achievement during undergraduate studies in a curriculum related to biochemistry, biological sciences, biotechnology, or a related discipline; or a bachelor's degree and one year of specialized experience in one of the above-listed disciplines

GS-9   A master's degree or two years of graduate-level education; or a bachelor's degree and one year of specialized experience equivalent to at least GS-7

GS-11   A Ph.D. or equivalent doctoral degree, or three years of graduate-level education; or a bachelor's degree and one year of specialized experience equivalent to at least GS-9

GS-12   A bachelor's degree and one year of specialized experience equivalent to GS-11

GS-13   A bachelor's degree and one year of specialized experience equivalent to GS-12

Chemist (Forensic Examiner)

Chemists are assigned to the FBI Laboratory, where they perform highly complex examinations of evidence in support of criminal investigations and foreign counterintelligence matters. The chemistry unit of the FBI Laboratory is divided into five subunits, whose analyses and functions vary substantially. The expertise of FBI chemists is often the basis for prosecutions of criminals for offenses ranging from homicide to bank robbery, drug trafficking, terrorism, product tampering, and financial fraud.

Overview of the Position

FBI chemists investigate, analyze, and interpret the composition, molecular structure, and properties of various substances, the transformations that they undergo, and the amounts of matter and energy included in these transformations. Their work can be hazardous because they are exposed periodically to hazardous materials, toxic substances, and bloodborne pathogens.

FBI chemists assigned to the laboratory's general chemistry subunit identify dyes, chemicals, and marking materials used in bank security devices; controlled substances associated with drug investigations; ink from pens, typewriters, stamp pads, and other sources; as well as other solids and liquids. In the toxicology subunit, they analyze biological specimens of food products for drugs, drug metabolites, pharmaceuticals, poisons, biological tissues and fluids, and substances associated with product tampering investigations. Analyses performed in the paints and polymers subunit include paint chips, plastics, petroleum products, tapes, adhesives, caulks, and sealants. This subunit maintains the National Automotive Paint File, which stores examples of car paints and is used to locate vehicles involved in hit-and-run accidents. Metallurgy Unit chemists can determine whether objects share a common origin or how metal fragments were formed; identify surface and structural characteristics, defects, mechanical properties, or fabrication marks; or determine whether a lamp bulb was illuminated when it was broken. Chemists assigned to the instrumentation operation and support subunit are responsible for calibrating and maintaining analytical instruments used to analyze and identify samples, maintaining databases, and evaluating new technologies.

As members of FBI evidence response teams that examine evidence at crime scenes, chemists locate, identify, reconstruct, and preserve pertinent items of evidence for examination and analysis in the laboratory. For example, in support of investigations involving bombing incidents and arson, they conduct comprehensive technical analyses of explosives, explosive residues, and accelerants. FBI chemists played a major role in the investigation of TWA Flight 800, which crashed into the ocean off Long Island Sound in 1996. Many of the one-million-plus pieces of aircraft debris were retrieved from the ocean and examined using sophisticated methods of chemical analysis. During the investigation, traces of high explosive chemicals were found on the wreckage. The FBI later determined that months before the crash, the St. Louis Airport Police conducted explosives training for canine units aboard the aircraft, which left explosive residues on the aircraft. Chemists also tested evidence recovered from the 1995 bombing of the Murrah Federal Building in Oklahoma City, and from the wreckage of EgyptAir Flight 990, which crashed off the Massachusetts coast in 1999.

Because all evidence must be carefully accounted for at all times in order to maintain the legal chain of custody, chemists are required to prepare accurate inventories of evidence under their control, and to make these available to FBI special agents, prosecuting attorneys, and grand juries. Their responsibilities also include preparing and presenting written reports and oral briefings that convey their opinions and findings, as well as testifying as an expert witness during evidentiary hearings and criminal trials. Chemists also provide scientific support to other federal, state, and local law enforcement agencies.

In an ongoing effort to expand the knowledge base in the field, chemists conduct scientific research at the FBI Laboratory's Forensic Science Research and Training Center, and present their findings and newly established procedures to the forensic science community. They also conduct training in examination techniques for prosecuting attorneys, judges, police officers, and forensics examiners of other law enforcement agencies.

Minimum Qualifications and Salary Requirements

To qualify for the chemist position, applicants must have one of the following:

A. A bachelor's degree in the physical sciences, life sciences, or engineering that included 30 semester hours in chemistry, supplemented by coursework in mathematics through differential and integral calculus, and at least six semester hours of physics.

B. A combination of education, experience, and coursework equivalent to a college major as outlined in item A, including at least 30 semester hours in chemistry, supplemented by coursework in mathematics through differential and integral calculus, and at least six semester hours of physics. To qualify under item B, the quality of the combination of education and experience must be sufficient to demonstrate that the applicant possesses the knowledge, skills, and abilities required to perform work in the occupation, and is comparable to that normally acquired through the completion of a four-year course of study with a major in the field.

Evaluation Criteria Examples

Applicants for chemist positions must respond to online application questions and submit details in a resume to address elements such as the following:

- Knowledge of chemical concepts, theories, and principles

- Skill in written and oral communication

- Skill in operating scientific instruments and interpreting data to analyze evidence

- Ability to organize, plan, and prioritize testing and analysis activities, and to evaluate information

Salary Grade Requirements

GS-7   One full year of graduate-level education, or superior academic achievement during undergraduate studies; or a bachelor's degree and one year of specialized experience

GS-9   A master's degree or two years of graduate-level education; or a bachelor's degree and one year of specialized experience equivalent to at least GS-7

GS-11   A Ph.D. or equivalent doctoral degree, or three years of graduate-level education; or a bachelor's degree and one year of specialized experience equivalent to at least GS-9

GS-12   A bachelor's degree and one year of specialized experience equivalent to GS-11

GS-13   A bachelor's degree and one year of specialized experience equivalent to GS-12

Community Outreach Specialist

The FBI Community Outreach Program (COP) is a comprehensive nationwide effort that addresses multiple interrelated societal problems, including violent crimes, terrorism, civil-rights violations, gang activity, drug abuse and trafficking, and other crimes in support of the Bureau's investigative mission. The Program was established to enhance communication between the FBI and America's communities, with emphasis on promoting the mission of the FBI and the Agency's crime-reduction efforts. Since 1988, the Bureau's outreach activities have expanded to include the Adopt-a-School Program, a speaker's bureau, the FBI Citizen's Academy, an assistance program for crime victims and witnesses, the Community Relations Executive Seminar Training Program, gun safety education, and other initiatives. Another important outreach effort supported by the COP is InfraGard, which is an alliance of private industry, colleges and universities, law enforcement agencies, and other participants committed to sharing information and intelligence to protect our nation's critical infrastructures.

Overview of the Position

The Bureau's community outreach specialists serve as the primary point of contact for all COP activities. Their responsibilities can vary from one field office to another, but generally involve conducting research and planning, organizing, implementing, and coordinating initiatives that are concerned with the FBI's crime prevention, intervention, and awareness programs.

Community outreach specialists develop and disseminate information, establish partnerships, speak to targeted groups, accompany key FBI staff to community events, and promote cooperation with representatives of government and law enforcement agencies, health and social service organizations, schools, local chapters of national organizations, and other community groups. These personnel participate in a variety of activities with family-centered organizations, such as Boys and Girls Clubs of America, National Family Partnership, Big Brothers Big Sisters, and the National Center for Missing and Exploited Children, among others. They also work with organizations such as the NAACP, National Council of Jewish Women, League of United Latin American Citizens, American-Arab Institute, and National Congress of American Indians to promote mutual understanding of issues, discuss concerns, and share perspectives.

Minimum Qualifications and Salary Requirements

The following evaluation criteria and salary grade requirements apply to candidates for the community outreach specialist position.

Evaluation Criteria Examples

Applicants for community outreach specialist positions must respond to assessment questions online and submit supporting details in a resume to address elements such as the following:

- Ability to plan and implement projects
- Ability to conduct research, compile and organize information, and prepare information for dissemination

- Ability to serve as a representative or speaker in the areas of crime, drug, gang, and violence prevention

- Knowledge of community affairs issues, health and social service organizations, government and law enforcement agencies, national organizations, and community groups

- Knowledge of liaison and public relations principles

Salary Grade Requirements

GS-7   One full year of graduate-level education, or superior academic achievement during undergraduate studies; or one year of specialized experience equivalent to at least GS-5

GS-9   A master's degree or two years of graduate-level education; or one year of specialized experience equivalent to at least GS-7

GS-11   A Ph.D. or equivalent doctoral degree, or three years of graduate-level education; or one year of specialized experience equivalent to at least GS-9

Cryptanalyst (Forensic Examiner)

Cryptanalysis is an important technical discipline within the U.S. Intelligence Community. This field entails the art and science of deciphering coded messages. Cryptanalysts, also known as "code-breakers," use mathematics, computer programming, engineering, foreign-language skills, other technologies, and creativity to systematically analyze codes and find solutions. In addition to the FBI, several federal agencies have cryptanalysts on staff, such as the National Security Agency, National Reconnaissance Office, Air Force, Navy, and Coast Guard.

Cryptanalysis has been used since ancient times. Some 20th-century examples include the following: In the 1920s, advanced crypto messages were used by alcohol smugglers to communicate with one another. During World War II, the Allies decoded the German Enigma Cipher Machine to read secret communications throughout the war. In 1969, the Zodiac Killer, who terrorized California's Bay Area during the 1960s and 1970s, sent coded messages to newspapers explaining his motive for killing. More recently, cryptology has been in the spotlight following speculation that terrorist organizations have communicated secret codes to their members through messages broadcast on television. Gangs also use coded messages in graffiti to communicate.

Overview of the Position

The career of FBI cryptanalysts is multifaceted. These personnel inventory, examine, analyze, and decrypt encoded text, clandestine documents, electronic data, tape recordings from undercover and covert surveillance activities, and other information obtained by the FBI and other law enforcement agencies in criminal and national security investigations. Much of their activity revolves around material relating to domestic and international terrorist organizations, individuals and organizations involved in counterespionage activities, drug trafficking and organized crime enterprises, illegal gambling and sports "bookmaking" operations, loan-sharking activities, money laundering and other financial crime activities, street and prison gangs, and violent criminals.

Criminals have a long history of maintaining records and communicating with one another using cipher systems, which involves the replacement of letters or numbers with different characters or the systematic rearrangement of letters to form encoded messages.

Cryptanalysts perform many analytical tasks with the aid of complicated software programs, supercomputers, and high-powered workstations. In addition, they occasionally develop custom computer hardware and software applications to decipher encoded information. They also can accomplish plenty with a pencil and paper. In many cases, cryptanalysts work closely with FBI language specialists, because evidence under examination often is written or spoken in foreign languages. Cryptanalysts conduct research; write comprehensive reports; brief various FBI personnel, other law enforcement officers, and prosecutors; and testify in court concerning their findings. The Bureau's cryptanalysts are based within the Analysis Section of the FBI Laboratory in Quantico, Virginia.

Minimum Qualifications and Salary Requirements

Basic eligibility requirements for the cryptanalyst position include a bachelor's degree in mathematics, computer science, business administration, banking, accounting, finance, forensic science, intelligence analysis, criminal justice, criminology, or law enforcement.

Applicants also can qualify with a combination of education and specialized experience. To qualify in this manner, the experience must be related to cryptanalysis (including mathematics, intelligence, or computer science); accounting, business, or banking (concerned with maintaining business records, cash flow, or accounting principles, or designation as a certified public accountant); or law enforcement (including work in forensic science or the investigation of terrorism, organized crime, gangs, drug crimes, gambling, money laundering, loan sharking, or prostitution).

Evaluation Criteria Examples

Cryptanalyst applicants must respond to online application questions and submit details in a resume to address elements such as the following:

- Ability to inventory, organize, and collate large amounts of hard-copy and electronic records; to evaluate the records for completeness and value; and to establish a methodology to conduct an analysis

- Knowledge of accounting and auditing principles, theories and techniques, including cash flow, cash receipts, disbursements, accounts receivable and accounts payable, bank deposit analysis, and net-worth analysis

- Knowledge of the procedures used in financial link analysis to trace the movement of money and the ownership of assets; and the principals of the investigation

- Ability to use, manipulate, and extract data from automated systems and other software applications for the preparation of financial worksheets, schedules, and reports

- Ability to apply critical-thinking and problem-solving skills to identify patterns and draw conclusions

- Ability to communicate in writing in support of analytical findings
- Ability to communicate orally in order to maintain liaison with FBI field divisions, other law enforcement agencies, and Assistant United States Attorneys

Salary Grade Requirements

GS-7   One full year of graduate-level education, or superior academic achievement during undergraduate studies; or a bachelor's degree and one year of specialized experience

GS-9   A master's degree or two years of graduate-level education; or a bachelor's degree and one year of specialized experience equivalent to at least GS-7

GS-11   A Ph.D. or equivalent doctoral degree, or three years of graduate-level education; or a bachelor's degree and one year of specialized experience equivalent to at least GS-9

GS-12   A bachelor's degree and one year of specialized experience equivalent to GS-11

GS-13   A bachelor's degree and one year of specialized experience equivalent to GS-12

Document Analyst (Forensic Examiner)

The skilled expertise of FBI document analysts is utilized by the Bureau—and other law enforcement agencies—in the investigation of crimes involving fraud against the government, check fraud, forgery, counterfeiting, bank robbery, threats, kidnapping, homicide, and many other offenses. As a result, examinations and opinions of these expert analysts are often the focal point of FBI investigations and prosecutions.

Overview of the Position

The work of FBI document analysts focuses primarily on the examination and comprehensive technical analyses of evidence seized at crime scenes or during the execution of search warrants; or obtained from individuals, government agencies, and private firms in response to subpoenas or through other investigative means. Examinations often focus on identifying common authorship of documents, as well as authenticity, alteration, obliterated writing, erasures, and mechanical impressions. Document analysts also conduct research or development projects on the identification and analysis of document evidence to improve technology and solve evidence problems.

Although physical examinations are performed on many types of surfaces, paper is the most common surface examined. Document analysts examine a wide range of documents, notes, letters, forms, paper, and paper products to identify characteristics of handwriting, hand printing, typewriting, indented writing, watermarks, dry seals, inks, and hidden security features. Depending on the nature of the investigation, these examinations focus on items such as counterfeit or altered checks, securities, contracts, loan documents, promissory notes, application forms, and a wide range of other documents, typically consisting of handwriting comparisons. These often consist of questioned and known documents submitted for side-by-side comparison. If the evidence submitted includes only writing of unknown origin, however, the examination could include only file searches, preservation of the evidence, and evaluation of the potential for future comparisons. The FBI Questioned Document Unit also maintains a number of databases, including the Anonymous Letter File, Bank Robbery Note File, National Fraudulent Check File, Office Equipment File, Shoeprint File, and Watermark File.

Aside from documents and other paper products, examinations are also performed on typewriter ribbons, printers, photocopiers, facsimiles, and other equipment and devices to identify the source of various writings and impressions. For example, document analysts could examine a typewriter ball to determine whether it was used to type a particular document or a portion of a document. During the investigation of the Unabomber, FBI document analysts performed approximately 400 examinations to compare documents to a typewriter that was seized during the search of Theodore Kaczynski's Montana cabin.

Document analysts perform examinations using a variety of imaging techniques that utilize computers, microscopes, chemical substances, photographic equipment, infrared technology, casts, and sequential morphological analysis. They also use this technology to examine shoeprints and tire-tread impressions to determine the brand name and manufacturer of the shoe or tire that made the impression. For example, an FBI document analyst utilized shoeprint identification techniques following the murders of Nicole Brown Simpson and Ronald Goldman in 1994, and later testified in the civil trial of O.J. Simpson. As a result, evidence presented in court linked impressions in blood outside of Simpson's home to the same brand and size of shoes owned by Simpson.

As with other FBI Laboratory personnel, document analysts prepare written reports that address their findings, and present these along with oral briefings to case agents and supervisors, assistant United States attorneys, grand juries, and law enforcement officers of other agencies. They also prepare court exhibits and testify as expert witnesses during trials and evidentiary hearings to explain forensic procedures that were followed and the results obtained.

Minimum Qualifications and Salary Requirements

As a condition of employment, FBI document analysts must successfully complete training necessary for certification as an FBI forensic examiner. They must also be willing to travel frequently, often on short notice, to conduct crime scene examinations. Applicants must be capable of lifting objects in excess of 50 pounds.

Evaluation Criteria Examples

Document analyst applicants must respond to online application questions and submit details in a resume to address elements such as the following:

- Knowledge of microscopic examination of materials, investigative techniques and detection procedures, printing, graphic arts, duplicating processes, and business machines

- Skill in photography and conducting scientific experiments

- Ability to examine and compare handwriting, printing, typewriting, and other mechanical impressions to determine their identity or genuineness

- Ability to analyze inks, papers, and recording instruments and materials by various scientific means
- Ability to write reports

Salary Grade Requirements

GS-7   One full year of graduate-level education, or superior academic achievement during undergraduate studies; or a bachelor's degree and one year of specialized experience

GS-9   A master's degree or two years of graduate-level education; or a bachelor's degree and one year of specialized experience equivalent to at least GS-7

GS-11   A Ph.D. or equivalent doctoral degree, or three years of graduate-level education; or a bachelor's degree and one year of specialized experience equivalent to at least GS-9; or certification by the American Board of Forensic Document Examiners

GS-12   A bachelor's degree and one year of specialized experience equivalent to GS-11

Electronic Surveillance Operations Technician

The electronic surveillance (ELSUR) of terrorists, other criminals, and foreign powers has proven to be one of the FBI's most effective and important tools. The Bureau's emphasis on counterterrorism, counterintelligence, and cyber activities has caused the agency to increase its use of complex technical surveillance tools to collect and analyze evidence. In 2002, the FBI established the Operational Technology Division to consolidate technical investigative support activities and increase the emphasis on future investigative technologies. The Bureau has since been steadily expanding its cadre of foreign-language specialists, intelligence analysts, and technical surveillance personnel—including electronic surveillance operations technicians. These personnel support ELSUR activities by carrying out crucial tasks associated with evidence-gathering in a variety of criminal cases and counterintelligence investigations.

Overview of the Position

The responsibilities of electronic surveillance operations technicians primarily revolve around the processing and control of evidence, as well as the documentation and reporting associated with highly classified ELSUR operations. These personnel are charged with ensuring that appropriate approvals and documentation are obtained prior to ELSUR operations in accordance with various laws and FBI policies. This requires a firm knowledge of approval options, which depend on the type of surveillance and monitoring techniques to be used—including the application of more than 50 types of audio, video, or digital electronic recording devices or methods.

Electronic surveillance operations technicians also maintain records and control systems to track surveillance targets, equipment installations, and evidence obtained, and conduct records searches to report on surveillance operations for various purposes. Some of these records are maintained in the Bureau's Electronic Surveillance Indices system, and are concerned with individuals who have been the target of direct electronic surveillance; those whose communications have been monitored or intercepted by FBI electronic surveillance; and those who own, lease, or license premises subjected to FBI electronic surveillance.

Once evidence has been obtained, electronic surveillance operations technicians maintain it separately from other evidence and ensure the chain of custody. This includes performing special sealing procedures, minimizing access to the evidence, controlling changes in custody, and preparing associated documentation. Their responsibilities also include preparing duplicate tapes or other media of original recordings made through surveillance, and assuring that recorded conversations are audible so that they can be transcribed accurately—and also so that members of juries will hear the evidence clearly.

Other tasks include providing advice and assistance to FBI special agents regarding ELSUR legal requirements, evidence processing and control, and recordkeeping. Electronic surveillance operations technicians serve as a resource regarding ELSUR matters, and consult with FBI attorneys or other legal advisors regarding interpretation of statutes and the legal requirements for specific investigations and installations. In some cases, they must testify in court regarding duplication and security of evidence, chain of custody, recordkeeping, and other aspects of ELSUR operations. These personnel also perform technical duties concerning the preparation and installation of equipment and resolution of technical problems.

Minimum Qualifications and Salary Requirements

Applicants for electronic surveillance operations technician positions must be willing to travel on FBI business periodically, and to work during the evening and on weekends when necessary. A driver's license also is required.

Evaluation Criteria Examples

When applying for electronic surveillance operations technician positions, candidates must respond to online application questions and submit details in a resume to address elements such as the following:

- Ability to research, analyze, and interpret policies and procedures
- Ability to monitor and maintain sensitive and confidential evidence or materials
- Ability to prepare and process complex forms, paperwork, authorizations, and records associated with the ELSUR process
- Knowledge of courtroom procedures
- Ability to testify in court concerning the chain of custody of evidence

Salary Grade Requirements

GS-6   One year of general experience equivalent to GS-5. This may include any responsible clerical, administrative, or technical work that indicates the ability to acquire the knowledge, skills, and abilities needed for successful performance of the ELSUR operations technician position

GS-7   One year of specialized experience equivalent to GS-6

GS-8   One year of specialized experience equivalent to GS-7

GS-9   One year of specialized experience equivalent to GS-8

Electronics Engineer

The work of the FBI—whether it involves catching criminals, providing assistance to other agencies, or developing new technologies—relies heavily on state-of-the-art electronic equipment and systems. The Bureau places a high priority on obtaining and utilizing the most advanced technology available to conduct investigations, maintain sensitive and national security information, and protect its operations and personnel. FBI electronics engineers form the backbone of the Bureau's efforts to sustain its electronic capabilities at the highest level possible.

Overview of the Position

The Bureau's electronics engineers perform research and development engineering studies on an assortment of technical projects that are geared toward the FBI's specialized electronic systems, equipment, investigative aids, and other devices. Their assignments cover a broad range of activities and engineering functions in areas such as telecommunications, security systems, audio and video system design, countermeasures, and covert electronic and physical surveillance system design. Electronics engineers are involved in many phases of applied engineering research, and are also responsible for the development of equipment prototypes that are designed for use in criminal investigations and for other purposes. They often specialize in one or more aspects of their broad field of work. The nature of assignments is largely dependent on the grade of the electronics engineer, with particularly difficult projects being assigned to those serving in GS-12 through GS-14 positions.

Their daily activities focus on designing circuits, breadboarding, performing computer-aided design and modeling tasks, mechanical layout functions, testing and evaluating prototypes, pre-production tasks, and the mass production of electronic equipment. They also determine requirements for special test equipment and perform troubleshooting functions to isolate and define specific engineering problems. Troubleshooting often involves investigating, analyzing, and preparing design layouts to resolve specific problems with equipment and electronic systems. Many assignments involve major problems that require extensive experimentation and the development of new approaches and technology.

To succeed in their day-to-day activities, electronics engineers maintain constant contact with local and national research institutions, associations, and professional organizations to exchange ideas and seek solutions to problems. Although much of their work is performed within FBI facilities, many projects are carried out at contractor locations.

Electronics engineers prepare engineering drawings and review contractors' drawings for accuracy and adequacy. They also conduct site surveys to determine what must be done to prepare the environment for new equipment, and specify the types of equipment to be used, power requirements, and whether structural modifications are necessary. Their responsibilities also include developing and evaluating the adequacy of maintenance programs, training equipment and materials, operating manuals, and repair procedures.

In furtherance of their mission to develop and improve technology for use by the Bureau and other law enforcement agencies, FBI electronics engineers write reports and author scientific papers for publication in peer-reviewed literature. These may also be presented at training seminars and academic conferences, or distributed for use by law enforcement agencies and others in the intelligence community. Many engineers serve on special agency and interagency committees that address long-range planning and the establishment of future research and development programs. They also maintain continuing liaison with law enforcement agencies, the intelligence community, and scientific groups in the private sector to exchange information and provide technical assistance.

Minimum Qualifications and Salary Requirements

Electronics engineer candidates can meet basic eligibility requirements either by possessing a bachelor's degree in engineering, or through a combination of education and experience, as follows:

Bachelor's degree in professional engineering. To be acceptable, the curriculum must: (A) be in a school of engineering that has at least one curriculum in professional engineering that is accredited by the Accreditation Board for Engineering and Technology in professional engineering; or (B) include differential and integral calculus and advanced courses in five of the following seven areas of engineering science or physics: (1) statics, dynamics; (2) strength of materials (stress-strain relationships); (3) fluid mechanics, hydraulics; (4) thermodynamics; (5) electrical fields and circuits; (6) nature and properties of materials (relating particle and aggregate structure to properties); and (7) any other comparable area of fundamental engineering science or physics, such as optics, heat transfer, soil mechanics, or electronics; OR,

A combination of education and experience. This includes college-level education, training, or technical experience that furnished a thorough knowledge of the physical and mathematical sciences underlying professional engineering, and a good understanding (both theoretical and practical) of the engineering sciences and techniques and their applications to one of the branches of engineering. The adequacy of a candidate's background must be demonstrated by one of the following:

- **Professional registration,** including current registration as a professional engineer by any state, the District of Columbia, Guam, or Puerto Rico.

- **A written test,** which requires evidence of achieving a passing score on the Fundamentals of Engineering Examination (formerly known as the Engineering-in-Training Exam), or a written test required for professional registration that was administered by the Boards of Engineering Examiners in the various states, the District of Columbia, Guam, or Puerto Rico.

- **Specified academic courses,** including successful completion of at least 60 semester hours of courses in the physical, mathematical, and engineering sciences that included the courses specified in the basic requirements of the vacancy announcement. The courses must be fully acceptable toward meeting the requirements of a professional engineering curriculum.

- **Related curriculum,** meaning that successful completion of a curriculum leading to a bachelor's degree in engineering technology or in an appropriate professional field (for example, physics, chemistry, architecture, computer science, mathematics, hydrology, or geology) may be accepted in lieu of a degree in engineering, provided that the applicant has had at least one year of professional engineering experience acquired under professional engineering supervision and guidance.

Evaluation Criteria Examples

Depending on the area of specialty for the position being filled, online application questions for the electronics engineer position are likely to focus on elements such as the following:

- Knowledge of audio and video technologies relating to advanced security, surveillance, and sensor systems

- Knowledge of computer technology, computer hardware, and software

- Knowledge of network communications systems, radio frequency systems, and digital signal processing

- Ability to conduct technical analyses and troubleshooting

- Ability to analyze, test, modify, and develop new technology

- Ability to write reports and prepare professional papers, and to communicate orally

Salary Grade Requirements

GS-7   One full year of graduate-level education, or superior academic achievement during undergraduate studies in a professional engineering curriculum; or a bachelor's degree and one year of specialized experience

GS-9   A master's degree or two years of graduate-level education; or a bachelor's degree and one year of specialized experience equivalent to at least GS-7

GS-11   A Ph.D. or equivalent doctoral degree, or three years of graduate-level education; or a bachelor's degree and one year of specialized experience equivalent to at least GS-9

GS-12   A bachelor's degree and one year of specialized experience equivalent to GS-11

GS-13   A bachelor's degree and one year of specialized experience equivalent to GS-12

GS-14   A bachelor's degree and one year of specialized experience equivalent to GS-13

Electronics Technician

Electronics technicians are assigned to FBI field offices, where they perform the installation and maintenance of specified portions of critical systems and subsystems of the Bureau's communications and intrusion-detection assets. The work of electronics technicians is similar in many ways to electronics engineers. However, whereas personnel in both positions must apply practical knowledge of engineering methods and techniques, electronics technicians are not required to have the full professional knowledge of engineering that is required for electronics engineer positions.

Overview of the Position

The primary responsibilities of electronics technicians revolve around the installation and preventative maintenance of transmitters, receivers, antenna systems, fixed-station units, audio amplifiers, and technical investigative equipment and systems. Maintenance of this equipment typically requires replacing or repairing defective components, adjusting transmitter outputs and modulation, realigning and adjusting FM receivers, and related tasks. Once maintenance work has been completed, electronics technicians inspect the work, furnish advice and assistance on maintenance problems, and conduct on-the-job training for various FBI personnel.

Additional responsibilities revolve around troubleshooting and redesigning complex electronic systems and interrelated subsystems. Electronics technicians perform repairs of all systems utilizing regular as well as highly specialized test equipment. They also assist in planning, organizing, and managing the field office preventative and corrective maintenance programs relating to electronic devices, equipment, and systems. Other tasks include the routine inspection and testing of equipment and systems to ensure technical integrity. They must also ensure that operational and standby systems and equipment are available and are in continuous and reliable operating condition for normal daily functions and emergencies.

In direct support of FBI field investigative operations, electronics technicians assist special agents in planning and carrying out a variety of assignments that require the use of mobile and technical investigative equipment. This could include the design, modification, repair, and testing of radio and electronics systems used in FBI vehicles, as well as video equipment, transmitters, and covert electronic surveillance devices. Their support of field operations ensures that technical equipment is maintained and utilized at optimum operational performance levels. In the course of search-warrant or arrest-warrant operations, or during major incidents, electronics technicians may set up command posts in the field to ensure reliable communication by radio, phone, and fax.

In support of the Bureau's administrative operations, electronics technicians install and provide limited maintenance of radio dispatching and computer equipment and systems. They also provide guidance and assistance in the installation and maintenance of active and passive intrusion-detection systems, which include closed-circuit television, infrared and photoelectric sensors, and a variety of system control panels. In addition, electronics technicians conduct training programs to instruct FBI special agents and support personnel on various types of equipment.

Some of the work of electronics technicians includes contact with high-voltage equipment. They may also be required to work irregular hours or to report to work in emergency situations. Other responsibilities include preparing reports, technical documentation, and diagrams; and reviewing technical publications to stay abreast of electronic technological improvements.

Minimum Qualifications and Salary Requirements

Electronics technician applicants must be capable of strenuous physical exertion, such as climbing, lifting, and crouching or crawling in small spaces. Applicants must also meet specific education requirements.

Physical Requirements

Electronics technician candidates are required to have a physical examination because they might be required to lift heavy objects or climb ladders, poles, towers, and other apparatuses to mount or service electronic equipment and devices. Eyesight requirements include uncorrected binocular vision of not less than 20/200 (Snellen), and corrected vision of 20/20 in one eye and 20/40 in the other. Applicants must also pass a color-vision test. A valid driver license is also required.

Education Requirements

For education to be acceptable, degrees and certification must have included major study in electronics engineering, electrical engineering, electronics engineering technology, electronics technology, or telecommunications.

Evaluation Criteria Examples

Applicants for the electronics technician position must respond to online application questions and submit details in a resume to address elements such as the following:

- Knowledge of theory, design characteristics, operation, and functions of electronic communications equipment
- Knowledge of electrical systems, electronics, mechanical equipment, security equipment, and telephone facilities
- Knowledge of professional electronic engineering concepts
- Ability to communicate orally and in writing with engineers, technicians, special agents, and professional support personnel

Salary Grade Requirements

GS-7   An associate degree or equivalent certificate program; or four years of military service in a technical Military Occupational Specialty (MOS) that required in-depth technical training; or one year of specialized experience equivalent to at least GS-5

GS-9   A bachelor's degree; or an associate degree, or completion of an equivalent certificate program and two years of specialized experience equivalent to the GS-7 level; or six years of military service in a technical MOS that required in-depth technical training; or one year of specialized experience equivalent to at least GS-7

GS-10   A bachelor's degree and one year of specialized experience equivalent to the GS-9 level; or an associate degree or equivalent certificate program and three years of specialized experience equivalent to the GS-9 level; or eight years of military service in a technical MOS that required in-depth technical training; or one year of specialized experience equivalent to at least GS-9

GS-11   A bachelor's degree and two years of specialized experience equivalent to the GS-10 level; or an associate degree or equivalent certificate program and four years of specialized experience equivalent to the GS-10 level; or 10 years of military service in a technical MOS that required in-depth technical training, or one year of specialized experience equivalent to at least GS-10

GS-12   A bachelor's degree and three years of specialized experience equivalent to the GS-11 level; or an associate degree or equivalent certificate program and four years of specialized experience equivalent to the GS-11 level; or 12 years of military service in a technical MOS that required in-depth technical training; or one year of specialized experience equivalent to at least GS-11.

Evidence Technician

The accurate and secure storage of evidence is critical to the integrity of FBI investigations, particularly as it relates to presentation during evidentiary hearings, plea negotiations, and trials. Seized evidence must be properly stored and accounted for so that it can be retrieved for examination or other use by laboratory technicians and specialists, special agents, and Assistant United States Attorneys.

Overview of the Position

The Bureau's evidence technicians perform a variety of functions associated with the receipt, retention, and disposition of evidence in the custody of the FBI. The integrity of evidence depends on evidence technicians and others to maintain a proper chain of custody at all times until final disposition of the case. Establishing the chain of custody requires accurate records and the diligence of skilled personnel to maintain them.

Evidence that is turned over to evidence technicians by special agents is obtained during the course of investigations, the execution of search warrants, seizures from arrested persons, and other circumstances. Once items have been received, evidence technicians first identify their contents and then ensure that numbering, labeling, and inventory procedures are carried out according to legal requirements and Bureau policies. Some items are also measured, weighed, or photographed, although this depends on the type of evidence and nature of the investigation. Certain items are heat-sealed to protect them from air, moisture, or other contamination.

Initial processing also requires evidence technicians to determine whether precautions or safety procedures are necessary for certain types of evidence, such as blood, semen, explosives and other hazardous materials, or other items that require refrigeration, freezing, or any form of special handling. Packaging and storage space requirements are also evaluated. Evidence technicians make appropriate log and computer entries whenever evidence is turned over to or received from special agents, FBI Laboratory personnel, or others. They are also responsible for following specific procedures to ensure the physical security of evidence-storage facilities. Evidence technicians may be called on to testify in court as witnesses or custodians of records concerning the security and chain of custody of evidence under their control.

As members of the Bureau's evidence response teams (ERTs), evidence technicians also respond to FBI operations in the field, where they assist special agents and other personnel with investigations involving white-collar crime, terrorism, drug offenses, homicide and other violent crimes, civil-rights violations, and many other offenses. In this capacity, they offer assistance with evidence processing at the scenes of crimes or disasters, or during the execution of search warrants. For example, evidence technicians were deployed to the scene of the Alfred P. Murrah Federal Building bombing in Oklahoma City, where they combed the bombing site along with special agents and conducted inventories of items seized. Evidence recovered at the scene was used to link Timothy McVeigh to the bombing, which led to his conviction. The skilled expertise of evidence technicians sometimes requires these personnel to be deployed overseas as well.

Minimum Qualifications and Salary Requirements

Applicants must be capable of lifting heavy packages or objects, and able to pass a pre-employment physical examination. The position also requires a willingness to handle potentially dangerous materials, such as explosives, poisons, corrosives, combustibles, or contaminated items or substances.

Evaluation Criteria Examples

Evidence technician applicants must respond to online application questions and submit details in a resume to address elements such as the following:

- Ability to read and interpret instructions and written information

- Ability to gather, assemble, and analyze information

- Ability to communicate orally, in order to provide information to other FBI personnel regarding evidence in custody, and to testify in court as a custodian of evidence

- Ability to communicate in writing, in order to maintain written accountability records and logs

Experience in following proper procedures for receiving, logging, storing, packaging, and shipping of evidentiary materials is also helpful. Knowledge of proper procedures for the handling and disposal of items such as weapons, narcotics, toxic substances, blood, and contaminated articles are a plus, and computer skills are also valuable.

Salary Grade Requirements

Evidence technicians normally are hired at the GS-5 salary level and progress to GS-7 and GS-9. To qualify for the position, applicants must have completed technical training or possess work experience that has equipped them with the particular knowledge, skills, and abilities to successfully perform the duties of the position. Applicants are rated on their experience, education, training, employment performance evaluations, and awards as they relate to the duties and qualifications of the position. A high school diploma or equivalent is also required.

Financial Analyst

The investigation of criminal activity—especially white-collar crime—often includes the assistance of financial analysts to crack the case. Their expertise is indispensable in making sense of complex financial information and transactions in a large proportion of FBI investigations.

Overview of the Position

FBI financial analysts are assigned to investigative squads, where they perform accounting and analytical tasks to assist special agents with investigations, particularly those requiring review and analysis of voluminous accounting and financial records. This often involves the preparation of financial spreadsheets based on information obtained through subpoenas and during the execution of search warrants.

FBI financial analysts have particular proficiency in following "money trails" to establish unreported income and the flow of assets. Their expertise is especially useful during the investigation of offenses involving money laundering, illegal political campaign contributions, bribery of public officials, illegal tax shelters, banking violations, bankruptcy fraud, healthcare and insurance fraud, and embezzlement. In many cases, these investigations focus on organized crime activities, high-level drug-trafficking enterprises, and public corruption. They also search property records, locate assets, and work with financial regulatory agencies in extracting pertinent information for use in bank failure investigations. Financial analyses often revolve around records obtained from domestic and international banks. In addition to assisting with investigations that lead to criminal prosecutions, financial analysts also perform tasks relating to the seizure and forfeiture of assets.

Financial analysts are responsible for developing financial profiles of suspects based on information gathered during investigations, and preparing special agents for interviews with witnesses and suspects. Occasionally, they accompany special agents during interviews to provide the benefit of their expertise. Many financial analysts also serve as members of multi-agency task force operations that focus on fraud against the government, environmental crimes, healthcare fraud, bank fraud and embezzlement, and other offenses. They also prepare investigative materials for presentation in court, and testify during criminal and civil trials. These personnel must be available for assignments that occasionally involve working at night or on weekends, and for temporary duty assignments away from their permanent office for anywhere from 30 days to 6 months.

Minimum Qualifications and Salary Requirements

Applicants must meet specific education requirements, including completion of core courses in accounting. Examples of acceptable core courses generally include Principles of Accounting, Intermediate Accounting, Advanced Accounting, Cost Accounting, Federal Income Tax, Auditing, International

Accounting, and Managerial Accounting. Courses in Business Law, Electronic Data Processing, Statistics, and other business administration courses are not acceptable substitutes for required accounting courses.

Evaluation Criteria Examples

Financial analyst applicants must respond to online application questions and submit details in a resume to address elements such as the following:

- Knowledge of accounting and finance principles and financial management organization operations and practices, in order to interpret and analyze financial documents and records

- Knowledge of the operations of banks and other financial institutions

- Knowledge of legal principles pertaining to subpoenas, search warrants, criminal procedure, and court proceedings

- Ability to communicate clearly and concisely in writing, in order to accurately present information and write factual investigative reports

- Ability to communicate orally, in order to deal effectively with employees in other government agencies, business corporations, banks, courts, and other entities

- Ability to research, collate, evaluate, and analyze information

Salary Grade Requirements

GS-5   A high school diploma or its equivalent, and three years of general experience, and a minimum of six semester hours of core accounting courses from an accredited college or university; or a bachelor's degree in business administration with a minimum of six semester hours of college-accredited accounting courses

GS-7   One year of graduate-level education, or a bachelor's degree and superior academic achievement, and six semester hours of core accounting courses

GS-9   Two full years of graduate-level education, either in business administration (with a strong emphasis in accounting or finance), or accounting, finance, economics, or a directly related subject; or a master's degree and a minimum of 12 semester hours of core accounting courses

GS-11   Three years of graduate-level education in one of the fields described in the preceding item, or a Ph.D. and 12 semester hours of core accounting courses

Fingerprint Specialist

Identifying criminals by their fingerprints is one of the most potent factors in apprehending those who might otherwise escape arrest and continue their criminal activities. Fingerprint identification consists of identifying the impressions made by the minute ridge formations or patterns found on the fingertips. No two persons have exactly the same arrangement of ridge patterns and— except in cases of injuries or mutilations—the patterns remain unchanged throughout life. By comparing fingerprints at the scene of a crime with those of suspects and those on file, FBI personnel can establish absolute proof of the presence or identity of a person. The FBI maintains the world's largest fingerprint repository—including more than 219 million fingerprint cards—as well as sophisticated computer databases.

Overview of the Position

FBI fingerprint specialists are responsible for classifying, searching, verifying, and filing fingerprints and other vestigial prints for identification in support of criminal investigations for the Bureau and other federal, state, and local law enforcement agencies. Their primary responsibilities include the examination of crime scene evidence to detect, develop, analyze, and preserve latent fingerprints, palm prints, footprints, and lip prints. They compare these latent prints with those of known suspects or victims, or those on file in the Bureau's Automated Fingerprint Identification System database. Fingerprint specialists employ a variety of techniques, including the use of chemicals, powders, lasers, alternative light sources, and other scientific methods.

Many fingerprint specialists assigned to the Bureau's Latent Print Unit also are members of the Bureau's disaster squad, which provides assistance in identifying deceased victims of accidents or catastrophes worldwide. When disaster strikes, this squad may be deployed on request from the ranking law enforcement official at the scene, the medical examiner or coroner in charge of victim identification, the ranking official of a public transportation carrier, the National Transportation Safety Board, the Federal Aviation Administration, or the U.S. Department of State in instances of foreign disasters involving U.S. citizens. Since 1940, the disaster squad has responded to more than 200 disasters worldwide and—with the assistance of FBI fingerprint specialists—has identified more than one-half of the victims by fingerprints or footprints. As members of the disaster squad, fingerprint specialists have participated in the identification of victims following the space shuttle *Challenger* explosion in 1986, as well as the Mount St. Helens volcano eruption in 1980, and the mass suicide of hundreds of members of the People's Temple cult in Jonestown, Guyana, in 1978. The identification of disaster victims sometimes involves the use of cleaners, tissue builders, formaldehyde, and other substances to prepare the fingers of dead persons for identification work. Depending on the situation, the identification of disaster victims could also include obtaining latent prints from their personal possessions.

Fingerprint specialists are also responsible for preparing detailed reports developed from their examination and analysis of evidence, and maintaining reports and other records. These are often used by special agents and prosecuting attorneys during criminal case preparation and in court. In many cases, fingerprint specialists are called on to testify in evidentiary hearings and criminal trials in support of their findings, for which they prepare and present charts and other exhibits for use in the courtroom. Their duties also include conducting research studies in latent fingerprint identification, which includes conducting experiments in new techniques and testing new equipment and technology. They also provide training in all aspects of latent print work to local, state, federal, and foreign law enforcement personnel.

Minimum Qualifications and Salary Requirements

The following evaluation criteria and salary grade requirements apply to candidates for the fingerprint specialist position.

Evaluation Criteria Examples

Areas to be addressed in online application questions for this position may include elements such as the following:

- Knowledge of chemicals, procedures, and equipment used in developing latent prints on a variety of substances and materials, and of techniques used in the preservation of latent prints

- Ability to communicate in writing, in order to prepare written laboratory reports based on interpretation and evaluation of fingerprint evidence, research papers, and instructional guides

- Ability to communicate orally, in order to brief supervisory personnel, special agents, prosecuting attorneys, and others, and to testify as an expert witness in criminal cases and administrative hearings to explain results of examinations

- Ability to use computers, as well as word-processing, database, and video-imaging software

Salary Grade Requirements

GS-7   One year of specialized experience equivalent to at least GS-5 that demonstrated the ability to classify inked fingerprints by the Henry and NCIC systems

GS-9   One year of specialized experience equivalent to at least GS-7 that provided knowledge of the techniques for comparing and lifting latent fingerprints on evidentiary materials, in photographing latent and inked prints, and in making photographic enlargements for court demonstrations

GS-11 One year of specialized experience equivalent to at least GS-9 performing complex latent fingerprint examinations, preparing written laboratory reports based on examinations, and testifying as an expert witness in the area of latent fingerprint examinations

GS-12 One year of specialized experience equivalent to at least GS-11 analyzing complex fingerprint cases and imperfect or partial latent fingerprint impressions that contain only the minimum number of points necessary to make an identification, and conducting methods-development projects to improve latent fingerprint examination capabilities

Foreign Operations Specialist

Foreign operations specialists are assigned to the FBI Office of International Operations (OIO). Based at FBI Headquarters in Washington, D.C., the OIO oversees the Legal Attaché (LEGAT) program, whose mission is to establish and maintain liaison with Interpol and principal law enforcement, intelligence, and security services worldwide. This program enables the FBI to investigate organized crime, international terrorism, foreign counterintelligence, and other major criminal activity on a global scale. LEGAT offices are established through mutual agreement with host countries and are situated in U.S. embassies or consulates. The liaison activities performed by LEGAT personnel are essential to the successful fulfillment of the international responsibilities of the FBI and to the interests of the United States. The Bureau's OIO personnel assist foreign

agencies with investigative requests in the United States to encourage reciprocal assistance in criminal and other matters.

Overview of the Position

FBI foreign operations specialists serve as experts on international terrorism
and criminal activity emanating from a particular LEGAT territory. They work
in teams to study the nature of the terrorism and criminal activity to determine how it affects or could affect the United States.

To accomplish this, foreign operations specialists conduct research and glean
information from a variety of databases, foreign law enforcement and intelligence services, open source information, U.S. Embassy economic and political reporting, and other means. They also develop contacts with counterparts
at FBI Headquarters and field offices, the U.S. State Department, the U.S.
Department of Defense, U.S. and foreign law enforcement agencies, and other
organizations to obtain and share intelligence information.

Foreign operations specialists summarize their findings in detailed written
reports and verbal briefings to FBI management and foreign officials concerning international terrorism and crime trends. These reports and briefings serve
as the basis for policy recommendations and the allocation of FBI personnel
around the world. Foreign operations specialists also compose correspondence
in response to inquiries from members of Congress and U.S. federal agencies,
FBI field and LEGAT offices, other FBI Headquarters divisions, foreign law
enforcement agencies, and U.S. and foreign embassies.

Minimum Qualifications and Salary Requirements

Applicants for this position must have one year of specialized experience in an
administrative, professional, technical, investigative, or intelligence position
that involved either: (a) conducting research, performing analytical tasks, and
preparing written products, or (b) international relations responsibilities. They
must also be willing to travel worldwide occasionally and to obtain a U.S. passport.

Evaluation Criteria Examples

Applicants for foreign operations specialist positions must respond to assessment questions online and submit supporting details in a resume to address
elements such as the following:

- Experience in creating written products, such as college term papers,
  research grant proposals, laboratory reports, policy documents, journal or
  newspaper articles, investigative or intelligence reports, form letters, position papers, or legal briefs

- Ability to create and modify work products using word-processing software, e-mail, spreadsheets, databases, Microsoft PowerPoint, Internet Web
  browsers, search engines, and so on

- Ability to communicate orally with internal and external customers,
  including coworkers and superiors

- Ability to collect information from a variety of sources and evaluate the
  similarities and disparities in the data

- Ability to analyze and interpret information, draw conclusions, and apply reasoning to resolve a problem, question, or issue

- Ability to analyze and evaluate data in a geographical or functional area

- Ability to respond to work requests, set priorities, organize information, and complete assignments in a timely manner

Salary Grade Requirements

GS-9   A master's degree or two years of graduate-level education; or a bachelor's degree and one year of specialized experience equivalent to at least GS-7

GS-11   A Ph.D. or equivalent doctoral degree, or three years of graduate-level education; or a bachelor's degree and one year of specialized experience equivalent to at least GS-9

GS-12   A bachelor's degree and one year of specialized experience equivalent to GS-11

GS-13   A bachelor's degree and one year of specialized experience equivalent to GS-12

Information Technology Specialist

Few occupations within the FBI cover as broad a range of responsibilities and areas of focus as information technology specialists. Personnel working under this position classification range from specialists who maintain computer hardware, to others who perform software engineering tasks, and to those who are directly involved in criminal investigations. To accomplish these and myriad other tasks, FBI information technology specialists are employed at FBI Headquarters; at the Bureau's Criminal Justice Information Services (CJIS) Division complex in Clarksburg, West Virginia; and at FBI field offices.

Overview of the Position

Generally speaking, FBI information technology specialists are responsible for programming and other tasks associated with the design, development, testing, implementation, and maintenance of the Bureau's information systems. Specialties in the information technology specialist classification include areas such as information security, systems analysis, applications software, operating systems, network services, data management, customer support, and systems administration.

A substantial proportion of the Bureau's information technology specialists are employed at the CJIS Division, which was established in 1992 to serve as the focal point and central repository for the Bureau's criminal justice information services. CJIS is the largest division within the FBI. Many of the Bureau's information technology programs are consolidated under the CJIS Division, such as the National Crime Information Center, Uniform Crime Reporting Program, National Instant Criminal Background Check System, Integrated Automated Fingerprint Identification System, and the National Incident-Based Reporting System.

Responsibilities of information technology specialists working at the CJIS vary widely depending on the functions of the unit they are assigned to. For example, those assigned to the CJIS software development unit are responsible for tasks such as the installation of commercial off-the-shelf software, applying patches supplied by software vendors, analyzing computer errors attributed to software, and communicating with software vendors to resolve technical problems. They also modify database structures and develop operational software for a variety of needs. In the engineering unit, information technology specialists perform systems engineering, hardware and software engineering, and telecommunications engineering, as well as other functions to ensure that modifications to CJIS computer systems meet operational requirements and standards. Information technology specialists in the technical maintenance unit provide preventative, corrective, and adaptive hardware maintenance for CJIS computer systems, networks, voice and security systems, and communications systems. Day-to-day monitoring of the CJIS system-of-systems is the responsibility of information technology specialists within the operations unit, including database administration, program analysis, system backup and restore functions, and response to error conditions.

In direct support of criminal investigations, many FBI information technology specialists are members of the Bureau's computer analysis and response team (CART). CART information technology specialists assist in the search and seizure of computer evidence, and also provide forensic examinations and technical support for FBI investigations involving computer intrusions and other crimes. Using a combination of proprietary tools, commercial off-the-shelf software, and commercial forensic tools, CART conducts computer forensic examinations on evidence seized in virtually all of the FBI's investigative programs. For example, CART information technology specialists analyzed and restored data during the Columbine High School shooting investigation, and assisted in the investigation of Theodore Kaczynski—known also as the Unabomber. They also were involved in the search and analysis of more than one million computer files in the investigation of Wen Ho Lee, a nuclear weapons engineer at the Los Alamos National Laboratory who was convicted of illegally downloading sensitive data from a classified computer system. CART information technology specialists are often hired into the CART program directly.

Because information technology management is an around-the-clock operation, some information technology specialist positions require shift work, which may include duty on weekends and holidays, as well as reporting for work during adverse weather conditions or emergency situations—even if federal agencies are closed in the immediate vicinity.

Minimum Qualifications and Salary Requirements

Information technology specialists must be willing to accept assignments that require occasional travel. The ability to lift objects in excess of 50 pounds also is required.

Evaluation Criteria Examples

Online application questions for information technology specialist positions may vary widely depending on the nature of positions being filled, including elements such as the following:

- Knowledge of network design, data recovery, and software integration
- Skill in database management, and in developing and testing information systems
- Skill in writing and debugging code, and in troubleshooting techniques
- Ability to analyze system requirements, determine computer system configuration, and analyze automated data-processing system design

Salary Grade Requirements

GS-7   One full year of graduate-level education; or superior academic achievement during undergraduate studies; or one year of specialized experience equivalent to at least GS-5

GS-9   A master's degree or two years of graduate-level education; or one year of specialized experience equivalent to at least GS-7

GS-11   A Ph.D. or equivalent doctoral degree; or three years of graduate-level education; or one year of specialized experience equivalent to at least GS-9

GS-12   One year of specialized experience equivalent to GS-11

GS-13   One year of specialized experience equivalent to GS-12

Qualifying education must include major study in computer science, information science, information systems management, mathematics, statistics, operations research, or engineering; or coursework that required the development or adaptation of computer programs and systems and provided knowledge equivalent to a major in the computer field.

Intelligence Analyst

The work of FBI intelligence analysts revolves around the collection, processing, and dissemination of national security or criminal intelligence information that focuses on four areas of interest, including counterterrorism, counterintelligence, cyber crime, and criminal investigations. These skilled professionals play a vital role in the Bureau's extensive intelligence operations by providing strategic analyses to FBI headquarters and direct operational support to special agents in the field.

In response to the September 11 attacks, the FBI established field intelligence groups in each of its 56 field offices to raise the priority of intelligence and to enhance collection, analysis, and dissemination of intelligence information at the local level. Each field intelligence group is responsible for managing its local intelligence resources. Field intelligence groups are comprised of intelligence analysts and special agents.

Overview of the Position

Until recently, the FBI had two categories of analysts, including intelligence operations specialists, who provided tactical analytic support to FBI special agents in managing individual cases, and intelligence research specialists, who were responsible for strategic analyses and were based primarily in analytical units that were farther removed from field-level operations. These positions were merged and combined with the newly created "reports officer" position, and the consolidated position was renamed "intelligence analyst." The Bureau implemented this change to standardize and integrate intelligence support for the FBI's highest priorities.

Presently, there are three separate roles within the intelligence analyst position, including all source analyst, operations specialist, and reports officer. The following sections include an overview of these specialties.

The All Source Analyst

FBI all source intelligence analysts are responsible for projects and activities that are geared to a specifically defined geographical or functional area in support of the criminal intelligence, foreign counterintelligence, counterterrorism, and organized crime missions of the FBI. Intelligence information is used for the preparation of strategic and operational analyses, espionage case studies, and threat assessments, which are distributed within the FBI and to other agencies. In addition to receiving and processing intelligence on investigative targets within the United States, all source analysts also obtain intelligence data concerning situations in foreign countries, such as implications of a recent presidential election, revolution, uprising, or coup. This may also include speculative intelligence that focuses primarily on projecting what future conditions will be.

Tasks carried out by all source analysts include accessing local and national intelligence information databases, analyzing investigative intelligence reports from various agencies, and recommending approval or disapproval regarding the dissemination of intelligence information within the FBI and to outside organizations. Much of their work revolves around recognizing complex patterns of behavior of individuals and groups, and making assessments of present and future terrorist, foreign intelligence, or criminal threats. Their responsibilities also include compiling information and assessing its importance, validity, and comprehensiveness, and apprising FBI personnel of activity that impacts the Bureau's tactical and strategic initiatives. In many cases, intelligence information collected by all source analysts is processed through sophisticated computer databases and various methods of data manipulation. They also provide analytical assistance to FBI special agents and other personnel to assist them with complex investigative issues and problems.

To assist organizations outside of the FBI, all source analysts routinely respond to requests for intelligence information from members of the U.S. Intelligence Community and law enforcement agencies. Maintaining effective working relationships with local, national, and international contacts within the intelligence and law enforcement communities is crucial to their success. They also are responsible for preparing and presenting briefings and training classes to FBI personnel, prosecuting attorneys, grand juries, high-level decision-makers within the government, and members of the Intelligence Community and other law enforcement agencies.

The Operations Specialist

In this specialty, intelligence operations specialists lend direct support to investigations by providing case management assistance and critical front-line intelligence. They participate along with FBI special agents in intelligence and investigative operations, including multi-agency task force operations, by collecting, analyzing, evaluating, and disseminating intelligence information.

The Bureau's operations specialists receive intelligence data through criminal investigations and sources such as seized documents, financial records, surveillance reports, photographs, witness interviews, cooperating sources, informants, and court-ordered wiretaps. They also review FBI case files and information obtained through covert sources of information, as well as intelligence reports, published materials, and other forms of communication. This information often includes up-to-the-minute details concerning local events and individuals or groups under investigation. Operations specialists carefully review and analyze the data to determine its significance and validity—and the reliability of the source—and to discover gaps in information that can be filled to the extent possible. They also summarize their findings into written reports, and present verbal briefings to special agents in the field and to other FBI personnel. Operations specialists assist special agents periodically in debriefing intelligence sources or arrested individuals. In other words, they work closely with FBI special agents in developing investigations on a day-to-day basis.

Carrying out these responsibilities requires operations specialists to maintain effective working relationships with their counterparts in the intelligence community, and with law enforcement officers from other federal, state, and local agencies. To perform these functions efficiently and effectively, specialists exchange information through various intelligence working groups that are dedicated to specific or mutual foreign intelligence, counterintelligence, counterterrorism, or other operational programs.

The Reports Officer

Intelligence analysts in this area of expertise are vital to the FBI's efforts to maximize the quantity and quality of information shared within the Bureau and with other law enforcement agencies. They are responsible for reviewing investigative and intelligence reports, briefing notes, bulletins, memoranda, correspondence, and other documents; summarizing the information; and formatting it for dissemination to intelligence and law enforcement agencies.

The FBI's reports officers determine intelligence collection requirements throughout the Bureau, including overseas Legal Attaché offices. Their responsibilities include developing sources of intelligence information and understanding the motivations, access, and reliability of the sources. On an ongoing basis, they receive all source intelligence reports and other data from the FBI, Department of Homeland Security, Defense Department, State Department, Department of Energy, Coast Guard, National Security Agency, Central Intelligence Agency, and other intelligence agencies and sources.

After evaluating, analyzing, and making decisions regarding the value of intelligence data they receive, reports officers write Intelligence Information Reports (IIRs) and prepare intelligence bulletins for dissemination throughout the U.S. Intelligence Community and to their international counterparts. They also sift through raw, unevaluated intelligence and disseminate it within the FBI and to other federal agencies for further processing. Among their most important roles, reports officers perform liaison tasks with U.S. and foreign law enforcement agencies, and represent the FBI at interagency conferences and within working groups and task force operations.

Minimum Qualifications and Salary Requirements

Applicants for intelligence analyst positions should have a fundamental knowledge of research and intelligence techniques, as well as an understanding of one or more of the natural or social sciences, political science, engineering, law enforcement, or military science. Experience that demonstrates the ability to analyze problems, gather pertinent data and recognize solutions, plan and organize projects, and communicate effectively can be particularly helpful.

Evaluation Criteria Examples

The FBI evaluates applicants for intelligence analyst positions based on knowledge, skills, and abilities such as the following:

- Ability to conduct research, evaluate and analyze raw data, apply inductive and deductive reasoning, and draw conclusions

- Knowledge of principles and methodology of research and analysis concerning political, economic, social, cultural, geographical, and military conditions

- Knowledge of foreign and domestic affairs as they relate to counterintelligence and counterterrorism, national security issues, law enforcement, and operational security

- Ability to communicate clearly and concisely in writing, in order to compose written intelligence reports in various formats

- Ability to communicate orally, in order to provide briefings to FBI personnel, members of the intelligence community, and other law enforcement agencies

Salary Grade Requirements

All applicants must possess at least one of the following qualifications:

1. A bachelor's degree in any discipline from an accredited college or university; OR,

2. A present or former federal employee assigned to a GS-0132 occupational (intelligence analysis) series position for a minimum of one year, or served in a temporary duty assignment to a GS-0132 position for a minimum of one year; OR,

3. At least one year of experience as an intelligence analyst; OR,

4. Experience in the United States Armed Services under an intelligence Military Occupational Specialty (MOS) code

In addition, the following salary grade requirements apply:

GS-7   One full year of graduate-level education, or superior academic achievement during undergraduate studies; AND either one year of specialized experience, or two years of experience in a position that involves the exercise of analytical ability, judgment, discretion, and personal responsibility equivalent to at least GS-5

GS-9 A master's degree, or a law degree (JD or LL.B), or two years of graduate-level education; AND either one year of specialized experience, or two years of experience in a position that involves the exercise of analytical ability, judgment, discretion, and personal responsibility equivalent to at least GS-7

GS-11 A Ph.D. or equivalent doctoral degree, or three years of graduate-level education; AND either one year of specialized experience, or two years of experience in a position that involves the exercise of analytical ability, judgment, discretion, and personal responsibility equivalent to at least GS-9

GS-12 One year of specialized experience equivalent to at least GS-11

GS-13 One year of specialized experience equivalent to at least GS-12

GS-14 One year of specialized experience equivalent to at least GS-13

GS-15 One year of specialized experience equivalent to at least GS-14

Investigative Communications Assistant

The success of the FBI depends largely on communication, whether internal, with the public, or with outside organizations. No manner of communication is more important than the work performed by FBI investigative communications assistants, whose responsibilities are vital to the success of the Bureau and other law enforcement agencies.

Overview of the Position

Investigative communications assistants carry out a variety of tasks to assist FBI special agents, joint task force personnel, and other law enforcement officers with investigations and intelligence-gathering activities. The majority of their duties are concerned with the operation of computer databases, whether obtaining data through searches or entering information for ready access by other law enforcement agencies. These personnel operate the Law Enforcement Communications Network (LECN), a national computerized information system comprised of the National Crime Information Center (NCIC-2000), the National Law Enforcement Telecommunications System (NLETS), state criminal justice system databases, and local law enforcement systems. The LECN contains records used by local, state, and federal law enforcement agencies.

Investigative communications assistants search these and other databases for personnel within the FBI and other law enforcement agencies to obtain information on fugitives, suspects, relatives of suspects, missing persons, unidentified deceased persons, criminal records, driver's license data, stolen property, counterfeit securities, vehicles, vehicle identification numbers, license plates, watercraft, and other persons or property. In some cases, completing these tasks involves radio communications with special agents in the field. Investigative communications assistants are responsible for radio dispatch and switchboard operations. They also enter information into the LECN and other databases, and provide day-to-day guidance to other authorized users of the LECN system.

Minimum Qualifications and Salary Requirements

Applicants for investigative communications assistant vacancies at the GS-7 level or higher must be state-certified NCIC operators. For GS-5 applicants, permanent placement in the position is contingent upon achieving state certification as an NCIC operator.

Evaluation Criteria Examples

Investigative communications assistant applicants must respond to online application questions and submit details in a resume to address elements such as the following:

- Ability to read and interpret data

- Ability to collect, compile, and retrieve information

- Ability to communicate orally in order to interact tactfully and courteously with personnel at all levels of responsibility

- Knowledge of policies, procedures, rules, and regulations governing the Law Enforcement Communications Network

Salary Grade Requirements

GS-5   One year of general experience that may include any responsible clerical, administrative, or technical work that indicates the ability to acquire the knowledge, skills, and abilities needed for successful performance of the investigative communications assistant position

GS-6   One year of specialized experience equivalent to GS-5

GS-7   One year of specialized experience equivalent to GS-6

GS-8   One year of specialized experience equivalent to GS-7

GS-9   One year of specialized experience equivalent to GS-8

Investigative Specialist

FBI personnel who serve as investigative specialists have a unique opportunity to be directly involved in street-level investigative operations without making arrests or performing other law enforcement tasks. Their role is critical to accomplishing the FBI's foreign counterintelligence and national security missions. The theft of U.S. technology and sensitive economic information by foreign intelligence services and competitors has been estimated by the White House and others to be valued up to $100 billion dollars annually.

Overview of the Position

The FBI is the lead foreign counterintelligence agency within the U.S. intelligence community. The Bureau's National Foreign Intelligence Program is tasked with preventing foreign espionage and economic espionage, and with investigating foreign counterintelligence cases. The program is also involved in international terrorism threats, weapons of mass destruction threats, and attacks on the nation's critical infrastructures such as communications, banking operations, and transportation systems. The FBI conducts espionage investigations anywhere in the world when the subject of the investigation is a U.S. citizen and is not under the jurisdiction of the Uniform Code of Military Justice. The primary mission of the FBI in foreign counterintelligence investigations is to identify, penetrate, and neutralize the threat posed—which is where the Bureau's elite team of covert investigative specialists lends its expertise.

Investigative specialists collect, analyze, and utilize intelligence information to assess and respond to the activities of foreign powers and their agents that could adversely affect national security. Specifically, they participate as members of teams that conduct discreet surveillance coverage in foreign counterintelligence and counterterrorism cases. For example, these investigations may focus on foreign powers that conduct intelligence activities to identify and collect national defense information from the U.S. Government or American corporations, or to obtain or use chemical, biological, or nuclear weapons and delivery systems. FBI Investigative specialists are assigned to the Bureau's Special Surveillance Group (SSG), and are known in counterespionage circles as the "The G's."

Surveillance missions are performed in a variety of environments and circumstances, and may involve observing individuals from static positions for hours or days at a time, or following surveillance targets on foot or in vehicles. Investigative specialists document their observations through surveillance logs, which provide a record of the activities of those under surveillance, as well as detailed written reports. They also provide periodic briefings to special agents in the field and other FBI personnel on a need-to-know basis. Investigative specialists draw on a variety of resources and techniques in carrying out surveillance tasks, including the use of sophisticated video and photographic equipment to document the activities of their surveillance targets, other technical investigative devices, and radio communications equipment. The work of investigative specialists sometimes involves surveillance activities on extended shifts, at night, and on weekends and holidays.

Minimum Qualifications and Salary Requirements

Unlike the majority of professional support positions, investigative specialists are required to be available for permanent transfers or temporary duty assignments wherever the needs of the FBI dictate. Applicants are required to sign an agreement in which they commit to remaining in the position for at least two years. They must also possess a valid driver's license and pass a physical examination.

Evaluation Criteria Examples

Applicants for investigative specialist positions must respond to online application questions and submit details in a resume to address elements such as the following:

- Knowledge of surveillance techniques
- Skill in gathering factual and visual information through questioning, observing, analyzing, drawing conclusions, making recommendations, following guidelines, and working independently
- Ability to operate photographic and radio communication equipment
- Written communication skills, in order to maintain surveillance logs and write detailed reports

- Oral communication skills, in order to communicate with other surveillance team members, and to provide verbal briefings to FBI special agents and other personnel

Salary Grade Requirements

GS-5   Completion of a four-year course of study leading to a bachelor's degree; or three years of general experience, one year of which was equivalent to at least GS-4. Preference is given to applicants whose major field of study is in the areas of political science, history, journalism, international studies, psychology, sociology, criminology, or certain foreign languages.

GS-7   One full year of graduate-level education, or superior academic achievement during undergraduate studies in the disciplines described in the preceding item; or a bachelor's degree and one year of specialized experience equivalent to at least GS-5.

GS-9   A master's degree or two years of graduate-level education in the disciplines described in the previous item; or a bachelor's degree and one year of specialized experience equivalent to at least GS-7.

GS-11   A Ph.D. or equivalent doctoral degree, or three years of graduate-level education in the disciplines described in the previous item; or a bachelor's degree and one year of specialized experience equivalent to at least GS-9.

GS-12   One year of specialized experience equivalent to at least GS-11.

GS-13   One year of specialized experience equivalent to at least GS-12.

Language Specialist

The FBI has an ongoing and ever-evolving need for personnel who speak foreign languages. Foreign-language needs vary from time to time, and from one office to another, depending on the nature of investigations and initiatives that are underway. For example, proficiency in Arabic might be in demand in Detroit and Los Angeles, whereas Spanish usually is at a premium in cities such as Chicago, New York, and McAllen, Texas. The New York Field Office typically requires support in a wide variety of foreign languages, including Cantonese, French, Hebrew, Italian, Japanese, Mandarin, Russian, and Yiddish. Other language proficiency sought by the Bureau includes Dutch, German, Haitian Creole, Hindi, Jamaican Patois, Korean, Punjabi, Thai, Turkish, Urdu, and Vietnamese. The need for language specialists with fluency in Arabic, Farsi, and Pashto reached a critical level following the attacks on the World Trade Center and the Pentagon on September 11, 2001.

In addition to language specialists, the FBI also employs contract linguists for foreign-language support. These personnel perform essentially the same tasks as language specialists, although they are not full-time FBI employees and do not receive federal benefits. Contract linguists are paid an hourly wage, depending on the language spoken and level of expertise, and are called upon on an as-needed basis. The FBI also meets its foreign-language needs with special agent linguists. Overall, more than 1,000 personnel who are fluent in more than 50 languages and dialects provide foreign-language support to the FBI.

Overview of the Position

FBI language specialists provide a wide range of linguistic support services to criminal investigations and national security matters under the Bureau's jurisdiction. Their work revolves around the translation of oral and written material from foreign languages into English in a wide range of settings and during all types of investigations. For example, they assist special agents with interviews of crime victims or witnesses, and during interrogations of criminals involved in organized crime, drug trafficking, white-collar crime, public corruption, and violations of other federal statutes. Language specialists also work closely with special agents involved in foreign counterintelligence work.

Language specialists also translate speech from audio and video recordings that were produced during electronic surveillance, wiretapping operations, and undercover transactions. In addition, FBI investigations that end up in court often require language specialists to translate testimony during hearings and trials. Language specialists also participate as members of the Bureau's evidence response teams in field offices nationwide because crime-scene investigations often require FBI personnel to communicate with victims and witnesses who speak little or no English. Language specialists also play a crucial role as members of the Bureau's terrorism squads because many terrorist groups are based outside of the United States, as well as various multi-agency task force operations.

The expertise of language specialists has been useful during a number of high-profile cases, such as the investigation of the crash of EgyptAir flight 990 in 1999. In this case, they worked for 130 hours to translate speech from the aircraft's cockpit voice recorder from Arabic into English. Language specialists also assisted FBI special agents during court hearings in the case against Mohamed Rashed Daoud Al-'Owhali, who—along with Osama Bin Laden—was charged with the 1998 bombings of the U.S. Embassies in Kenya and Tanzania. The indictments accused Bin Laden, Al-'Owhali, and other members of the al Qaeda terrorist group of killing a total of 224 people in the bombings. Language specialists also respond to bombings and other crime scenes worldwide as members of the Bureau's rapid deployment teams.

Minimum Qualifications and Salary Requirements

Language specialist candidates are required to undergo a hearing test because they must have satisfactory hearing to translate live and recorded speech. They must also be willing to accept permanent transfers or temporary duty assignments wherever the needs of the FBI dictate.

Evaluation Criteria Examples

Each candidate's language proficiency is measured by a battery of language tests, which include written translations from the foreign language into English, and oral tests in both languages. These tests focus on listening comprehension, reading comprehension, and translation. (Passing an equivalent Defense Language Proficiency test is also acceptable.) The FBI adheres to the Interagency Language Roundtable (ILR) Skill Level Descriptions for listening, reading, writing, speaking, and translation, which serve as the government-wide standard. Candidates are required to provide a self-assessment of their expertise, which is based on ILR language proficiency standards (see appendix E for the Language Proficiency Self-Assessment Chart). In addition to language skills, knowledge of law enforcement and street jargon is also a plus.

Salary Grade Requirements

Whereas contract linguists receive an hourly wage, language specialists are paid according to the General Schedule salary scale. Requirements for various salary grades include the following:

GS-5   Proficiency in a foreign language (and in English) needed by the FBI that is sufficient to attain passing language-test scores.

GS-7   Four years of college-level education; or four years of specialized experience. At the GS-7 level, specialized experience may include life experience from residing in a non-native–language culture. Where English is the applicant's nonnative language, residence in the United States qualifies.

GS-9   Five years of college-level education; or five years of specialized experience; or a master's degree in the needed foreign language or a related subject (such as English, foreign affairs, country area studies, and so on).

GS-10   Six years of college-level education; or six years of specialized experience. Advanced education must be related to the needed foreign language or country area studies.

GS-11   Seven years of college-level education; or a Ph.D. related to the needed foreign language or country area studies; or seven years of specialized experience.

Specialized experience for all levels includes any work with a foreign language, such as translating, teaching, interpreting, editing foreign-language manuscripts, or experience in positions that require a bilingual capability.

Paralegal Specialist (Asset Forfeiture)

The mission of the FBI's Asset Forfeiture Program is to seize and forfeit property under civil and criminal statutes to undermine the economic infrastructure of criminal enterprises. Many criminals are motivated by greed and the acquisition of material goods. Therefore, the ability of the government to forfeit property connected with criminal activity can be an effective law enforcement tool by reducing the incentive for illegal conduct. Asset forfeiture can remove the tools, equipment, cash flow, profit, and illegal goods bought and sold, rendering criminal organizations powerless to operate. In other words, asset forfeiture takes the profit out of crime by helping to eliminate the ability of criminals to command resources necessary to continue their illegal activities.

To accomplish its goals, the Asset Forfeiture Program provides training, resources, and operational assistance to FBI field offices and Headquarters to ensure that asset forfeiture is incorporated into as many investigations as possible to deter criminal activity and dismantle criminal enterprises. Asset Forfeiture Program staff also serve as the point of contact with the Department of Justice and other federal, state, and local law enforcement agencies pertaining to the use of asset forfeiture in FBI investigations.

Overview of the Position

The expertise of FBI paralegal specialists is critical to the success of the FBI Asset Forfeiture Program. These skilled and highly trained personnel are responsible for all aspects associated with seized property and forfeiture in cases relating to drug-related offenses, sexual exploitation of children, counterfeiting, copyright matters, illegal gambling, money laundering, and other crimes. For example, they analyze documentation to ensure there is sufficient evidence to support forfeiture action, determine the need for additional information, identify all persons requiring legal notice of the forfeiture action, and prepare notice letters and newspaper advertisements associated with the forfeiture action.

FBI paralegal specialists perform legal research; review precedent case law; prepare legal pleadings necessary to commence forfeiture proceedings and subsequent motions; propose orders to accomplish forfeiture, settlement, or dismissal; and testify in federal courts. They also determine the suitability of placing seized property into official use, transmit official use documentation to appropriate FBI managers, review requests from outside agencies for sharing of forfeited property, coordinate the disposition of forfeited property between the Bureau and the U.S. Marshals Service, and enter information into forfeiture database systems. Paralegal specialists also conduct training seminars for FBI personnel relating to forfeiture proceedings and the Asset Forfeiture Program.

FBI paralegal specialists work closely with the United States Attorney's Office and during joint investigations with agencies such as the Drug Enforcement Administration, Bureau of Immigration and Customs Enforcement, the Internal Revenue Service Criminal Investigation Division, and various Inspector General agencies, among others.

Minimum Qualifications and Salary Requirements

Applicants for this position must have one year of specialized experience relating to the examination of legal documents, acquisition and disposal of real property, appraisal and review of real or personal property interests, property valuation, and preparation of forfeiture cases for litigation.

Evaluation Criteria Examples

Applicants for paralegal specialist (asset forfeiture) positions must respond to assessment questions online and submit supporting details in a resume to address elements such as the following:

- Ability to analyze facts and legal issues, conduct legal research, and establish and maintain legal file systems

- Ability to review case documents and evidence to determine the nature of violations and potential for forfeiture action

- Ability to draft legal documents and correspondence

- Knowledge of precedent court and administrative decisions, litigation procedures, and court processes and rules

- Skill in the use of office-automation software and hardware, and automated legal research and case management systems

Salary Grade Requirements

GS-9   A master's degree or two years of graduate-level education; or a bachelor's degree and one year of specialized experience equivalent to at least GS-7

GS-11   A Ph.D. or equivalent doctoral degree, or three years of graduate-level education; or a bachelor's degree and one year of specialized experience equivalent to at least GS-9

GS-12   A bachelor's degree and one year of specialized experience equivalent to GS-11

GS-13   A bachelor's degree and one year of specialized experience equivalent to GS-12

Personnel Security Specialist

The FBI employs personnel security specialists to assess the reliability, loyalty, suitability, and trustworthiness of persons who have access to sensitive or classified information, resources, and material that could adversely affect the national security, public welfare, or efficiency of the FBI.

Overview of the Position

FBI personnel specialists conduct a variety of inquiries to determine whether Bureau personnel—or applicants for employment with the Bureau—meet security standards to the extent that their retention, hiring, or access to classified information or work sites is consistent with FBI standards and policies. Tasks these personnel perform also focus on security clearance determinations for contractors who perform work for the FBI.

The responsibilities of personnel security specialists include reviewing and evaluating investigative reports, personnel files, and other information; determining the degree and extent of investigative inquiry that is required to resolve allegations of adverse information; and conducting interviews and other investigative tasks to obtain information relating to minor derogatory allegations against FBI personnel. They also develop detailed and objective summaries of the information considered, and recommend approval or denial of security clearances based on their findings. Although background investigations are performed mostly by special investigators under contract with the FBI, personnel security specialists are responsible for conducting certain components of background investigations, such as indices checks, criminal record inquiries, and other related tasks.

Their administrative responsibilities include developing and implementing policies and procedures for the FBI's personnel security program, and advising FBI officials on personnel security policies and the impact of personnel security requirements on the Bureau's mission. They also administer programs for continuous security evaluation of FBI personnel and security awareness. Personnel security specialists are called upon occasionally to testify at formal hearings regarding security clearance processes, criteria, and justification for adverse actions. They are also responsible for ensuring the proper storage and safeguarding of classified information under their control.

Minimum Qualifications and Salary Requirements

The following evaluation criteria and salary grade requirements apply to candidates for the personnel security specialist position.

Evaluation Criteria Examples

Applicants for this position must respond to online application questions and submit details in a resume to address elements such as the following:

- Knowledge of laws, regulations, and precedents governing personnel security programs

- Knowledge of personnel security programs, concepts, and principles; and of investigative procedures

- Knowledge of medical, legal, and law enforcement terminology for analysis of expert opinions

- Ability to develop information and apply the significance of information to adjudicative determinations

- Ability to communicate effectively orally and in writing

Salary Grade Requirements

GS-5   Completion of a four-year course of study leading to a bachelor's degree; or three years of general experience, one year of which was equivalent to at least GS-4

GS-7   One full year of graduate-level education, or superior academic achievement during undergraduate studies; or one year of specialized experience equivalent to at least GS-5

GS-9   A master's degree or two years of graduate-level education; or one year of specialized experience equivalent to at least GS-7

GS-11   A Ph.D. or equivalent doctoral degree, or three years of graduate-level education; or one year of specialized experience equivalent to at least GS-9

GS-12   One year of specialized experience equivalent to at least GS-11

GS-13   One year of specialized experience equivalent to at least GS-12

Photographer

Photography plays a significant role in the FBI's mission to investigate violations of criminal law and conduct foreign counterintelligence operations. The Bureau employs skilled photographers who capture, process, analyze, and disseminate images relating to crime scenes, forensics, surveillance, tactical operations, courtroom testimony, and training purposes.

Overview of the Position

FBI photographers perform investigative and noninvestigative photographic assignments in a broad range of conditions and environments. Much of their work involves photographing evidence at crime scenes in both indoor and outdoor settings. In this capacity, FBI photographers choose the appropriate equipment and determine the selection, exposure, positioning, angle, background, and lighting sources for each item to be photographed. They are also responsible for marking items of photographed evidence, such as jewelry, furs, oil paintings, motor vehicles, equipment, weapons, documents, notes, damaged property, drugs and contraband, cash, and other goods. Photographers capture images at crime scenes to show the condition and location of evidence, as well as its position relative to other evidence or objects. They work closely with special agents and other FBI specialists to photograph latent fingerprints, footprints, shoe prints, tire prints, grease prints, and other evidence susceptible to photographic enhancement. Photographers apply a range of specialized technical methods to bring up fine details, sharpen images, or eliminate certain colors or features when processing photographic renditions that can be used in court. They must also prepare a log that records all photographs taken, and a description and location of evidence. Depending on the nature of the case, photographers might also photograph victims at crime scenes or at offsite locations.

The Bureau's photographers also perform a wide range of static and moving surveillance photography during the course of criminal investigations, which sometimes involves the use of concealed cameras. These activities often include covert photography of crime suspects who are engaged in criminal activity or interacting with criminal associates. In some cases, photographers are called upon to take photographs from aircraft, including aerial mapping and surveillance applications, and during the execution of search warrants. FBI photographers use an assortment of equipment in accomplishing their missions, such as medium-format cameras, zoom lenses, image intensifiers, 2X and 3X extenders, cable and electronic release mechanisms, remote tripping devices, tripods, infrared flash equipment, high- and low-contrast films, infrared films, and various lens filters. They also adapt standard and special techniques in processing black-and-white film to meet the requirements of specific photographic projects.

As members of the Bureau's evidence response teams, FBI photographers have responded to many incidents around the world to provide their expertise. For example, photographers were deployed to Yemen following the bombing of the *USS Cole* guided-missile destroyer in October 2000, where they photographed the impact of the explosion and assisted in identifying the victims. In the attack, two suicide bombers in a small fiberglass boat blew a 40-by-40–foot hole in the side of the destroyer, killing 17 American sailors and wounding 39. In 1983, FBI photographers traveled to Grenada, where they produced approximately 1,000 images of skeletal remains that were buried in U.S. military body bags found in unmarked graves. In this case, the government of Grenada wanted to determine whether the bags contained the remains of Maurice Bishop, the former prime minister of Grenada, who was assassinated along with 18 government officials. Laboratory examinations disclosed that none of the exhumed bodies included remains of Maurice Bishop. In 1993, photographers were deployed to massacre sites in Kosovo, where they photographed bodies and other evidence in support of war-crimes prosecutions of Slobodan Milosevic. FBI photographers also photographed important evidence in the 1995 bombing of the Murrah Federal Building in Oklahoma City, and during the 1993 siege of the Branch Davidian complex in Waco, Texas.

FBI photographers must also testify in court and present photographic exhibits during evidentiary hearings and trials to explain their photographs as well as the photographic and film-processing techniques they applied.

Minimum Qualifications and Salary Requirements

The following evaluation criteria and salary grade requirements apply to candidates for the photographer position.

Evaluation Criteria Examples

When applying for FBI photographer positions, candidates must respond to online application questions and submit details in a resume to address elements such as the following:

- Ability to photograph moving and stationary objects
- Ability to operate photographic processing equipment, to process photographic films and prints, and to enhance photographic images
- Ability to use equipment developed or adapted for use at crime scenes and in surveillance situations, including flash devices, telephoto lenses, tripods, concealed cameras, and other equipment
- Ability to take aerial photographs

Salary Grade Requirements

GS-8   One year of specialized experience equivalent to at least GS-7

GS-9   One year of specialized experience equivalent to at least GS-8

GS-10   One year of specialized experience equivalent to at least GS-9

GS-11   One year of specialized experience equivalent to at least GS-10

Physical Security Specialist

Physical security is concerned primarily with preventative measures designed to safeguard sensitive or classified information, facilities, equipment, personnel, visitors, and materials from criminal, terrorist, or hostile intelligence activities. With national security and the integrity of FBI investigations and other operations at stake, it is crucial for the Bureau to protect FBI Headquarters, field offices, resident agencies, Legal Attaché offices, off-site locations, and its personnel through its extensive physical security program.

Overview of the Position

The FBI's physical security specialists develop security policy and procedures, and design, develop, evaluate, and maintain intrusion prevention and detection systems to ensure that sensitive information, equipment, and other material is not compromised, sabotaged, stolen, misused, or damaged. Physical security specialists provide technical expertise and hands-on support in the areas of physical security, fire safety, and chemical, biological, and radiological (CBR) countermeasures.

Their responsibilities include conducting physical security surveys; determining the need for safes, alarms, locking devices, and markings needed to effectively secure various sites; and defining restricted, controlled, or secure areas. They also establish procedures for the movement, handling, storage, and protection of national security information, sensitive compartmented information, and other sensitive documents or materials, and inspect facilities where national security data and equipment will be located.

To protect FBI employees and visitors, physical security specialists conduct fire safety surveys, evaluate fire protection systems, implement personnel evacuation plans, and develop countermeasures to explosive and CBR threats against FBI personnel and facilities. Security surveys are designed to evaluate elements such as the use of X-ray and magnetometer devices to screen packages and visitors, the presence and visibility of uniformed officers, personnel access systems, visitor-control procedures, proximity of parking to FBI facilities, building construction and design, exterior lighting and security barriers, closed-circuit television monitoring systems, and backup systems for security devices. To protect FBI personnel from explosives and hazardous materials, physical security specialists develop procedures for screening mail, packages, and cargo that are delivered to the FBI. They are also responsible for analyzing technical problems associated with the Bureau's security equipment and systems, and developing appropriate solutions.

To ensure that the physical security program is operating properly, physical security specialists periodically conduct security compliance reviews to verify adherence to FBI security regulations and policies, and write reports to ensure the proper application of the Bureau's security requirements. Physical security specialists conduct risk and threat assessments on a continuous basis in order to respond to criminal and terrorist threats.

As members of the Bureau's rapid deployment teams, physical security specialists are prepared to respond within four hours to bombings and other high-profile incidents under the FBI's jurisdiction worldwide. In this capacity, when they arrive at the crime scene they are responsible for reporting on the threat level to other responding FBI personnel, as well as the need for additional physical security at the scene and housing for FBI personnel.

Minimum Qualifications and Salary Requirements

Physical security specialists sometimes are required to travel on temporary duty assignments, or to respond to crime scenes or work sites involving hazardous materials or weapons of mass destruction.

Evaluation Criteria Examples

Applicants for this position must respond to online application questions and submit details in a resume to address elements such as the following:

- Knowledge of physical security programs, concepts, and principles
- Knowledge of access-control systems, locking devices, closed-circuit television systems, fire safety, and other security devices and systems
- Knowledge of laws and regulations relating to physical security
- Knowledge of procedures regarding the safeguarding and handling of sensitive compartmented information and other classified or sensitive information
- Ability to conduct security surveys
- Ability to communicate effectively orally and in writing

Salary Grade Requirements

GS-5   Completion of a four-year course of study leading to a bachelor's degree; or three years of general experience, one year of which was equivalent to at least GS-4

GS-7   One full year of graduate-level education, or superior academic achievement during undergraduate studies; or one year of specialized experience equivalent to at least GS-5

GS-9   A master's degree or two years of graduate-level education; or one year of specialized experience equivalent to at least GS-7

GS-11   A Ph.D. or equivalent doctoral degree, or three years of graduate-level education; or one year of specialized experience equivalent to at least GS-9

GS-12   One year of specialized experience equivalent to at least GS-11

GS-13   One year of specialized experience equivalent to at least GS-12

Police Officer

In addition to maintaining a professional staff of physical security specialists, the FBI also has uniformed officers who are committed to protecting Bureau personnel, property, and national security information from acts of assault, terrorism, sabotage, espionage, trespass, theft, fire, and accidental damage or malicious destruction.

Overview of the Position

The FBI maintains a force of uniformed police officers whose primary mission is to maintain law and order, and to protect life, property, and the civil rights of Bureau employees and visitors. FBI police officers are stationed at the Bureau's Headquarters building in Washington, D.C.; the Washington, D.C., Field Office; the FBI Training Academy in Quantico, Virginia; two buildings occupied by the New York City Field Office; and at the Bureau's Criminal Justice Information Services Division complex in Clarksburg, West Virginia. They are assigned to fixed posts, roving patrols, and control-desk duties on rotating shifts around the clock.

FBI police officers conduct patrols on foot and in vehicles to check for unsecured windows and doors, detect and prevent illegal entry, identify suspicious persons and vehicles, and respond to other conditions. They also answer calls for service, respond to crimes in progress and emergency situations, conduct physical security escorts, and administer first aid and CPR to sick or injured persons. When crimes are detected, officers secure crime scenes, collect and preserve evidence, interview victims and witnesses, and process prisoners. Fixed-post duty revolves around access-control tasks, such as checking the identification of FBI employees and screening visitors seeking access to secure areas. Officers are also assigned to a control desk where they monitor electronic intrusion-detection systems and communications systems. FBI police officers are authorized to carry firearms and make arrests.

Many officers have the opportunity to participate in special operations, such as providing security at the 2002 Winter Olympic Games in Salt Lake City, Utah. FBI police officers also provided on-site security during the investigation of TWA Flight 800, which crashed near Long Island in 1996. Occasionally, the Bureau's police officers assist the Metropolitan Police of the District of Columbia (MPDC) with calls for service, arrest situations, and other law enforcement matters. Officers must be willing to accept temporary duty assignments away from their permanent office, at locations wherever the needs of the FBI dictate.

FBI police officers also are eligible to participate in the Bureau's canine (K-9) program, which provides support to criminal investigations and response to disaster situations. The K-9 program affords FBI police officers, special agents, and special agent bomb technicians the opportunity to serve as dog handlers on the Bureau's evidence response teams or to assist FBI field offices nationwide with situations that require the expertise of K-9 teams. Each handler works with a dog that is specially trained to detect narcotics, explosives and the components used in explosives, firearms, currency, or people. K-9 teams carry out assignments such as searching for victims under rubble at the scenes of explosions, or detecting bombs or illegal drugs in cars, trucks, buses, boats, aircraft, houses and apartments, or commercial buildings. The teams also provide support at major events such as the Super Bowl, the Olympic Games, and the Goodwill Games.

Minimum Qualifications and Salary Requirements

Applicants must be a high school graduate or have earned a General Education Development (GED) certificate, be at least 21 years of age, and possess a valid driver's license. Candidates must pass a physical examination, including eyesight and hearing tests.

Eyesight Requirements

Eyesight standards for police officer applicants are the same as for candidates seeking special agent positions. These include uncorrected vision not worse than 20/200 (Snellen), and corrected vision not worse than 20/20 in one eye and 20/40 in the other eye. All candidates must also pass a color-vision test. Applicants who have undergone surgical vision correction are evaluated on a case-by-case basis by the FBI's Health Care Programs Unit. The Bureau has accepted applicants who have had LASIK laser vision correction in the past, although these candidates must wait one year from the time of surgery to be considered.

Hearing Requirements

Hearing requirements also mirror those for the special agent position. Hearing loss must not exceed: (a) average hearing loss of 25 decibels (ANSI) at 1000, 2000, and 3000 Hertz; (b) a single reading of 35 decibels at 1000, 2000, and 3000 Hertz; (c) a single reading of 35 decibels at 500 Hertz; and (d) a single reading of 45 decibels at 4000 Hertz. An audiometer test is used to determine whether police officer candidates meet minimum hearing requirements.

Physical Requirements

All candidates must meet either a standardized weight-to-height ratio or body fat requirement to be qualified for appointment, although they are not required to meet both standards. In other words, those who fall outside of the weight-to-height ratio can qualify by meeting the body fat standard, and vice versa. (Appendix D is a chart of the desirable weight ranges and body fat requirements.)

Evaluation Criteria Examples

Applicants for police officer positions must respond to online application questions and submit details in a resume to address elements such as the following:

- Ability to gather and analyze facts, draw conclusions, and devise solutions to problems
- Ability to use good judgment and make appropriate decisions
- Ability to plan, organize, and coordinate work
- Ability to establish rapport and deal effectively with the public, co-workers, management, and others
- Ability to communicate effectively orally and in writing

Salary Grade Requirements

GS-5   Completion of four years of undergraduate coursework leading to a bachelor's degree related to law enforcement, criminal investigation, or criminology; or one year of specialized experience equivalent to at least GS-4

GS-6   One year of specialized experience equivalent to GS-5

GS-7   One year of specialized experience equivalent to GS-6

GS-8   One year of specialized experience equivalent to GS-7

GS-9   One year of specialized experience equivalent to GS-8

Surveillance Specialist

The FBI relies deeply on surveillance to carry out criminal investigations and sensitive counterterrorism and counterintelligence activities. The Bureau's surveillance staff and resources have increased significantly since the September 11 attacks, reflecting the agency's increased focus on preventing terrorism and threats to national security. The FBI's surveillance activities also have been enhanced through provisions of the USA PATRIOT Act and an increase in the application of surveillance techniques authorized under the Foreign Intelligence Surveillance Act. Among other benefits, these efforts have resulted in an improvement in intelligence-gathering operations and the disruption of terrorist plots.

The work of surveillance specialists is crucial to the FBI's mission to protect the United States from terrorist attacks, foreign intelligence operations, and espionage. Indeed, in November 2004 the National Commission on Terrorist Attacks Upon the United States made the following recommendation:

A specialized and integrated national security workforce should be established at the FBI consisting of agents, analysts, linguists, and surveillance specialists who are recruited, trained, rewarded, and retained to ensure the development of an institutional culture imbued with a deep expertise in intelligence and national security.

The inclusion of FBI surveillance specialists in the 9/11 Commission's equation is a clear and convincing indication of the importance of these professionals to the Bureau and the nation.

Overview of the Position

Although many details concerning the functions of these personnel are classified, surveillance specialists generally are responsible for observing, evaluating, and gathering information about the targets of FBI investigations, and reporting their findings. Unlike FBI investigative specialists, who perform primarily mobile surveillance in vehicles and on foot, the Bureau's surveillance specialists carry out their mission only from stationary positions such as apartments, houses, offices, commercial buildings, hotel rooms, specially equipped vans, other vehicles, and other observation points. Many missions require surveillance specialists to observe investigative targets around the clock, seven days a week.

Depending on the assignment, surveillance specialists observe locations such as homes, businesses, other buildings, parking lots, parks, or other settings to determine the nature of activity occurring there. Typically, assignments begin with the examination of intelligence reports and the review of information provided by other surveillance operatives concerning their activities and findings. Surveillance results must be summarized in written reports and verbal briefings, and maintained in written logs. These communications normally include details such as the identity, description, and activities of targeted individuals and their associates; dates, times, and locations of activities; descriptions of vehicles and license plates observed; weather conditions; and any other pertinent information obtained during surveillance operations. Surveillance specialists also are responsible for operating a variety of technical investigative devices and equipment such as cameras, video equipment, radio transmitters and receivers, listening devices, binoculars, night-vision equipment, and computers.

Minimum Qualifications and Salary Requirements

Unlike the majority of professional support positions, surveillance specialists are required to be available for permanent transfers or temporary duty assignments wherever the needs of the FBI dictate. Applicants are required to sign an agreement in which they commit to remaining in the position for at least two years. They must also possess a valid driver's license and pass a physical examination.

Evaluation Criteria Examples

Surveillance specialist applicants must respond to online application questions and submit details in a resume to address elements such as the following:

- Ability to operate technical equipment such as computers, radios, cameras, video equipment, and other devices

- Ability to carry out assignments with initiative and minimal supervision

- Ability to communicate in writing in order to produce reports and logs, document findings, and so on

Salary Grade Requirements

GS-5   One year of general experience, which may include administrative, clerical, security, or other responsible work

GS-7   One full year of graduate-level education, or superior academic achievement during undergraduate studies; or a bachelor's degree and one year of specialized experience

GS-9   A master's degree or two years of graduate-level education; or a bachelor's degree and one year of specialized experience equivalent to at least GS-7

GS-11   A Ph.D. or equivalent doctoral degree, or three years of graduate-level education; or a bachelor's degree and one year of specialized experience equivalent to at least GS-9

Technical Information Specialist

The work of FBI technical information specialists is crucial to the success of the Bureau's operations within its 56 field offices and approximately 400 resident agency locations nationwide. Field office and resident agency operations are at the heart of the FBI's mission to protect and defend the United States against terrorist and foreign intelligence threats and investigate criminal activity. Technical information specialists work directly with FBI special agents during intelligence-gathering operations and criminal investigations concerning terrorist activities, organized crime, public corruption, computer intrusions and other cyber crime, white-collar fraud, violent crime, gang activity, civil-rights violations, and other crimes. These personnel are involved in the Bureau's field-level investigative and intelligence operations, "where the rubber meets the road," by conducting research and providing a variety of critical information to FBI special agents around the clock.

Overview of the Position

The Bureau's technical information specialists are experts at searching for and retrieving information from automated databases and open-source applications. They conduct complex short-term and long-term research projects by operating a wide variety of specialized automated informational sources, including FBI, local and state law enforcement databases, and other tools. These personnel are responsible for obtaining, evaluating, analyzing, and disseminating information to FBI special agents, the Bureau's intelligence specialists, and other law enforcement officers during investigations, intelligence-gathering projects, crisis operations, planned inter-agency activities, and all special operations undertaken within FBI field offices and resident agencies.

Technical information specialists must first identify relevant and essential information that is significant to the requester, and oftentimes locate additional data to provide more precise, specialized, or customized information to meet the needs of individual research projects. These personnel glean information from FBI databases, computerized cross-reference telephone directories, and other public-source materials and prepare analytical reports that are formatted to meet the requirements of each requester. They also input and manage data stored in various FBI database systems. In addition, the Bureau's technical information specialists serve as a point-of-contact or team member for all informational services provided to the FBI and other local, state, and federal law enforcement agency personnel during FBI Command Post operations.

Minimum Qualifications and Salary Requirements

Applicants for this position must have one year of specialized experience that required the knowledge of the principles, theories, practices, techniques, and terminology related to accessing and disseminating intelligence or other specialized information. They also must be willing to work nights, weekends, and holidays, and to report for duty during periods of adverse weather conditions or during emergency situations.

Evaluation Criteria Examples

Applicants for technical information specialist positions must respond to assessment questions online and submit supporting details in a resume to address elements such as the following:

- Ability to use automated databases, including inputting and extracting information

- Ability to respond to telephonic, electronic, and written requests for information from individuals at various levels of responsibility

- Experience in creating and maintaining records in accordance with established policies and procedures

- Ability to perform research and analytical assignments, and summarizing information in a standardized format

- Skill at preparing official correspondence that requires knowledge of grammar, punctuation, and spelling

- Ability to create and modify work products using word-processing software, e-mail, spreadsheets, databases, Microsoft PowerPoint, and so on

Salary Grade Requirements

GS-7   One full year of graduate-level education or superior academic achievement during undergraduate studies; or one year of specialized experience equivalent to at least GS-5

GS-9   A master's degree or two years of graduate-level education; or a bachelor's degree and one year of specialized experience equivalent to at least GS-7

GS-11   A Ph.D. or equivalent doctoral degree, or three years of graduate-level education; or a bachelor's degree and one year of specialized experience equivalent to at least GS-9

GS-12   A bachelor's degree and one year of specialized experience equivalent to GS-11

Telecommunications Specialist

The installation, operation, and maintenance of voice, data, and video communication systems are at the core of the Bureau's ability to exchange information internally and with outside organizations. To this end, FBI telecommunications specialists ensure the efficient movement of information from one location to another. The Bureau relies on the technical and analytical abilities of these personnel at FBI Headquarters and field offices nationwide to accomplish its mission and to "stay connected."

Overview of the Position

In coordination with FBI electronics technicians and other technical experts, telecommunications specialists are responsible for the testing, integration, installation, and modification of covert and overt telecommunications systems throughout the FBI. These personnel serve as the point of contact for a variety of services concerning telecommunications systems used for investigative and administrative operations. Their responsibilities include the acquisition, installation, storage, inspection, and maintenance of all telecommunications equipment. These include radio networks, telephones (including cellular), voice-mail systems, pagers, digital communication systems used for data transmission between computers, facsimile stations, and teleconferencing systems. They often accomplish these tasks in cooperation with representatives of regional and local telephone companies and various equipment vendors. Many telecommunications specialists also are responsible for maintaining equipment that provides data on pen registers, trap and trace devices, Title III wiretaps, and other intercept devices.

Telecommunications specialists accomplish many of these tasks by working and establishing liaisons with various commercial carriers and vendors. Their responsibilities also include scheduling downtime to perform backup recovery tasks. To ensure the appropriate use of the various telecommunication systems, they present training to the Bureau's personnel in the procedures, techniques, policies, instructions, and software used in FBI telecommunications centers. They must also maintain an inventory of all telecommunications equipment, which is achieved through the application of an automated inventory tracking program. A variety of administrative duties also are required, such as preparing reports on system information, invoice processing and bill payment, conducting a weekly review of budget information, and maintaining detailed records regarding the configuration of data circuits. The duties of telecommunications specialists vary considerably according to the needs of each office and the grade level of individual personnel.

Minimum Qualifications and Salary Requirements

Education may be substituted for experience if it involved major study in electrical or electronic engineering, mathematics, physics, public utilities, statistics, computer science, telecommunications management, information systems management, business administration, industrial management, or another field related to the position.

Evaluation Criteria Examples

Telecommunications specialist applicants must respond to online application questions and submit details in a resume to address elements such as the following:

- Knowledge of telecommunications equipment, concepts, principles, practices, procedures, and operational requirements

- Knowledge of computer software, equipment, and operating systems

- Ability to communicate in writing in order to prepare correspondence and written reports

- Ability to communicate orally in order to deal tactfully and courteously with people at all levels of responsibility

- Ability to interpret and apply policies, procedures, and regulations

Salary Grade Requirements

GS-7   One full year of graduate-level education, or superior academic achievement during undergraduate studies; or a bachelor's degree and one year of specialized experience

GS-9   A master's degree or two years of graduate-level education; or a bachelor's degree and one year of specialized experience equivalent to at least GS-7

GS-11   A Ph.D. or equivalent doctoral degree, or three years of graduate-level education; or a bachelor's degree and one year of specialized experience equivalent to at least GS-9

GS-12   A bachelor's degree and one year of specialized experience equivalent to GS-11

GS-13   A bachelor's degree and one year of specialized experience equivalent to GS-12

Victim Specialist

The FBI takes very seriously its responsibility to crime victims by enforcing their legal rights, including them in criminal-justice-system processes, making referrals to appropriate organizations for victim services, and holding criminals accountable. To properly address the rights and needs of those victimized by crimes investigated by the FBI, the Bureau employs victim specialists to ensure that victims are treated with respect, fairness, and compassion in the criminal justice system, in accordance with the law.

Overview of the Position

Under the direction of the FBI Office for Victim Assistance, victim specialists are responsible for ensuring that all victims of crimes investigated by the FBI are identified, are offered assistance, and have the opportunity to receive information about case events and court hearings. Among their most important responsibilities, victim specialists personally assist victims by providing information about a wide range of available assistance, as well as referrals to the organizations that provide these services. Some of these include state crime victim compensation programs, homicide bereavement support groups, mental health counseling, rape crisis center support, and a variety of special services for child victims. Victim specialists also maintain contact with victims during investigations to notify them about events such as the arrest of a suspect, whether the case is declined for prosecution, or if the case is being referred to state or local authorities. When more than one federal agency is involved in an investigation, victim specialists work closely with other agencies to ensure that victims receive appropriate assistance.

Other interesting responsibilities of victim specialists include making certain that resources and services are available to victims in cases of terrorism and crimes against American citizens that occur outside of the United States. For example, they have worked with more than 10,000 victims and family members of the 9/11 attacks, and created a special Internet Web site to share information with them. In cases involving overseas homicide of American citizens, victim specialists also arrange for transportation of the victim's remains to the United States; coordinate the autopsy and collect dental records and DNA from family members, if necessary; ensure that family members receive the victim's personal effects and death certificates; and provide additional comfort and support.

To further ensure that victims are afforded appropriate services and information, victim specialists also develop and maintain a library of resource materials for use by victims and FBI staff, and conduct research studies to evaluate and enhance the FBI's victim assistance program. In addition, they present training and information to FBI special agents, other Bureau personnel, and other law enforcement agencies to assist them in working effectively with victims. They also speak to public, civic, and special-interest groups about victims' issues, and present related training at regional, national, and international professional conferences. In some cases, victim specialists respond to crime scenes to provide crisis intervention and information to victims about services they may be eligible to receive.

Minimum Qualifications and Salary Requirements

Specialized experience is qualifying if it was gained by working for an agency or organization that provided services to victims of crimes. Examples of qualifying experience include providing child or adult protective services, sexual assault victim services, alcohol or drug abuse counseling, victims of crime compensation services, crisis intervention services, or social work.

Evaluation Criteria Examples

Applicants for victim specialist employment must respond to online application questions and submit details in a resume to address elements such as the following:

- Knowledge of victimology and victim assistance issues and resources, as well as policies and procedures relating to federal victim assistance programs (including Attorney General Guidelines for Victim and Witness Assistance)

- Ability to establish and maintain effective working relationships with FBI special agents and other Bureau staff, other law enforcement officers, attorneys, and representatives of other organizations

- Ability to communicate effectively orally and in writing

- Knowledge of the criminal justice system, including the roles of investigators, prosecutors, the judiciary, and corrections personnel

- Ability to locate and develop resources for crime victims

Salary Grade Requirements

GS-9   A master's degree or two years of graduate-level education; or a bachelor's degree and one year of specialized experience equivalent to at least GS-7

GS-11 A Ph.D. or equivalent doctoral degree, or three years of graduate-level education; or a bachelor's degree and one year of specialized experience equivalent to at least GS-9

GS-12 A bachelor's degree and one year of specialized experience equivalent to GS-11

CHAPTER 6

The Hiring Process for Professional Support Positions

"Blessed is he who has found his work. Let him ask no other blessedness."

—Thomas Carlyle

As discussed in chapter 4, the hiring process for the special agent position is clearly defined, standardized, and systematic for all applicants nationwide. This approach ensures that candidates are evaluated equally, based on the same criteria and according to merit principles. The hiring process for FBI professional support personnel is also designed to provide equal opportunity to all applicants, although with less uniformity than the special agent process. Although support personnel candidates must clear many of the same hurdles as special agent candidates, applicant processing for support positions varies from one position to another, depending on the type and location of positions being filled. For example, applicants for some positions must take an examination, and the format of personal interviews can vary widely. Nonetheless, there are more similarities than differences. After all, every Bureau employee must qualify for a top-secret security clearance, and standards relating to loyalty, integrity, drug use, and other criteria also are the same.

This chapter provides an overview of applicant processing for administrative, professional, technical, clerical, and other FBI careers. Specific strategies that applicants can use to describe their knowledge, skills, and abilities in application materials are presented in chapter 7, "Standing Out from the Crowd." Qualification requirements for various positions are reviewed in chapter 5, "Professional Support Career Opportunities."

FBI Hiring Policies

It is widely known that the FBI has established employment policies to safeguard the rights of applicants and ensure that the Bureau recruits, hires, and retains the most qualified special agents. These principles and practices also apply to professional support applicants and employees. The FBI Employment Drug Policy, for example, applies to all Bureau personnel—from special agents to automotive workers. Truthfulness during the hiring process is also required of applicants for professional support positions. Applicants with disabilities are provided all protections afforded under the Rehabilitation Act of 1973, including entitlement to reasonable accommodation in the hiring process. Applicants for professional support positions are provided equal employment opportunity also, free from discrimination based on their color, race, religion, national origin, political affiliation, marital status, disability, age, sex, sexual orientation, or membership or non-membership in an employee organization; or on the basis of personal favoritism.

An Overview of Applicant Processing

Hiring processes for FBI professional support positions are similar to special agent applicant processing, although there are notable differences. For example, there are slight variations in application processes for certain technical careers, depending on the positions' qualification requirements. In addition, although special agent candidates must take a written examination, the vast majority of professional support career vacancies are filled without testing of any kind.

Final screening of candidates for support positions is similar to the special agent hiring process and includes a security interview, background investigation, polygraph examination, and urinalysis drug screening. Applicants for certain other positions must also undergo a physical examination.

The remainder of this chapter provides a step-by-step breakdown of applicant processing for support positions.

Step One: Initial Application

To begin the hiring process, you must conduct research, gather information about your background, submit a great deal of paperwork, and wait for the Bureau to screen your application. The following sections discuss the components of the first step in the application process.

The FBI Vacancy Announcement

The first step toward landing a support job with the FBI is to obtain information about the position you seek and the application procedures. The FBI generates a detailed vacancy announcement for every professional support position it needs to fill. (See "Sources of Job Vacancy Information" later in this chapter for details on how to find vacancy announcements.) These announcements provide details about the duties and responsibilities of each job, as well as information concerning qualification requirements, selection criteria, and how to apply. Most FBI vacancy announcements consist of the same components, although some include additional elements to facilitate hiring for certain positions. Vacancy announcements typically provide the following information.

Position Title and Announcement Number

The top portion of the vacancy announcement lists the position title and also the vacancy announcement number. The announcement number is used to facilitate the processing of application materials and recordkeeping functions.

Open Period

The period in which applications are accepted is marked by the opening and closing dates specified in the vacancy announcement, which is known as the "open period." The opening date is the first day in which candidates are permitted to submit application materials. Applications must be received by the closing date in order to receive consideration. FBI vacancy announcements normally remain open for about two to three weeks, although announcements for some hard-to-fill positions remain open indefinitely.

Job Series, Salary Range and Grade, and Promotion Potential

The job series and salary grade normally are listed in a format such as *GS-0080-09*. In this example, the position is classified in the General Schedule GS-0080 Security Specialist job series, with a salary grade of GS-09. When only one salary grade is shown, such as GS-09, applicants must meet the minimum qualifications for the specified grade level and cannot be hired at any other grade. Many vacancy announcements specify a range of salary grades, such as GS-07/09/11, which allows the FBI to fill vacancies at the highest grade level for which appointees are qualified—in this case, GS-7, GS-9, or GS-11. (See chapter 2 for an explanation of the GS pay scale and a listing of salaries for each grade level.) The promotion potential is the highest grade to which an employee could expect to advance, provided that his or her job performance is satisfactory. In many cases, personnel have an opportunity to advance to supervisory and management positions above the highest grade specified in the vacancy announcement.

Hiring Agency and Duty Location

The hiring agency is the FBI, of course, which is a component of the U.S. Department of Justice. Therefore, this is shown as *Department of Justice/Federal Bureau of Investigation* on the top of the first page of the vacancy announcement. The location where the job will be performed is included under the "Duty Location" heading. When vacancies exist in more than one field office or resident agency, including those that are being filled nationwide, applicants must specify where they are willing to work.

Who May Be Considered

Information under this heading specifies who is eligible to apply for a particular vacancy, such as FBI personnel only, current federal personnel, former federal employees with reinstatement privileges, those who reside in a particular geographic area, or other qualified candidates.

Job Summary, Division/Section/Unit, Location, Area Information, and Working Hours

Information under these headings offers details concerning the work location and conditions. These items include the city and state where the office is located; information concerning the FBI division, section, and unit under which the selectee will be assigned; an overview of physical demands required of the position; demographic and climate particulars pertaining to the office location; and sometimes other details. Some vacancy announcements do not include details under all of these headings.

Statement of Major Position Duties

A summary of the duties and responsibilities is provided in this item. This statement typically includes examples of the assignments and tasks required of the job, and sometimes provides additional details about the division, branch, or unit where the selectee will serve.

Qualifications

An outline of the eligibility standards for each position is incorporated under this heading. This section provides a description of basic qualifications, including required specialized experience, education, training, and other qualifications. Applicants must meet minimum requirements to be given further consideration in the application process. FBI human resources specialists use minimum qualification standards to evaluate candidates' eligibility for positions and to eliminate those who do not qualify. Positions advertised under multiple salary grades usually include a breakdown of minimum requirements for each grade.

Evaluation Criteria

Applicants who meet basic eligibility requirements are rated on the basis of whether they possess specific attributes needed for the positions being filled. Ratings are based on particular knowledge, skills, and abilities (KSAs) that are required to perform the duties of the position. Applicants must provide responses to an online questionnaire or write a narrative statement indicating how their experience, education, and training have provided them with the required KSAs. The number of KSAs applicants must address varies from one vacancy announcement to the next. Some applications require candidates to respond to only three or four KSAs, whereas others might ask for eight to ten responses. (Detailed guidance for completing KSA statements is included in chapter 7, "Standing Out from the Crowd.")

Application Instructions

The "How to Apply" and "Required Documents" sections provide detailed instructions on completing an application online and supporting documentation that must also be submitted, as well as other information concerning application procedures. Typically, applicants must submit a resume, complete an online questionnaire, and submit copies of documents such as college transcripts, proof of Veterans' Preference eligibility, performance appraisals, and so on.

What to Expect Next, Agency Contact, Benefits, and Additional Information

Information under these headings explains how applicants can check the status of applications; indicates the name, address, phone number, and e-mail address of an FBI human resources specialist who can assist with questions and other inquiries; and lists some of the fringe benefits FBI employees receive. The "Additional Information" section offers details concerning forms that must be completed later in the application process, a notice relating to registration for the Selective Service System, details on claiming Veterans' Preference and submitting related forms, and other information regarding the application process.

Submitting Application Materials

Although job application processes in the private sector often require candidates to submit little more than basic information about their education and experience, this is only the tip of the iceberg in the FBI hiring process. In addition to biographical information, applicants for FBI professional support positions must submit a narrative statement that addresses their qualifications and suitability for employment, a resume, military and security clearance information, details about citizenship, and sometimes college transcripts and a variety of other forms.

Completing the Online Application Form

In the past, the FBI has permitted candidates for professional support positions to submit a typewritten application form or resume when applying for employment. These options are now available only on a limited basis or in unusual circumstances, as the Bureau has fully implemented online application processing through its Web site. This process provides a measure of uniformity and facilitates the efficient collection of information needed to evaluate applicants. Any candidate without direct access to the Internet can apply online at almost any public or college library, or through federal, state, and local government-sponsored employment offices.

Although there are minor differences in the information requested in the online application for some positions, the application generally requires candidates to submit the following:

- **Biographical information,** which consists of the applicant's name, address, home and work telephone numbers, e-mail address, Social Security number, and date of birth.

- **Citizenship status,** which requires applicants to indicate whether they are U.S. citizens. (U.S. citizenship is required for FBI employment.)

- **Military service and Veterans' Preference information,** indicating whether the applicant has served on active duty in the U.S. military, the branch of service and dates of active duty, military school attendance, and whether Veterans' Preference is claimed.

- **Employment data,** including information concerning current or previous federal employment, permission to contact the applicant's current supervisor for a reference, and other details.

- **Security clearance information,** including details relating to the agency that previously issued a security clearance to the applicant.

- **Demographic information,** including data concerning ethnicity, race, gender, and physical disabilities.

- **Assignment location and grade selection,** which includes the lowest grade for which an applicant is willing to be considered and the location of the field office or resident agency where the applicant is seeking employment, as well as whether the applicant is willing to relocate to the office at his or her own expense if the FBI is unwilling to pay for relocation.

- **History of illegal drug use,** including marijuana use during the preceding three years, other illegal drug use, distribution or sale of illegal drugs, and so on.

- **Group membership information,** such as foreign or domestic organizations that are totalitarian, fascist, communist, or subversive in nature, or groups that advocate acts of force or violence to deny persons their rights under the U.S. Constitution.

- **Employment experience data,** including responses to many specific questions concerning previous experience relating to the position applied for.

Submitting a Resume

Applicants are required to type or paste a text copy of their resumes into a box provided in the online application form. The resume should include information relating to previous employment, such as the following:

- Job titles

- Series and grade of federal employment

- Names, addresses, and telephone numbers of current and previous employers

- Starting and ending dates of employment

- A description of duties and accomplishments

- The average number of hours worked for each position

- The number of people supervised

- Salary details

See chapter 7, "Standing Out from the Crowd," for tips and samples for creating an outstanding federal resume.

Submitting a KSA Statement

Applicants for some positions are also required to submit a detailed statement of their knowledge, skills, and abilities relating to the selection criteria for the position. Like the resume, this statement can be typed or pasted into the appropriate block of the online application. (See chapter 7, "Standing Out from the Crowd," for guidance on composing a KSA statement.)

Submitting College Transcripts

Many professional support positions, particularly those that involve technical or scientific work, require applicants to submit copies of their college transcripts along with the application form and resume. For example, applicants who apply for financial analyst, intelligence operations specialist, electronics technician, or computer specialist positions are required to submit their college transcripts to the FBI. Vacancy announcements specify the manner in which transcripts must be submitted, which typically involves faxing them to a particular person at a telephone number listed in the announcement. When faxing transcripts and other documentation to the FBI, it is important to include the vacancy announcement number on the cover sheet and every page submitted. In many instances, the online application questionnaire automatically creates a fax cover sheet for use in submitting college transcripts.

Submitting Other Documents

Some applicants, such as federal employees and certain veterans, must submit additional materials with their application packages. Federal employees, for example, are required to submit their latest SF-50 Notification of Personnel Action and their most recent Performance Appraisal. In addition, candidates seeking Veterans' Preference must also submit supporting documentation for their claim. Vacancy announcements specify the names and form numbers of documents that must be included in application materials. As with college transcripts, the FBI normally requires applicants to fax these materials to a particular person, and online application questionnaires often create fax cover sheets for use in submitting these documents.

Selection of Candidates for Further Processing

To conclude the initial application phase, the FBI reviews all application materials and excludes those candidates who do not meet basic requirements. Of those remaining, only candidates whom the Bureau determines to be most competitive will be invited to continue in the hiring process.

Step Two: Written Examinations

The application process for some FBI professional support positions includes either a written or practical skills examination. Until recently, many candidates for clerical positions were required to take the Clerical and Administrative Support Examination. This exam is no longer given. Instead, questions asked in the online application process are used to identify each applicant's knowledge, skills, abilities, and experience.

Certain candidates for FBI professional support employment must take examinations that are geared specifically to the nature of the positions sought. For example, electronics engineer candidates must have passed the Fundamentals of Engineering Examination (formerly known as the Engineering-in-Training Exam), or a written test required for professional registration administered by the boards of engineering examiners in the various states. Language specialist and contract linguist candidates must achieve passing scores on a hearing test arranged by the Bureau, as well as a battery of FBI language tests that focus on listening comprehension, reading comprehension, and translation. Applicants should carefully review vacancy announcements to determine whether testing is required.

Step Three: The Questionnaire for National Security Positions (SF-86)

After the FBI reviews application forms, resumes, and test results, only the most competitive candidates are asked to take the next step in the selection process. Competitiveness is based not only on applicants' background, but also on the hiring needs of the FBI at the time.

Those selected to continue will be asked to submit the SF-86 Questionnaire for National Security Positions, a 17-page form that is used to gather additional information relating to applicants' qualifications and background. Information provided by applicants on the SF-86 is also used to conduct the background investigation and for security clearance determinations.

The SF-86 requests information relating to birth and citizenship, places of residence, employment history, educational background, association membership, references and social acquaintances, relatives, roommates, military service, foreign travel, passport information, financial status, civil and criminal court record, alcohol and drug use, and security clearances previously held. Attachments to the SF-86 also include a general Authorization for Release of Information and an Authorization for Release of Medical Information that permits the Bureau to obtain limited information from health practitioners. Copies of the SF-86 and attachments are provided in appendix B.

Step Four: The Personal Interview

The personal interview phase of the professional support personnel selection process differs in many ways from special agent hiring procedures. Unlike the special agent hiring process, during which interviewers follow a standard list of questions, interviews of professional support candidates tend to vary from one position to another, both in style and the level of formality.

A variety of interviewing formats are utilized, involving personnel from various operational divisions or units. Techniques also range from structured panel interviews to less-formal one-on-one discussions. Depending on the position being filled, panel interviews could include peers from the field of expertise, whereas other interviews might be conducted by a single supervisor or manager representing the division or unit where the selectee will serve.

Structured Interviews

Candidates for certain FBI positions must undergo a structured interview in this phase of the hiring process. During structured interviews, the interviewers ask all candidates a standard set of questions. This method allows interviewers to compare and evaluate candidates on a level playing field, and to determine which candidates possess the knowledge, skills, and abilities that are required of the position being filled. The FBI conducts structured interviews when filling clerical vacancies—including jobs such as clerk, secretary, and typist—and other positions.

Semi-Structured Interviews

Other interviews for professional support positions tend to be semi-structured in nature, meaning they are less formal than structured interviews. These often include a combination of standard questions—similar to the format of a structured interview—and questions that have not been predetermined. Semi-structured interviews are effective in the selection of technical and scientific personnel, where detailed answers are often required. The semi-structured approach allows interviewers to probe, explore, and revisit applicants' responses to a variety of open-ended questions that are tailored to each position.

Step Five: Final Screening

The final screening phase includes procedures that are similar to those followed during special agent applicant processing. Tentative appointees receive a conditional letter of appointment, and must also pass a polygraph examination, personnel security interview, drug test, and background investigation, and submit to fingerprinting. In addition, some candidates must pass a physical examination.

Conditional Offer of Appointment

To begin this phase, successful candidates receive a letter from the FBI notifying them that they will be hired if the outcome of the final screening process is satisfactory. Final appointment is contingent on budgetary limitations, authorized positions, and the results of a background investigation, polygraph exam, and urinalysis drug screening. The letter provides tentative appointees with details concerning the background investigation and other information relating to final screening.

Personnel Security Interview

Professional support candidates must complete a personnel security interview prior to appointment. The interview focuses on the veracity of the information contained in employment application forms, the SF-86 Questionnaire for National Security Positions, drug use by the applicant, foreign travel and contacts, financial status and obligations, and various national security issues. Applicants must bring photo identification to the interview, and might be asked to bring their Social Security card, birth certificate, or other documents.

Polygraph Exam and Drug Testing

All tentative appointees are administered a polygraph exam, during which information provided during the Personnel Security Interview is verified and other areas are explored. The exam includes questions relating to national security and counterintelligence issues, illegal drug use and activity, and the truthfulness of information provided during the hiring process. (Details concerning functions and phases of the polygraph exam are discussed in chapter 4, "The Special Agent Hiring Process.") Prior to appointment, all FBI applicants are required to submit to a urinalysis drug test, which screens for illegal drug use.

Background Investigation

All FBI professional support personnel must hold a top-secret security clearance as a condition of employment. Therefore, the background of all tentative appointees is thoroughly investigated by the FBI prior to appointment. Background investigations normally are conducted by special investigators under contract with the Bureau.

During the background investigation, the FBI verifies employment, credentials, educational background, citizenship and birth records, residency, military service, and medical history; interviews friends, neighbors, references, and employers; and inquires into an applicant's credit history and criminal record. The background investigation is used to explore a number of issues relating to suitability for employment and a top-secret security clearance.

These include an applicant's character, associates, reputation, loyalty, ability, financial responsibility, biases or prejudice, and alcohol or drug abuse. (Further discussion of these issues is provided in chapter 4, "The Special Agent Hiring Process.")

Applicants are provided written notification of the outcome of their background investigation. Those who would like to obtain a copy of their background investigation report should send a written request to the FBI's Freedom of Information/Privacy Act Section at FBI Headquarters in Washington, D.C.

Pre-employment Physical Examinations

Most professional support personnel candidates are not given a pre-employment physical examination. Considering the physical demands and hazardous work conditions of some positions, however, the FBI must ensure that certain personnel are physically fit for duty. Physical exams are performed to rule out any medical issue or condition that could potentially affect an applicant's ability to perform the basic functions of the position for which they have applied.

For example, electronics technician candidates must have a physical exam because they might be required to lift heavy objects or climb ladders, poles, towers, and other apparatuses to mount or service electronic equipment and devices. Due to the strenuous nature of law enforcement work, FBI police officer applicants also must pass a physical exam. Language specialist candidates are required to undergo a hearing test because these personnel must have adequate hearing in order to translate live and recorded speech.

Physical examinations sometimes reveal medical issues or conditions that require applicants to undergo additional examination. Applicants who are required to have a physical examination are also subject to a review of their medical history. Each candidate's health and fitness is reviewed on an individual, case-by-case basis. These reviews sometimes result in delay of the final processing for employment. Although input or copies of medical records might be requested from an applicant's doctor, the final decision as to an applicant's physical ability rests with the FBI's Chief Medical Officer.

Sources of Job Vacancy Information

Information relating to professional support position vacancies is available on the Internet and in published materials from the FBI, the U.S. Office of Personnel Management, and a number of private sources.

FBI Resources

FBI vacancy announcements and other professional support position recruiting details are posted online at the Bureau's employment Internet Web site (www. fbijobs.com). More information concerning the FBI Web site is provided at the end of this chapter (see "Additional Online Resources"). Information concerning vacancies and position details can also be obtained over the telephone by contacting the recruiter or applicant coordinator for professional support positions at any FBI field office. In addition, vacancy announcements are available for viewing at some field offices. A list of FBI field offices and resident agencies is shown in appendix J.

U.S. Office of Personnel Management (OPM) Resources

The U.S. Office of Personnel Management oversees human resources management for the federal government. OPM disseminates employment information and job vacancy announcements for many government agencies—including the FBI—and establishes basic qualification standards for federal occupations. The public can access information about employment with the FBI and other agencies online and at OPM offices nationwide.

USAJOBS Web Site

The USAJOBS Web site, which is maintained by OPM, posts information relating to current job openings not only with the FBI, but also with other federal agencies. This Web site displays full-text vacancy announcements that you can print. The USAJOBS address is www.usajobs.gov.

USAJOBS by Phone

OPM's USAJOBS by Phone is a telephone-based system that provides instant access to current information on federal job opportunities worldwide, including positions with the FBI. Users are guided through a series of prompts that allow searches for position vacancies by occupational category, job series, agency, or position title. Requested information is normally mailed or faxed within 24 hours. USAJOBS by Phone can be reached by telephone at (703) 724-1850, 24 hours a day, 7 days a week.

Federal Job Information Touch-Screen Computers

OPM also maintains a network of computers that utilize touch-screen technology to disseminate job vacancy information. These kiosks are located at OPM Federal Employment Information Centers in major cities nationwide, at many state employment service centers and social service agencies, and within job placement offices at some colleges and universities.

Federal Job Publications

Many printed and online publications provide information about federal job vacancies worldwide. Two popular publications, *Federal Career Opportunities* and *Federal Jobs Digest,* are discussed in the following sections.

Federal Career Opportunities

The *Federal Career Opportunities* newspaper is a biweekly publication that contains details on federal job vacancies, including professional support positions with the FBI. *Federal Career Opportunities* is published every two weeks, and is available from Federal Research Service, P.O. Box 1708; Annandale, VA 22003. Federal Research Service can be reached by phone at (800) 822-5027. An online version is also accessible by subscription at www.fedjobs.com.

Federal Jobs Digest

Another publication that contains details on vacancies with the FBI and other agencies is *Federal Jobs Digest.* This publication is available in bookstores, libraries, and schools, or from Federal Jobs Digest, 1503 Radcliffe Ct.; Newtown Square, PA 19073. *Federal Jobs Digest* can be reached by telephone at (800) 824-5000. The *Federal Jobs Digest* Web site is located at www.jobsfed.com.

Additional Online Resources

Many Web sites offer information for those interested in working for the FBI or other federal law enforcement agencies. Locating these resources is as easy as typing keywords into search engine text boxes, although locating current and reliable information presents an entirely different challenge. Most college and university criminal justice programs host Web sites that provide general information on the FBI and links to federal law enforcement agencies, and many commercial Web sites and message boards contain a mixed bag of information that varies from current and accurate to outdated and inaccurate. The following Web sites are among the best and have proven helpful to many FBI career seekers.

The 911HotJobs.com Employment Portal

The 911HotJobs.com Web site was created in 1997 by Robert Amaral, a police officer who realized it was difficult to find police department employment information on the Internet and wanted to make it easier for job seekers. Over the years, Amaral's Web site has expanded to include job postings for positions with law enforcement agencies, fire departments, and emergency medical service providers at the municipal, county, state, and federal levels. A wide range of federal agencies have posted job vacancy announcements on the 911HotJobs.com Web site, including the FBI. The site also offers for sale more than 100 employment books; dozens of videotapes, CDs, and DVDs; software; and an assortment of online practice tests.

The 911JobForums.com Message Board

In February 2000, the 911HotJobs.com Web site added an interactive message board for job seekers interested in exchanging information on employment opportunities. Today, 911JobForums.com has more than 20 employment forums and other interactive specialty areas concerned with federal law enforcement, state police and highway patrol, sheriff's departments, corrections, probation and parole, the military, fire and emergency medical services, dispatch, physical fitness, firearms and equipment, news, and other topics. Message board members can post questions and answers relating to employment issues and other subjects, read responses posted by other members, poll members about their job search experiences and concerns, and contact one another through a private message system. About one-half of employment-related message board activity revolves around federal law enforcement, of which much pertains to FBI matters. More than 30 volunteer moderators—all seasoned veterans in their particular areas of expertise—monitor message board activity, answer questions, and offer their assistance. Membership is free.

The FBI Web Site

The official FBI Web site (www.fbi.gov) offers an extensive assortment of interesting information concerning the Bureau's history, mission, responsibilities, investigative activities, publications, budget, statistics, Ten Most Wanted Fugitives, and Freedom of Information Act requests. This site also includes a Press Room that features links to local and national press releases, congressional testimony, breaking news stories, and FBI contact information. A particularly interesting area of the site is the Electronic Reading Room, which includes access to many historical FBI documents, investigative reports, files relating to famous persons investigated by the bureau, and other interesting records.

The FBIjobs.com Web Site

The Employment portal of the FBI Web site leads to www.FBIjobs.com, a site where anyone interested in a career with the Bureau can find out about job vacancies for all FBI positions, internships, career fairs attended by the FBI, the location of field offices, and how to apply for job vacancies online. Although the FBIjobs.com Web site presents information that usually is current and accurate, details tend to be limited and out-of-date information often remains on the site, which means Web surfers could be left with more questions than answers. Nonetheless, the FBIjobs.com Web site is a good start, especially for information on vacancies for professional support positions.

The FBIcareers.com Web Site

FBIcareers.com—the companion Web site to this book—provides valuable and timely information for those seeking employment opportunities with the Bureau and other agencies. This Web site also includes links to many useful Internet resources for federal law enforcement officers and job seekers, such as FederalCareers.com, the companion Web site to the popular *Federal Law Enforcement Careers* book (also published by JIST Publishing).

CHAPTER 7

Standing Out from the Crowd

"Genius is one percent inspiration and ninety-nine percent perspiration."

—Thomas Edison

The FBI workforce is diverse, talented, and well trained. To maintain excellence and prepare for future challenges, the Bureau recruits special agents and support personnel with a variety of skills and experience. Given its broad mission and commitment to diversity, the Bureau does not maintain a single "profile" of the ideal special agent or professional support employee. Instead, criteria for the selection of FBI personnel are based on the knowledge, skills, and abilities needed for the specific jobs being filled, while taking into consideration the Bureau's particular needs at any given time. Although there is no secret formula for landing a position as one of America's finest, there are things you can do to stand out from the crowd. This chapter presents a number of strategies you can apply before and during the hiring process to increase your chances of getting hired as an FBI special agent or other Bureau professional.

Are You Right for the FBI?

One of the most common questions those who are interested in working for the FBI ask is "What sort of background is the FBI looking for?" To begin to answer this question, it is important to note that your background encompasses far more than employment experience and education. In other words, your background also is concerned with your character, reputation, training, abilities, involvement in civic and community activities, military service, financial matters, criminal history, and many other aspects of your life. Although the requirements for employment vary from one position to another, the Bureau is always looking for bright individuals who possess "Fidelity, Bravery, and Integrity," which is the motto and motivating force behind the men and women of the FBI.

Character Issues

The most important thing you can do prior to applying for employment with the FBI is to carry out your personal affairs and professional business in a responsible manner. Character, honesty, integrity, and loyalty are far more

169

important to the Bureau than any amount of experience, education, or skill that applicants may have. In fact, many applicants who otherwise meet basic qualification standards for FBI jobs either fail the drug test or polygraph examination or are disqualified for other reasons. In addition to unlawful drug use, the FBI disqualifies applicants who have been convicted of felony or major misdemeanor offenses, have defaulted on student loans, or have failed to pay income taxes. Candidates with bad credit also face an uphill battle, and those who show a lack of candor or falsify information during the hiring process are routinely disqualified. Lying, cheating, and stealing are wholly inconsistent with everything the FBI stands for. In other words, the best way to prepare for a career with the FBI is to "keep it clean" before submitting your application.

Experience and Education

The Bureau's personnel needs change from time to time depending on the expertise on staff and projected needs for the future. For example, the FBI recently announced that special agent applicants with knowledge, skills, and abilities in several critical skill areas would be given special consideration. These areas include the following:

- Accounting and finance
- Computer science and other information technology specialties
- Engineering
- Foreign-language proficiency
- Intelligence experience
- Law experience
- Law enforcement or other investigative work
- Military experience
- Physical sciences (physics, chemistry, and biology)
- Tactical Operations and Special Forces

Occasionally, the FBI processes special agent applications only from candidates who possess certain critical skills and experience. At other times anyone may apply, although the Bureau may give special consideration to applicants with backgrounds in certain areas. When the application process is open to candidates lacking preferred critical skills and experience, those with education, training, and experience in other areas should not hesitate to apply because a substantial proportion of special agent recruits will not have expertise in these areas.

For example, in filling special agent vacancies the Bureau will always place a premium on applicants with accounting experience and education because a significant percentage of the Bureau's criminal investigations revolve around white-collar crime. Similarly, the FBI is likely to continue seeking law school graduates because lawyers tend to be proficient at problem-solving and sorting out legal issues during investigations. Indeed, two of the Bureau's entry programs are geared to recruiting candidates with accounting and legal skills. Language proficiency will always be helpful, although language needs vary from time to time and from one office to another. Also, considering the changes in mission and organization the FBI has made since the terrorist attacks of 9/11, it appears likely that the Bureau will favor applicants with intelligence experience for years to come. Finally, through its diversified entry program, the Bureau will continue to recruit talented individuals who have expertise in many other areas or who otherwise show great potential to succeed as special agents. These candidates range from store managers to school teachers, dental hygienists, nurses, real estate agents, paramedics, journalists, stock brokers, and many others.

As far as college education is concerned, the FBI does not have a preference for certain college courses or diplomas earned from any particular schools when hiring special agents. Instead, the Bureau prefers candidates who have completed a course of study that develops communication, research, and analytical skills. Some of the college majors that develop these skills include psychology, sociology, criminal justice, nursing, medicine, business, journalism, forensic science, engineering, computer science, and political science. In a nutshell, although the criteria for determining the most qualified candidates are constantly evolving, certain skills and experience will always be in demand.

On the other hand, professional support position applicants often are required to have education and experience in particular areas of study or expertise. This is especially true where scientific or technical careers are concerned, including positions such as biologist, chemist, electronics engineer, information technology specialist, and financial analyst. Although many schools have earned an exceptional reputation for academic programs that prepare students for law enforcement support careers, the FBI places greater emphasis on hiring talented individuals who are team players and dedicated to their professions than focusing on candidates who attended certain schools. This is not to say that a degree from a prestigious school or program will go unnoticed; it's just that the Bureau takes much more into consideration than the top line of a diploma when hiring support personnel.

Volunteer Work and Community Service

The FBI recognizes that volunteer work and community service provide valuable experience that is unavailable in most traditional employment settings. These activities demonstrate a commitment to the community and important causes, while also providing an opportunity to develop skills in communication, leadership, planning, administrative tasks, and decision-making, among other skills. In fact, a recent article in the *Wall Street Journal* pointed out that five years of volunteer work provides management experience most corporations couldn't provide in 20 years. Volunteer work with hospitals, churches, synagogues, animal shelters, public broadcasting stations, the American Red Cross, and other nonprofit organizations provides a sense of accomplishment and builds character. Community service as a volunteer firefighter, coach, scout leader, police reserve officer, Parent-Teacher Association board member, or in other positions is rewarding—and worthy of recognition. Volunteer work and community service also provide additional employment references and demonstrate a strong work ethic. Therefore, you should not omit this experience on FBI application forms or during interviews.

Military Service

Service in the military is a definite plus. Experience in the armed forces provides structure, discipline, exceptional training, skill development, and technical knowledge that are transferable to many careers in the FBI. In addition, military service builds responsibility, leadership skills, camaraderie, loyalty, values, and other traits the FBI looks for in its employees. Many of the Bureau's intelligence specialists, electronics technicians, electronics engineers, language specialists, special agents, and others developed their skills in the armed forces prior to hiring on with the FBI.

Internships

Anyone who is serious about making a career in the FBI should take full advantage of internship opportunities that become available during college. These provide an opportunity for students to enhance their education and make practical application of classroom theory. They also enable students to explore their career interests under actual working conditions, and to make informed choices before moving into the workforce. The FBI and many other federal law enforcement agencies offer internships that allow students to perform some of the primary duties that special agents and professional support personnel carry out. For example, many agencies allow interns to participate in interviews, review financial records and create spreadsheets, conduct surveillance, operate technical investigative equipment, assist with the execution of search warrants, recover and process evidence, and meet with Assistant United States Attorneys, among other tasks.

Applicants interested in FBI professional support positions can participate in college internships that are geared toward virtually every position in the Bureau. In many instances, interns also participate in training exercises alongside full-time personnel. These experiences are valuable in demonstrating your skills and potential when you are seeking employment with the FBI or other organizations. See chapter 9, "FBI Internship Programs," for information concerning FBI internship opportunities.

Completing the Special Agent Online Application

Getting started in the special agent hiring process is much different today than in the recent past, now that applying for FBI employment has made a complete transition to online processing. Although most of the paper forms are gone and the process is now a bit easier to navigate, it is still as important to be organized, thorough, precise, and truthful when submitting information to the Bureau. Oddly enough, many applicants underestimate the importance of completing Online Application materials accurately and completely, or they do not understand certain questions and how to respond to them. This can easily spell failure, because submitting incomplete or incorrect information is likely to delay the processing of your application or cause the FBI to eliminate you from the applicant pool.

This section includes a discussion of many questions and issues that could arise when completing the Online Application, as well as a few pointers you can use along the way.

Applicant Personal Data

Although there is not much that could be considered rocket science concerning the personal data you submit to the FBI, your answers to certain questions in this area could raise red flags or otherwise call unwanted attention to your application nonetheless.

Your Name

Even submitting your name might not be as simple as it appears. The application requests your first, middle, and last names, so be sure to submit your current *legal* name. Otherwise, if the name you submit does not match up with current driver's license records, employment information, occupational licenses, credit report details, and other important data, you could be asking for trouble. For example, if your legal name is John, do not use Jack, even if you have been commonly known as Jack your entire life. Although this might seem like common sense, many applicants have made the mistake of submitting nicknames, middle names, or initials in place of their legal first names without giving it much thought.

Of course, your current legal name might not be the same as shown on diplomas, military records, court documents, or other records as a result of marriage or legal action, or for other reasons. So, to avoid confusion, the SF-86 Questionnaire for National Security Positions asks whether you have used nicknames, maiden names, names by a former marriage, aliases, or any other names. This clarification on the SF-86 also is useful during the background investigation, especially where maiden names are concerned. In regard to nicknames, such as the scenario discussed in the preceding paragraph, the background investigator would know that Jack and John are one and the same when obtaining records or interviewing neighbors.

Home Address

Submitting a current address with your Online Application is straightforward enough. However, what happens if the address you provide changes while you are in the midst of the hiring process? In this case, you must notify the applicant coordinator at the FBI field office that processed your application. If your new residence is in the same area, the applicant coordinator will simply update your file. If you move to an area under the jurisdiction of a different FBI field office, the Bureau will forward your materials to the field office covering your new place of residence for further processing of your application.

Citizenship

Although United States citizenship is required for FBI employment, U.S. citizens who possess dual citizenship may face additional challenges. The Online Application requires applicants to indicate whether they are U.S. citizens, and also asks those with dual citizenship whether they are willing to renounce their foreign citizenship. Online application responses concerning dual citizenship, foreign preference, or loyalty to the United States are addressed on an individual, case-by-case basis. Keep in mind that dual citizenship will result in additional examination of your suitability for FBI employment and possibly a delay in the background investigation. (See chapter 3 for additional discussion of dual-citizenship issues.)

Military Service

The Online Application includes several questions concerning military service, requiring applicants to identify the branch served, dates of service, and Veterans' Preference eligibility. It is important to include starting and ending dates of military service, not only for verification purposes, but also because certain categories of Veterans' Preference eligibility depend on dates of service.

Veterans' Preference eligibility is an area of concern and sometimes confusion in this segment of the application, where applicants must correctly place themselves among more than 10 possible categories depending on service-connected disability, period and length of service, discharge conditions, relationship to a veteran, and other considerations. Veterans who are uncertain about hiring preference should correctly identify their eligibility prior to answering military service questions. "Vet Guide," published by the U.S. Office of Personnel Management (OPM), is an excellent handbook that explains the rights and privileges of veterans concerning federal employment, including details on military service categories shown in the FBI Online Application. This publication is available free of charge on OPM's Web site at www.opm.gov. The U.S. Department of Veterans Affairs also offers many exceptional resources that address Veterans' Preference eligibility.

Local FBI Field Office

In this segment, applicants are asked to identify the FBI field office nearest their residence, and also how they found out about the position they are applying for.

Applicants who plan to move to another residence shortly after applying for FBI employment often question whether to identify the field office nearest their current or future residence when responding to this item. Considering that a change of address during the hiring process will cause the FBI to make changes to your file and possibly transfer your application to another field office, many applicant coordinators suggest waiting until after you have moved to submit your application if the move will take place early in the process.

If you are uncertain as to which field office to identify or when to apply, contact the applicant coordinator at the field office nearest your current residence.

Applicant Demographic Survey

Information requested in this portion of the application pertains to race, ethnicity, gender, and disabilities. One question asks whether any "Targeted Disability" is claimed, although the application presently offers no explanation or definition of qualifying disabilities. The Equal Employment Opportunity Commission (EEOC) defines targeted disabilities as "...deafness, blindness, missing extremities, partial paralysis, complete paralysis, convulsive disorders, mental retardation, mental illness, and genetic or physical conditions affecting limbs or the spine...." Individuals with physical and mental disabilities are eligible for FBI employment if they can perform the essential functions of the job with or without reasonable accommodation.

Job Requirements

There are several questions geared toward various job requirements and difficult aspects of the special agent position. These require applicants to certify either that they understand certain conditions of FBI special agent employment, or that they are willing and able to perform various job functions. The questions focus on a wide range of concerns, such as defending against physical attacks, participating in raids and arrests, witnessing heinous crimes, working an average of 10 hours per day, willingness to relocate or accept assignments anywhere within the FBI's jurisdiction, completing basic training, and serving a two-year probationary period. Any response indicating unwillingness or inability to carry out essential functions of the job will raise a red flag. Therefore, it is critical to read these questions very carefully and fully understand the conditions of employment and requirements of the position. A negative response to a single question could put you on a fast track to disqualification from the hiring process.

Employment Suitability and Disqualifiers

The first item of the Employment Suitability and Disqualifiers section adequately summarizes the nature of this portion of the application: "I understand that my answers to the following questions determine my suitability for application to any position with the FBI." Questions in this area focus on matters such as drug use, criminal convictions, default on student loans, membership in subversive or extremist organizations, and willingness to undergo a variety of pre-employment screening processes. When answering these questions, keep in mind that your responses will be verified through the polygraph, medical examination, urinalysis drug test, and background investigation.

Application and Testing Process

Questions in this segment are designed to confirm that applicants understand what to expect during the application and testing process, and that they will follow related instructions and rules. These questions are quite simple and straightforward.

Federal Employment and Security Clearances Held

If you have been employed by the federal government or held a security clearance, you will need to provide certain details in this section of the application. Data you must be prepared to submit include your pay plan, highest grade level held, dates of employment, and level of security clearance held.

Previous FBI Employment

This is another section that requires some research, but not much thought. If you are a current or former FBI employee, you must indicate which field office processed your application, your duty station, and dates of employment. Candidates also are asked whether they have participated in the FBI Honors Internship Program. You must also disclose whether you have ever applied for federal employment and the date of application (if any).

Minimum Education and Experience Requirements

Although there is only one question in this segment, your answer will determine whether your application is rejected right from the start. Several combinations of education, experience, and professional certifications are presented in this item, and you must correctly identify where you fit in. Be sure to examine the selections carefully to ensure that at least one of the combinations is consistent with your background. Otherwise, selecting "I do not meet any of the above" will disqualify you from the hiring process.

Special Skills, Education, and Experience

Your responses in this portion of the application can move you past other applicants and straight to the front of the line if you possess certain skills and experience the FBI is particularly interested in at the time. Although the skill sets in demand change periodically, one thing that remains constant is that the FBI seeks applicants from a wide range of backgrounds.

Be prepared to provide details about your skills, education, and experience in areas such as engineering, aviation, accounting, finance, law, computers and information technology, the physical sciences, counterintelligence, counterterrorism, international studies, the military, law enforcement, investigations, special forces, and other areas of expertise. You will have an opportunity to submit more than multiple-choice responses, because short-answer and essay questions also are included. Considering the importance of this portion of the application, it is critical that you provide sufficient details to set yourself apart from other applicants, especially in submitting answers to essay questions. Therefore, you must take the time to compose organized and thorough responses, even if this requires closing the application temporarily and returning to it a day or two later.

Foreign-Language Proficiency

Similarly to special skills, education, and experience discussed in the preceding section, foreign-language proficiency also can put you on the fast track to the front of the line. Questions relating to languages of special interest to the FBI are used to identify applicants with skills in Spanish, Japanese, Chinese, Korean, Vietnamese, Russian, Hebrew, Arabic, Farsi/Persian, Hindi, Pashto, Punjabi, Urdu, and other languages. Applicants who claim proficiency in languages of interest are asked additional questions concerning their ability to read, write, and speak the language (see appendix E to assess your proficiency before answering these questions).

Resume Attachment

As discussed in chapter 4, applicants must prepare a resume early in the application process through the Resume Builder feature of the USAJOBS Web site. This is a critical opportunity to stand out from the crowd and make a pitch for advancement to the phase I testing process. In addition to submitting biographical information, your resume should include details concerning your education, degrees received, employment experience, job-related honors and awards, special accomplishments, training completed, computer skills, membership in professional organizations and honor societies, and any other information that articulates your value to the FBI. It is critical to describe your accomplishments, not just your job responsibilities, and to place particular emphasis on special skills, education, training, and experience that the FBI is particularly interested in at the time. Also be sure that information included in your resume is consistent with details you provide in the Online Application and SF-86 Questionnaire for National Security Positions.

Volunteer work, community service, and internships are among the most commonly overlooked resume entries, even though they often involve valuable hands-on experience and transferable skills. You should list these and describe them as employment in the same manner as you do for paid positions. In other words, do not include them on a list of extracurricular activities; this approach does not provide an adequate accounting of your accomplishments or responsibilities. Instead, under separate headings for each position, provide details of your activities and place emphasis on the specific tasks you performed and your achievements. This is especially important when describing internships, where it is critical that you identify exactly what you did rather than what you observed.

Your resume should be well organized and written in plain English. As far as formatting is concerned, simple is best. Keep in mind that you will be pasting information into online text boxes, and that special formatting is likely to be lost. Therefore, you should not use bold, italics, underlining, bullets, indenting, or centering of lines or text. Plain fonts, such as Arial or Times New Roman, tend to work best.

Your resume serves as a closing argument that supplements the Online Application and offers important details that could propel you over the first hurdle in the FBI hiring process. Make no mistake about it; the Bureau combines information provided in your resume with answers to Online Application questions to assess your qualifications and competitiveness for the special agent position. With this in mind, your resume has to be exceptional. There are many excellent books on resume writing that are well written and very helpful. *Federal Resume Guidebook,* published by JIST Publishing, is worth its weight in gold and absolutely the best choice for federal job seekers. Nearly all bookstores, public libraries, college libraries, and career resource centers have resume books on hand.

Filling Out the Questionnaire for National Security Positions (SF-86)

The SF-86 Questionnaire for National Security Positions is used by the FBI and other federal agencies primarily as the basis for the background investigation. As a result, completing this form is the first step toward eventual determination of eligibility for a security clearance and access to classified information.

As with the FBI Online Application, the importance of filling out the SF-86 accurately and completely cannot be overstated. In other words, it is critical that you include your Social Security number, middle name, maiden name, employment information, previous addresses, telephone numbers with area codes, and other requested information, or you will cause a delay in the processing of your application and possibly elimination from the applicant pool. The following areas deserve special attention when completing the SF-86.

Time Period Covered

More than a dozen questions on the SF-86 request information pertaining to employment, mental health, financial history, and other matters beginning with the present and working back seven years. However, the FBI requires applicants to provide information addressed in these questions going back to age 18. These questions are presented in the following sections:

- Section 11: Where You Have Lived
- Section 12: Where You Went to School
- Section 13: Employment Activities
- Section 16: People Who Know You Well
- Section 19: Foreign Contacts
- Section 20: Foreign Activities
- Section 21: Mental and Emotional Health
- Section 22: Police Record
- Section 23: Illegal Use of Drugs or Drug Activity
- Section 24: Use of Alcohol
- Section 25: Investigations and Clearance Held
- Section 26: Financial Record
- Section 27: Use of Information Technology Systems
- Section 28: Involvement in Non-Criminal Court Actions
- Section 29: Association Record

Using Continuation Sheets or Attachments

It is important to note that the residence, education, and employment sections of the SF-86 may not provide adequate space for the information requested. For example, the employment section affords enough space for six jobs, even though many applicants have worked for more than six employers. The FBI provides a continuation sheet for the SF-86 that you can use to furnish additional information on employment, education, and residences. You can find it online at https://www.fbijobs.gov/Employment/SF86A.pdf. However, no such form exists for other information. If you need additional space to answer other questions in addition to the lines at the bottom of page 9, type your responses on plain paper and attach them to the form. Be sure to record your name and Social Security number at the top of every attachment.

Where You Have Lived

Residence information is among the most common omissions on the SF-86. Although the *Where You Have Lived* section of this form asks applicants to provide details on all residences for the past 7 years, remember that the FBI requires you to list your home addresses going back to age 18. Many applicants fail to provide information on campus and summer housing and on- and off-base addresses during military service. List your residence information in chronological order, with all time periods accounted for. Leaving gaps in time periods could call unwanted attention to your application and cause a delay in processing.

Where You Went to School

The *Where You Went to School* section asks for academic information beginning with the most recent school and working back seven years. As discussed previously, in this section you must provide details for all schools you attended since age 18. Considering that the SF-86 allows enough space for only three entries, you should record details of additional education and training programs you completed on the SF-86 Continuation Sheet.

Employment Activities

The Employment block requires a listing of all full- and part-time jobs you have held, as well as military service, self-employment, other paid work, and all aspects of unemployment. The fastest way to raise a "red flag" in this section is to leave unexplained gaps in employment, even if you omit part-time jobs. If you were unemployed while attending college or for any other reason, indicate this by filling out an employment block, indicating the appropriate unemployment code, and listing the name of someone who can provide verification. Be sure to include volunteer work, community service, and internship experience as well. Also, do not omit entries relating to jobs you held with companies that are no longer in business. For these positions, the FBI requires you to list as much information as possible. Failure to do so may also create a gap in employment. As discussed earlier in this section, you probably will need to fill out continuation sheets or attachments to adequately account for your employment history.

People Who Know You Well

In this section, you must list three people who know you well and live in the United States. Common omissions include full names, complete addresses, and phone numbers including area codes. As with other sections, do not omit any information; doing so may cause a delay in your background investigation. You should not list relatives or anyone listed elsewhere on the form. For example, do not list your spouse or former spouse(s) in the first three blocks because they must be included at the end of this section. Similarly, do not list past or present employers because they should already be included in the Employment section.

Relatives

Many applicants are concerned that they will automatically be disqualified from consideration for FBI employment if one of their relatives has an arrest record. This is not true. Do not throw in the towel if your brother-in-law was arrested for tax evasion or your mother was convicted of drunk driving. The Bureau looks very carefully at each situation, including your relationship to the person and any involvement you might have had, and makes determinations on a case-by-case basis. In this section, be sure to include all middle names, maiden names, complete addresses, birth dates, and places of birth. Attach an explanation if you are unable to determine information about relatives with whom you have had no contact for several years.

Foreign Contacts and Activities

Make no mistake about it—these sections are not intended to determine whether you are a well-rounded world traveler with extraordinary life experiences. The Bureau is interested primarily in your contacts with people and places that might be relevant to national security issues. You should not be concerned if you have taken a family vacation to Sweden. On the other hand, if you spent six months in Afghanistan attending tactical training, you should be prepared to answer all sorts of questions later in the hiring process.

Police Record

The FBI is interested in any criminal actions you have been a part of, including the location and results. Note that the Bureau wants to know whether you have been arrested or charged with a criminal offense. Do not make the mistake of omitting information relating to arrests or criminal charges just because you were not convicted. Withholding this information could result in disqualification—even if you were innocent.

Financial Record

The questions in this section are concerned with your financial and credit history. The FBI will review your credit report during the background investigation. Although bad credit can be cause for disqualification, these determinations are made on a case-by-case basis and perfect credit is not required. You should attach an explanation and supporting documentation concerning any loan defaults, serious delinquencies, liens, judgments, property repossessions, bankruptcies, or failure to pay taxes.

False Statements

Applicants must be aware that providing any false statements to the FBI during the hiring process not only will be cause for disqualification from consideration for employment, but may also result in criminal prosecution. Title 18 of the United States Code, Section 1001, provides that knowingly falsifying or concealing a material fact is a felony that may result in fines of up to $10,000 or five years in prison, or both. In addition, if false statements are discovered after you are hired, your employment can be terminated. The FBI verifies information you provide on application materials through your associates, your former employers, criminal record checks, fingerprint records, a drug test, a polygraph examination, and through other means.

Strategies for Special Agent Phase I Testing

Three examinations are given to special agent applicants during phase I of the hiring process, including the Biodata Inventory Test, Situational Judgment Test, and Logical Reasoning Test. Applicant coordinators or staffing assistants from FBI field offices coordinate the testing, which is administered nationwide. Candidates normally are contacted by the FBI about two to four weeks prior to testing and are given the date, time, and location of the testing session. The FBI advises applicants to wear casual, comfortable clothing that would be suitable for an office environment. Phase I tests are of the paper-and-pencil variety and are machine-scored. The tests are graded on a "pass or fail" basis, and the FBI does not disclose numerical scores. Applicants are notified in writing within two weeks whether they passed or failed. In some cases, those who fail can repeat phase I testing six months later (see chapter 4 for more information on the retest process).

General Test-Taking Tips

The special agent phase I hiring process includes multiple-choice tests that are designed to test your ability to recognize and sort out information and to apply facts and concepts. Here are some strategies for succeeding on these tests:

- **Follow directions.** Read and listen to all directions carefully before starting the test. One of the most important test-taking skills is the ability to follow directions. Some candidates are so anxious to get the test over with that they skip the directions, which is often a costly mistake.

- **Read the questions and choices carefully.** As much as multiple-choice questions examine your knowledge and problem-solving skills, they are also designed to test your ability to review information carefully and thoroughly. Failure to read questions carefully is a common cause for selecting incorrect answers on multiple-choice tests. Read difficult or confusing questions more than once, if necessary, and resist the temptation to jump to conclusions about what you think the questions ask. Instead, rely only on the information presented and decide which answers are best. Also, read all of the answers before making a selection, even if the first or second choice appears correct; the best answer might be listed last. In other words, keep in mind that more than one correct answer may be presented and that you must choose the best answer from among the choices.

- **Make educated guesses.** The FBI phase I tests are scored on the total number of correct answers. Therefore, because there is no penalty for guessing, you should answer every question—even if you have to guess. If you do not know the answer, keep in mind that eliminating only one or two of the choices will increase the probability of selecting the correct answer.

- **Pace yourself.** Work through questions quickly but also carefully. If you come to a question that you can't answer or are unsure about, it is best to skip the question for the time being and to return to it after answering the other questions. Tackling difficult questions is often easier when you are more relaxed after answering easier questions. In addition, your answers to easier questions may provide clues to those that are more difficult.

- **Fill in answers carefully.** The FBI tests are administered using test booklets and separate answer sheets. Therefore, it is critical that you make sure that the number you are answering corresponds to the number of the question. If you skip a question, be sure to leave the space for that question blank. Although this is a matter of common sense, many test takers have been thrown off by one question in a sequence and marked one incorrect answer after another. Also be sure to fill in the answer ovals completely so that the machine that grades the test can easily record your responses.

Managing Test Anxiety

Many special agent applicants experience what is commonly known as test anxiety prior to phase I and phase II testing. After all, it's not every day that they voluntarily subject themselves to intense examination by the world's best-known law enforcement agency. Test anxiety is merely a reaction to stress that accompanies test taking. Some applicants experience symptoms such as nervousness, muscle tension, headaches, stomach discomfort, rapid heartbeat, or sweating. The most detrimental of symptoms is mental blocking, which can affect memory, reasoning skills, perception, and the ability to focus.

Test anxiety is not necessarily bad news. According to many prominent research studies, a moderate amount of pretest stress actually boosts performance, although either too little or excessive amounts can diminish performance. In other words, applicants who are able to recognize, manage, and channel test anxiety can actually use it to their advantage. To accomplish this, consider the techniques in the following sections.

Confront Your Fears

For most people, test anxiety ultimately boils down to a fear of failure. Recognizing that fear is the culprit and confronting your fear are the primary challenges in conquering test anxiety. Although it is easier said than done, many test-takers succeed in overcoming pretest fear simply by putting the outcome of the FBI hiring process into perspective. It is important to keep in mind that, in the worst-case scenario, failure to be selected by the FBI will not bring an end to the world. If you fail the phase I test, nobody will take away your college degree, you will not lose your job, and your pets will still worship you. In addition, considering that you were among the few that the FBI selected to take the test, you might have an opportunity to retest at a later date. So, although you should do everything within reason to ensure your success in the hiring process, be sure to maintain proper perspective overall.

Be Fully Prepared

Perhaps the most important tool for conquering test anxiety is to have a firm understanding of what lies ahead. Oftentimes the most stressful part of an event—whether you're going out on a blind date or moving your family across the country—boils down to fear of the unknown. After the event is over, you often find that the stress was for naught. Adequate preparation also leads to an increase in confidence. It is far easier to have confidence going into a situation if you understand the challenges you're facing and expect to succeed.

You can best prepare for phase I and phase II tests by studying this book, studying books that cover logical reasoning questions and general test-taking strategies, and gaining insights from others who have completed the FBI hiring process or similar employment application experiences. Also, study with someone else periodically. Discussing the material with others is not only an effective tool for reinforcing the information, it also reduces test anxiety. In addition, review the strategies for mastering multiple-choice exams discussed in the preceding section, as well as test-taking tips offered in the remainder of this chapter. Following these strategies can lead to higher scores also.

Avoid Cramming for the Tests

It is very important to space studying over a period of weeks or months instead of cramming for the test the night before. Cramming is most often the result of procrastination. Unfortunately, cramming increases anxiety, which interferes with clear thinking. Procrastination itself also increases stress—and excessive stress reduces test scores. On the other hand, studies have repeatedly shown that students absorb more information when studying takes place over a period of time.

Reduce Stress Prior to the Tests

To the greatest extent possible, try to reduce stress in your life for the days and weeks leading up to testing. This could include tactics such as getting organized, working fewer hours, following a nutritious diet, exercising, and getting plenty of rest. It is also important to get enough sleep the night before and to eat breakfast on the day of the tests. Visualizing success and maintaining a positive attitude can also be very helpful. Of course, all of these should be part of your everyday routines, but that's a topic for another discussion.

Use Relaxation Techniques

Many people find that relaxation techniques are useful in reducing test anxiety and other forms of stress. A common method of relaxing tense muscles is known as the Progressive Muscular Relaxation (PMR) technique, which has proven effective in studies by university researchers. The PMR technique involves tightening a group of muscles for a few seconds at a time, holding them in a state of tension for a few seconds, and then relaxing them completely. You can achieve this best by working head to toe and waiting about 30 seconds between muscle groups. You can use PMR in conjunction with slow, deep breathing, which also aids in relaxation.

The Biodata Inventory Test

The FBI administers a Biodata Inventory Test during phase I of the hiring process as a supplement to cognitive testing. Biodata tests are useful for predicting aspects of job performance—such as interpersonal relationships with coworkers, communicating with the public, personality, and motivation—that cannot be predicted by cognitive measures. These tests have been used in many fields to predict everything from salesmanship of life insurance agents to productivity of research scientists, turnover of bank clerks, proficiency of naval personnel in diver training, and many other performance issues.

Biodata questions may ask about academic achievements, leisure activities, hobbies, interests, community service, goals, preferences for working in groups or alone, or other variables. Research has demonstrated that biodata inventory tests are reliable predictors of job performance in groups ranging from unskilled workers to office clerks, service station workers, chemists, engineers, and high-level executives. The underlying assumption of biodata is that past behavior is a valid predictor of future behavior. More specifically, these tests have shown that information obtained from job applicants about their backgrounds, previous work experience, education, and interests can be used to predict job performance.

The Biodata Inventory Test consists of 40 questions that measure motivation and initiative, ability to prioritize and adapt to changing situations, organization and planning skills, and judgment abilities. The questions must be answered within 45 minutes, which provides plenty of time for most applicants. All responses are recorded on answer sheets that are scored by a computer.

Sample Biodata Inventory Questions

The following are examples of the types of biodata questions that you might encounter on the test:

1. In connection with your work, in which of the following have you taken the most pride?

    A. Having been able to avoid any major controversies.

    B. Having gotten where you are on your own.

    C. Having been able to work smoothly with people.

    D. Having provided a lot of new ideas, good or bad.

    E. Having been able to do well whatever management has requested.

2. Which has provided your greatest source of motivation on the job?

    A. Praise from your supervisors.

    B. Receiving good scores on performance evaluations.

    C. Satisfaction accompanied by assisting others with their problems.

    D. Devising new ways to accomplish various tasks.

    E. Allowing enough free time to concentrate on personal interests.

3. When carrying out your work assignments, would you prefer:

    A. To work alone.

    B. To work in small groups.

    C. To lead small groups.

    D. To work in large groups.

    E. To lead large groups.

Tips for Taking the Biodata Inventory Test

As you can see from the sample questions, there are no correct or incorrect answers. Instead, responses to these questions provide an indication of whether the respondent will fit in with the FBI. Keep in mind that the hiring process is geared to identify candidates who are well adjusted, well rounded, and likely to succeed. When taking the Biodata Inventory Test, resist the temptation to outsmart the exam by marking answers you believe the FBI considers correct. This could spell disaster. Instead, selecting the answers you believe are best will provide the most accurate characterization of yourself.

If the biodata inventory was designed to test knowledge of mathematics or grammar, or even law enforcement practices or investigative techniques, applicants could take a fairly straightforward approach to preparing for the test. However, the Biodata Inventory Test evaluates nonacademic elements for which it is virtually impossible to study. After all, the Bureau administers the test to determine which applicants have the motivation, attitude, and personal characteristics that are best suited for the work of FBI special agents—qualities that are difficult to hone through study guides. In other words, there is no magic formula for success with this test. The best approach you can take is to answer biodata questions honestly, based on common sense and a genuine assessment of the problems, situations, or issues presented.

The Situational Judgment Test

Situational judgment tests are commonly used for selecting law enforcement officers and other workers—from school principals to military personnel—to evaluate critical thinking, decision-making skills, integrity, and other attributes. In these tests, brief descriptions of realistic scenarios are followed by a number of options for handling various situations. These types of questions enable employers to assess candidates' abilities to evaluate information, prioritize, adapt, and decide on a course of action. The FBI uses a situational judgment test to forecast the likelihood of applicants' job success by evaluating their behavior in various situations.

The Situational Judgment Test is a 45-minute examination that is given during the phase I testing process. It consists of questions that present a range of problem scenarios and a list of actions that could be taken. After carefully evaluating the facts, respondents must rate the effectiveness of each action using a 1–7 rating scale, where 7 is highly effective and 1 is completely ineffective.

Sample Situational Judgment Questions

The Situational Judgment Test includes questions that are similar to the following examples:

1. You are standing in line at a bank when a man approaches a teller and announces a robbery. You are armed and wearing business attire. What would you do?

    A. Nothing, as you do not want to get involved in the incident.

    B. Remain in line and observe the robber until he leaves, then call the police.

    C. Rush out of the bank and call the police.

    D. Wait until the robber leaves, then follow him until he settles somewhere.

    E. Try to apprehend the robber.

2. While you are interviewing a fraud suspect at his residence, the suspect offers you a $500 cash bribe to "make the investigation go away." You and the suspect are alone in the residence. What would you do?

    A. Decline the suspect's offer, complete the interview, and continue the investigation as if the bribery attempt had not occurred.

    B. Decline the suspect's offer, complete the interview, and contact your supervisor immediately after you leave the residence.

   C. Accept the $500 payment, terminate the interview, and contact your supervisor immediately after you leave the residence.

   D. Decline the offer, complete the interview, arrest the suspect as soon as the interview has been completed, and contact your supervisor immediately.

   E. Arrest the suspect when the bribe is offered and contact your supervisor immediately.

3. While you are off duty and driving through a grocery store parking lot, you observe a vehicle in front of you strike a man who was loading groceries into a car. The driver speeds away, leaving the man lying injured on the pavement. What would you do?

   A. Observe what you can about the vehicle and immediately give aid to the injured man.

   B. Run into the store to call the police and then return to the parking lot and give aid to the injured man.

   C. Catch up to the vehicle, get a good look at the driver, then return to the scene to aid the injured man.

   D. Pull in front of the vehicle to prevent the driver from escaping and then arrest the driver.

   E. Follow the vehicle and arrest the driver when he stops somewhere.

Tips for the Situational Judgment Test

Responses to situational judgment questions depend on the unique perspectives and priorities of each applicant. Although the questions typically are straightforward, the answers require intense analysis of problems and the underlying issues. The best strategy involves *carefully* reading each question, imagining yourself in the situation, recognizing signs of danger or ethical issues, analyzing the problem overall, and applying common sense. Many experts suggest deciding on a course of action before reading the answers, and then seeking the chosen response among the answers. This approach makes sense, although its effectiveness varies from one person to another.

As a rule of thumb, officer safety and providing emergency aid take precedence over enforcing the law. Therefore, making an arrest probably would not be the best approach in either of the preceding scenarios. Ultimately, if your chosen actions are professional, free from emotional or biased behavior, and based on commonly accepted protocols, they probably will be correct.

The Logical Reasoning Test

Logical reasoning is the most important competency for successful performance of FBI special agents, intelligence specialists, and other key personnel. The Bureau administers the Logical Reasoning Test to ensure that newly appointed special agents can apply appropriate reasoning, decision-making, and problem solving throughout their careers. Logical reasoning tests are widely used during the hiring process by many federal law enforcement agencies and police departments as a reliable predictor of future job performance.

The Logical Reasoning Test is a 90-minute examination that is designed to measure your ability to understand complicated written material and to derive correct conclusions from it. The test requires you to make logical conclusions based on facts you are given in a brief passage. The passages are followed by a lead-in phrase that introduces five response choices. Your conclusions and the responses you select must be based only on facts in the passages.

It is important to read the passages, lead-in phrases, and responses very carefully and to focus on the information that is given and *not* given. Keep in mind that the test measures your ability to reason on the basis of given facts and not on your independent knowledge of the subject matter of questions.

Each passage is drawn from subject matter that is relevant to work of FBI special agents, although knowledge of the special agent position is not required. It is important to keep in mind that the procedures and other information presented in the passages are not necessarily accurate. Nonetheless, you must accept every fact in the passages as true.

Lead-in phrases can be either positive or negative. For example, a positive phrase could read, "From the information given above, it CAN be validly concluded that...," while a negative phrase could read, "From the information given above, it CANNOT be validly concluded that...." Positive lead-in phrases are followed by four invalid conclusions and one valid conclusion. On the other hand, negative lead-in phrases are followed by four valid conclusions and one invalid conclusion.

Sample Logical Reasoning Questions

The following examples are similar to questions presented in the FBI Logical Reasoning Test.

1. FBI special agents were led to believe that many weapons sold at a certain gun store were sold illegally. Upon investigating the lead, the agents learned that all of the weapons sold by the store that were made by Precision Arms were sold legally. Also, none of the illegally sold weapons were .45 caliber.

   From the information given above, it CAN be validly concluded that, concerning the weapons sold at the store:

   A. All of the .45-caliber weapons were made by Precision Arms.

   B. None of the .45-caliber weapons were made by Precision Arms.

   C. Some of the weapons made by Precision Arms were .45-caliber weapons.

   D. All of the .45-caliber weapons were sold legally.

   E. Some of the weapons made by Precision Arms were sold illegally.

2. Impressions made by the ridges on the ends of the fingers and thumbs are useful means of identification, because no two persons have the same pattern of ridges. If finger patterns from fingerprints are not decipherable, then they cannot be classified by general shape and contour or by pattern type. If they cannot be classified by these characteristics, then it is impossible to identify the person to whom the fingerprints belong.

From the information given above, it CANNOT be validly concluded that:

A. If it is possible to identify the person to whom fingerprints belong, then the fingerprints are decipherable.

B. If finger patterns from fingerprints are not decipherable, then it is impossible to identify the person to whom the fingerprints belong.

C. If fingerprints are decipherable, then it is impossible to identify the person to whom they belong.

D. If fingerprints can be classified by general shape and contour or by pattern type, then they are decipherable.

E. If it is possible to identify the person to whom fingerprints belong, then the fingerprints can be classified by general shape and contour or pattern type.

3. Explosives are substances or devices capable of producing a volume of rapidly expanding gases that exert a sudden pressure on their surroundings. Chemical explosives are the most commonly used, although there are mechanical and nuclear explosives. All mechanical explosives are devices in which a physical reaction is produced, such as that caused by overloading a container with compressed air. While nuclear explosives are by far the most powerful, all nuclear explosives have been restricted to military weapons.

From the information given above, it CAN be validly concluded that:

A. All explosives that have been restricted to military weapons are nuclear explosives.

B. No mechanical explosives are devices in which a physical reaction is produced, such as that caused by overloading a container with compressed air.

C. Some nuclear explosives have not been restricted to military weapons.

D. All mechanical explosives have been restricted to military weapons.

E. Some devices in which a physical reaction is produced, such as that caused by overloading a container with compressed air, are mechanical explosives.

4. The printed output of some computer-driven printers can be recognized by forensic analysts. The "Acme Model 200" printer was manufactured using two different inking mechanisms, one of which yields a "Type A" micropattern of ink spray around its characters. Of all Acme Model 200 printers, 70 percent produce this Type A micropattern, which is also characteristic of some models of other printers. Forensic analysts at a crime lab have been examining a kidnap ransom note that clearly exhibits the Type A micropattern.

From the information given above, it CAN be validly concluded that this note:

A. Was printed on an Acme Model 200 printer, with a probability of 70 percent.

B. Was printed on an Acme Model 200 printer, with a probability of 30 percent.

C. Was not printed on an Acme Model 200 printer, with a probability of 70 percent.

D. Was not printed on an Acme Model 200 printer, with a probability of 30 percent.

E. Might have been printed on an Acme Model 200 printer, but the probability cannot be estimated.

Logical Reasoning Test Answers

1. The correct response is D.

   The second and last sentences are the two main premises in the passage. These sentences provide information about three categories of weapons, including (1) weapons made by Precision Arms, (2) weapons sold legally, and (3) .45-caliber weapons.

   The last sentence states that none of the illegally sold weapons were .45 caliber. This means that none of the .45-caliber weapons were sold illegally. Notice that this statement is a double negative. In affirmative form, the statement means that all .45-caliber weapons were sold legally, response D.

   Information in the last sentence that all .45-caliber weapons were sold legally, combined with the information in the second sentence that all weapons made by Precision Arms were sold legally, allows us to draw no valid conclusions about the relationship between the .45-caliber weapons and the weapons made by Precision Arms.

   There is insufficient information about the entire group of weapons sold legally to know whether the group of .45-caliber weapons and the group of weapons made by Precision Arms overlapped entirely (response A), partially (response C), or not at all (response B). Response E contradicts the second sentence and is, therefore, invalid.

2. The correct response is C.

   This question asks for the response option that CANNOT be validly concluded from the information in the passage. Response C is invalid because the passage does not provide enough information to conclude whether it would be possible to identify the person to whom the fingerprints belong from the mere fact that the fingerprints are decipherable.

   Response A refers to a condition where it is possible to identify the person to whom fingerprints belong. Based on the final sentence in the passage, this condition of fingerprints means that the fingerprints could be classified by general shape and contour or by pattern type. Based on the second sentence, the ability to classify the fingerprints means that the fingerprints are decipherable.

   Because response B refers to a condition in which finger patterns from fingerprints are not decipherable, we know from the second sentence that, in that circumstance, they cannot be classified by general shape and contour or by pattern type. From the final sentence in the passage, we can infer that because they cannot be classified by these characteristics, then it is impossible to identify the person to whom the fingerprints belong.

According to the second sentence, fingerprints cannot be classified by general shape and contour or by pattern type when they are not decipherable. Therefore, if fingerprints can be classified by general shape and contour or by pattern type, then the fingerprints must be decipherable (response D).

According to the third sentence, it is impossible to identify the owner of a set of fingerprints when the fingerprints cannot be classified by general shape and contour or by pattern type. Therefore, if it is possible to identify the person to whom fingerprints belong, then the fingerprints must be able to be classified by general shape and contour or pattern type (response E). Responses D and E are valid based on the same type of reasoning. The first and second statements of the second sentence were made opposite and reversed in response D, and the first and second statements of the final sentence were made opposite and reversed in response E.

3. The correct response is E.

The third sentence demonstrates the overlap between all mechanical explosives and devices in which a physical reaction is produced, such as that caused by overloading a container with compressed air. From this, we can conclude that some devices in which a physical reaction is produced, such as that caused by overloading a container with compressed air, are mechanical explosives.

Response A is incorrect because the passage does not provide sufficient information to validly conclude that all explosives that have been restricted to military weapons are nuclear weapons. It could be that some types of explosives other than nuclear weapons also have been restricted to military weapons.

Responses B and C are incorrect because they contradict the passage. Response B contradicts the third sentence, and response C contradicts the last sentence. Response D is incorrect because the passage provides no information about whether mechanical explosives are restricted to military weapons.

4. The correct response is E.

We know from the third sentence that the Type A micropattern exists in 70 percent of all Acme Model 200 printers and in some other models of printers. However, we know neither how many other models nor what percentage of other models produce the Type A micropattern.

Hence, the probability that the note was printed on the Acme Model 200 printer cannot be determined. For that reason, responses A, B, C, and D are incorrect because the probability is based only on the characteristic of the one model printer that we know, the Acme Model 200, and not on all of the printer models that contain the Type A micropattern.

Tips for Taking the Logical Reasoning Test

To prepare for the Logical Reasoning Test, you must fully understand the format of the test and what is expected of you. It is especially important to understand that in reading the passages you are drawing logical conclusions instead of determining the general meaning. In other words, analytical reading is different than ordinary reading, and it is critical that you carefully evaluate the information and pay attention to detail.

The following tips should be helpful with Logical Reasoning Test questions.

- In questions with positive lead statements, always choose the *only* conclusion that can definitely be drawn from the information given in the passage.

- Remember *not* to use any outside factual information to reach your conclusion. Take into consideration only the information provided in the passages.

- Always read the passage and lead-in sentence very carefully.

- Be sure to read *all* response choices before you make your selection.

- Pay particular attention to words and phrases such as "all," "most," "some," "none," "other than," "unless," "except," "sometimes," "never," and "only." These words and phrases help to define the facts from which you must draw conclusions.

- Also pay special attention to negative prefixes such as "non," "un," or "dis," or a negative verb such as "disconnect" or "unfasten." These may be crucial to understanding the basic facts in the passage.

- Ignore any advice you might have received in the past about avoiding a response that contains the words "all" or "none." These words could be signs of an incorrect response in some tests, but not necessarily in the FBI Logical Reasoning Test. These words appear in both correct and incorrect responses in this test.

- Use a study guide. Study guides that are geared to the Graduate Management Admission Test (GMAT) are useful in preparing for the logical reasoning portion of the FBI phase I test, because the questions are similar on both tests. This type of question is known as "critical reasoning" on the GMAT. Virtually all GMAT preparation guides include full-length practice tests, answers, analyses, and other useful features.

Strategies for Special Agent Phase II Testing

The most competitive applicants who passed phase I testing are invited to compete in the phase II process, which consists of a structured personal interview and a written exercise. The following sections discuss strategies for performing well during these segments of the process.

The Structured Interview

Structured interviews are used by the FBI, other law enforcement agencies, and firms in the private sector to evaluate job candidates by asking each of them identical questions under the same conditions. During phase II of the special agent hiring process, structured interviews provide the FBI with an assessment of candidates' communications skills, judgment, integrity, priorities, initiative, flexibility, and other attributes that special agents must have to meet FBI standards and succeed in federal law enforcement.

About the Interview

The structured interview takes place at an FBI field office on the same day as the written exercise. The interview is designed primarily to evaluate each candidate's previous behavior in a variety of actual situations to predict their potential for success as an FBI special agent. This approach is commonly known as *behavioral interviewing*.

What Is Behavioral Interviewing?

Behavioral interviewing appears similar to traditional interviewing, although is far different. It is based on the concept that examples of your behavior in previous circumstances provide more accurate information concerning the presence or absence of skills than traditional interview questions, and also a more reliable indication of how you will behave in similar circumstances in the future.

Traditional interview questions often require "yes" or "no" answers, or ask you to describe what you would do in a particular situation. These questions only require you to *speculate* how you would behave, which offers much less insight than information about how you *actually behaved* in a given set of circumstances. For example, a traditional interview could include a question such as this:

> *"How would you react if one of your co-workers disagreed with you about the best way to approach a problem?"*

This question asks you to imagine yourself in the situation and to predict your response. In traditional interviews, questions of this variety tend to be answered with only a brief supposition of the best way to handle the matter—often based on the interviewee's perception of what the interviewer would like to hear—after which the interviewer moves on to the next question. On the other hand, a similar behavioral interview question could be presented like this:

> *"Tell me about an actual situation you have experienced during which one of your co-workers disagreed with you about the best way to approach a problem."*

As you can see, behavioral questions are designed to provide actual evidence of your ability to perform and succeed on the job—or your lack of these abilities—as opposed to mere guesswork. In addition, considering that behavioral questions require you to describe actual experiences instead of making a quick guess, *you* will do most of the talking and the interviewer will do most of the listening, rather than the other way around.

Of course, it is well known that past behavior does not always predict future behavior, and that people can and do change their previous behavior patterns. Nonetheless, behavioral interviewing is widely acknowledged as superior to traditional interviewing in determining whether job applicants have attained particular knowledge, skills, and abilities. As a result, behavioral interviewing is more reliable than traditional interviewing as a basis for predicting future behavior and job success.

Structured Interview Format

During the interview, which lasts about one hour, a panel of three FBI special agents asks each applicant a series of 13 questions and rates the responses based on predetermined criteria. To ensure objectiveness in scoring, the panel is not provided with any information about applicants' backgrounds, such as their phase I test scores, work history, education, skills, or other qualifications.

Although the interview consists of 13 standard questions, there is a good chance you will face follow-up questions as well. Whether follow-up questions are asked depends on factors such as the amount of time remaining, whether additional information is needed to clarify answers, or whether the interviewers are curious or interested in hearing more about your stories. There is no conventional wisdom as to whether the presence or lack of follow-up questions is a positive or negative indication of your performance. For example, you might be asked a follow-up question if an interviewer enjoyed your response and wanted additional information, or because your answer included gaps or inconsistencies that need further explanation. On the other hand, a lack of follow-up questions could indicate either that your answers were right on the money and additional information was not needed, or that you were so far off base that follow-up questions would be a waste of time.

Sample Structured Interview Questions

The following are examples of behavioral interview questions that correspond to the critical skills and abilities measured during the phase II interview. Taking the time to consider your answers to these questions prior to the interview is a good investment because you will be better prepared when it is your turn in the hot seat.

Ability to Communicate Orally

1. Give an example of a situation during which you used your communication skills to present complex information so that it was easy to understand.

2. Tell about an occasion when you made a decision that was not supported initially and how you later received support.

3. Tell about a successful oral presentation or speech you made.

4. Give an example of a time you approached someone to discuss a difficult or unpleasant situation, and how you handled the matter.

5. Tell about a time during which your verbal communication skills allowed you to express yourself about an issue or concern that was important to you.

Ability to Organize, Plan, and Prioritize

6. Tell about a time when being organized and prepared resulted in your success.

7. Give an example of a situation that required you to gather a great deal of information to solve a problem or present a proposal.

8. Tell about an occasion when you analyzed a situation and identified the appropriate steps to take to achieve positive results.

9. Discuss how you completed a project on schedule because you prioritized tasks effectively.

10. Describe a successful project that required you to focus on many tasks at the same time.

Ability to Relate Effectively with Others

11. Give an example of a situation during which you successfully motivated others.

12. Tell about a time when you established rapport or a positive relationship with a difficult person.

13. Tell about a time during which a group of people you worked with had a serious conflict or could not agree on a course of action, and how you approached the matter.

14. Describe a situation that required you to compromise in order to resolve a problem or disagreement.

15. Describe a situation during which you used diplomacy to resolve a problem.

Ability to Maintain a Positive Image

16. Give an example of your success in building morale.

17. Tell about a time when your efforts improved teamwork.

18. Give an example of a time during which you maintained a positive attitude when others did not.

19. Describe an occasion during which your organization was looked upon favorably as a result of your actions.

20. Tell about a time during which you received special recognition or acknowledgement for your leadership abilities.

Ability to Evaluate Information and Make Judgment Decisions

21. Describe a situation when you prevented a small problem from becoming a large problem.

22. Give an example of a time during which your attention to detail was the key to success.

23. Describe a significant mistake you have made, how you could have avoided it, and what you learned from the experience.

24. Tell about a situation during which you solved a problem or achieved other positive results by using your analytical abilities.

25. Give an example of circumstances that required you to weigh various options to make an important decision.

Initiative and Motivation

26. Give an example of a significant personal goal you set and how you accomplished it.

27. Tell about an occasion when you used a creative idea to solve a problem.

28. Give an example of an award or recognition you have received for making a positive change.

29. Tell about a time during which you took on extra duties, worked additional hours, or made sacrifices for an employer or organization you served.

30. Give an example of an important idea or project that was implemented primarily as a result of your efforts.

Ability to Adapt to Changing Situations

31. Describe a situation that caused you to modify your planned actions in order to respond to the needs of another person.

32. Tell about a situation when you made a quick decision under difficult or dangerous circumstances.

33. Give an example of a situation that caused you a great deal of stress, and how you reacted to the situation and the stress.

34. Tell about a situation during which you reacted successfully to circumstances that were changing rapidly and beyond your control.

35. Describe a time when you helped someone to accept change and make adjustments to move forward.

Integrity

36. Tell about an occasion when you conformed to a policy or followed a supervisor's orders even though you disagreed with the policy or order.

37. Give an example of a challenging situation during which you exercised integrity.

38. Discuss a time when you dealt with a problem concerning honesty, ethics, or fairness.

39. Tell about a time during which your values had a positive impact on someone.

40. Give an example of a situation during which you abided by an obligation or promise to maintain confidentiality.

Physical Requirements

41. Discuss what you have done to maintain physical fitness and good health.

42. Discuss any concerns you have concerning your ability to meet the FBI's physical requirements.

43. Discuss your efforts to prepare for the pre-employment physical fitness test.

44. Discuss how you plan to prepare for the physical aspects of New Agent Training.

45. Discuss how you plan to maintain physical fitness and good health in the future.

Tips for the Structured Interview

There are many steps you can take to prepare for the phase II interview that will improve your performance. These revolve around knowing in advance what you would like to discuss, presenting your answers in an appropriate format, getting the most mileage out of your experiences, putting your best foot forward, listening, and not attempting to be anyone but yourself.

Take Stock of Your Experiences

In preparation for the phase II interview, keep in mind that you will be asked to discuss your life experiences in a wide range of situations. A very effective method of preparing for behavioral interview questions is to recall incidents that required you to evaluate a situation and choose a course of action while you were under stress, in difficult or emotional circumstances, responding to emergencies, or faced with moral or ethical dilemmas. It is also important to present your responses in an organized manner, including an introduction to the situation, a detailed description of your actions, and an explanation of the outcome.

Although many behavioral questions are tailor-made for responses based on your experience in the workplace, many questions also lend themselves to experience that is not career-related. For example, many of your responses could revolve around your experience as a student, parent, member or coach of an athletic team, instructor, member or leader of a Girl Scout or Boy Scout troop, Parent-Teacher Association board member, volunteer police officer or firefighter, homeowner's association board member, or other position. In other words, just about any experience that involves employment, community service, education, troubleshooting, problem-solving, teamwork, coaching, teaching, leadership, responding to emergencies, or thinking on your feet is likely to fit in nicely. Give careful thought to how your experiences match these and similar environments and it should pay off during the phase II interview. Among other benefits, discussing your experiences outside of the workplace should give the impression that you are well-rounded.

Use the STAR Technique

An excellent method you can use to prepare for and answer phase II interview questions is the STAR technique. The acronym STAR stands for

- Situation
- Task
- Action
- Result

To apply the STAR technique, follow these steps:

1. First describe the **situation** or **task** you encountered. For example, you could discuss a conflict between two of your co-workers and how you helped them to resolve it. Be sure to provide sufficient detail so that the interviewers understand the circumstances completely.

2. Next, explain the specific **action** you took toward resolving the situation. The focus of the action should be on what you actually did or suggested. In the scenario involving your co-workers, you could describe a compromise that you suggested.

3. Finally, describe the **result** of the situation. In this case, you could discuss the terms of the compromise and how each worker accepted the outcome, as well as what you accomplished or learned from the incident. In a nutshell, the STAR technique allows you to frame your responses to behavioral questions in a straightforward, organized, and informative manner.

As a rule of thumb, your description of the situation or task should encompass about 20 to 25 percent of your response overall; your explanation of the action taken should cover about 50 to 60 percent of your response; and describing the results should comprise the remaining 20 to 25 percent. The following example illustrates the STAR technique in action:

Interviewer's Question:

"Describe a situation in which you exercised good judgment and integrity."

Situation or Task:

"Last month, I participated in the execution of a search warrant at a convenience store in Chicago that was involved in food stamp trafficking. I was assigned to search a small office at the rear of the store. While I was alone in the office, I opened a desk drawer and discovered a cigar box that contained more than $100,000 in cash."

Action:

"I am aware that being alone in the room could have resulted in baseless accusations by the suspect that I took some of the cash. Of course, this sort of accusation—even if unfounded—could have caused a great deal of unnecessary discussion between the defense attorney, the prosecutor, and my agency, and almost certainly would have cast a dark cloud over the investigation. I also had an obligation to follow my agency's policy concerning the handling of cash evidence. So, as soon as I noticed that the cigar box contained cash, I placed it back in the drawer, stood in the doorway leading into the office, and notified the team leader of my discovery. I remained in the doorway until he arrived, explained the circumstances, and then pointed out the box. After I photographed it, we counted the cash together and seized it in accordance with our agency's policy manual."

Result:

"Considering that I didn't handle, count, or seize the cash until a witness was present, it is unlikely that anyone will question whether I pocketed any of the money. Not only did I use good judgment and maintain my integrity in the situation, the integrity of the evidence—including the chain of custody—also was maintained at all times. In other words, I acted within the law and agency policies, and the prosecutor intends to use the cash as evidence."

In this example, the STAR technique allows the candidate to respond to the question clearly, concisely, and in an organized manner. In addition to addressing judgment and integrity, the response also focuses on other traits the

FBI looks for during the interview, such as oral communication skills, ability to evaluate and adapt to changing situations, and maintaining a positive image.

To take full advantage of the STAR technique, prior to the interview you must think carefully about several scenarios in which you have been involved, including the action you took and the outcome, and write down the details. Writing about the incidents will help you to collect and organize the details. The STAR technique should pay big dividends during the interview because you will already have a number of situations in mind when you are asked to discuss your experiences. This exercise might seem like a lot of work, but the rewards are well worth it.

Leave Your Modesty at Home

Many special agent applicants find it difficult to toot their own horns during the phase II interview because they are uncomfortable spending one hour bragging to three strangers. Forget about it. The structured interview is your only face-to-face opportunity to sell yourself to the FBI, and this is not the time to hold back.

Therefore, without appearing egotistical or arrogant, discuss your accomplishments completely as they relate to the critical skills and abilities the FBI is interested in. In addition, it is important to emphasize what *you* accomplished, even if your accomplishments were achieved in a team setting. Many applicants make the mistake of highlighting their role as a member of a team instead of focusing on their individual contribution to the team. Nonetheless, don't hesitate to discuss the value of teamwork and your ability to work as a team player; just be sure to provide complete details of *your* contributions and accomplishments.

Turn Negatives into Positives

Although some of the questions could focus on your successes in evaluating, responding to, and adapting to various circumstances, it is likely that you will be asked about experiences that resulted in negative outcomes. In other words, be prepared to discuss situations in which your actions brought results that were somehow unsatisfactory, and any shortcomings that might have caused negative results. The interviewers realize that no applicant has led a life of perfection, and they will be interested in how you address negative outcomes. If you are asked these types of questions, it is best to readily admit to your failures and to explain what you learned from your mistakes. This will give you a golden opportunity to turn negatives into positives, and also to exhibit maturity and humbleness. Rest assured that the interviewers neither want nor expect to hear that you have never made poor choices or otherwise taken the wrong path. If nothing else, failing to admit your mistakes will convince the interviewers that you are not the kind of person they will want to work with.

Present a Positive and Professional Image

A considerable amount of research has shown that job interviewers evaluate applicants not only on their responses to questions, but also on their appearance and demeanor. The saying, "you never get a second chance to make a good first impression," is quite true. It is very important to wear professional business attire to the interview, such as a suit and tie for males and a suit, dress, or pantsuit for females. You must be aware that every aspect of your performance will be judged, including the manner in which you present yourself.

Be sure to greet the interviewers with confidence and a firm handshake, and to maintain good posture throughout the interview. You should also maintain eye contact with every member of the interview panel in an alternating manner while you are answering questions.

Listen Carefully

Many candidates are so anxious to respond to questions during the interview that they overlook the importance of good listening skills. You must listen carefully to each question to understand the meaning and context presented. Do not hesitate to ask the interviewers to repeat questions, if necessary. Also, it is often wise to take a few seconds to think things over before responding to questions instead of blurting out answers you might regret later. The interviewers are interested not only in your answers, but also in the manner in which you construct your answers. Also consider that the interviewers expect you to give adequate thought to the questions, and that a moment of silence after each question will not hurt your score. Pausing to collect your thoughts and prepare a response—even if only briefly—usually results in better-organized answers.

Be Yourself

One of the most common mistakes that applicants make during phase II interviews is to anticipate what the interviewers would like to hear rather than answering questions with sincerity and candor. As a result, attempting to out-guess the interview panel often is the fastest way to fail the interview. Keep in mind that there are no "right" and "wrong" answers to the questions, and that every candidate is evaluated on whether they possess the critical skills, abilities, maturity, judgment, and personality traits that FBI special agents must have. Let's face it, the interviewers would like to know whether you are honest, down-to-earth, sincere, intelligent, and—perhaps most important of all—the kind of person they would like to work with down the road. In other words, if you have what it takes, you will be much better off providing a true snapshot of yourself than putting on an act.

The Written Exercise

The other portion of phase II testing consists of a written exercise that applicants complete in the presence of FBI test administrators. The written exercise is administered on the same day as the structured interview, and takes 90 minutes to complete.

Format and Scoring of the Written Exercise

To begin the examination, the FBI provides applicants with an assortment of materials that describe a problem or scenario. For example, the materials could include an introduction to the facts or circumstances, statements, charts, records, letters, memoranda, articles, contracts, and other supporting documents. You must carefully review the information provided and write a response that addresses the issues presented. For example, a previous written exercise instructed applicants to write a report to the editor of a newspaper to persuade her that an emerging situation should be investigated. Although the Bureau changes the situations or themes from time to time, the format of the written exercise still boils down to analyzing and reporting on a problem or scenario.

There are no "correct" answers or positions you can take in this examination. Unlike the multiple-choice tests administered during phase I, the written exercise is an open-ended essay examination that gives applicants considerable latitude in formulating their responses. Completed essays are scored by specially trained FBI agents who evaluate how well you analyze the facts and develop an articulate and compelling case in support of your position.

The Purpose of the Written Exercise

This portion of phase II testing is administered to measure skills and abilities that are crucial to carrying out the duties of special agents. The written exercise is similar to testing instruments used in most bar exams for law school graduates, and focuses on the following:

- **Organization.** You must be organized and focused to successfully complete this exercise. One of the most important aspects of the written exercise is your ability to follow directions. Therefore, make sure to read the instructions first and resist the temptation to immerse yourself in the test materials right out of the gate. After reading the instructions and reviewing the materials, take a moment to develop a plan for drafting a well-written composition within the time allotted.

- **Factual analysis and reasoning.** The next step includes a careful evaluation of the materials to sort out the facts and identify the problem or scenario. The factual analysis and reasoning process involves assessing not only relevant facts, but also information that might be irrelevant, vague, incomplete, or contradictory. This step also involves organization skills, which are needed throughout the exercise.

- **Decision-making and problem solving.** Another important aspect of the written exercise—and the work of FBI special agents—involves formulating strategies for reaching a solution to the problem or accomplishing an objective. In this step, you must determine how you are most likely to succeed in achieving positive results and which facts to discuss in your response.

- **Attention to detail.** One of the greatest challenges of the written exercise is sorting out a great deal of information and focusing on important details without being distracted by unimportant or irrelevant information. It is critical that you include an accurate analysis of the problem or scenario and all appropriate details that are necessary to support your position.

- **Written communication skills.** Of course, the exercise is designed to determine whether you have adequate written communication skills necessary to perform successfully as an FBI special agent. Therefore, your composition should be similar to papers you submitted to your eighth-grade English teacher—well organized, logical, intelligible, and grammatically correct.

A Sample Written Exercise Question

You are a member of your local school board. The school board is studying ways to reduce vandalism at the buildings within the school district. You have been appointed to write a report to the school superintendent about the problem of vandalism and how to solve it.

To help you get started, the school board has given you the following chart, which provides information about the extent of vandalism within the school district over the last seven years. Common acts of vandalism have included damaged furniture, broken windows, graffiti, damaged trees and athletic fields, slashed vehicle tires, and damaged fences. Sixty-five percent of those arrested and convicted of committing the vandalism have been members of local teen gangs within the school district. According to the United States Department of Justice, community policing and police-school liaison programs have been very effective in reducing vandalism and other crimes at schools nationwide.

The school board wants you to discuss ways to prevent some of the different types of vandalism in the school district. In your report, describe the extent of vandalism and discuss what you think are the primary causes. Then present the board with a plan to stop these crimes and solve the problem.

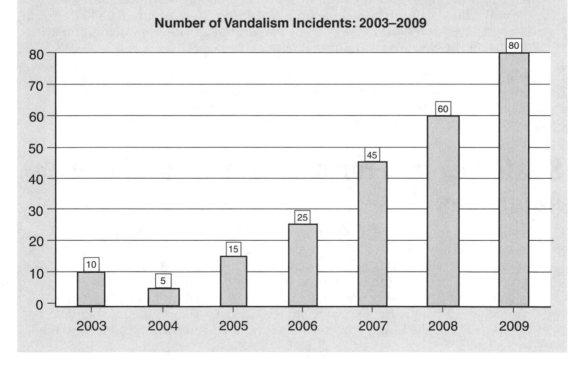

Number of Vandalism Incidents: 2003–2009

Additional Tips for the Written Exercise

Before beginning the exercise, read the situation and instructions very carefully—more than once, if necessary—to ensure that you understand the exercise. If you have any questions about the examination, ask the test administrator for information or clarification.

Although your approach to the written exercise is clearly a matter of personal preference and style, well-written essays are likely to share a number of common qualities. After you have read the introductory materials, do not rush into writing the essay immediately. Instead, take some time to prepare and outline an organized and logical presentation. If it is practical to do so, give prime consideration to summarizing your position in the first paragraph, and then carefully develop your position over the remainder of the essay. Summarizing your position in the final paragraph also is a good idea.

Overall, your essay should provide a thorough and detailed argument for your strategy or course of action based on common sense and accurate analysis of the issues. Whenever possible, support your position with specific examples or discussion of expected outcomes. Most importantly, remember to stay focused and articulate your ideas clearly using standard English.

Preparing for FBI New Agent Training

Now that phase I and phase II testing is out of the way and your background investigation has been initiated, you will need to pass the Physical Fitness Test (PFT). The Bureau is looking for a reasonable assurance that you will succeed in physical fitness activities during New Agent Training, and sending you through the PFT beforehand is the best way to find out whether you have what it takes. Therefore, as discussed in chapter 4, you must successfully complete four events—including push-ups, sit-ups, a 300-meter timed sprint, and a 1.5-mile timed run—to be eligible for a seat at the FBI Academy. The PFT also is given three times during New Agent Training (see chapter 8 for additional details on the New Agent Training program).

You must be in excellent physical condition before reporting to Quantico because there will not be enough time available to get into shape. After all, the first of the three PFTs held during New Agent Training is given during the first week.

Strategies for Professional Support Position Applicants

As discussed in chapter 6, the hiring process for professional support positions differs in some ways from the special agent hiring process. Among the primary differences, they must participate in job interviews that could differ widely from one position to another. In addition to the tips discussed at the beginning of this chapter relating to application forms, professional support candidates can apply the following strategies when tackling the most critical components of the hiring process: the online application and resume, and the interview.

Tips for Completing the Online Application and Resume

The most significant difference between hiring processes carried out by the federal government and those of private-sector firms is the use of Knowledge, Skills, and Abilities (KSA) statements to evaluate applicants' qualifications. Although the FBI no longer requests KSA statements, applicants still must describe their education, experience, training, accomplishments, and awards as they relate to the selection criteria for various positions and submit it to the FBI online. This is accomplished through questions asked in the online application, and the information also is provided in the resume you cut and paste into the online application. In other words, although KSA statements are a thing of the past, you must submit the same information formerly addressed in KSA statements to be a competitive applicant, although in a different format.

For example, depending on the setting of the position, an FBI biologist (forensic examiner) applicant must answer online application questions and include details in his or her resume to address elements such as the following:

- Knowledge of biological principles and practices
- Skill in interpreting test results and evaluating data
- Skill in oral and written communication
- Ability to operate various scientific instruments
- Ability to organize, plan, and prioritize testing and analysis activities

The importance of matching your knowledge, skills, and abilities to those the FBI is seeking cannot be overstated. The bottom line is that although the job interview often serves as the deciding factor in hiring decisions, you are not likely to make it to the interview stage if your online application responses and resume do not set you apart as one of the most competitive applicants in the pool. Whether you are applying for employment with the FBI or any other federal agency, you can actually outshine more qualified competition if you take the time to properly match your knowledge, skills, and abilities to the selection criteria.

Evaluating Your Knowledge, Skills, and Abilities

Before answering online application questions and preparing your resume, you must carefully evaluate your background and experience to determine what career skills you have to offer. It is critical that you carefully analyze the tasks you performed and your accomplishments at each job you held.

The next step is to create an exhaustive list of the skills you developed. Do not limit the list to full-time employment experience. Also include any part-time or volunteer work, internship experience, and co-op positions. Make a list of all professional memberships, achievements, awards, certificates, licenses, leadership activities, proficiency in foreign languages, special skills, public-speaking experience, and other relevant activities. Examine each item on the list and think about the skills or talents they require. Virtually all jobs, internships, extracurricular activities, hobbies, and other pursuits require particular knowledge, skills, and abilities, many of which might be transferable to the position you are seeking. Write them all down. Also list the schools, training seminars, and workshops you attended (including dates and locations), and any degrees, honors, fellowships, and certificates you have received. The accuracy of your online application responses and quality of your resume depends mostly on the depth and thoroughness of your effort in this step. Don't skimp here.

Matching Your KSAs to the Position

After you have prepared a list of your knowledge, skills, and abilities, you must match them to the job tasks discussed in the "Major Duties" section of the vacancy announcements, and also to the KSAs discussed in the online application questions. If you *carefully* read the Major Duties section and online application questions, you will know *exactly* what the FBI is looking for and the criteria with which applicants will be evaluated.

It is critical that you tailor your resume to the specific requirements of each targeted position, highlighting all of your education, training, experience, talents, and accomplishments that demonstrate your ability to perform the job skills. Do not make the mistake of providing generic job descriptions that present little or no information about your individual accomplishments. Instead, clearly describe your specific responsibilities and achievements. Also, do not overlook any experience and accomplishments that are related in any way to the career you are pursuing. These could include interacting with the public, gathering and organizing information, resolving complaints, troubleshooting, solving problems, writing reports, making oral presentations, using computers, establishing and attaining goals, following organizational policies and procedures, and coordinating projects with other people or organizations. Also highlight any experience that demonstrates communication skills, initiative, leadership, dependability, persistence, innovation, and the ability to perform in stressful situations.

A sample resume with the proper format for pasting into the FBI Online Application is shown in figure 7.1. This is a resume for an actual applicant for a support position with the FBI, although the name has been changed. It was written by federal resume writer Cory Edwards of Partnering for Success in Sterling, Virginia.

Jason P. Shelby
105 E. Fike's Lane; Sterling, VA 20164
(703) 444-7712
jpshelby@aol.com

SSN: 228-98-1212
Federal Status: N/A
Citizenship: U.S.
Veterans' Preference: N/A
Announcement Number: 2005-IT-2435-B4

PROFESSIONAL SUMMARY

Current college student with expertise in computer programming and networking systems. Successfully completed all Honors courses in General Education. Proven ability to troubleshoot and resolve technical problems. Strong team member, making significant team and individual contributions. Track record of innovative, creative solutions. Outstanding customer service skills. DoD Top Secret Security Clearance with NRO Counter-Intelligence Polygraph.

QUALIFICATIONS

* Proficient in programming with C/C++, PERL, SQL, Java, RISC Assembly Language, Flex/Lex, Yacc/Bison, JavaScript, and HTML
* Familiar with Bash, Lisp, and ColdFusion
* Outstanding ability to quickly research, learn, and use new skills necessary to complete tasks
* Proficient in Web protocols and technologies and database system design
* Experience performing systems administration, software testing and integration, software project lifecycle development, and network/information security
* Excellent written and oral communication skills
* Ability to work efficiently as part of a team or independently

ADDITIONAL TECHNICAL SKILLS

* Highly Skilled in UNIX; Solaris; Linux; Windows 2000, 2003, XP; Apache, MS Office Products.
* Experienced in Concurrent Versions System, Wireless Networking Technologies, Network Protocol Design and Implementation, Cisco Internetworking Equipment, Internet Filtering and Proxying Technologies.
* Familiar with Visual C++, MS IIS, Oracle, Thin Client technologies.

EDUCATION

Bachelor of Science, Computer Science
George Mason University, August 2006
Related classes successfully completed: C++ levels 1-3, Computer Systems Architecture, Software Design Theory, Unified Modeling Language, Advanced Network Programming, Database Design, Data Structures and Analysis of Algorithms, Introduction to Artificial Intelligence, Operating System Design, Compiler Design, and technical writing classes.

RELATED EMPLOYMENT EXPERIENCE

Systems Programmer
Blue Data Solutions; Sterling, VA
7/2002-12/2002 / 40 hours per week
Salary: $35,000 per year
Supervisor: Jeff Jones (571) 123-9384
* Developed replacement system to automatically manage and interpret incoming e-mail. System successfully designed to determine contents of e-mail and take appropriate actions based on customer's requests. New system increased processing efficiency tenfold, allowing thousands of messages to be processed per minute with far greater accuracy.

(continued)

Figure 7.1: A sample resume for an FBI support position applicant.

(continued)

* Designed and collaborated in implementation of enhanced server network, including configuring and installing multiple pieces of Cisco networking equipment. Design consisted of gigabit backbone connecting multiple subnets with separate connections to Internet. System was designed with automatic failover capabilities, successfully minimizing impact of equipment failure.

Contract Programmer
Traveling Wheels, Inc.; Manassas, VA
Summer 2002 / 15 hours per week
Salary: Varied
Supervisor: Paulette Myers (703) 234-9586
* Developed Web-based system to track and process orders from multiple suppliers, track daily register receipts, and compute company bonuses, significantly improving efficiency and accuracy.

Network Administrator
XYZ Desktop Solutions; Fairfax, VA
Summer 2000 / 40 hours per week
Salary: $27,000 per year
Supervisor: Jeff Dinzel (703) 471-0473
* Formulated, designed, tested, and successfully implemented plan to restructure physical computer network, resulting in increased efficiency, usability, and security.
* Handled day-to-day network activities, including recognizing problems and needs and developing, testing, and implementing applicable solutions.

Information Technology Volunteer
Fairfax Church; Sterling, VA
1996-present / 10-15 hours per week
Salary: None (volunteer)
Supervisor: Frank Zelnick (703) 402-9281
* Manage in-house network duties, including server maintenance and addition, Website management, Internet connectivity, and general network infrastructure management.
* Developed several Web-based administration tools in PERL and C++ to facilitate easier management of network facilities and generate real-time custom log reports.
* Designed, built, and continue to maintain Website using PERL, MySQL, and various templating techniques to provide a front end to more than 20 years of teachings. Website includes session management, members-only sections, and permissions-based administrative functions.

COMPUTER-RELATED SKILLS

* More than 7 years of experience using Linux for many server-related tasks.
* Extremely proficient with all Microsoft-based operating systems.
* Skilled in using most office applications, including Microsoft Office, OpenOffice, and StarOffice.
* Experience using Adobe Acrobat and Microsoft Visio to create technical documentation and other related documents.
* Experience configuring and installing Cisco Networking Equipment.

HONORS AND AWARDS

* Crew Most Valuable Player (MVP) Award, Blue Data Solutions (2002)
* Technician of the Year Award, XYZ Desktop Solutions (2000)
* Dean's List, all semesters, George Mason University (2000-2004)

Tips for Professional Support Interviews

As discussed in chapter 6, the most competitive professional support applicants must participate in either structured or semi-structured interviews toward the end of the application process. Considering that most FBI careers require confidence and interpersonal skills, interviewers will evaluate these attributes carefully, in addition to other criteria. Personal interviews provide knowledgeable and well-prepared applicants with a golden opportunity to showcase their qualifications. The following strategies are useful in making a positive impression.

Interview Preparation

The first step in preparing for the personal interview is to learn about the FBI and the position being filled. If you are knowledgeable in these areas, you will be far more likely to adequately articulate what you have to offer, while also sending the message that you are serious about a career with the Bureau. Some applicants conduct no more than minimal research about the careers they are seeking, and it shows. It is best to present yourself in the most positive light by showing that you have done your homework. Remember that your goal is to demonstrate that you are the best fit for the job, so it only stands to reason that you will make a more positive impact if you are knowledgeable about the division or unit filling the position and how it can use your skills.

Be sure to review your resume and application prior to the interview because many interview questions are likely to be based on information you provided in these documents. Interviewers often start off by confirming information that applicants provided months prior to the interview. Brush up on the details so as not to provide contradictory information. In addition, be prepared to discuss any significant changes that occurred after you submitted your resume and application. These could include developments such as a promotion or other change of positions, a change of employers, degrees or professional certifications you earned, or any awards or professional recognition you received.

Also be prepared to ask questions during the interview. A one-way job interview that consists only of questions asked by the employer and none by the applicant is more of an interrogation than an interview. An exchange of information is appropriate for virtually all job interviews, and applicants should be prepared to ask meaningful questions about the FBI, the division, and the position.

During the Interview

One of the most effective strategies you can apply is to focus on the positive during the interview. In other words, answer questions in a direct and positive manner and speak positively of present and former employers whenever possible. You can express a positive attitude and interest in the position using information you gathered to prepare for the interview. Explain how your experience, education, and training will make you productive in the shortest time with minimal supervision. Sell yourself with specific examples of your skills and accomplishments.

Candidates who perform well during job interviews owe much of their success to good listening skills. Those who make an effort to listen attentively for information about the position and the agency also tend to ask better questions, which sets them apart from others. Always listen carefully and take a brief moment to think about each question before responding.

Considering that job interviews are designed to provide an exchange of information, feel free to ask questions during the interview. The interviewers will expect you to ask questions about the FBI, working conditions, training programs, advancement opportunities, job performance measures, and other issues. Having the confidence to ask appropriate questions during an interview will not only make a positive impression, but will also allow you to become more informed about the Bureau and the position.

After the Interview

It is possible that the interviewers will ask you to provide copies of references, certificates, diplomas, transcripts, or any other credentials that were not requested prior to the interview. Be sure to provide these documents or any other requested information as soon as possible after an interview; otherwise, you might lose consideration for the position. Also send a brief letter of appreciation to thank the participants for their time and reiterate your interest in the position. Finally, in an effort to make each interview a learning experience, evaluate your performance by asking yourself whether you prepared adequately, presented your qualifications effectively, listened well, asked appropriate questions, and learned all that you needed to know about the position. By answering these questions as objectively as possible, you will be able to identify specific ways you can improve your interviewing skills.

Strategies for Internship Applicants

For many full-time FBI personnel, the road to the Bureau began with an FBI internship. Whether you pursue an FBI Honors Internship, National Center for the Analysis of Violent Crime Internship, FBI Academy Internship, or any other Bureau internship, you must put your best foot forward to be competitive in the selection process. Consider the following strategies to increase your chances of landing an internship with the world's best-known law enforcement agency.

Information Is Power

Unfortunately, many college students who are interested in landing a full-time career with the FBI or another law enforcement agency are unaware of FBI internship opportunities that are available to graduate and undergraduate students. This can be good news for you, however, because you are holding the information in your hands. Chapter 9 provides an overview of each FBI internship program, including eligibility, application procedures, selection processes, intern assignments, and training. You can also learn about FBI internship opportunities by visiting career fairs that the Bureau attends, or by contacting applicant coordinators at FBI field offices. (A list of field offices is in appendix J.) When you know what is available and how to take the steps to land an internship, you are halfway there.

Make Your Own Opportunities

The second step to landing an FBI internship—or any internship—is to realize that you must get the ball rolling on your own. Countless college students who are close to graduation approach professors and expect to obtain an internship on the way out the door. As a result, these students almost always graduate with no internship or practical experience under their belts, and often with little direction in their career search. Similar to internships with other agencies, the application process for FBI internships starts 10 to 12 months prior to the starting date. You must meet specific deadlines. You must also realize that college professors and internship coordinators typically are swamped with myriad responsibilities, and that internships most often go to students who are persistent and willing to do much of the legwork themselves. Although academic transcripts, letters of recommendation, or other documents must be submitted by the college, FBI internship application processes must be initiated by the student.

Application Materials

As discussed at the beginning of this chapter, it is important to provide truthful and accurate information in all application materials; otherwise, your application might be delayed or rejected. In addition, be sure to meet all application deadlines, including those for the submission of forms, transcripts, and recommendation letters that others have been asked to submit on your behalf. In other words, stay abreast of things throughout the application process.

Describing Your Experience

Similar to applying for full-time positions with the FBI, you must submit a resume or a detailed application form (or both) to begin the selection process. Carefully evaluate your experience and education before completing these materials, including all full-time and any part-time employment, volunteer work, community service you have performed, and your involvement in professional organizations. Also be sure to provide details of any achievements, awards, leadership activities, licenses or certificates, or special skills you possess. (For additional tips on what to include, see "Strategies for Professional Support Position Applicants," earlier in this chapter.)

Describing Previous Internships

Many applicants for FBI internships have already completed internships with other agencies, firms, or organizations. Always list internships as separate positions on your application or resume, similar to regular employment, so that you will have adequate space to describe your experiences in detail. In doing so, it is critical that you describe exactly what you did rather than what you observed. Under separate headings for each internship, provide complete details of your activities and place emphasis on the specific tasks you performed and any accomplishments. These often provide valuable hands-on experience that could place you ahead of other applicants.

Submitting Application Materials

After you have spent hours putting together your application package, it would be unfortunate if it was misdirected or lost. One of the most important aspects of the application process is to be sure that you send the package to the right address. Mail that is misdirected—either at the FBI or on the way there—could be delayed for days or weeks before it ends up in the right hands. Also, submit all of your application materials via first-class mail or through a major package courier service, such as UPS or FedEx. Mailed packages should be sent either certified with "return receipt" service, or by Priority Mail with "delivery confirmation" service. UPS and FedEx provide both tracking and delivery confirmation automatically. Spending a few extra pennies will give you assurance (and supporting details) that your materials were received by the FBI, as well as peace of mind.

Tips for Internship Interviews

The next step in the process involves a personal interview, at the FBI field office that processes your application for the Honors Internship; at FBI Headquarters for Presidential Management Fellows (PMF) candidates; or in the Quantico, Virginia, area for NCAVC and FBI Academy internships. In some cases, the FBI conducts interactive televised interviews with candidates who would otherwise be required to travel to Washington or Quantico. For these interviews, candidates report to a local television station and the interview is broadcast live via satellite.

Interview Questions

The nature of interview questions depends mostly on the type of internship for which you are applying. For example, interviews for PMF candidates are likely to be more elaborate than those conducted for FBI Academy, Honors, and NCAVC applicants because these internships lead directly to full-time positions with the FBI. Therefore, PMF candidates are likely to be asked more detailed questions that focus on their career interests and qualifications. On the other hand, interviews for FBI Academy, Honors, and NCAVC internships are similar to job interviews for many entry-level positions. In other words, the FBI does not expect these internship applicants to have extensive experience. In addition to answering questions that are targeted specifically to the internship they are seeking, candidates should be prepared to answer a number of general questions, such as the following:

- What can you tell me about yourself?
- What can you tell me about this division?
- What would you like to accomplish during the internship?
- Do you have any particular qualities that will be helpful during your internship?
- What are your major strengths and weaknesses?
- What accomplishment are you most proud of?
- What kinds of tasks, assignments, or projects motivate you the most?
- Why have you chosen to pursue a career in this field?

- What are your career goals?

- How would your most recent supervisor describe you?

- What can you tell me about yourself that is not on your resume or application?

- Do you have any questions about the internship?

In addition to the "traditional" questions in the preceding list, it also is possible that you will be asked behavioral questions during the internship interview. Therefore, you should review the special agent phase II examples shown previously in this chapter so that you will have a general idea of what to expect. Regardless of the interview format, if you keep in mind the knowledge, skills, and abilities the interviewers are looking for, you should be able to predict many—if not most—of the questions, which should serve you well.

Questions You Should Ask

Regardless of the internship you have applied for, you will be given an opportunity toward the end of the interview to ask questions. Asking questions serves not only as a means of gathering information, but also demonstrates your interest in the internship. Be careful, however, not to ask questions that have already been answered during the interview or questions with obvious answers. Interviewers can assess your maturity, communication skills, and professionalism based on your questions, so it is important to be prepared and to ask questions that you truly would like answered. Also, have several questions in mind, because the interviewer might answer some of them during the interview. Generally speaking, your questions should be geared toward learning more about the internship and the division to which you will be assigned. Here are a few examples of questions you could ask:

- Could you describe a typical day for interns in this division?

- What sort of assignments or projects do interns work on?

- Are interns rotated to other divisions?

- Do interns have an opportunity to participate in training or seminars?

- What have interns found to be most satisfying or rewarding in their internships?

- How do you measure the performance of interns?

Other Interviewing Tips

Preparation, eye contact, listening skills, and a positive attitude are crucial to your success during internship interviews. For guidance on these and other aspects of the interview process, see "Tips for Professional Support Interviews," under "Strategies for Professional Support Position Applicants," earlier in this chapter.

CHAPTER 8

FBI Training

"Anyone can shoot a gun. What counts is how well you stand up when someone is shooting back at you."

—Louis L'Amour

O ne of the Bureau's most important functions is training FBI special agents, support employees, and personnel from other law enforcement agencies. The FBI is widely recognized as one of the finest providers of law enforcement training in the world. The Bureau's training functions are managed by its training division, which is based at the FBI Academy in Quantico, Virginia. This division is responsible for training all new employees and providing continuing education for the existing FBI workforce. The division conducts advanced training for state and local law enforcement personnel at every level and in many disciplines, and also manages the FBI Academy. In response to the growth of international crime and terrorism, many of the Bureau's training programs are also offered in foreign countries to our international law enforcement allies. To maintain a skilled and professional workforce, and to meet the needs of other law enforcement agencies, training will continue to be one of the FBI's most urgent priorities.

The FBI Academy

Since its opening in 1972, the FBI Academy has remained on the cutting edge of law enforcement training, assistance, and research as one of the world's most highly regarded law enforcement training centers. The Academy trains three primary groups of students, including newly hired FBI and Drug Enforcement Administration (DEA) special agents participating in basic training programs, Bureau personnel who attend professional development courses and seminars throughout their careers, and representatives of other law enforcement agencies who attend a variety of specialized programs.

FBI Academy Facilities

The FBI Academy is located about 40 miles southwest of Washington, D.C., on the United States Marine Corps base at Quantico, Virginia. The Academy grounds encompass nearly 400 wooded acres of land and more than 20 buildings. The primary training complex includes a classroom building, audiovisual facilities, administrative offices, three dormitory buildings, a dining hall, a library, research facilities, a 1,000-seat auditorium, a chapel, a gymnasium, and an outside track. In addition to the main complex, there is a mock city known as "Hogan's Alley" that is used for practical training, as well as indoor and outdoor firearms ranges, a 1.1-mile pursuit and defensive driving track, and a fully equipped garage. The DEA training academy is also on site and shares the FBI's facilities.

Operational Units at the FBI Academy

Five sections and two dozen units are based at the FBI Academy, where they provide support to a variety of Academy training functions and operations in the field. The following sections summarize the primary functions of these components.

The New Agents' Training Program Section

This section is composed of the components that are responsible for presenting the FBI New Agents' Training Program, including the New Agents' Training Unit, Practical Applications Unit, Physical Training Unit, Firearms Training Unit, Investigative Training Unit, and Defensive Systems Unit.

New Agents' Training Unit

The New Agents' Training Unit coordinates the 21-week New Agents' Training program. The training curriculum is broken down into investigative and tactical, noninvestigative, and administrative training components. Staff from this unit oversee the program, which consists of academics, firearms instruction, physical training, defensive tactics, and practical exercises. They are also responsible for evaluating trainees as to their suitability to be FBI special agents.

Practical Applications Unit

The Practical Applications Unit manages a wide variety of practical training events and problem exercises that the FBI Academy carries out. This unit provides instruction in areas such as surveillance, arrest procedures, and tactical street survival techniques. Practical Applications Unit staff present training programs to new agent trainees, veteran FBI agents, and law enforcement officers from other agencies, such as the Bureau's Law Enforcement Training for Safety and Survival Program and the Tactical Emergency Vehicle Operators Course.

Physical Training Unit

This FBI Academy component manages the Bureau's physical fitness and defensive tactics programs. Physical Training Unit instructors conduct training for newly appointed FBI special agents, FBI National Academy attendees, the Bureau's in-service training program participants, and state and local law enforcement officers attending FBI Academy training programs. This unit's instructional staff consists of permanently assigned fitness advisors, defensive tactics instructors, and nutrition advisors.

Firearms Training Unit

Firearms training at the FBI Academy is carried out by the Firearms Training Unit, which is also responsible for administering training programs for special agents in the field and conducting a variety of firearms-related research projects. Firearms Training Unit instructors teach new agent trainees to shoot all Bureau-issued weapons safely and efficiently, and provide advanced firearms training to special agents and task force members in the field.

Investigative Training Unit

The Investigative Training Unit offers instruction to new agent trainees, National Academy students, intelligence analysts, and others concerning investigative and intelligence techniques, national security investigation methods, and case management. Instructors in this unit teach white-collar crime, organized crime, drug trafficking, domestic and international terrorism, informant development, and other topics to prepare FBI special agents to conduct criminal investigations in these areas. Members of the Investigative Training Unit also teach courses attended by police commanders at the FBI National Academy, by Bureau personnel during in-service training programs, and off-site by law enforcement personnel throughout the United States and internationally.

Defensive Systems Unit

The FBI Academy's Defensive Systems Unit provides services, equipment, and supplies for New Agents' training, and also administers the FBI's weapons, ammunitions, and related equipment programs. This unit is responsible for the procurement of handguns, shotguns, submachine guns, other weapons, ammunition, and related equipment, and for the maintenance and inventory of the FBI's firearms. Defensive Systems Unit personnel also are tasked with the continuous evaluation of all weapons issued to FBI personnel.

The Intelligence Training Section

The Intelligence Training Section is responsible for all basic and advanced intelligence training carried out at the FBI Academy. This section includes the following operational units.

Basic Analyst Training Unit

The FBI Academy's Basic Analyst Training Unit instructors ensure that special agents and intelligence analysts receive the highest-quality intelligence, counterterrorism, and counterintelligence training available. This unit administers the Intelligence Basic Course for the Bureau's newly appointed intelligence analysts.

Advanced Analyst Training Unit

Advanced Analyst Training Unit staff present a variety of training programs to all levels of personnel from the FBI and other law enforcement agencies. This unit is responsible for administering all coursework related to the Intelligence Community Advanced Analyst Program, analytic leadership courses, and other advanced intelligence programs at the FBI Academy, interagency partnering schools, and the National Intelligence University network.

HUMINT Operations Training Unit

Human Intelligence (HUMINT) training is the responsibility of the FBI Academy's HUMINT Operations Training Unit. This unit provides training to FBI personnel relating to the collection of intelligence information from human sources in support of the FBI's criminal investigative and national security missions. Training presented by this unit focuses on the collection of information openly, as when FBI special agents interview witnesses or suspects, and also through covert means.

The Law Enforcement Programs Section

This section is responsible for the majority of the Bureau's leadership development training programs for FBI personnel and outside agencies, and includes the following units.

Law Enforcement Communication Unit

The Law Enforcement Communication Unit teaches courses pertaining to oral and written communication. In the New Agents' Training Program, instruction is geared to interviewing, informant development, and field office communications. Courses presented for the National Academy include interviewing and interrogation, instructor development, public speaking, media relations, contemporary issues in law enforcement, and effective writing. This unit presents in-service training to FBI personnel and instruction in various police training programs. It also publishes the *FBI Law Enforcement Bulletin*—the most widely read law enforcement publication in the world—which is distributed to domestic and foreign law enforcement agencies and professionals in the criminal justice field.

National Academy Unit

Since 1935, the FBI National Academy has provided leadership and management training for mid- and upper-level police commanders from around the world. The FBI National Academy program focuses on leadership development, behavioral science, law, communication, health and fitness, and forensic science. Among these disciplines, attendees can take courses in white-collar crime, youth and gang crime, hate crimes, racial profiling, community policing, computer crime, communication skills, abnormal psychology, budgeting and finance, stress management, ethics, and other subjects. Instructors in the program include permanent staff of the FBI Academy, personnel from various FBI field offices, and visiting scholars who are recognized experts in their fields. More than 42,000 law enforcement officers from the United States and more than 150 countries have graduated from the program since its inception in 1935.

International Training and Assistance Unit

The Bureau's international training efforts are managed and coordinated by the International Training and Assistance Unit. This FBI Academy component develops training programs for international law enforcement agencies to successfully combat and prevent terrorist acts against U.S. citizens and institutions in the United States and worldwide. The International Training and Assistance Unit works with other FBI operational divisions, such as the Office of International Operations, FBI Legal Attaché offices abroad, the Department of Justice's Office of International Programs, the State Department, and U.S. embassies overseas.

Behavioral Science Unit

Training programs, research, and consultation in the behavioral and social sciences for the FBI, other law enforcement agencies, and the military are carried out by the Behavioral Science Unit. This unit conducts research and presents instruction relating to criminal and forensic psychology, crime analysis, death investigation, community policing and problem-solving strategies, gangs and gang behavior, interpersonal violence, law enforcement officers killed and assaulted in the line of duty, and stress management in law enforcement.

FBI Leadership Training Unit

The FBI Leadership Training Unit teaches leadership skills and concepts to Bureau employees, including ethical leadership training to new agents and intelligence analysts. This unit also establishes a leadership development vision within the FBI and works to implement that vision through various training programs. The Leadership Training Unit teaches leadership in the context of domestic and international law enforcement cooperation, intelligence, and counterterrorism to FBI employees as they progress through their careers.

Community Leadership Development Unit

This unit provides professional liaison, consultation, and executive leadership education to the FBI and other law enforcement agencies. The Community Leadership Development Unit leads or supports programs such as the FBI National Academy, National Executive Institute, Law Enforcement Executive Development Seminar, Regional Command Colleges, and the Domestic Security Executive Academy.

The Office of Technology Research and Curriculum Development

The Office of Technology Research and Curriculum Development ensures that FBI training is designed and implemented using the most effective and up-to-date technology and learning methods available. This section includes the Curriculum Development and Evaluation Unit, the Distance Learning Unit, the Virtual Academy Unit, and the FBI Library Unit.

Curriculum Development and Evaluation Unit

The Curriculum Development and Evaluation Unit directs, designs, and develops instructional learning materials for traditional classroom instruction and distance education for the FBI and its criminal justice and intelligence partners. It also evaluates existing training, helps assess course or program strategies, and provides instructor training to FBI personnel and law enforcement officers from other agencies.

Distance Learning Technology Unit

This unit identifies and uses various technologies to create audio, video, graphics, Internet, and simulation productions to facilitate a variety of self-paced and instructor-led training programs to meet the training and job performance needs of the FBI and other agencies. The Distance Learning Technology Unit offers multimedia-based instruction, satellite broadcasts, teleconferencing, and videotape instruction services.

Virtual Academy Unit

This unit develops, manages, and operates the FBI Virtual Academy, the Bureau's computer-based training system that hosts 5,000 online courses. The FBI Virtual Academy is used to train FBI employees worldwide through a mix of commercial and custom technology tools. Courses presented through the Virtual Academy are designed to replace many instructor-led classes. FBI Virtual Academy registration is open to all personnel serving in any agency within the criminal justice or intelligence community, including federal, state, local, tribal, and international law enforcement, forensic laboratories, and public safety organizations.

FBI Library Unit

The FBI Library maintains the most complete and up-to-date law enforcement library in the world. The FBI Library is used by Academy students, Training Division staff, other FBI personnel, and other representatives of the law enforcement community. As a primary information center for the FBI and other agencies, the FBI Library provides access to resources reflecting a broad range of perspectives, viewpoints, and approaches. It also offers professional reference services in response to research requests and promotes communication and cooperation among libraries in order to share law enforcement information and resources.

Resource Management Section

Administrative support and resource allocation for the FBI Academy is handled by the Resource Management Section. This section includes the following operational units that are critical to the success of FBI Academy operations.

Strategic Planning and Policy Unit

The mission of the Strategic Planning and Policy Unit is to effectively manage the development of plans, policies, procedures, strategies, accreditation, and resources in support of FBI Academy Training initiatives. This unit works closely with other FBI Academy components to ensure that the Bureau's Training and Development Division initiatives are in alignment with its strategic planning goals.

Financial Management Unit

The mission of the FBI Academy's Financial Management Unit is to support the training objectives of the Director of the FBI by managing the budget of the FBI's Training and Development Division. This includes budget formulation, execution, and reporting activities.

Administrative Services Unit

The Administrative Services Unit provides assistance, guidance, coordination, and the implementation of human resources and other administrative services necessary to support the mission of the FBI Academy. This unit also oversees resource management and personnel actions, and is responsible for FBI Training and Development Division records management.

Training Services Unit

The FBI Academy's Training Services Unit is responsible for managing regional training conferences and seminars, and for scheduling FBI Training and Development Division classes and dormitory rooms in support of the New Agents' Training Program, the FBI National Academy, the Center for Intelligence Training, and other training programs.

Training for FBI Special Agents

The FBI Academy is responsible for training special agent recruits, veteran agents, and professional support personnel through instructional programs that are presented to staff at all levels of the Bureau's workforce. These programs range from the 21-week New Agents' Training program, which provides basic training in a multitude of disciplines, to a variety of courses and seminars that are geared to specific tasks. This section provides an overview of training programs for the Bureau's special agents.

The New Agents' Training Program

All newly appointed special agent candidates are required to complete basic training at the FBI Academy in Quantico, Virginia, regardless of their previous experience, education, or training. Although the trainees are considered full-time FBI employees, their basic training effectively serves as the final stage of the special agent hiring process. The training atmosphere is similar to that of a college campus. A maximum of 50 trainees are assigned to each New Agents' Training class. FBI Academy staff carefully evaluate every aspect of trainees' performance—from their test scores to character and attitude—before they are permitted to graduate from the program. The New Agents' Training program is designed to push trainees' minds and bodies to their limits, leaving them with new tools, a few dozen close friends, and a keen sense of accomplishment and pride.

The graduation ceremony serves as their final assignment at the Academy, during which they are issued their badges and credentials and are sworn in as FBI special agents. During the ceremony, an award is given to the trainees who achieved the highest score in academics, weapons proficiency, and physical fitness. In addition, each graduating class selects a member of the class to receive the *Fidelity, Bravery, and Integrity (FBI) Award*. This is the highest award for a new special agent and recognizes the recipient's commitment to law enforcement ethics, professionalism, and the FBI's core values.

Overview of the Training Curriculum

The FBI New Agents' Training program includes 21 weeks of intensive instruction involving three components, including investigative and tactical training, noninvestigative training, and administrative matters. The program is designed to provide trainees with the basic knowledge and skills they will need to effectively carry out their responsibilities after they are assigned to one of the FBI's field offices. New agents' training consists of about 900 hours of classroom and practical instruction that is spread over four major concentrations, including academics, firearms, physical training and defensive tactics, and practical applications. The program uses a building-block approach, in which lessons and practical exercise are presented in a carefully planned sequence. Following is an overview of the primary subjects of the curriculum.

Investigative and Tactical Subjects

- Defensive Tactics, Arrest Techniques, and Physical Training
- Firearms Training and Qualification
- Legal Subjects
- Interviewing and Interrogation
- Practical Exercises and Management of Integrated Case Scenarios
- Counterterrorism, National Security, and Intelligence Subjects
- Forensic Sciences
- Computer Skills, Data Analysis, and Information Security
- Financial Investigation Tools and Techniques
- Surveillance
- Behavioral Sciences
- Online Sources of Information
- Consensual Monitoring and Title III Wiretaps
- Espionage and Sensitive Operations
- Sources of Information
- Drug Identification and DEA Briefing
- National Crime Information Center
- Background Investigations
- Case Management
- Civil Rights
- Command Post Operations
- Criminal Enterprise Theory
- International Investigations
- Investigative Technology
- Liaison
- Reactive Investigations
- Security Awareness
- Telephone Records Analysis
- Undercover Operations

Noninvestigative Subjects

- Ethical Leadership
- First-Aid, CPR, and Bloodborne Pathogens
- Cultural Diversity
- FBI Office of Professional Responsibility
- Employee Assistance Program
- Equal Employment Opportunity
- New Agents' Training Unit Briefing
- Training Section Chief Briefing
- Victim and Witness Assistance Programs
- FBI Ombudsman

Administrative Subjects

- Federal Employees Retirement System
- FBI Transfer Policy
- Relocation Management
- Vouchers Information
- Nurse Briefing
- Oath of Office

Academics

Academics in the New Agents' Training program consist of a wide range of subject areas that provide a foundation for trainees to build upon throughout their careers. The largest academic block revolves around legal instruction, including more than 70 hours of training on topics such as criminal law, civil law, constitutional law, laws of arrest, admissions and confessions, and civil liability. Trainees also receive more than 70 hours of training in law enforcement communications, which is concerned primarily with interviewing and interrogation, effective writing, and field office communications. Other large training blocks focus on tactical procedures, forensic sciences, counterterrorism and counterintelligence, computer skills, surveillance, and informants.

The FBI has significantly expanded counterterrorism and counterintelligence instruction in the New Agents' Training program since the September 11 terrorist attacks. Prior to 9/11, special agent trainees received only 23 hours of classroom instruction in these areas. The curriculum expanded after the attacks to include 55 hours of counterterrorism and counterintelligence coursework, and has since grown to more than 100 hours. The expansion has resulted in the addition of classes covering FBI intelligence mandates, the intelligence cycle, the U.S. Intelligence Community, intelligence reporting and dissemination procedures, Middle Eastern terrorist threats, the role of FBI intelligence analysts, and other related topics.

Much of the counterterrorism and counterintelligence coursework added since 9/11 was incorporated into the innovative Integrated Case Scenario (ICS). The ICS is an ongoing exercise that begins around the fourth week of training and ends only a few days prior to graduation. This portion of the program includes classroom instruction and practical exercises relating to subjects such as interviewing and interrogation, informant development, financial crimes, data analysis, law, tactical procedures, and FBI paperwork. To begin the exercise, information that serves as the basis for a mock investigation is given to the trainees. From this point forward, they develop additional information through interviews, following leads, surveillance, intelligence-gathering, consensual monitoring, wiretapping operations, and other methods. The exercise culminates with a practical exercise at the Hogan's Alley complex that results in multiple arrests. The ICS exercise provides critical hands-on experience that is carefully designed to prepare the trainees for their responsibilities as special agents.

The remainder of the academic portion of the program covers subjects such as the history of the FBI, behavioral sciences, case management, civil rights, ethics, first-aid and CPR, information security, international investigations, and undercover operations. Noninvestigative training is headlined by ethics instruction, which covers FBI ethics standards, the ethical basis of the Constitution, classic philosophy on ethics, the nature of criminal and noncriminal misconduct, and the functions of the FBI Office of Professional Responsibility. Ethics coursework focuses on corruption, deception, ethical problems unique to law enforcement, and the standards of conduct for executive branch personnel. This training also includes a lesson concerning the Holocaust, in which six million Jews were killed and others were persecuted in Nazi-controlled territory, so that trainees will understand the consequences when law enforcement fails to protect citizens, their civil rights and dignity, and their moral and humane values. During Hitler's reign, German police officers rounded up Jews, political adversaries, and other targeted groups.

The Holocaust lesson includes a guided tour of the United States Holocaust Memorial Museum in Washington, D.C., where trainees learn further about the role the police played during the Holocaust.

Firearms Training

Firearms training is the largest single block of instruction in the program. Special agent trainees spend more than 100 hours developing their firearms skills at an indoor firing range, eight outdoor firing ranges, four skeet ranges, and a 200-yard rifle range. This training is designed to teach familiarity and confidence with semiautomatic pistols, shotguns, and submachine guns. Instruction is broken into three areas, consisting of fundamental marksmanship, combat survival shooting, and judgmental shooting. Various techniques are taught, including shooting at stationary and moving targets; from behind barricades and other forms of cover or concealment; from standing, kneeling, and prone positions; and when moving into various positions. Each trainee fires about 4,000 rounds of ammunition during the program, and trainees are responsible for maintaining and cleaning their own weapons. Those who either handle weapons in an unsafe manner—regardless of their shooting proficiency or qualifications scores—or fail to qualify in all firearms courses by the 12th week are dismissed.

Firearms training goes beyond skill development and includes instruction in the Bureau's deadly force policy and judgmental shooting exercises. These areas are examined during one of the most important and stressful segments of the training, during which Firearms Automated Training System (FATS) scenarios are introduced. FATS training consists of a full spectrum of realistic scenarios that are projected on a large video screen in front of participants. In these computerized scenarios, trainees are effectively placed in the midst of incidents, requiring them to respond to various threats and situations, many of which require them to draw or fire simulated firearms at the screen to protect themselves or others. The primary purpose of FATS scenarios is to test participants' judgment, including adherence to the Bureau's deadly force policy. FATS equipment also keeps track of shooters' reaction time and accuracy.

Practical Applications

Practical application exercises provide realistic, hands-on application of material covered in the classroom. In addition to focusing on skill development, these multidisciplinary exercises help trainees to build confidence, overcome obstacles, and learn how to work with others as a team. Most of these exercises—known as "practicals" or "case exercises"—are conducted in the Hogan's Alley complex, where academics, firearms, defensive tactics, communications skills, and legal knowledge are collectively put to the test. Hogan's Alley consists of facades and buildings replicating a small town, including a bank, movie theater, drugstore, post office, courthouse, used car lot, and other facilities. Behind the facades are fully functioning classrooms, audiovisual facilities, storage areas, and administrative and maintenance offices. The Practical Applications Unit manages practical instruction throughout the program.

Practical scenarios carried out in the Hogan's Alley complex focus primarily on surveillance techniques, arrest procedures, and tactical street survival skills. In these exercises, trainees are taken through realistic scenarios revolving around bank robberies, assaults, hostage situations, illegal drug transactions, kidnapping incidents, daytime and nighttime surveillance of criminal suspects, felony traffic stops, the execution of search and arrest warrants, and other situations. Some of these exercises require trainees to use guns that fire artificial bullets (containing soap or paint) in order to test their tactical skills. Bureau vehicles, two-way radios, surveillance devices, and other equipment are provided to scenario participants. To increase the level of realism, professional role-players confront the trainees with a variety of problems and situations. Since the terrorist attacks of 9/11, the FBI has incorporated many additional practical scenarios into the New Agents' Training curriculum—including Integrated Case Scenario exercises—in which trainees work with intelligence analysts and use intelligence information.

Other practical exercises carried out within and beyond the Hogan's Alley complex focus on informant development, undercover operations, intelligence gathering, physical and electronic surveillance, driving, interviewing techniques, defensive tactics, firearms proficiency, and other law enforcement skills. For example, surveillance training is conducted on public streets and highways in cities such as Washington, D.C.; Richmond, Virginia; and in other areas. These daytime and nighttime scenarios require trainees to keep sight of suspects who are involved in various activities in vehicles and on foot, and to maintain proper radio communications with one another as a team. Interviewing scenarios are carried out in a variety of settings, including rooms that are outfitted with video cameras. Instructors use videotapes of interviews to evaluate and discuss trainees' questioning and listening skills. Practical training also includes testifying on the witness stand during moot court exercises, during which actual lawyers question trainees about their roles during other training exercises.

Physical Training, Defensive Tactics, and Tactical Subjects

Training that focuses on health, physical fitness, defensive tactics (DT), and other tactical procedures has always been popular with new agent trainees—and an eye-opener. These subjects, which collectively account for more than 100 hours of the program, are taught by fitness advisors, defensive tactics instructors, and nutrition experts from the Academy's Physical Training Unit. Health and fitness training focuses primarily on proper nutrition and the development of muscular strength, flexibility, endurance, agility, and aerobic capacity. Height, weight, and body fat levels are checked at the beginning, middle, and end of the program.

Physical training includes plenty of running, including the grueling "Yellow Brick Road" endurance and obstacle course that was depicted in the movie *The Silence of the Lambs*. To complete this challenging course, informally known as the "Hell Run," trainees must navigate a wooded trail and overcome log hurdles, a tall rope net structure, walls, roped cliffs, barbed wire, rough terrain, and other obstacles. Inspirational signs posted along the route—which is more than six miles long—include messages such as "hurt," "agony," "pain," "pride," "attitude," and "loyalty." The course got its name from the yellow bricks, inscribed with the class numbers from the FBI National Academy, that serve as markers along the way.

Defensive tactics, arrest techniques, and other tactical training revolves around various kicks and strikes, arrest procedures, handcuffing, subject-control holds, pressure-point tactics, boxing, ground fighting, weapon retention and disarming, searching of subjects, building entry principles, and other DT techniques. The use of oleoresin capsicum (OC) "pepper" spray is also covered; during practical exercises, the trainees must be able to make an arrest after being sprayed in the face with OC. Trainees must demonstrate their proficiency in these areas during two DT tests. Tactical training is presented in the always-demanding "Concepts and Tactics for Survival" component.

Supervision and Evaluation of New Agent Trainees

The New Agents' Training program is overseen by supervisory special agents who serve as class supervisors, as well as special agents who serve as field counselors. Class supervisors are permanently assigned to the FBI Academy, whereas field counselors are detailed temporarily to the Academy from FBI field offices for 21 weeks. Field counselors play an important role by providing leadership and serving as mentors to trainees during their early development as special agents. Class supervisors and field counselors also carefully observe and evaluate trainees throughout the program to determine their suitability to perform as FBI special agents.

Requirements for Graduation

To graduate from the program, new agent trainees must pass academic and physical fitness tests, qualify with firearms, pass physical fitness and defensive tactics examinations, and otherwise demonstrate their suitability to serve as FBI special agents. Trainees must pass nine academic examinations (with a score of 85 percent or better) in three legal disciplines, interviewing, national security investigations, criminal investigations, and interrogation.

Trainees are given a physical fitness test (PFT) during the first week, and again around the 7th and 15th weeks of training. This test consists of four events including push-ups, sit-ups, a 300-meter timed sprint, and a 1.5 mile timed run. A fifth event—pull-ups—is added at the end of the test, although this event is not scored for pass/fail purposes. PFT events are scored on a point system, with up to 10 points possible in each event. To pass the PFT, trainees must score at least one point in each event and at least 12 points total (out of a possible 40) on the test. (PFT scoring scales are included in chapter 4.) The PFT not only measures physical fitness, but also provides an indication of trainees' commitment to improve their scores, which demonstrates attributes such as character, initiative, judgment, and maturity. To pass the firearms segment, you must qualify twice with a semiautomatic pistol and once with a shotgun and also demonstrate familiarity with a submachine gun. You must also pass two defensive tactics tests by demonstrating proficiency in various DT skills.

In addition to achieving passing scores in academics, physical fitness, firearms, and defensive tactics, trainees must also demonstrate adherence to the FBI's core values throughout the training program in order to graduate. In other words, test scores alone will not be sufficient if a trainee does not meet the Bureau's standards relating to character, integrity, fairness, and other related criteria. Character and suitability issues are evaluated constantly by class supervisors and field counselors, and also by the Academy's New Agent Review Board in cases where corrective action—including dismissal—is possible.

Professional Development Training for Special Agents

FBI special agents receive periodic professional development training, also known as *in-service training,* to acquire new skills and enhance their knowledge and capabilities throughout their careers. The nature of in-service training depends largely on the needs of individual agents, their responsibilities and special assignments, and the needs of the Bureau at any given time. In-service courses focus on topics such as leadership, management, supervision, ethics, counterterrorism, driving, information technology, and critical-incident stress counseling, among others. Many special agents who serve on special response teams and joint task forces also attend the Bureau's Law Enforcement Safety and Survival Course, which is commonly known as "street survival training."

FBI special agents assigned to counterterrorism and counterintelligence duties after graduating from the New Agents' Training program must complete an additional four weeks of training to prepare them for their first assignment. New agents who assume cybercrime responsibilities after Quantico are given a one-week introductory cybercrime course. Experienced agents who are reassigned to counterterrorism functions attend a one-week terrorism course, and those reassigned to counterintelligence responsibilities complete a four-week interactive CD-ROM training program. Special agents participating in Joint Terrorism Task Force operations also receive additional training.

All special agents are required to complete at least 15 hours of in-service training annually. Training in subjects such as Middle Eastern terrorism, national security matters, financial underpinnings of crime, hate crimes, and bloodborne pathogens is common. All FBI field offices provide eight hours of counterterrorism awareness training for their personnel. FBI special agents and intelligence analysts also receive in-service training concerning the USA PATRIOT Act and the Foreign Intelligence Surveillance Act, which includes details on legal and operational requirements, procedures, and tools that are useful in counterterrorism and national security investigations. In addition, all special agents receive in-service training on the recruitment, development, and management of informants.

Training for Special Response Teams

The Bureau's special response teams require specialized training to develop the particular knowledge and skills they need to succeed in their respective operations. Much of the training attended by team members is held at the FBI Academy, although other sources of training are utilized nationwide and in other countries. This section includes a brief overview of training that is provided to special response teams.

Scuba Team Training

Members of the FBI's scuba team are highly trained and experienced special agents who must maintain stringent physical fitness and watercraft skills that far exceed recreational diving standards. Many team members are scuba instructors. Ongoing training focuses on skills relating to underwater crime scene investigation, evidence collection, search and recovery operations, photography, searching for explosives, diving in varying degrees of currents, night diving, under-ice operations, deep-water diving, helicopter water entries, and diving in zero-visibility conditions. Scuba team members are also trained to use specialized equipment such as scuba regulators, dive computers, underwater scooters, metal detectors, sonar units, global positioning system (GPS) satellite navigation units, underwater communications systems, hand-held underwater video and still cameras, dive watches, wet and dry suits, and surface-supplied air systems.

Evidence Response Team Training

All members of the Bureau's evidence response teams (ERTs), which include special agents and support personnel, attend an 80-hour basic course that provides instruction in crime scene photography, evidence photography, latent fingerprint subjects, crime scene management and documentation, and general physical evidence recovery matters. After they have completed the basic course, ERT members are eligible to attend advanced courses covering topics such as recovery of human remains, blood spatter analysis, and post-blast investigation techniques at bombing crime scenes. ERT training is presented by the FBI and other forensic experts.

Hazardous Materials Response Unit Training

Personnel assigned to the Hazardous Materials Response Unit are trained to safely and effectively respond to criminal acts and other incidents involving hazardous materials, including chemical, biological, and radiological materials. The Hazardous Materials Response Unit trains its personnel in areas such as terrorism, weapons of mass destruction, chemical agents, biological agents, nuclear devices and radiological weapons, hazardous materials regulations, hazardous materials labels, personal protective equipment, breathing devices, decontamination procedures, crime scene preservation and evidence collection, conventional explosives as weapons of mass destruction, downwind hazard analysis, planning for hazardous materials incidents, and the role of first responders. Training in these areas typically includes lectures, multimedia presentations, and practical exercises.

Hostage Rescue Team Training

FBI Hostage Rescue Team training begins with a rigorous two-week selection course, in which prospective team members are carefully evaluated to determine whether they possess the knowledge, skills, and abilities necessary for hostage rescue assignments. Once selected, team members attend a four-month initial training program at the FBI Academy that consists of highly specialized tactical law enforcement instruction. The primary subjects covered during this program and ongoing in-service training include hostage rescue fundamentals and planning, barricaded subject incidents, execution of high-risk arrest and search operations, firearms and defensive tactics, rappelling, weapons of mass destruction, maritime operations, helicopter operations, mobile assaults, and cold weather operations. When team members are not engaged in hostage rescue operations, they participate in full-time training at the FBI Academy and other locations. In order to be prepared for deployment to a wide range of climates and conditions, they also attend training at sites throughout the United States and its territories year-round.

Crisis Negotiation Unit Training

The FBI Crisis Negotiation Unit must be prepared and trained to respond immediately to crisis situations anywhere in the world, 24 hours a day, seven days a week. Initial training for the Bureau's negotiators includes a two-week negotiation course at the FBI Academy. Negotiators also participate in advanced and periodic update training at the FBI Academy, at other sites nationwide, and worldwide in cooperation with foreign law enforcement agencies. The Crisis Negotiation Unit has exchange programs in place through which it conducts training with British, Canadian, Australian, Israeli, German, and South African law enforcement agencies. Crisis negotiation training includes instruction in areas such as incident management, negotiation concepts and techniques, communication skills, behavioral sciences, abnormal psychology, crisis assessment and intervention, suicide intervention, active listening skills, coordination with tactical teams, terrorism, case studies in crisis negotiation, post-incident debriefing, and role-playing scenarios. FBI negotiators are also trained through computer-based simulation training programs that present realistic scenarios involving real-time negotiation dialogue and decision-making applications.

Special Weapons and Tactics Team Training

Special weapons and tactics (SWAT) training prepares FBI SWAT team members for the execution of high-risk arrest and search operations, drug raids, barricaded suspect incidents, sniper assaults, dignitary protection details, and other crisis situations and tactical operations. This training is conducted at the FBI Academy, in various FBI field offices, at law enforcement academies and agencies, and in other locations. To prepare for these incidents, FBI SWAT teams nationwide are trained in intelligence gathering, operational planning, command and control operations, communications, threat assessment methods, strength and conditioning, and legal issues. The teams also participate in ongoing practical training in areas such as building-entry and room-clearing techniques, containment techniques, arrest and subject-control tactics, diversionary techniques, rappelling, vehicle stops and assaults, weapons of mass destruction incidents, and tactical first-aid. Weapons training carried out by SWAT team members includes subjects such as tactical firearms skills, low-light shooting techniques, cover and concealment principles, impact weapons, weapon retention, use of chemical agents, and countersniper issues.

Canine Team Training

FBI canine teams train year-round to develop and maintain the skills required of the dogs and dog handlers to perform their invaluable service for the Bureau. Canine teams attend training provided by state and local police departments; other federal law enforcement agencies; the U.S. Customs and Border Protection's Canine Enforcement Training Center in Front Royal, Virginia; and organizations such as the North American Police Work Dog Association and the United States Police Canine Association. Training focuses primarily on the teams' particular areas of expertise, including the detection of explosives, explosives residues, firearms, marijuana, hashish, cocaine, methamphetamine, and heroin, as well as tracking fleeing criminals and locating missing persons and cadavers. Their training also is concentrated in areas such as animal obedience and behavior, search sequences and techniques, and the recovery and preservation of evidence.

Training for Professional Support Personnel

The FBI ensures that professional support personnel stay abreast of trends and developments in their respective areas of expertise through a variety of training programs. Unlike training for special agents, the majority of FBI personnel who serve in professional support positions do not attend lengthy introductory basic training programs. Instead, those who are hired into entry-level jobs receive on-the-job training. Experienced employees attend periodic professional-development training.

Courses for support personnel are offered at the FBI Academy and various facilities nationwide, within mobile classrooms, through distance-learning applications such as Web-based programs and satellite teleconferences, through interactive video programs, and on CD-ROM. Many of the Bureau's distance-learning programs are created and produced by the FBI Training Network at the FBI Academy, which offers training to FBI personnel and law enforcement officers worldwide. The FBI Training Network is a component of the Academy's Training Development Unit, which carries out broadcast and studio production operations from a television studio located in Hogan's Alley. The remainder of this chapter provides examples of training that is offered to the Bureau's professional support employees.

Auditor Training

To ensure that FBI auditors have the knowledge, skills, and abilities to carry out their responsibilities in an efficient and productive manner, the Bureau offers in-service and on-the-job training, including opportunities to attend professional development seminars and conferences. These focus on subjects such as audit planning, setting accounting and auditing standards, report writing, interviewing, internal auditing best practices, internal controls, computer-assisted audit techniques, audit software, audit project management, audit tracking, performance measures, continuous auditing, information security concepts, emerging trends, and quality assessment of the audit activity. Auditor training and development is offered by the FBI, Web-based training providers, colleges and universities, and organizations such as the Institute of Internal Auditors, Inspectors General Auditor Training Institute, USDA Graduate School, and Association of Government Accountants.

Aviation Investigative Specialist Training

The Bureau's aviation investigative specialists attend a broad range of courses, workshops, seminars, and briefings to ensure that they remain current in all aspects of airborne surveillance operations. Training for these professionals encompasses flight operations, technical investigative equipment, and surveillance techniques, and may include daylight and nighttime practical exercises. This training focuses on topics such as aircrew safety and survival, air and ground operations, night confined-area operations, airspace security, electronic surveillance devices, surveillance photography, photographic equipment maintenance, night-vision photography, metering, scaling, infrared devices, airborne thermal imaging, thermal search warrants, legal updates, courtroom testimony, and investigative techniques.

In addition to training offered by the Bureau's Aviation and Surveillance Operations Section and the FBI Academy, aviation investigative specialists also may attend courses and seminars presented by organizations such as the

Airborne Law Enforcement Association, Law Enforcement Thermographers Association, National Technical Investigators' Association, Federal Law Enforcement Training Center, and other law enforcement agencies.

Biologist (Forensic Examiner) Training

Biologists/forensic examiners in the FBI Laboratory must successfully complete a combination of on-the-job and in-service training to be certified as FBI forensic examiners. Training for biologists is designed to expand their knowledge and skills relating to various scientific theories and principles, serological techniques, biochemical analysis, mitochondrial DNA analysis, preserving evidence, courtroom testimony, and other areas. Training topics might revolve around the identification of hair, bones, blood, saliva, and other biological samples. Examiners also receive training that prepares them to use the latest technology, instruments, and equipment in the laboratory. Some of these courses are presented by FBI staff at the Bureau's Forensic Science Research and Training Center, a component of the FBI Academy. Classes and seminars also are available at colleges and universities, and through other organizations.

Chemist (Forensic Examiner) Training

Similar to the training of FBI biologists, chemists/forensic examiners assigned to the FBI Laboratory attend a variety of professional seminars, workshops, and courses throughout their careers that focus on laboratory techniques and procedures utilized in the examination and analysis of evidence. These personnel must also complete training to be certified as FBI forensic examiners. In-service training for chemists/forensic examiners could focus on scientific techniques used to identify various chemicals, poisons, controlled substances, explosives residues, paints, petroleum products, and many other substances. They are also trained in the use and maintenance of scientific instruments, and also in various computer hardware and software that is used in chemical analyses. The Forensic Science Research and Training Center at the FBI Academy also offers training to the Bureau's chemists.

Community Outreach Specialist Training

To ensure that FBI community outreach specialists are knowledgeable and fully prepared to carry out their responsibilities in an effective manner, the Bureau offers ongoing in-service and on-the-job training to these personnel, including opportunities to attend professional development seminars and conferences. These focus on subjects such as crime prevention, community policing strategies, victimology, gang violence, drug abuse prevention, research and data collection methods, public speaking, interviewing techniques, public relations, and community partnership issues. Other training topics could include crisis intervention, mental health issues, problem-solving strategies, health and social service organizations and programs, mentoring, interpersonal and cross-cultural communication, civil-rights matters, and liaison strategies.

Cryptanalyst (Forensic Examiner) Training

Like most other FBI professional support personnel, FBI cryptanalysts have opportunities to attend various professional conferences, seminars, and classes. Nonetheless, the Bureau's cryptanalysts learn a great deal from one another, and also by listening carefully to FBI special agents and intelligence analysts, police detectives, and other law enforcement officers who deal with gang members, drug traffickers, organized gambling and prostitution rings, and other criminals on a regular basis. On a more formal scale, cryptanalysts can attend training in computer hardware and software applications, cryptology research, and various scientific methods used in cryptology. Training also is available through the FBI Laboratory's Cryptanalysis and Racketeering Records Analysis Unit, from affiliates of the National Alliance of Gang Investigators, and also from organizations such as the American Cryptogram Association.

Document Analyst (Forensic Examiner) Training

Newly hired FBI document analysts complete a two-year apprenticeship program that includes classroom training and actual document examinations under the guidance and evaluation of experienced FBI document analysts. Some of the classroom portions of the program can be shortened or modified for trainees who have prior experience in the field. In addition to subjects relating to the examination and analysis of handwriting, typewriting, shoeprints, and tire treads, document analyst trainees also participate in moot court exercises to qualify for certification as FBI forensic examiners. In-service training for these personnel includes courses and professional seminars that are presented by FBI staff, academic institutions, firms associated with the ink and paper industry, and related professional organizations. Instruction focuses on subjects such as ink and paper chemistry and dating procedures, various printing processes, laboratory techniques, and other aspects of forensic document examination.

Electronic Surveillance Operations Technician Training

Initial training for electronic surveillance (ELSUR) operations technicians includes instruction by FBI staff in four categories that focus on electronic surveillance technology, evidentiary requirements, legal matters, and recordkeeping systems and responsibilities. Training in these areas provides a foundation for carrying out the basic responsibilities of the position. ELSUR operations technicians also receive ongoing on-the-job and in-house training on subjects such as evidence processing methods, evidence inventory procedures, chain of custody requirements, Title III wiretap requirements and other legal updates, courtroom testimony, safeguarding electronic surveillance records, technical investigative equipment operation, equipment inventory and security, computer system hardware and software, FBI policies and procedures, and other relevant topics.

Electronics Engineer Training

Professional development for electronics engineers covers a wide range of technologies. Depending on their expertise and area of specialty, electronics engineers receive ongoing in-service training that is geared to areas such as covert electronic and physical surveillance system design, countermeasures, telecommunications, audio and video system design, security systems, and other areas. Material covered in these training programs focuses on topics such as circuit configurations, alternating current and direct current, electronic circuit applications, circuit protection, switches and relays, semiconductors, project management, signal processing, and troubleshooting. Although the FBI conducts formal and on-the-job training in these and other areas for its personnel, electronics engineers can also take advantage of training that is offered by academic institutions and organizations such as the Institute of Electrical and Electronics Engineers and the National Technical Investigators' Association.

Electronics Technician Training

FBI electronics technicians attend a variety of courses, seminars, and conferences throughout their careers that focus on the assembly, installation, disguising, application, maintenance, and repair of technical investigative equipment and other electronic devices the FBI uses. These programs are often geared to the design, modification, repair, testing, and troubleshooting of transmitters, audio and video equipment, radio and electronics systems used in FBI vehicles, as well as video equipment, transmitters, covert electronic surveillance devices, radio and electronics systems used in FBI vehicles, and other electronic surveillance technologies. Instruction could also focus on the development and advancement of new technical surveillance techniques, electronic audio and video surveillance devices, and other technical investigative equipment. Training is presented by the FBI; colleges and universities; organizations such as the National Technical Investigators' Association; and companies that manufacture, sell, or service electronic devices and other equipment. Some of the training for electronics technicians is similar to programs attended by electronics engineers.

Evidence Technician Training

Most of the career development for FBI evidence technicians is provided by the FBI through on-the-job training in the areas of evidence handling and tracking procedures, chain of custody requirements, computer system hardware and software, Bureau policies and regulations, and other related topics. These personnel could also attend training offered by organizations such as the International Association of Chiefs of Police and the International Association for Property and Evidence. Material covered during formal classroom training could focus on evidence handling, documentation, inventory control, record-keeping, chain of custody issues, legal guidelines, civil liability, evidence packaging and shipping, evidence destruction, security practices, biohazards, and safety procedures. Evidence technicians who are members of the Bureau's evidence response teams also receive 80 hours of training to prepare them for their responsibilities with the team, such as instruction concerning evidence-collection techniques and preparing crime scene diagrams.

Financial Analyst Training

To enhance their knowledge and skills pertaining to white-collar crime and criminal investigations, FBI financial analysts attend conferences and seminars that are conducted by organizations such as the Association of Certified Fraud Examiners, the International Association of Financial Crimes Investigators, and the United States Attorney's Office. Training presented by these and other organizations focuses on subjects such as forensic accounting and auditing techniques, criminal law, rules of evidence, white-collar crime investigation, healthcare and insurance fraud, financial institution and securities fraud, interviewing techniques, fraud schemes, locating hidden assets, asset forfeiture, computer fraud, sources of information, contract and procurement fraud, and courtroom testimony.

Fingerprint Specialist Training

FBI fingerprint examiners attend an in-house training program that revolves around the examination and classification of fingerprints, fingerprint identification procedures, and FBI policies and procedures relating to fingerprint classification. They also complete a period of supervised on-the-job training and can attend courses, seminars, and conferences conducted by organizations such as the International Association for Identification or the American Academy of Forensic Sciences, academic institutions, and the FBI Academy. Fingerprint specialists assigned to the FBI disaster squad or evidence response teams also attend training programs to enhance their fingerprint identification skills and assist them in carrying out other responsibilities relating to these special assignments. For example, this training could focus on methods for obtaining fingerprints, palm prints, and footprints from deceased victims.

Foreign Operations Specialist Training

The Bureau's foreign operations specialists attend a broad range of courses, workshops, seminars, and briefings to ensure that they remain current in the issues relating to terrorism threats and major criminal activity in areas covered by the Bureau's LEGAT offices. Training for these professionals could address international terrorism groups, counterterrorism, crime trends, national security issues, weapons of mass destruction, foreign counterintelligence and espionage, public corruption issues, human intelligence, organized criminal enterprises, foreign affairs and political systems, foreign law enforcement and intelligence services, and liaison strategies. Training also could focus on research methods, analytical methodologies, intelligence gathering, data analysis, law enforcement databases, open-source information, and report writing, among other subjects.

Information Technology Specialist Training

The nature of training for FBI information technology specialists depends mostly on their area of expertise. For example, members of the Bureau's Computer Analysis and Response teams could receive a wide range of specialized training concerning computer crimes and the search and seizure of computers, data recovery, information linking, and other computer forensic techniques. Depending on their responsibilities and areas of focus, information technology specialists could also complete training relating to commercial and proprietary forensic tools, Internet investigations, software development, Web design, data networks, computer security, computer system maintenance and repair, and data management. Training for information technology specialists is conducted by staff of the Computer Training Unit at the FBI Academy and also by various computer hardware and software manufacturers, private firms that specialize in various facets of information technology, colleges and universities, and law enforcement training academies.

Intelligence Analyst Training

Training for FBI intelligence analysts begins with a seven-week Analytical Cadre Education Strategy (ACES) course at the FBI Academy in Quantico, Virginia. Instruction is held at the College of Analytical Studies, which was established by the Bureau in 2001 to train new and experienced analysts, joint terrorism task force members, and other law enforcement personnel. The ACES course is designed to expose new intelligence analysts to the intelligence cycle—which revolves around the components of intelligence requirements, collection, analysis, reporting, and dissemination—and how intelligence advances national security goals. This course also includes instruction on how to use strategic and tactical analysis effectively, asset vetting, report writing, the Intelligence Community, and various analytical methodologies.

In-service training for intelligence analysts varies widely depending on analysts' particular area of specialty and unit of assignment. For example, those assigned to the Counterterrorism Division could receive ongoing training concerning terrorist groups, sleeper cells, weapons of mass destruction, animal rights and environmental extremists operating in the United States, and other terrorism matters. Similarly, analysts who serve in the Counterintelligence Division may receive training in areas such as the Economic Espionage Act of 1996 and other pertinent laws, theft of U.S. technology and sensitive economic information by foreign intelligence services, attacks on the nation's critical infrastructure, and other national security issues. On the other hand, analysts assigned to the Bureau's Jewelry and Gem program could receive training relating to gemology, handling jewelry and gems, and related subjects. Training for analysts based in the Bureau's field offices also would depend on their areas of interest and level of experience, although it could focus on subjects such as gang activity, organized criminal enterprises, healthcare fraud, cyber crime, insurance fraud, the behavioral sciences, terrorist threats, and other topics.

As with other professional support personnel, in-service training programs for analysts are sponsored by educational institutions, private firms, member organizations of the Intelligence Community, other government agencies, organizations such as the International Association of Law Enforcement Intelligence Analysts or the International Association of Chiefs of Police, and other groups. Analysts also can attend advanced versions of the ACES course and other programs at the FBI Academy.

Investigative Communications Assistant Training

Throughout their careers, investigative communications assistants receive on-the-job, Web-based, and formal classroom training that focuses primarily on computerized criminal-justice databases such as the Law Enforcement Communications Network (LECN), National Crime Information Center (NCIC-2000), and National Law Enforcement Telecommunications System (NLETS). These programs are presented by organizations such as the FBI's Criminal Justice Information Services Division, NLETS, and Regional Information Sharing System affiliates. This training includes updates on interstate telecommunications networks and various databases used by the FBI, and topics such as data-entry codes and abbreviations, search parameters, clearing information stored in criminal justice information databases, database access and security policies, and XML technology. Training also is available concerning databases such as the Internet Crime Complaint Center, the Wildlife Crime Information System, the Interstate Criminal Intelligence Index System, the National Drug Pointer Index Program, the Convicted Sex Offender Registry, the National Instant Criminal Background Check System, and the National Weather Wire Service.

Investigative Specialist Training

Initial basic training for FBI investigative specialists consists of an eight-week course at the FBI Academy that covers fundamentals of surveillance, foreign counterintelligence, and defensive driving techniques. Basic and in-service training for investigative specialists is likely to concentrate on subjects such as foreign counterintelligence operations, national security issues, economic espionage, terrorism, and weapons of mass destruction. Depending on the nature of assignments and expertise of individual investigative specialists, instruction in surveillance methods could focus on surveillance planning, mobile and static surveillance techniques, foot surveillance, countersurveillance, observation skills, daytime and nighttime operations, urban and rural surveillance techniques, covert photography and video techniques, technical investigative equipment, electronic surveillance countermeasures, radio communications, law enforcement computer databases, legal subjects, defensive tactics, and report writing. In-service training is available from the FBI Academy, Federal Law Enforcement Training Center, other law enforcement agencies, and organizations such as the National Technical Investigators' Association.

Language Specialist Training

Training for FBI language specialists varies widely depending on the languages spoken and level of expertise of individual personnel. In general, this training could focus on skill development relating to the translation of written and oral material from various foreign languages into English, listening skills, reading comprehension, vocabulary, translating testimony during court hearings and trials, and providing testimony in the courtroom concerning their translating activities. Language specialists who are members of the Bureau's evidence response teams also receive 80 hours of training pertaining to the operations of the team and their responsibilities. Similarly, those who are members of the FBI's counterterrorism squads or rapid deployment teams could also receive additional training in these areas.

Paralegal Specialist (Asset Forfeiture) Training

A variety of seminars, conferences, and courses are available to paralegal specialists who are responsible for the Bureau's Asset Forfeiture Program. Throughout their careers, these personnel receive training relating to subjects such as asset forfeiture fundamentals, national and international asset tracing, hidden and commingled assets, forfeiture statutes, criminal and civil procedure, evidentiary requirements, administrative forfeiture, money laundering, bulk cash smuggling, the Bank Secrecy Act and U.S.A. Patriot Act, Internet banking, Suspicious Activity Reports, the Financial Crimes Enforcement Network, and terrorism financing. Training topics also could focus on computer software programs, automated database management, forensic accounting techniques, cooperation between U.S. and foreign law enforcement agencies and governments, U.S. Department of Justice initiatives, ethics, administrative procedures, budget concerns, and other related subjects. Asset forfeiture training is presented by organizations such as the criminal and civil divisions of the U.S. Department of Justice, the United States Attorney's Offices, the U.S. Drug Enforcement Administration, the Federal Law Enforcement Training Center, and the International Association for Asset Recovery.

Personnel Security Specialist Training

To ensure that FBI personnel security specialists have the tools they need to carry out their responsibilities, in-service and on-the-job training for these employees consists of instruction in areas such as agency personnel standards, security clearance eligibility requirements, position sensitivity and security suitability determinations, adverse personnel action and derogatory information, interviewing techniques, report writing, agency policies and procedures, and other subjects. To remain current in applicable laws and regulations, these personnel also receive ongoing legal updates. Personnel security specialists can attend courses presented by FBI staff; by the Federal Law Enforcement Training Center; by various federal, state, or local law enforcement agencies, training programs, or academies; by colleges or universities; and by other organizations.

Photographer Training

FBI photographers attend a wide range of training courses, seminars, and workshops throughout their careers to expand their knowledge and hone their skills. These programs focus on subjects such as crime scene and arson photography, flash photography, infrared photography, photographic surveillance equipment and techniques, night-vision photography, darkroom techniques, film processing, camera systems and meters, special films, lenses, filters, lighting techniques, photographic equipment maintenance, and other topics. Although the Bureau presents training to photographers at the FBI Academy, these personnel can also take advantage of training programs offered by other law enforcement training academies, colleges and universities, organizations such as the Evidence Photographers International Council, and various firms in the photographic industry. Photographers who are assigned to the Bureau's evidence response teams also receive 80 hours of training to prepare them for tasks they will perform with the team.

Physical Security Specialist Training

FBI physical security specialists attend a variety of in-service training programs depending on their areas of expertise, including nuclear security, explosive operations, security countermeasures, and other specialties. Generally speaking, training for personnel security specialists covers agency policies and directives and subjects such as intrusion-detection systems and devices, security awareness, access-control systems, physical-security surveys, crime prevention, terrorism, applicable laws and regulations, legal updates, investigative techniques, report writing, interviewing techniques, and other training topics that are geared to the responsibilities of individual specialists. Some of these training programs are presented by FBI staff, although others could be presented by the Federal Law Enforcement Training Center, other law enforcement training programs or academies, academic institutions, and organizations such as the American Society for Industrial Security.

Police Officer Training

Initial basic training for FBI police officers includes the 12-week Uniformed Police Training Program at the Federal Law Enforcement Training Center (FLETC) in Glynco, Georgia. Topics covered in this program include patrol procedures, emergency response driving, high-risk vehicle stops, crowd control, hostage situations, critical-incident response, radio communications, legal subjects, crime scene preservation, interviewing techniques, courtroom testimony, report writing, narcotics, terrorism overview, terrorist strategies and tactics, vehicle-borne improvised explosive devices, and criminal intelligence. This program also includes instruction in firearms safety and marksmanship, bombs and explosives, self-defense, nonlethal control techniques, impact weapons control, physical conditioning, first-aid and CPR, and many other law enforcement subjects. After completing the 12-week program at FLETC, FBI police officers attend a four-week training program at the FBI Academy that focuses on FBI policies, procedures, and directives and other agency-specific topics. Ongoing in-service training covers a wide range of topics relating to patrol techniques, vehicle operation, weapons proficiency, response to emergency situations, law, and the development of other law enforcement skills.

Surveillance Specialist Training

Training for FBI surveillance specialists begins with a three-week in-house introductory course that provides an overview of surveillance specialists' mission, basic surveillance techniques, legal matters, and FBI policies and procedures pertinent to the work of surveillance specialists. Continuous on-the-job and in-service training covers subjects such as surveillance planning, static observation posts, observation skills, daytime and nighttime operations, countersurveillance, covert video systems, still photography, electronic surveillance, electronic surveillance countermeasures, use and maintenance of operational equipment, legal updates, and national security issues. Training in these and other subjects is presented by the FBI Academy, and is available from the Federal Law Enforcement Training Center, organizations such as the National Technical Investigators' Association, and other law enforcement agencies.

Technical Information Specialist Training

To ensure that FBI technical information specialists are knowledgeable and prepared to carry out their responsibilities in an efficient and effective manner, the Bureau offers ongoing in-service and on-the-job training to these personnel, including opportunities to attend professional development seminars and conferences. These focus on subjects such as databases, including the National Crime Information Center database, the National Instant Criminal Background Check System, the Integrated Automated Fingerprint Identification System, and other FBI information systems. Additional training could focus on state driver and vehicle record systems, prison system databases, probation and parole databases, sex offender registries, mug-shot records, enhanced name searches, missing persons records, information linking, real estate records, open-source databases, cross-reference telephone directories, database and records management, the Privacy Act of 1974, legal requirements, FBI Criminal Justice Information Services operations, report writing, and ethics, among other subjects.

Telecommunications Specialist Training

FBI telecommunications specialists receive ongoing in-service and on-the-job training throughout their careers. This training focuses on technical and analytical functions pertaining to the planning, development, acquisition, testing, integration, installation, use, modification, and repair of telecommunications systems and technical investigative equipment. Some of the subjects covered include troubleshooting, radio frequencies, wireless communications systems, electrical circuits, wiring diagrams, equipment maintenance, functions and requirements of the Federal Communications Commission and the National Telecommunications and Information Administration, computer operating systems and software applications, inventory management, report writing, legal updates, and courtroom testimony. Some instruction is available from telecommunications equipment manufacturers. Other training opportunities are available from FBI staff, various law enforcement and government agencies, and other organizations.

Victim Specialist Training

FBI victim specialists have opportunities to broaden their knowledge of victim assistance programs and associated legal requirements though training offered by the FBI, other government agencies, professional associations, and academic organizations. Several federal agencies offer courses and seminars to victim program personnel, such as the Federal Law Enforcement Training Center; the Drug Enforcement Administration; the U.S. Department of Defense; the Office for Victims of Crime, U.S. Department of Justice; and various U.S. Attorneys' Offices. Many academic and professional organizations also offer training, such as the National Center for Victims of Crime, the National Organization for Victim Assistance, the National Crime Victims Research and Treatment Center, and the National Victim Assistance Academy.

Training programs for victim specialists focus on topics such as victimology, crisis intervention, handling cases, federal jurisdiction and initiatives, federal victim assistance programs, the Federal Crime Victims' Bill of Rights, victim services innovations, victim program policies, program management, research methods, report writing, and interviewing techniques. To remain current in legal requirements and changes, victim specialists receive training in the Attorney General Guidelines for Victim and Witness Assistance, and laws such as the Victim and Witness Protection Act of 1982, the Crime Control Act of 1990, the Victims' Rights and Restitution Act of 1990, the Victims of Child Abuse Act of 1990, the Violent Crime Control and Law Enforcement Act of 1994, the Mandatory Victims Restitution Act of 1996, the Victim Rights Clarification Act of 1997, and the Victims of Trafficking and Violence Protection Act of 2000.

CHAPTER 9

FBI Internship Programs

"Success only breeds a new goal."

—Bette Davis

The FBI offers a wide range of internship programs that afford students a unique opportunity to enhance their education and make practical application of classroom theory. Some of these include the FBI Honors Internship, Presidential Management Internship, Fellows Program, National Center for the Analysis of Violent Crime Internship, National Security Internship, and FBI Laboratory Internship. In addition, the FBI Academy offers more than a dozen one-of-a-kind internship programs that involve everything from fine-tuning the New Agent's Training Program curriculum, to conducting research in the Behavioral Science Unit, to working in the FBI Academy Library. These dynamic programs enable participants to explore their career interests under actual working conditions and to make informed choices before moving into the workforce.

FBI internships provide students with hands-on experience and an exceptional resume builder, as well as an outstanding opportunity to showcase their skills, abilities, and potential to one of the most respected and sophisticated law enforcement agencies in the world. These internships also offer college students a unique opportunity to obtain FBI employment following graduation. The FBI has always shown considerable interest in retaining its interns who seek a long-term professional career with the Bureau. For those who pursue careers with other organizations, experience as an FBI intern can lead to a positive and prestigious professional reference when seeking employment with other law enforcement and government agencies or firms in the private sector.

Presidential Management Fellows and Honors Interns receive a salary, whereas interns serving other FBI components are not paid. Although the FBI does not pay for housing expenses, Headquarters personnel provide interns with information and assistance in securing housing in the Washington, D.C. area.

Many FBI field offices also offer volunteer internship opportunities that provide priceless hands-on experience working for the Bureau. Field office internships typically are offered to college undergraduate juniors and seniors, and graduate students. Some of the field offices presently offering internships include Boston, Denver, Houston, Los Angeles, Memphis, New York,

Philadelphia, San Diego, Seattle, and Washington, D.C. Students interested in these internships should contact the applicant coordinator at the nearest FBI field office.

The following sections provide details concerning FBI internships that result in unique opportunities for more than 200 students each year. Every form that you will need to submit to apply for FBI internships is shown in the appendixes at the end of this book.

FBI Honors Internship Program

Approximately 100 college undergraduate and graduate students are selected to participate each summer in the 10-week FBI Honors Internship Program in Washington, D.C. The program was started in 1985 to provide students with an overview of FBI operations and a chance to explore career opportunities within the Bureau. Honors Interns work side-by-side with FBI Special Agents and professional support personnel on important cases and assignments. The program also enhances the FBI's visibility and recruitment efforts at colleges and universities nationwide. The Honors Internship Program, which is conducted only during the summer, begins in early June and ends in mid-August. Undergraduate Honors Interns are paid at the GS-6 grade level on the federal government pay scale (presently about $713 per week), whereas graduate Honors Interns are paid at the GS-7 grade level (about $793 per week). In addition, the FBI pays for all travel expenses to and from Washington, D.C.

Eligibility

To be considered, applicants must possess strong academic credentials, outstanding character, and a high degree of motivation. Minimum qualifications include the following:

- United States citizenship.

- A cumulative grade-point average of 3.0 or better.

- Undergraduate students must be attending school full time and should be enrolled in their junior year at the time they apply to the program.

- Graduate students must be attending a college or university on a full-time basis.

- Applicants must plan to return to their school for at least one semester after participating in the program.

- Suitability under the FBI's Employment Drug Policy (see chapter 4). records.

- Candidates for the Middle Eastern Foreign Language Honors Internship must also possess listening comprehension and translation proficiency of a Middle Eastern language.

The Application Process

The application process for Honors Internships is coordinated through the FBI field office nearest the school the applicant is attending. Interested students must complete and submit application forms and other materials to be considered for Honors Intern positions. Applicants can obtain forms from any FBI field office, and you can find copies of them in the appendixes of this book and online at www.fbijobs.com. The following applications and supporting information must be submitted:

- An FD-646a Preliminary Application Form
- An FD-804 Applicant Background Survey
- An FD-956 School Certification Form
- An SF-86 Questionnaire for National Security Positions
- A Program Term Acknowledgment Form
- A current academic transcript
- A resume
- A professional 2×2–inch photograph (passport-style) of the applicant with his or her name and the date of the photo printed on back
- A written letter of recommendation from the appropriate dean or department head
- A 500-word essay expressing interest in the program
- Applicants who have served in the military must submit a Form DD-214, Certificate of Release or Discharge from Active Duty.

The application process begins about one year prior to the start of the program. Here are the steps you should follow and the timeframe for doing so:

- **July:** Obtain an application package from the FBI field office nearest your campus. Request a letter of recommendation from your dean or department head. Obtain a copy of your current academic transcript.

- **August to September:** Complete your application, prepare your resume, write a 500-word essay, and obtain the letter of recommendation from your dean or department head.

- **September:** Review your Honors Internship brochure to ensure that you have obtained and completed all the necessary documents.

    Ensure that you have completed all application forms and submitted them to the FBI office nearest your school campus by September 30.

The Selection Process

After applications have been received at each field office, FBI representatives from that field office will arrange interviews with competitive candidates. Not all candidates will be interviewed. Interviews generally take place in October. Each field office then nominates a designated number of candidates to the Administrative Services Division at FBI Headquarters in Washington, D.C., by early November. A selection committee at Headquarters then reviews application packages and selects finalists.

Appointments are based on academic achievement, area of study, and both life and work experiences. Candidates who possess specific skills and educational backgrounds may be given special consideration, depending on the FBI's specific long-range needs. For example, the FBI is particularly interested in candidates with skills and education in areas such as engineering, computer science, foreign languages, political science, law, accounting, intelligence, counterterrorism, and the physical sciences. The FBI also actively seeks women, minorities, and persons with disabilities for participation in the program.

Final decisions are generally made in November, and selected candidates receive a conditional job offer soon thereafter. The initial offer is conditional because candidates selected must undergo an FBI background investigation and receive a Top Secret security clearance to be eligible to participate in the program. Final screening includes a drug test, polygraph examination, and fingerprinting.

Assignment

The Honors Internship Program normally starts on the first Monday in June, beginning with an orientation at FBI Headquarters. Interns are assigned to a Headquarters division based on their academic disciplines, potential contributions to the division, and the needs of the Bureau. Tasks that interns perform vary widely, depending on projects or initiatives underway at the time. The following are examples of assignments undertaken by Honors Interns:

- Interns whose discipline is in the physical sciences may be assigned to the Forensic Science Research and Training Center at the FBI Laboratory. There they could assist scientists in the development and validation of forensic technologies and procedures.

- In furtherance of the FBI's information technology strategies, the Information Resources Division could assign an intern who possesses exceptional computer skills to evaluate computer hardware and software, or to participate in other projects that focus on the Bureau's collection, management, and use of information.

- Interns with a legal background may be assigned to the Office of General Counsel (OGC). In this office, they could participate in legal research regarding law enforcement and national security matters, including the defense of civil litigation and administrative claims involving the FBI, its personnel, and its records.

- Accounting skills and education could land an intern an assignment to a unit within the Financial Crimes Section. In this section, they could contribute to the investigation of healthcare fraud, public corruption, government fraud, environmental fraud, telemarketing fraud, or other offenses.

- Interns with proficiency in certain languages (for example, Arabic, Farsi, Pashto, Hebrew, or Mandarin) can participate in the FBI Foreign Language Honors Internship, which includes assignment to a unit within the Directorate of Intelligence, such as a Joint Terrorism Task Force. These interns have responsibilities relating to counterterrorism, counterintelligence, weapons of mass destruction, cybercrime, organized criminal enterprises, and other national security matters.

Interns work alongside Special Agents and professional support personnel under the supervision of the Assistant Director of their assigned division. Field trips to locations such as the FBI Academy in Quantico, Virginia; the Criminal

Justice Information Services Division in Clarksburg, West Virginia; and various FBI field offices are also common. The Honors Internship experience provides participants with a thorough understanding of the inner workings of the FBI, as well as an overview of various career opportunities within the Bureau.

Training

Training begins with an orientation at FBI Headquarters that focuses on internship rules and procedures. Interns receive progressive on-the-job training. About once a week, they attend executive briefings conducted by FBI division directors that focus on various aspects of Bureau operations. FBI personnel and representatives of other agencies also provide instruction at Headquarters and the FBI Academy throughout the internship experience. Additional training is provided through field trips to the Washington, D.C. Field Office and other facilities. Interns also receive firearms training, including instruction in safety procedures, familiarization with various firearms, target practice, and other live-fire scenarios. The nature of other training depends on the functions and current activities of the unit to which interns are assigned.

Presidential Management Fellows Program

The Presidential Management Fellows (PMF) Program was established by President Carter in 1977 to attract graduate students from various academic disciplines who are interested in careers in federal government. PMFs receive an initial two-year full-time excepted-service appointment, after which they are eligible for conversion to a permanent federal government position. The PMF program is a government-wide undertaking administered by the U.S. Office of Personnel Management (OPM). Although PMFs are ultimately hired by individual agencies for their two-year appointments, OPM conducts the nomination and selection process.

The FBI has participated in the program since 1987, through which it has hired dozens of interns for placement in various divisions of the Bureau. These interns participate in training provided by the FBI and other government agencies, as well as executive briefings by senior-level FBI and Department of Justice management, including the Attorney General. Their duties might also include field trips to the FBI Academy and various FBI field offices, special tours of FBI Headquarters, temporary assignments to other federal agencies, and international travel.

PMFs are hired at the GS-9 grade level, which presently is about $50,400 per year. After successfully completing the first year, PMFs are eligible for promotion to GS-11, which is about $61,000 per year. As employees of the federal government, they also earn annual leave and sick leave, paid federal holidays, and coverage under the Federal Employees Retirement System (FERS). They are also eligible to participate in the Thrift Savings Plan and to obtain life insurance and health insurance coverage. As an added benefit, PMFs are also provided full access to the gym and workout facilities at FBI Headquarters.

Many of the permanent positions offered to PMFs who have completed the internship extend to the GS-15 level, providing substantial future promotional potential.

Divisions that Employ PMFs

The FBI has sought PMFs with diverse backgrounds ranging from international relations, to budget and program management, to cyber and computer technology. This diversity has enabled PMFs to contribute to the goals and mission of the FBI and other agencies in the U.S. Intelligence Community. Some of the FBI divisions that may utilize PMFs include the Counterterrorism Division, the Finance Division, the Training Division, and the Office of Public Affairs. Positions within these divisions are located at FBI Headquarters in Washington, D.C. The following sections provide overviews of each of these divisions.

Counterterrorism Division

All FBI counterterrorism initiatives are consolidated under the Counterterrorism Division, which includes the National Infrastructure Protection Center (NIPC) and the National Domestic Preparedness Office (NDPO). The NIPC serves as the government's focal point for threat assessment, warning, investigation, and response for threats or attacks against the United States. The NDPO coordinates all federal efforts to assist state and local first responders with planning, training, and equipment needs necessary to respond to an incident involving conventional or nonconventional weapons of mass destruction. The FBI shifted additional resources to the Counterterrorism Division following the September 11, 2001, terrorist attacks on the World Trade Center and the Pentagon, which could lead to appointment of additional PMFs in this division.

Finance Division

The Finance Division manages FBI budget and accounting matters, the strategic planning process, voucher and payroll functions, the procurement process, forfeiture and seized property process, property management, automotive management, and relocation and transportation services. This division also carries out competition advocacy functions to ensure fair and open competition in the Bureau's contracting and procurement processes. Provisions of the Chief Financial Officer Act of 1990 are also overseen by the Finance Division, which includes preparation and auditing of the Bureau's financial statements, overall financial management of FBI operations in accordance with the act, and other responsibilities.

Training and Development Division

The Training and Development Division designs and delivers training programs for all types and levels of FBI personnel, such as newly hired special agents, veteran field agents, supervisory special agents, and managers; professional support personnel; scientists, laboratory staff, technical support personnel, police officers, middle managers, and chiefs of U.S. police departments; and representatives of foreign law enforcement agencies, among others. Depending on the activities and needs of the Training Division at any given time, PMFs could be assigned to FBI Academy units such as the Training Development Unit, the New Agents' Training Unit, the Behavioral Science Unit, the International Training and Assistance Unit, the Curriculum Planning and Evaluation Unit, the Leadership Development Institute, or other components.

Office of Public Affairs

The Office of Public Affairs communicates information on FBI investigations, services, programs, policy, and accomplishments to the public and the media. It manages relations with the electronic and print media; prepares FBI speeches, reports, and publications; answers verbal and written inquiries from the general public, scholars, and authors regarding the FBI; oversees the FBI's prepublication review process; oversees the FBI's fugitive publicity program, including the "Ten Most Wanted" program; manages the FBI's Web site; and operates the Headquarters tour.

The PMF Career Path

Although PMFs represent only a small segment of the Bureau's professional workforce, their contributions have been substantial. Once appointed, PMFs must serve a two-year probation period, which is the duration of the Internship. After two years, PMFs are eligible for conversion to career employment status. Retention of PMFs is high, and the majority of PMFs that convert to permanent positions remain with the Bureau. The FBI encourages career development for PMFs, and several PMFs have achieved management positions within the FBI and other federal agencies. Any PMF who is interested in becoming an FBI special agent must apply through the standard special agent application process.

Eligibility

To be eligible for the PMF Program, you must be a graduate student completing or expecting to complete a master's or doctorate degree from an accredited college or university during the current academic year. No particular grade-point average is required, although school officials establish competitive campus nominating processes to ensure that the best candidates from their programs are nominated. The FBI seeks PMF candidates who have excellent writing skills, critical thinking abilities, and a commitment to public service.

Students from a wide variety of academic disciplines are encouraged to apply, although candidates must have a clear interest in, and a commitment to, a career in the analysis and management of public policies and programs. The majority of previous PMFs have had no prior experience in law enforcement or intelligence. Like all FBI applicants, those applying for PMF positions must meet the criteria of the Bureau's Employment Drug Policy (see chapter 4) and must be U.S. citizens.

The Application and Selection Process

Selection as a PMF finalist is based on nomination, interviews, review of information provided in the written application, and a one-day structured assessment center process that focuses on oral and written communication skills. The length of the application process typically ranges from 9 to 12 months from submission of the application to appointment, although it can take up to 14 months. Those who want to apply for PMF positions with more than one FBI unit must contact each unit for instructions because individual units might conduct the hiring process differently.

The basic stages in the PMF hiring process are outlined in the following sections.

Nomination

PMF candidates must be nominated by the appropriate dean, director, or chairperson of their graduate academic program. Nominations from individual professors, advisors, or placement counselors will not be accepted. Once nominated, PMF candidates compete nationwide with other eligible graduate-level students.

PMF Application Materials

Candidates must submit a PMF online application and resume to OPM, along with nomination materials completed by the school. Internet access to the application is available on OPM's PMF Web site beginning September 1 each year, and must be submitted online by October 15 for the following year. Although the application is likely to change from year to year, a sample application (in PDF) is posted on the Web at www.pmf.opm.gov/Documents/SampleApp.pdf.

Assessment Center Process

All nominees who meet minimum qualification standards are invited to participate in a one-day assessment center process that is held in January or February. The process is made up of three segments, including a group discussion, an oral presentation by the nominee, and a written exercise. OPM notifies those selected as finalists in late February or early March.

Interviews and Initial Selection

After they receive information relating to finalists from OPM, the Bureau invites competitive candidates to personal interviews at FBI Headquarters. The interview format may vary from one section to another. Some sections hiring PMFs might conduct informal interviews with the Unit Chief or Supervisor, whereas others might convene formal panel interviews.

FBI Application Materials

Applicants who pass the initial interview are invited to submit a written application to the FBI. Background screening, which is the next phase in the application process, cannot begin until the applicant has filled out the written application completely and returned it to the Bureau. Each applicant is assigned a local applicant coordinator in his geographic area. Applicant coordinators inform candidates of their status in the application process and describe related personnel procedures.

Initial Background Screening

After applications have been received and processed, candidates are eligible to receive a conditional offer of PMF employment by the FBI, which is contingent on successful completion of a full background investigation. Those who accept the conditional offer of employment are scheduled for a polygraph examination, urinalysis drug screening, and fingerprinting.

Background Investigation

During the background investigation, investigators contact former and current employers, references, social acquaintances, and neighbors. They also review school, credit, arrest, medical, and military records, and possibly other records. The completed background investigation is assessed at FBI Headquarters before a final decision is made to offer employment. All applicants are informed of the outcome of their investigation in writing. Like all FBI employees, PMFs receive a Top Secret security clearance.

Enter on Duty

Upon successful completion of the full background investigation, candidates are extended a formal offer of employment, or *appointment,* and are assigned an enter-on-duty (EOD) date. As a general rule, PMFs are appointed about four to six months after submitting their initial applications to the FBI. When they report for duty on their EOD, newly hired PMFs receive two days of employment processing and orientation before reporting to their assigned units.

Assignment

As with other FBI internships, assignments vary widely according to the skills, educations, and career goals of individual interns, as well as the projects or initiatives underway with various Headquarters divisions and units at the time. Here are some examples of possible assignments:

- PMFs with accounting backgrounds could be assigned to the Finance Division, where their responsibilities would revolve around the coordination and administration of the FBI's budgetary and fiscal matters, financial planning, voucher and payroll matters, and property and procurement activities.

- The Counterterrorism Division might utilize PMFs for support of FBI counterterrorism initiatives, which could include activities with the National Infrastructure Protection Center or the National Domestic Preparedness Office. Responsibilities within this division could revolve around terrorism threat assessment and investigation, as well as planning and training relating to incidents involving weapons of mass destruction.

- PMFs assigned to the Counterintelligence Division could have responsibilities associated with the protection of the United States against foreign intelligence operations and espionage. Much of the work in this Division is focused on interaction with the U.S. law enforcement and intelligence communities to neutralize the intelligence activities of foreign countries and entities that pose a significant threat to the United States.

In the past, many PMFs have visited other FBI field offices, and some have traveled internationally. Many PMFs have also had opportunities to participate in projects at agencies and departments such as the Central Intelligence Agency, Defense Intelligence Agency, Department of Energy, and Department of State, among others.

Training

Training and career development are fundamental components of the PMF Program, and the FBI is committed to assisting and training PMFs to develop the skills necessary to perform at the highest level of competence. The FBI offers its PMF employees at least 80 hours of training each year. Training begins with a three-day Orientation Training Program, conducted by OPM, which provides an overall perspective on how the Federal Government operates.

Throughout the Internship, PMFs attend courses at the FBI Academy, as well as training conducted by other agencies in the U.S. Intelligence Community, various law enforcement organizations, the U.S. Department of State, other federal agencies, and commercial vendors. PMFs also receive continuous on-the-job training and participate in other developmental opportunities such as seminars, briefings, and conferences. The content of the training is tailored to the specific learning objectives that will qualify the PMF intern for the target position at the end of the internship. The FBI works with each intern to develop a written outline of core competencies and technical skills the intern must gain before conversion to a target position.

NCAVC Volunteer Internship Program

The FBI's National Center for the Analysis of Violent Crime (NCAVC) offers full-time unpaid internships to undergraduate and graduate students. These are offered twice each year, starting either the first week in September (immediately after Labor Day) or the second week in January. These internships last 14 weeks.

The NCAVC was established in 1984 at the FBI National Academy in Quantico, Virginia, and originally concentrated on unsolved murder cases. Four years later, although the NCAVC already had an outstanding reputation in the law enforcement community, the Thomas Harris book *Silence of the Lambs* brought worldwide attention to the unit. As a component of the FBI's Critical Incident Response Group, the NCAVC provides investigative support to law enforcement agencies around the world in crimes such as serial murder, child abduction or exploitation, bombing, arson, terrorism, threats, serial rape, and public corruption. Services the NCAVC provides include profiling of unknown offenders, crime analysis, investigative strategies, interview and interrogation strategies, trial preparation and prosecutorial strategies, expert testimony, and coordination of other resources. The NCAVC also conducts research and provides training regarding high-risk, bizarre, vicious, or repetitive violent crimes.

Eligibility

Undergraduate applicants must be at least a college junior with a minimum grade-point average of 3.0, and must have student status during the internship. Students may be studying any discipline, although the most relevant majors are psychology, sociology, criminology, criminal justice, forensic science, terrorism, Middle-Eastern studies, and law. Additional requirements include excellent writing skills, analytical abilities, computer skills, and U.S. citizenship.

Applicants must also be aware that they will be exposed to investigative information and materials that are graphic and violent in nature. Interns are exposed to details of investigations, including written statements, audio- or videotaped interviews, and crime-scene and autopsy photographs. These investigations and related research often involve child victims and graphic sexual details.

The Application and Selection Process

As with other FBI internships, the NCAVC requires applicants to submit forms and other documents prior to established deadlines, to participate in a personal interview, and to undergo a background investigation. This section provides a list of application materials you must submit to be considered for an NCAVC internship position, and an overview of the application process.

Application Materials

Students who are interested in these internships must submit the following materials directly to the NCAVC:

- An FD-646c Preliminary Application for FBI Employment

- A completed SF-86 Questionnaire for National Security Positions

- A resume (1 to 3 pages)

- An essay (1 to 2 pages) indicating background, interests, goals, and reasons for wanting to participate in the internship

- Two letters of recommendation, including at least one from a department faculty member

- Transcripts of credits earned at all colleges attended

- A copy of a college term/research paper written by the applicant

- A letter of sponsorship from a school official confirming that the applicant is in good standing and identifying the sponsor's contact information

- A 2×2–inch passport-style photograph

Application Deadlines

Application materials for NCAVC internships must be submitted 10 months in advance. Applications for internships starting in September must be submitted by November 1. Applications for internships starting in January must be submitted by March 1.

Interviews

Finalists must participate in a personal interview at the NCAVC offices near Quantico, Virginia, and must travel to the interview at their own expense. Interviews are conducted about four to six weeks after application deadlines. In some cases, interviews can be conducted via video teleconferencing.

Background Investigation

Selection is contingent on passing a background investigation, which includes a review of school, credit, arrest, medical, and military records, and contact with current and former employers, references, social acquaintances, and neighbors. Applicants must qualify under other FBI employee standards, including policy regarding the use of illegal drugs, and must also pass a polygraph and drug-screening test.

Assignment

The NCAVC internship is designed around research, case consultations, interaction and networking, and classroom instruction, including the following tasks, assignments, and activities.

Research

Interns carry out significant and challenging social science research assignments, depending on their academic level and research experience. These assignments focus on all phases of the research process, including research design, resource material development, literature search and review, data collection and entry, offender timeline creation, case information coding, and the analysis and publication of research findings. Some interns have had the opportunity to author or coauthor articles for publication in the *FBI Law Enforcement Bulletin* and scientific or academic journals.

Case Consultations

NCAVC interns have opportunities to observe the case consultations carried out within the unit, through which they gain appreciation for the teamwork and cooperation among Unit members. This experience allows them to acquire a realistic understanding of the criminal "profiling" process and other services performed by the NCAVC, in contrast to portrayals characterized in movies, on television, or in books.

Interaction and Networking

Another critical aspect of the internship experience is the opportunity interns have to work and network with NCAVC staff members and to meet others at consultations or training sessions. Not surprisingly, the NCAVC staff come from a broad range of academic and employment backgrounds, and they are eager to discuss their experiences and suggest career options interns may want to consider.

Classroom Instruction

An important and heavily emphasized feature of the NCAVC internship is the opportunity for interns to attend a variety of class sessions at the FBI Academy. These focus on a wide range of topics presented by NCAVC staff and other Academy instructors, of which many involve violent crimes and the offenders who commit them.

Training

The NCAVC provides interns with a range of training instruction, including a variety of courses, seminars, and symposia, as well as continuous on-the-job training. About once per week, interns attend two-hour lectures conducted by NCAVC staff, FBI Academy instructors, directors of various FBI divisions, or other trainers. Training typically focuses on the behavioral sciences and subjects such as victimology, threat analysis, stalking, unusual or repetitive violent crimes, child abduction and other crimes against children, sexual assault, serial murder, evidence collection, DNA analysis, and terrorism, among other topics. Training is augmented by field trips to other government agencies and facilities such as hospitals, crime laboratories, and medical examiner offices.

National Security Internship Program

In 2008, the FBI and the U.S. Department of Homeland Security (DHS) joined forces with George Washington University (GWU) to create the National Security Internship (NSI) program, a unique experience for college students who speak or are studying Arabic and have declared a major or minor in international relations, homeland security, intelligence, political science, or area studies. The goal of this internship is to build a national security workforce by providing a direct career path to the FBI or DHS for students who possess a high degree of cultural competency. The NSI program is offered annually, during the summer.

National Security Internship participants receive paid lodging and meals at GWU, tuition for 11 college credits, and potential opportunities for continued internships in local FBI and DHS field offices following completion of the internship. NSI program participants also are given preferred access to employment with the FBI and DHS. To date, more than 80 percent of these interns have been offered full-time career positions with the FBI or DHS after graduation from college.

Eligibility

The NSI internship is open to undergraduate and graduate students. Applicants must be a citizen of the United States and at least 18 years of age. The following minimum requirements must also be met:

- College junior, senior, or graduate school standing
- Pursuing (or possess) a degree with a major or minor in international relations, homeland security, political science, or area studies (Middle East, Near East, or South Asia)
- Minimum 3.0 grade-point average (GPA)
- Arabic language skills, including a rating score of 1+ or higher in speaking proficiency as measured according to the Interagency Language Roundtable (ILR) skill level description

Candidates who have lived, worked, or studied abroad are in particular demand. Experience working with ethnic or religious minority groups also is a plus.

The Application and Selection Process

NSI interns are selected based on academic achievement, foreign-language abilities, demonstrated and expressed skills, and life experience. Intern selections normally are made within one month of the application deadline. Language testing typically begins about two weeks thereafter.

Application Materials

Candidates must submit the following materials prior to the application deadline:

- A program application

- Two letters of recommendation (at least one from a faculty member at the applicant's school)

- An essay (1,000 words maximum) indicating the student's background, interests, aspirations, and reasons for wanting to participate in the internship

- A resume that outlines educational background, language abilities, overseas experience, employment, awards, and achievements

- College academic transcripts from all schools attended

Application Deadline

Applications for internships beginning in June normally must be submitted by September 30 of the preceding year.

Background Investigation

Students selected for the internship are given a conditional offer of employment, contingent upon the successful completion of a background investigation, and are contacted by the nearest FBI field office for further processing. Information provided on the SF-86 Questionnaire for National Security Positions is verified and used during the background investigation. In addition, the FBI normally contacts fellow students, professors, employers, coworkers, neighbors, relatives, and others. FBI personnel standards pertaining to drug use and qualifying for a security clearance also apply to NSI internship applicants. A drug test, personnel security interview, polygraph examination, and fingerprinting also are part of the background investigation. Results of the background investigation are provided to FBI Headquarters for adjudication of a Top Secret clearance.

Assignment

This intensive nine-week summer program combines Arabic language, Middle Eastern studies, homeland security and intelligence seminars, and on-the-job training at the FBI or DHS headquarters. Many social and cultural activities also are undertaken. The internship's focus is four-pronged:

1. **Arabic Language:** Intensive immersion coursework in Arabic

2. **Arab Film and Cultural Studies:** Viewing, study, and discussion of a variety of Arab films, along with the study of relevant cultures in history

3. **National Security Seminars:** Includes topics such as bioterrorism, cybercrime, homeland security (intelligence and analysis), modern terrorism, Islam, Arab Culture, radicalization, weapons of mass destruction, and so on

4. **On-the-Job Experience:** Includes various projects in one or more DHS and FBI units related to concurrent on-campus coursework

Interns attend a variety of lectures at George Washington University through-out the program. Previous lecturers have included a GWU Department of Religion professor, a GWU professor of Gulf and Arabian Affairs, the president of the Moroccan-American Trade and Investment Council, a U.S. Congressman, a Department of Homeland Security chief of staff, and an FBI expert on weapons of mass destruction. Interns earn 11 college credits, includ-ing six credits in Arabic Language, three credits in National Security Seminars, and two credits in Arabic Film and Culture. Field activities include visits to the CIA museum, U.S. Congress, the White House, the FBI Academy, Dulles International Airport, the National Media Exploitation Center, the National Cryptologic Museum, and the International Spy Museum, among other loca-tions.

FBI Records Management Division Volunteer Internship Program

The Bureau's Records Management Division (RMD) components in Winchester and Alexandria, Virginia, offer a challenging internship program that affords qualified high school and college students an excellent opportunity to obtain valuable experience and earn school credits while serving the FBI.

Eligibility

The RMD internship is open to high school students and college undergradu-ate and graduate students. Applicants must be a citizen of the United States and at least 16 years of age. The following minimum requirements must also be met:

- Students must be enrolled at least part-time in an accredited high school, college, or university.

- High school students must have a minimum cumulative grade-point aver-age (GPA) of 2.5 or above on a 4.0 scale and be in good standing with their school.

- College students must have a minimum cumulative grade-point average (GPA) of 3.0 or above on a 4.0 scale and be in good standing with their school.

- Candidates must have strong writing skills and analytical abilities.

The FBI does not limit the applicant pool to specific areas of study. Some examples of academic disciplines that can be applicable to this internship include business management, accounting, finance, global studies, English, international relations, computer science, visual arts, education, criminal jus-tice, criminology, international studies, history, journalism, human resources, public administration, political science, sociology, psychology, social work, archaeology, art history, anthropology, law, organizational psychology, library science, marketing, advertising, and public relations.

The Application and Selection Process

The RMD internship committee makes selections based on academic achieve-ment, skills, abilities, and life experience. Intern selections normally are made within three months of the application deadline.

Application Materials

The following documents must be submitted to the Records Management Division internship coordinator prior to the application deadline:

- An FD-646c Preliminary Application for Employment

- A letter of faculty sponsorship from the applicant's college or university confirming the school's willingness to sponsor the student and communicate with the FBI prior to and during the internship as necessary

- Two letters of recommendation (at least one from a faculty member at the applicant's school)

- An essay (of no more than two pages) indicating the student's background, interests, goals, and reasons for wanting to participate in the RMD internship program

- A resume that outlines educational background, work experience, awards, and achievements

- Academic transcripts from all high schools and colleges attended where three or more classes were taken

- A professional 2×2–inch photograph (passport-style) of the applicant with his or her name and the date of the photo printed on the back

Application Deadline

Applications for spring internships must be submitted by September of the preceding year. Summer internship applicants must submit required materials by March of the same year. Applications for fall internships must be submitted no later than May of the same year.

Background Investigation

Students selected for the internship are given a conditional offer of employment, contingent upon the successful completion of a background investigation, and are contacted by the nearest FBI field office for further processing. Information provided on the SF-86 Questionnaire for National Security Positions is verified and used during the background investigation. In addition, the FBI normally contacts fellow students, professors, employers, coworkers, neighbors, relatives, and others. FBI personnel standards pertaining to drug use and qualifying for a security clearance also apply to RMD internship applicants. A drug test, personnel security interview, polygraph examination, and fingerprinting also are part of the background investigation. Results of the background investigation are provided to FBI Headquarters for adjudication of a Top Secret clearance.

Assignment

RMD interns work side-by-side with special agents and professional support personnel in the FBI's information hub to ensure that the Bureau's records are created, made readily available, and disposed of in accordance with prevailing policies and procedures, legal authorities, professional standards, and best business practices. They assist RMD archive specialists, management and program analysts, editors, legal assistants, records conversion specialists, research analysts, and others with the day-to-day operation of the division.

Interns are involved in a broad range of projects relating to large-scale records scanning operations and file management. Some tasks include assisting in file inventory processes using software and barcoding applications, participating in training development and video production, marketing, and working with various electronic media. RMD interns also could participate in the dissemination of FBI information responsive to requests made under the Freedom of Information Act and the Privacy Act, and provide information to FBI field offices and headquarters.

FBI Laboratory Volunteer Internship Program

The FBI Laboratory is one of the largest and most comprehensive crime laboratories in the world. It provides forensic and technical services to the FBI and other law enforcement agencies to support investigative and intelligence priorities. The Laboratory Division offers a full-time, 12-week (minimum) volunteer internship program that encourages students to seek careers at the FBI Laboratory after graduation.

Eligibility

Undergraduate and graduate students with strong academic credentials, outstanding character, and a high degree of motivation are encouraged to apply for the FBI Laboratory internship. Applicants must be a citizen of the United States and at least 18 years of age. The following minimum requirements must also be met:

- Undergraduate and graduate students must be in their junior or senior year, attending college at least part-time

- Minimum 3.0 grade-point average (GPA)

- Excellent writing skills and analytical abilities

- Proficiency with computers (for example, Microsoft Word, Excel, Access, and so on)

Depending on the particular field of interest, the most useful educational background for the Laboratory internship is forensic science, in particular biology and chemistry. Various other educational backgrounds in areas such as photography, firearms, hazardous materials, and explosives are also advantageous. Applicants do not have to be returning to their respective schools immediately following the completion of the internship.

The Application and Selection Process

Candidates must submit an application package to the FBI about 10 months prior to the starting date of the internship. Based on the application packages, the most competitive applicants will be selected directly or invited to participate in an interview. Interviews are conducted about one month after the application deadline.

Application Materials

Candidates must submit the following to the FBI Laboratory internship coordinator prior to the application deadline:

- An FD-646c Preliminary Application for Employment

- A letter of faculty sponsorship from the applicant's college or university confirming the school's willingness to sponsor the student and communicate with the FBI prior to and during the internship as necessary

- Two letters of recommendation (at least one from a faculty member at the applicant's school)

- An essay (of no more than two pages) indicating the student's background, interests, goals, and reasons for wanting to participate in the FBI Laboratory internship program

- A resume that outlines educational background, work experience, awards, and achievements

- Academic transcripts from all colleges attended where three or more classes were taken

- A professional 2×2–inch photograph (passport-style) of the applicant with their name and the date of the photo printed on the back

- Copy of a college term paper, thesis, or other substantial piece written solely by the applicant

Application Deadline

Applications for spring internships (beginning in January) must be submitted by March 1 of the preceding year. Summer internship (beginning in May) applicants must submit required materials by July 1 of the preceding year. Applications for fall internships (beginning in September) must be submitted no later than November 1 of the preceding year.

Background Investigation

Students selected for the internship are given a conditional offer of employment, contingent upon the successful completion of a background investigation, and are contacted by the nearest FBI field office for further processing. Information provided on the SF-86 Questionnaire for National Security Positions is verified and used during the background investigation. In addition, the FBI normally contacts fellow students, professors, employers, coworkers, neighbors, relatives, and others. FBI personnel standards pertaining to drug use and qualifying for a security clearance also apply to FBI Laboratory internship applicants. A drug test, personnel security interview, polygraph examination, and fingerprinting also are part of the background investigation. Results of the background investigation are provided to FBI Headquarters for adjudication of a Top Secret clearance.

Assignment

This internship is carried out at the FBI Laboratory on the Marine Corps Base in Quantico, Virginia, adjacent to the FBI training academy. Interns are assigned to various sections within the Laboratory Division, including the Scientific Analysis Section, the Latent Fingerprint Section, the Special Projects Section, the Forensic Science Research and Training Center, and the Investigative Operations and Support Section.

FBI Laboratory interns are involved in a variety of activities in support of the Bureau and other law enforcement agencies. These could include tasks related to crime scene searches, special surveillance photography, and latent-fingerprint examinations. They also can participate in forensic examinations of evidence ranging from blood, hair, and other biological materials to explosives, drugs, firearms, fibers, glass, paint, paper, and other materials. Interns also perform tasks in support of court testimony and the deployment of specially trained teams to assist domestic and international law enforcement agencies in large-scale investigations and disasters. Other activities could include tasks relating to the training of FBI staff and various state and local crime laboratory and law enforcement personnel.

FBI Laboratory interns typically work about 40 hours per week, normally from 8:00 a.m. to 4:30 p.m., Monday through Friday. The length of the internship can vary from a minimum of 12 weeks up to two years, depending on the intern's schedule and arrangements with the school, as well as projects or initiatives underway at any given time. Interns are responsible for expenses incurred relating to transportation, housing, meals, and incidentals. Although the FBI does not pay for housing accommodations, the Bureau will assist interns with locating affordable housing accommodations.

FBI Academy Volunteer Internship Program

The Bureau operates a popular and exciting unpaid internship program at the FBI Academy in Quantico, Virginia. These full-time internships are offered during three semesters per year to undergraduate and graduate students, and are open to applicants studying a variety of academic disciplines. Internships offered during the fall semester begin the second week in September, while spring-semester internships begin the second week in January and summer-semester internships begin the third week in May. Internships normally last 12 to 16 weeks, although they can be arranged for longer periods. The FBI Academy Internship Program provides experience with one of the world's premier institutions of higher learning, where FBI personnel and other members of the law enforcement community receive state-of-the-art training. Interns must pay for their housing, meals, and incidental expenses during the internship.

Eligibility

The FBI Academy seeks interns majoring in many disciplines, and the list of academic majors preferred varies periodically depending on the needs and of the Bureau and participating FBI Academy operational units. As a general rule, however, academic majors in particular demand include criminal justice, sociology, accounting, adult education, behavioral sciences, English, international relations, international business, hotel management, human resource management, communications, media and television studio production, library science, fitness and health management, physical education, human nutrition, and sports medicine, among others.

Undergraduate applicants must be at least a college junior with a minimum grade-point average of 3.0, and must be enrolled at least part-time at an accredited college or university. Applicants must also be in good standing academically, and meet all FBI employment standards. Excellent writing skills, analytical abilities, and computer proficiency are also required. Applicants must be U.S. citizens and at least 18 years of age.

The Application and Selection Process

FBI Academy internship application and selection procedures are similar to those of other FBI internships. The following section provides a summary of the process.

Application Materials

Internship candidates must submit the following application materials directly to the FBI Academy:

- A resume outlining educational background, employment experience, awards, and achievements

- An essay (one to two pages) indicating background, interests, goals, and reasons for wanting to participate in the internship program

- A copy of a college term paper, thesis, or other writing example written by the applicant

- Transcripts of credits earned at all colleges attended

- A professional 2×2–inch photograph (passport-style) of the applicant with their name and the date of the photo printed on the back

- A letter of faculty sponsorship from the applicant's college or university confirming the school's willingness to sponsor the student and communicate with the FBI prior to and during the internship as necessary

- Two letters of recommendation, including at least one from a department faculty member

- A completed SF-86 Questionnaire for National Security Positions

Application Deadlines

Candidates must submit all application materials about one year in advance. Applications for fall-semester internships starting in September must be submitted by September 1 of the preceding year. Applications for spring-semester internships beginning in January must be submitted by January 1 of the preceding year. Applications for summer-semester internships beginning in May must be submitted by May 1 of the preceding year.

Interviews

Internship finalists will be interviewed at the FBI Academy in Quantico, Virginia. Applicants must travel at their own expense for the interview.

Background Investigation

Students selected for the internship are given a conditional offer of employment, contingent upon the successful completion of a background investigation, and are contacted by the nearest FBI field office for further processing. Information provided on the SF-86 Questionnaire for National Security Positions is verified and used during the background investigation. In addition, the FBI normally contacts fellow students, professors, employers, coworkers, neighbors, relatives, and others. FBI personnel standards pertaining to drug use and qualifying for a security clearance also apply to internship applicants. A drug test, personnel security interview, polygraph examination, and fingerprinting also are part of the background investigation. Results of the background investigation are provided to FBI Headquarters for adjudication of a Top Secret clearance.

Assignment

Individual training units assign duties and responsibilities depending on the background and education of the intern and the current needs and activities of the unit to which they are assigned. Responsibilities frequently involve research, curriculum development, and lending support on various projects underway at the time. The internship experience usually is geared to the student's educational endeavors and interests. In addition, interns typically visit other units and groups to observe their activities and gain an overall prospective of Academy operations. Working hours normally are from 8:00 a.m. to 4:30 p.m., Monday through Friday, usually amounting to about 40 hours per week. FBI Academy units employing interns are discussed in the following section, including examples of assignments interns may complete.

Academy interns have many opportunities to participate in formal and on-the-job training. The nature of training provided depends mostly on the unit interns are assigned to. Training typically includes attending lectures, seminars, special presentations, or conferences at the academy; auditing courses attended by upper- and mid-level law enforcement officers in the FBI National Academy Program or other courses presented for law enforcement executives; observing classes, firearms practice and qualification, defensive tactics exercises, or other practical training in the New Agent Training program; and other on-the-job training geared to the specific functions of individual units and the intern's career aspirations. Field trips to FBI Headquarters or field offices also are possible. Many previous interns have had an opportunity to participate in firearms training and practical exercises, and to take an active role in other aspects of FBI Academy training programs.

New Agents' Training Unit Internship

FBI special agent recruits complete a basic training course known as the New Agents' Training (NAT) program. This rigorous 20-week course is designed and coordinated by experienced FBI special agents who evaluate new agent trainees as they progress through the program.

Interns assigned to the New Agents' Training Unit (NATU) assist with the coordination of all aspects of the NAT program, as well as other tasks associated with FBI recruiting and hiring initiatives. For example, NATU interns support the unit by working on projects relating to classroom and practical training, measuring success and gathering statistics concerning the NAT program, conducting longitudinal surveys, studying the hiring progression for FBI special agents, developing forecasts for future hiring of special agents, and exploring trends and other aspects of FBI basic training. Interns are provided ongoing opportunities to attend lectures and observe practical exercises dealing with subjects such as organized crime, domestic and international terrorism, undercover operations, informants, technical investigative equipment, information security, behavioral sciences, drug enforcement, law enforcement communication, ethics, and other topics.

Internship candidates should have an interest in human performance. A background in statistics and data analysis, and experience working with computers (for example, Microsoft Word, Excel, Access, PowerPoint, and so on) is a plus.

Behavioral Science Unit Research Internship

The Behavioral Science Unit (BSU) develops and provides training programs, research, and consultation in the behavioral and social sciences in support of the FBI and other law enforcement and intelligence agencies. The unit's personnel are experienced instructors and veteran police officers with advanced degrees in disciplines such as psychology, criminology, and sociology.

BSU interns assist with the development of training programs, course materials, and research in areas such as criminal psychology and profiling, forensic psychology, community policing, crime analysis, death investigation, gangs and gang behavior, domestic violence, law enforcement officers killed and assaulted in the line of duty, stress management in law enforcement, serial crimes, counterterrorism, and hate crimes. Interns participate in a variety of research projects and perform literature searches and reviews; research design tasks; data collection, coding, entry, and analysis; crime analysis; and related tasks.

The Behavioral Science Unit is especially interested in students majoring in criminal justice, criminology, sociology, psychology, or forensic science for the BSU internship, although they may consider applicants majoring in other disciplines. Applicants with a background in statistics and data analysis, and experience working with computers (for example, Microsoft Word, Excel, Access, PowerPoint, and so on), should be especially competitive.

Distance Learning Technology Unit Internship

Interns who are interested in Web-based training provide support to the Distance Learning Technology Unit (DLTU), where they assist with the development of courses and tools using a variety of traditional and technology-based instructional media, and provide production support for FBI training.

DLTU interns assist with the coordination and development of the FBI's Virtual Academy, which serves as a Web delivery model for training to all FBI employees. This coordination involves developing training functions, such as

Web-based learning, computer-based learning, virtual classrooms, and digital collaboration environments within the FBI Virtual Academy. Interns also assist with content development for the Virtual Academy.

Applicants majoring in disciplines concerning Web site development, instructional technology, television production, computer science, telecommunications, and related fields will be especially competitive, although students pursuing other majors also may be considered. Experience working with computers (for example, Microsoft Word, Excel, Access, PowerPoint, and so on) is a plus.

Investigative Training Unit Research Internship

The Investigative Training Unit (ITU) presents instruction to every category of student at the FBI Academy. Among other subjects, ITU instructors teach courses concerning basic and advanced investigative and intelligence techniques, national security investigations, case management, white-collar crime, organized crime, financial investigations, espionage, undercover operations, drug trafficking, national security investigations, domestic and international terrorism, and international investigations.

ITU interns assist with projects designed to teach FBI New Agent Training students how to investigate these offenses and other violations of federal law. For example, interns perform tasks such as updating academy curricula and instructional manuals, assisting instructors with class preparation, researching law enforcement topics for use in the classroom or FBI publications, and conducting legal research of court cases related to subject matter presented to trainees. Many of these tasks involve the application of word-processing and other computer software programs such as Microsoft PowerPoint, Excel, and Access.

Experience with computers is a plus, inasmuch as ITU staff also teach courses relating to computer databases, digital analysis, searching and seizing computers, and other information technology subjects.

Leadership Training Unit Internship

The FBI Academy's Leadership Training Unit (LTU) designs and conducts training programs for all levels of FBI personnel, as well as executive development programs for state, county, municipal, and international law enforcement agency managers. Interns serving in this Academy component conduct research and assist LTU instructors with ongoing projects and curriculum development relating to FBI New Agent Training, the FBI National Academy, the National Executive Institute, the Law Enforcement Executive Development Seminar, and other law enforcement management training programs.

Some of the tasks LTU interns perform include revising handouts and other course materials; working on PowerPoint presentations that are used in the classroom; designing marketing surveys; conducting research relating to leadership and management, and analyzing the data; and assisting LTU instructors with the development of distance-learning programs.

Preference will be given to internship applicants majoring in disciplines such as business administration, management, human resources, marketing, and adult learning, although students pursuing degrees in other disciplines also may be considered. Knowledge of distance learning initiatives and program planning also are required, and experience with computers (for example, Microsoft Word, Excel, Access, PowerPoint, and so on) is a plus.

Law Enforcement Communication Unit Research Internship

Serving the Law Enforcement Communication Unit (LECU) provides interns with outstanding experience in the fields of law enforcement training and publishing. LECU staff are responsible not only for training special agent recruits and FBI National Academy students, but also for publishing the *FBI Law Enforcement Bulletin,* the most widely read law enforcement publication in the world.

Within this framework, LECU interns assist instructors with lesson plans, student practical exercises, and role-playing scenarios in subjects such as media relations, interviewing and interrogation, statement analysis, informant development, field office communications, effective writing, and public speaking. They also assist *FBI Law Enforcement Bulletin* staff with articles submitted by law enforcement professionals for publication, which involves proofreading and editing material through all stages of production leading up to the finished publication. Other tasks interns perform focus on literature searches, preparing annotated bibliographies or summaries of articles, developing and collating information for writing and editing assignments, and assisting in the analysis of information collected in research projects.

The Law Enforcement Communication Unit is particularly interested in recruiting candidates with an educational background in criminal justice, communications, or English, although the unit may also consider applicants with other academic majors. Proficiency with Microsoft Word, Excel, and Access also is desired.

Curriculum Development and Evaluation Unit Internship

Located at FBI Headquarters, the Curriculum Development and Evaluation Unit (CDEU) is the only component of the FBI Training Division that is not located in Quantico. Based at FBI Headquarters in Washington, D.C., CDEU personnel rely on the assistance of student interns to ensure that the content and design of all FBI Academy programs meet the present and future needs of FBI personnel and other Academy students.

Many of the tasks interns perform revolve around the analysis of FBI training programs, which includes curriculum and needs assessment, task analysis, definition of learning objectives, analyzing training delivery methods, and evaluating course outlines. Interns also are responsible for conducting research and participating in projects concerning course design and development, course materials, instructional strategies, learning methodologies, and course evaluations. Some research is performed at the Library of Congress, as well as college, university, and local libraries. Projects carried out by interns also may involve coordination with the FBI Academy's Distance Learning Technology Unit and other components.

Preference will be given to students majoring in education or a closely related field, although students with other majors may be considered on a case-by-case basis. Applicants must have experience with Microsoft Word, Excel, and PowerPoint computer software programs. Candidates with knowledge of database and statistical packages such as SPSS and Microsoft Access will be especially competitive.

Physical Training Unit Internship

FBI special agent trainees learn physical fitness and defensive tactics techniques from the Physical Training Unit (PTU). This unit manages the Bureau's physical fitness and defensive tactics programs and instructs new agent trainees and National Academy students in defensive tactics and the principles of health and fitness. PTU staff also develop and deliver training for FBI employees (and their spouses) being deployed overseas. Much of this internship is served in the FBI Academy gymnasium, where PTU instructors prepare new agent trainees physically and mentally for the challenges they will face after graduation.

PTU interns are involved in projects that focus on educating special agent recruits about defensive tactics skills, use of force laws, and FBI policies they will need to master to carry out their responsibilities in a safe, effective, and legal manner. Interns also assist in the effort to educate trainees concerning the benefits of regular exercise and maintaining a healthy lifestyle. Although interns do not have teaching responsibilities, they may be asked to assist with physical challenges and events new agent trainees and National Academy students participate in, such as the obstacle course and endurance runs. Depending on projects in progress at the time, interns may also assist PTU instructors with downloading articles, periodicals, and video via the Internet, or with development of the FBI defensive tactics manual.

Ideal candidates for this internship include those majoring in criminal justice, physical education, or exercise physiology, although PTU staff also will consider applicants studying other majors.

International Training and Assistance Unit Research Internship

The International Training and Assistance Unit (ITAU) internship involves students in training programs the FBI presents to international police officials at the FBI Academy and other sites throughout the world, including the International Law Enforcement Academy in Budapest, Hungary. The FBI's international training initiatives are designed to protect U.S. interests at home and overseas, and also to assist foreign police agencies in their efforts to combat international criminal activity. Courses presented by FBI instructors focus on international terrorism, financial fraud, money laundering, organized crime, drug trafficking, white-collar crime, and other international criminal matters.

Interns conduct research and prepare briefings for instructors concerning activities and issues in various regions of the world that will be the focus of FBI training programs. These could involve tasks such as composing country background information, highlighting current events, gathering data on recent terrorist attacks, and conducting research regarding special holidays and anniversaries of significant events. ITAU interns also compose reports relating to the training courses, enabling them to gain insight regarding the Bureau's contribution to combating terrorism and other crime through international training. Interns attend lectures, special presentations, and briefings; assist instructors with seminars held at the FBI Academy; and may have an opportunity to travel internationally.

Preferred majors include foreign relations, international finance, international government, and related areas of study, although other majors may be considered. Experience with computers (for example, Microsoft Word, Excel, Access, PowerPoint, and so on) and proficient writing skills also are desired. Applicants should have a valid passport and willingness to travel abroad, as well as an interest in foreign relations, international finance, and international government.

Administrative Services Unit Internship

Students assigned to the FBI Academy's Administrative Services Unit (ASU) are directly involved in the Bureau's effort to control administrative information and provide human resources support for all units at the Academy.

This internship offers opportunities to assist Academy staff with many records-management functions and tasks such as maintaining policy and procedure information, creating position descriptions, coordinating job interviews with prospective employees, preparing briefing reports to be used by the FBI Director, keeping track of FBI firearms and ammunition, and working on computer databases designed to process and control files and other information. ASU interns also perform a broad range of training support tasks associated with the FBI Academy's International Training and Assistance Unit, such as determining whether prospective students qualify to attend FBI Academy training programs and making arrangements for their attendance.

Applicants should be motivated and possess exceptional organization skills. Preferred majors include computer science, information technology, data processing, and related areas of study. Competitive candidates will have a significant background in computer sciences and networking, and knowledge of software applications such as Microsoft Word, PowerPoint, Excel, Access, and WordPerfect, and SPSS.

Library Unit Internship

Interns assigned to the FBI Academy Library work in an impressive facility that is situated in the center of the Academy dormitory complex. The library holds 45,000 volumes and other open-source materials pertaining to law enforcement, criminal justice, and government.

This internship involves a broad range of library science assignments, such as working with the library's special collections; archival functions; acquisitions tasks; assisting with requests for information from FBI Academy staff, other FBI components and field offices, and other law enforcement agencies; and working with other libraries to exchange materials through inter-library loan systems. Interns also update and prepare bibliographies on contemporary law enforcement and criminal justice topics, process U.S. Government Printing Office documents, manage circulation and cataloging functions, plan and implement Web site content and design, and participate in library planning functions.

Applicants for this internship must be enrolled in a graduate program working toward a Master's degree in library science. Although the library is open 24 hours a day, interns work only during regular daytime business hours, Monday through Friday.

Financial Management Unit Internship

The FBI Academy's Financial Management Unit (FMU) offers a unique internship for undergraduate and graduate students interested in pursuing a career in accounting or business management.

Interns serving the FMU apply government accounting principles and assist FBI administrative staff with an extensive assortment of financial, accounting, auditing, budgeting, and recordkeeping functions carried out by and for the FBI Academy. For example, the duties of FMU accounting interns may involve auditing Academy financial records; analyzing account information; creating and improving spreadsheet programs used to track accounting data; processing travel vouchers filed by Academy personnel and students, and auditing associated travel accounts; auditing procurement accounts; researching Academy budget appropriations; creating computer databases; and assisting Academy auditors with many other projects and initiatives underway at the time.

The Financial Management Unit is particularly interested in undergraduate and graduate students majoring in business administration, accounting, or related areas of study, although other majors also may be considered. Applicants also should have a solid working knowledge of Microsoft Excel and Microsoft Access software programs.

Practical Applications Unit Internship

The FBI Academy's Practical Applications Unit (PAU) provides new agent trainees, special agents, professional support personnel, and law enforcement officers from other agencies with practical training to enhance their ability to conduct investigations in a safe and effective manner. This unit is located within the Hogan's Alley complex at the FBI Academy (see chapter 8 for more information).

PAU interns apply their knowledge, skills, and abilities in various projects pertaining to the FBI's New Agent Training program and other courses. The primary responsibilities of PAU interns revolve around practical applications for New Agent Program trainees, and presentation of the Law Enforcement Safety and Survival training program, the Tactical Emergency Vehicle Operations course, and the Overseas Antiterrorism and Force Protection training program. The tasks interns perform vary widely, although they could include curriculum review, analyzing training delivery methods, evaluating course outlines, conducting research, updating course materials, and other activities. Projects carried out by interns also may involve coordination with other FBI Academy units.

Applications for the PAU Internship are accepted from candidates majoring in criminal justice, criminology, and other majors. Applicants must have a sincere interest in the education and training of new FBI agents and other law enforcement personnel. Proficient writing skills are necessary. Applicants also must be computer literate, motivated, well organized, capable of balancing multiple tasks, and able to work with minimal supervision.

Strategic Planning and Policy Unit Internship

The Strategic Planning and Policy Unit (SPPU) manages and develops plans, procedures, strategies, and resources to support all FBI Academy training, accreditation, and Training and Development Division initiatives in alignment with the Bureau's strategic priorities.

Although the duties of SPPU interns vary in accordance with the needs of the unit and each intern's skills, interests, and abilities, tasks generally are related to FBI Academy instructional support, policy research, strategic planning and reporting, and the FBI Citizens' Academy. SPPU interns could conduct research and analyze the data, perform Internet searches, evaluate course outlines, revise handouts and other materials, work on PowerPoint presentations, and assist SPPU staff with a variety of other tasks. Projects carried out by interns also may involve coordination with other FBI Academy units.

A broad range of college majors are preferred, including criminal justice, public administration, computer science, information technology, communications, education, and media or graphic design. Intern applicants must have proficiency with computers sufficient to download articles and video segments, and prepare instructional materials and presentations with graphics. Proficiency with Microsoft Word, Excel, PowerPoint, and Access is a plus.

PART 3

APPENDIXES

APPENDIX A

Online Application for the Special Agent Position

The online application includes more than 100 questions that are designed to screen out applicants who do not meet minimum requirements, to evaluate applicants' qualifications, and to ensure that applicants fully understand what is expected of them during the application process and on the job. In addition to submitting basic biographical information, applicants must answer questions and furnish information relating to their citizenship, military service, employment history, community service and volunteer work, education, professional certifications earned, awards and professional recognition, special skills, and foreign-language proficiency. Applicants must also certify that they are willing to undergo a background investigation, urinalysis drug screening, and medical examination, and also that they understand and accept a number of job requirements. Information obtained from online applications is used to establish competitiveness, which serves as the basis for determining which candidates are invited to complete phase I testing.

This appendix provides a listing of questions asked and information requested in the online application. To enhance user-friendliness of this appendix, questions presented during the online application registration process have been combined with the body of the application, headings have been added to categorize the nature of information requested, and the order of some questions has been changed so that questions concerning similar topics and issues are grouped together.

Applicant Personal Data

1. Applicant information._____

    a. Name _____

    b. Date of birth_____

    c. Social Security number _____

    d. Address_____

    _____

    e. Phone number_____

    f. E-mail address _____

2. Are you a United States citizen?

   a. Yes

   b. No

3. Do you have dual citizenship?

   a. Yes

   b. No

3.1. If you answered "yes" to the previous question, are you willing to renounce your foreign citizenship?

   a. Yes

   b. No

4. Military Service and Veterans' Preference (select one):

   a. Not a veteran.

   b. 30 percent or more compensably disabled veteran.

   c. 10-point compensable veteran. You must have an existing compensable service-connected disability of 10 percent or more.

   d. Other 10-point veteran. To select (d), you must be one of the following:

      (1) A disabled veteran or a veteran who was awarded the Purple Heart for wounds or injuries received in action

      (2) A veteran's widow or widower who has not remarried

      (3) The wife or husband of a veteran who has a service-connected disability which disqualified the veteran for civil service appointments

      (4) The widowed, divorced, or separated mother of an ex-service son or daughter who died in action, or who is totally and permanently disabled

   e. 5-point veteran. To select (e), you must have been discharged under honorable conditions and had one of the following:

      (1) Active duty in the Armed Forces of the United States, in a war or during the period 04/28/52 to 07/01/55

      (2) Active duty for more than 180 consecutive days other than for training, any part of which occurred during the period between 02/01/55 to 10/14/76

      (3) Active duty during the Gulf War sometime between 08/02/1990 and 01/02/1992

      (4) Active duty in a campaign or expedition for which a campaign badge has been authorized

   f. Had active duty or reserve service which does not meet any of the above.

5. If you are or were active military, please identify the branch of service.

   a. I am not nor have I been active military.

   b. Air Force

   c. Army

   d. Coast Guard

   e. Marines

   f. Navy

6. If you are a veteran, supply service dates below:

   a. Start of service: _____

   b. End of service: _____

   c. Not applicable

7. If you are not in the U.S. military, are you a U.S. government employee currently on assignment overseas?

   a. Yes

   b. No

8. If you are a male at least 18 years of age, born after December 31, 1959, have you registered with the Selective Service System?

   a. Yes

   b. No

   c. Not applicable

9. If you are a male at least 18 years of age, born after December 31, 1959, AND you have not registered with the Selective Service System, do you have an approved exemption?

   a. Yes

   b. No

10. Do you possess a valid U.S. driver's license and drive a motor vehicle?

    a. Yes

    b. No

Previous Federal Employment

1. Are you now, or have you ever been, a civilian Federal employee?

   a. Yes

   b. No

2. If you are or were a civilian Federal employee, by what agency and organization are or were you employed?

   a. Federal Bureau of Investigation

   b. Other

   c. Not applicable

2.1. If you selected "Other," please enter the agency and organization.

_____

3. If you are a current Federal employee, what is your duty station?

_____

4. If you are currently a Federal employee, under what type of appointment are you serving?

   a. Permanent-Career, competitive service

   b. Career-Conditional, competitive service

   c. Temporary (Time-Limited Appointment, not to exceed one year, may become permanent)

   d. Term (Time-Limited Appointment, more than one year, not more than four years and may become permanent)

   e. Excepted Service (FBI employees, students that may become permanent, PMI, disability, etc.)

   f. Other

   g. Not Applicable

5. If you are NOT currently serving as a permanent Federal employee, have you previously held a permanent appointment or a time-limited appointment eligible for conversion to a permanent appointment in the Federal government?

   a. Yes

   b. No

6. If you are or ever were a Federal civilian employee, please indicate the pay plan, series, and grade of the highest graded position you held (i.e., GS-0343-14).

_____

7. If you are a current civilian Federal employee, please indicate the level of security clearance you hold.

   a. Secret

   b. Top Secret

   c. Top Secret with SCI access

   d. Not Applicable

8. Are you a retiree receiving a Federal annuity, either military or civilian?

   a. Yes

   b. No

   c. Not Applicable

   Note: If you are an annuitant, your salary or annuity may be reduced upon employment.

9. Have you accepted a buyout from a Federal agency within the past 5 years?

   a. Yes

   b. No

   c. Not Applicable

   Note: If you have accepted a Federal buyout, you may be required to repay a pro-rated portion upon employment with the FBI.

Employment Suitability and Disqualifiers

1. I understand that my answers to the following questions determine my suitability for application to ANY position with the FBI.

   a. Yes

   b. No

2. I am willing to undergo a comprehensive background investigation which includes, but is not limited to, contact with all references, employers, coworkers, close personal associates, etc.; review of my driving record; credit history; criminal history; and service in the military.

   a. Yes

   b. No

3. I am willing to undergo a pre-employment polygraph, physical examination, and a urinalysis drug test. Refusal to submit to an FBI urinalysis (drug test) or polygraph examination is grounds for disqualification from the applicant process.

   a. Yes

   b. No

4. Are you currently in default (failed to make payments) on a student loan insured by the U.S. Government?

   a. Yes

   b. No

5. Have you ever been convicted of a felony?

   a. Yes

   b. No

6. Have you used marijuana/cannabis during the last three (3) years or have you extensively used marijuana/cannabis over a substantial period of time?

   a. Yes

   b. No

7. Have you used any illegal drugs(s) or combination of illegal drugs, other than marijuana, during the past ten (10) years or engaged in more than minimal experimentation in your lifetime? (For the purpose of this question, the term "illegal drugs" includes the use of anabolic steroids

after February 27, 1991, unless the steroids were prescribed by a physician for your use alone to alleviate a medical condition.)

    a. Yes

    b. No

8. Have you used any illegal drug(s) while employed in any law enforcement or prosecutorial position; or while employed in a position which carries with it a high level of responsibility or public trust; or while holding a security clearance?

    a. Yes

    b. No

9. Have you ever distributed or sold any illegal drugs for profit?

    a. Yes

    b. No

10. Are you a member of any foreign or domestic organization, association, movement, group, or combination of persons which is totalitarian, fascist, communist, or subversive, or which has adopted, or shows a policy of advocating or approving the commission of acts of force or violence to deny other persons their rights under the Constitution of the United States, or which seeks to alter the form of Government of the U.S. by unconstitutional means?

    a. Yes

    b. No

11. Do you have a physical or mental impairment that limits one or more major life activities AND has been certified by the State Department of Vocational Services or Veterans Administration?

    a. Yes

    b. No

Demographic Information

Applicants are requested to provide the following information for statistical purposes only. The information will be used to evaluate recruitment and hiring activities. Public Law 93-579 (Privacy Act of 1974) permits solicitation of personal information. SUBMISSION OF THIS INFORMATION IS VOLUNTARY. Your failure to do so will not affect the processing of your application. Your cooperation is appreciated.

1. Ethnicity:

    a. Hispanic or Latino

    b. Not Hispanic or Latino

2. Race (check all that apply):

    a. American Indian or Alaska Native

    b. Asian

    c. Black or African American

   d. Native Hawaiian or Other Pacific Islander

   e. White

   f. Hispanic In Puerto Rico

   g. Not Hispanic In Puerto Rico

3. Gender:

   a. Male

   b. Female

4. Do you have any physical disabilities?

   a. Yes

   b. No

4.1. If yes, do you have a targeted disability?

   a. Yes

   b. No

Education and Critical Skills

1. Choose one answer that best describes your education as related to the basic qualification requirements for this position:

   a. I have a four-year degree from an accredited college or university.

   b. I do not possess the education requirement described above.

2. In addition to meeting the basic eligibility requirement of an undergraduate degree, applicants must possess the experience and/or education relative to one or more Critical Skills/Selective Placement Factors (SPF) to be considered for this position. Failure to meet the SPF will result in the applicant not receiving further consideration for this position. Applicants who do not meet the SPF will be rated ineligible.

FBI SPECIAL AGENT CRITICAL SKILLS

- Accounting/Finance
- Computer Science/Information Technology
- Engineering
- Foreign Language proficiency
- Intelligence
- Law
- Law Enforcement or Military
- Physical Science
- Diversified

Do you possess at least one of the selective placement factors listed above?

   a. Yes

   b. No

3. Please identify the selective placement factor(s) for which you possess experience and/or education.

   Check all that apply:

   a. Accounting/Finance

   b. Computer Science/Information Technology

   c. Engineering

   d. Foreign Language proficiency

   e. Intelligence

   f. Law

   g. Law Enforcement or Military

   h. Physical Science

   i. Diversified

   j. None

4. Do you have a Juris Doctorate degree from an accredited law school?

   a. Yes

   b. No

5. Have you ever been admitted to the Bar of any U.S. state or jurisdiction?

   a. Yes

   b. No

6. Have you successfully completed the FBI Honors Internship Program?

   a. Yes

   b. No

6.1. When did you complete the program?_____

_____

7. If you currently have a Pilot's License, please identify the type(s). You will be asked to provide proof of ratings at a later date.

   a. I have a Fixed Wing/Single Engine License

   b. I have a Multi-Engine Pilot's License

   c. I do not currently have a Pilot's License

8. Which of the following best describes your education or experience in Accounting and/or Finance?

   a. I do not have education or experience in Accounting and/or Finance

   b. I have a Bachelor's Degree in Accounting and/or Finance

   c. I have a Master's Degree or higher in Accounting and/or Finance

   d. I am a Certified Public Accountant (CPA)

   e. I have at least 3 years of relevant Accounting/Finance experience

8.1. Please briefly describe your 3 years of Accounting and/or Finance experience. More detailed information should be included in your resume.

_____

_____

9. Which of the following best describes your education and/or certification in Computer Science and/or Information Technology?

a. I have a Bachelor's Degree in Computer Science and/or Information Technology or related discipline

b. I have a Master's Degree or higher in Computer Science and/or Information Technology

c. I am a Cisco Certified Network Professional (CCNP) and/or Cisco Certified Internet Expert (CCIE)

d. I am not CCNP or CCIE certified but have at least 2 years of relevant Computer Science and/or Information Technology experience

e. I do not have education or experience in Computer Science and/or Information Technology

10. Which of the following best describes your education in the Physical Sciences (such as physics, chemistry, biology, etc.)?

a. I do not have education in the Physical Sciences

b. I have a Bachelor's Degree in the Physical Sciences

c. I have a Master's Degree or higher in the Physical Sciences

10.1. If you have a degree in the Physical Sciences, please specify the discipline of the highest degree obtained.

a. Physics

b. Chemistry

c. Biology

d. Other

11. Which of the following best describes your experience and/or education in Engineering?

a. I have a Bachelor's Degree in Engineering

b. I have a Master's Degree or higher in Engineering

c. I do not have education in Engineering

11.1. If you have a degree in Engineering, please specify the discipline of the highest degree obtained.

a. Mechanical

b. Electrical

c. Chemical

d. Other

12. In order to qualify for a Diversified critical skill, you must have a four-year degree from an accredited college/university AND three years of full-time work experience; OR possess an advanced degree from an accredited college/university AND two years of full-time work experience. Do you possess the education and/or experience as stated above?

    a. Yes

    b. No

12.1. Please provide examples from your experience that support your answer choice. You are encouraged to include specific accomplishments in your responses. Please cross-reference this information to your resume.

    _____

    _____

13. Do you have at least two years of full-time experience in the intelligence field?

    a. Yes

    b. No

13.1. Please select the area(s) in which you have operational intelligence experience.

    Check all that apply:

    a. Foreign Counterintelligence

    b. Counterterrorism

    c. Military Intelligence

13.2. Please provide examples from your experience that support your answer choice. You are encouraged to include specific accomplishments in your responses. Please cross-reference this information to your resume.

    _____

    _____

14. Do you have at least two years of full-time experience in Law Enforcement or other Criminal Investigative areas?

    a. Yes

    b. No

14.1. Please provide examples from your experience that support your answer choice. You are encouraged to include specific accomplishments in your responses. Please cross-reference this information to your resume.

    _____

    _____

15. Do you have at least 3 years of Special Operations experience in the U.S. Military, or at least 3 years of specialized law enforcement tactical experience?

    a. Yes

    b. No

15.1. Please briefly explain your Special Operations experience, including any certifications or education you may have. Do not enter classified information.

_____

_____

16. Are you fluent in any foreign languages?

a. Yes

b. No

16.1. What foreign language are you proficient in?

1. Achinese	29. French
2. Afrikaans	30. Fulani
3. Albanian	31. Ga
4. Amharic	32. Georgian
5. Arabic	33. German
6. Aramaic	34. Greek
7. Armenian	35. Gujarati
8. Assyrian	36. Haitian Creole
9. Azerbaijani	37. Hakka
10. Bambara	38. Hausa
11. Bengali	39. Hebrew
12. Bosnian	40. Hindi
13. Bulgarian	41. Hmong
14. Burmese	42. Hungarian
15. Cambodian/Khmer	43. Ibo
16. Cantonese	44. Ilocano
17. Cebuano	45. Indonesian
18. Chavacano	46. Italian
19. Chechen	47. Jamaican Patois
20. Croatian	48. Japanese
21. Czech	49. Kazakh
22. Danish	50. Kirghiz
23. Dari	51. Korean
24. Dutch	52. Kurdish—Kermanji
25. Estonian	53. Kurdish—Sorani
26. Farsi	54. Lao
27. Finnish	55. Latvian
28. Flemish	56. Lithuanian

57. Macedonian
58. Malay
59. Malayalam
60. Malinke
61. Maltese
62. Mandarin
63. Marathi
64. Mongolian
65. Nepalese
66. Northern Min/Fuzhou
67. Norwegian
68. Pashto
69. Polish
70. Portuguese
71. Punjabi
72. Romanian
73. Russian
74. Ruthenian
75. Samoan
76. Serbian
77. Shanghai
78. Sicilian
79. Sindhi
80. Sinhalese
81. Slovak
82. Slovenian

83. Somali
84. Soninke
85. Spanish
86. Southern Min/Amoy/ Taiwanese
87. Sundanese
88. Swahili
89. Swedish
90. Tagalog
91. Tajik
92. Tamil
93. Tausug
94. Telugu
95. Thai
96. Tigrinya
97. Tongan
98. Turkish
99. Turkmen
100. Twi
101. Uighur
102. Ukrainian
103. Urdu
104. Uzbek
105. Vietnamese
106. Wolof
107. Yiddish
108. Yoruba

16.2. What is your self-declared SPEAKING proficiency in this language?

a. 0
b. 0+
c. 1
d. 1+
e. 2
f. 2+
g. 3

h. 3+

i. 4

j. 4+

k. 5

Special Agent Career Path

After the successful completion of a background investigation and prior to entry into New Agents' Training, Special Agent applicants will be designated into one of the following five (5) career paths: Intelligence, Counterintelligence, Counterterrorism, Criminal, or Cyber. In addition, applicants designated to either Counterintelligence or Counterterrorism may receive a further specialty designation to Weapons of Mass Destruction matters based upon their education and/or prior employment.

1. Please indicate your first choice of preference in the Special Agent Career path:

   a. Intelligence

   b. Counterintelligence

   c. Counterterrorism

   d. Criminal

   e. Cyber

2. Please indicate your second choice of preference in the Special Agent Career path:

   a. Intelligence

   b. Counterintelligence

   c. Counterterrorism

   d. Criminal

   e. Cyber

3. Please indicate your third choice of preference in the Special Agent Career path:

   a. Intelligence

   b. Counterintelligence

   c. Counterterrorism

   d. Criminal

   e. Cyber

4. Please indicate your fourth choice of preference in the Special Agent Career path:

   a. Intelligence

   b. Counterintelligence

   c. Counterterrorism

   d. Criminal

   e. Cyber

5. Please indicate your fifth choice of preference in the Special Agent Career path:

   a. Intelligence

   b. Counterintelligence

   c. Counterterrorism

   d. Criminal

   e. Cyber

6. If your final Career Path designation is not your preferred selection, are you willing to be considered for the Special Agent position?

NOTE: If you answer "NO" to this question, you will not be allowed to continue processing for the Special Agent position as all Special Agent applicants must be willing to work in the Career Path deemed most beneficial to the needs of the FBI.

   a. Yes

   b. No

Application Process Requirements

1. Federal Law requires Special Agent applicants to be able to achieve 20 years of service prior to mandatory retirement at age 57. Please select the response that best describes how you meet this requirement:

   a. I am currently between 23 and 36 years of age

   b. I am currently assigned in a Federal Law Enforcement or other Federal position which requires mandatory retirement at age 57

   c. None of the above

2. I understand that the FBI may disqualify me at any time during the application process should it be determined that I will reach age 37 before completion of the process (this does not apply to individuals currently employed in federal law enforcement positions).

   a. Yes

   b. No

3. I am aware that as an applicant for the Special Agent position, I will be required to pass a Physical Fitness Test (PFT) which consists of four events (sit-ups, 300-meter sprint, push-ups, and one and one-half mile run).

   a. Yes

   b. No

4. I am aware that as a Special Agent I will be required to accept no more than a two-week notice to report to New Agent Training upon

successful completion of the application process, and that failure to do so may result in disqualification for future consideration.

a. Yes

b. No

Job Requirements

1. I am aware that as a Special Agent I will be required to routinely carry firearms and use them, as appropriate, in a variety of life-threatening situations.

    a. Yes

    b. No

2. I am aware that as a Special Agent I will be required to engage in strenuous and potentially dangerous duties including witness heinous crimes or crime scenes, participate in raids and arrests, and use of defensive tactics.

    a. Yes

    b. No

3. I am aware that as a Special Agent I will be required to work an average of 10 hours per day, work overtime, or work an irregular schedule as required.

    a. Yes

    b. No

4. I am aware that as a Special Agent I will occupy a "Key Federal Employee" position and therefore may not be a member of, or rejoin during FBI employment, a military Ready Reserve unit.

    a. Yes

    b. No

5. I am aware that as a Special Agent I must successfully complete New Agent Training at the FBI Academy in Quantico, Virginia, for 21 weeks which includes physical fitness, firearms, defensive tactics, academics, practical exercises, self-study, and teamwork, or I will be terminated from the FBI.

    a. Yes

    b. No

6. I will commit to serving the FBI as a Special Agent for three years to meet the service agreement for training (this includes the initial two-year probationary period).

    a. Yes

    b. No

7. If appointed as Special Agent, I will accept assignment and relocate anywhere within the FBI's jurisdiction.

    a. Yes

    b. No

8. I have discussed my potential transfer with my spouse, significant other, and/or family. They know and understand that I must be willing to relocate as a requirement of the Special Agent position.

    a. Yes

    b. No

Notice to Applicants

This is a federal job application system. Providing false information, creating fake identification, or failing to answer all questions truthfully and completely may be grounds for not hiring, for disbarment from federal employment, or for dismissal after the applicant begins work. Falsifying a federal job application, attempting to violate the privacy of others, or attempting to compromise the operation of this system may be punishable by fine or imprisonment (Title 18, U.S. Code, section 1001).

Questionnaire for National Security Positions (SF-86)

The Questionnaire for National Security Positions is a 21-page form that requests a great deal of detailed information about your background. The FBI and other federal agencies use this form as the basis for the background investigation and to determine eligibility for a security clearance and access to classified information.

On this form, you must provide information relating to birth and citizenship, places of residence, educational achievements, employment history, military service, references and social acquaintances, foreign travel, association membership, civil and criminal court record, financial status, relatives, roommates, alcohol and drug use, passport information, and security clearances previously held. Although instructions on the SF-86 ask you to go back seven years from the present concerning where you have lived, worked, attended school, and conducted other activities, the FBI requires all applicants to go back to age 18 for background investigation and security clearance purposes.

It is critical that you fill out the Questionnaire for National Security Positions accurately and completely. Submitting an incomplete form could result not only in a delay in the processing of your application, but also your elimination from employment consideration.

Standard Form 86
Revised July 2008
U.S. Office of Personnel Management
5 CFR Parts 731, 732, and 736

Form approved:
OMB No. 3206 0005
NSN 7540-00 634-4036
86-111

Questionnaire for National Security Positions

Follow instructions fully or we cannot process your form. If you have any questions, contact the office that gave you the form.

Purpose of this Form

The United States (U.S.) Government conducts background investigations and reinvestigations of persons under consideration for or retention in national security positions as defined in 5 CFR 732 and for positions requiring access to classified information under Executive Order 12968.

Giving us this information is voluntary. If you do not provide each item of requested information, however, we will not be able to complete your investigation, which will adversely affect your eligibility for a national security position. Any information that you provide is evaluated on the basis of its recency, seriousness, relevance to the position and duties, and consistency with all other information about you.

Withholding, misrepresenting, or falsifying information will have an impact on a security clearance, employment prospects, or job status, up to and including denial or revocation of your security clearance, or your removal and debarment from Federal Service.

This form is a permanent document that may be used as the basis for future investigations, security clearance determinations, and determinations of your suitability for employment. Your responses to this form may be compared with previous security questionnaires. It is imperative that the information provided be true and accurate to the best of your knowledge.

Authority to Request this Information

Depending upon the purpose of your investigation, the U.S. Government is authorized to ask for this information under Executive Orders 10450, 10865, 12333, and 12968; sections 3301, 3302, and 9101 of title 5, U.S. Code (U.S.C.); sections 2165 and 2201 of title 42, U.S.C.; chapter 23 of title 50, U.S.C.; and parts 2, 5, 731, 732, and 736 of title 5, Code of Federal Regulations.

Your Social Security Number (SSN) is needed to identify your unique records. Although disclosure of your SSN is not mandatory, failure to disclose your SSN may prevent or delay the processing of your background investigation. The authority for soliciting and verifying your SSN is Executive Order 9397.

The Investigative Process

Background investigations for national security positions are conducted to gather information to show whether you are reliable, trustworthy, of good conduct and character, and loyal to the U.S. The information that you provide on this form may be confirmed during the investigation. The investigation may extend beyond the time covered by this form when necessary to resolve issues. Your current employer may be contacted as part of the investigation, even if you have previously indicated on applications or other forms that you do not want your current employer to be contacted.

In addition to the questions on this form, inquiry also is made about your adherence to security requirements, honesty and integrity, vulnerability to exploitation or coercion, falsification, misrepresentation, and any other behavior, activities, or associations that tend to show the person is not reliable, trustworthy, or loyal. Checks of Federal agency records may be made about your spouse or other cohabitant.

Your Personal Interview

Some investigations will include an interview with you as a routine part of the investigative process. The investigator may ask you to explain your answers to any question on this form. This provides you the opportunity to update, clarify, and explain information on your form more completely, which often helps to complete your investigation faster. It is important that the interview be conducted as soon as possible after you are contacted. Postponements will delay the processing of your investigation, and declining to be interviewed may result in your investigation being delayed or canceled.

For the interview, you will be asked to bring identification with your picture on it, such as a valid state driver's license. There are other documents you may be asked to bring to verify your identity as well. These may include documentation of any legal name change, Social Security card, passport, and/ or your birth certificate.

You may also be asked to bring documents about information you provided on the form or about other matters requiring specific attention. These matters include (a) alien registration or naturalization documentation; (b) delinquent loans or taxes, bankruptcies, judgments, liens, or other financial obligations; (c) agreements involving child custody or support, alimony, or property settlements; (d) arrests, convictions, probation, and/or parole; or (e) other matters described in court records.

Special Instructions for Completing this Form

Questions on this form related to residence, employment, and education will require 7 years of information except that Single-Scope Background Investigations (SSBI) will require 10 years of information.

Provide 7 years of information unless you have been instructed to provide 10 years to satisfy SSBI requirements. If you are unsure as to the amount of information to provide, contact the office that gave you this form.

The instructions for these questions specify a 10-year time frame when an SSBI is required. If you have any questions about this investigative request or whether the 7-year time frame or the 10-year time frame applies to your responses to these questions, contact the office that gave you this form.

Instructions for Completing this Form

1. Follow the instructions given to you by the office that gave you this form and any other clarifying instructions furnished by that office to assist you in completion of this form. You must sign and date, in ink, the original and each copy you submit. **You should retain a copy of the completed form for your records.**

2. Type or legibly print your answers in ink (if the form is not legible, it will not be accepted). You may also be asked to submit your form using the approved electronic format.

3. All questions on this form must be answered. If no response is necessary or applicable, indicate this on the form with "N/A" unless otherwise noted.

4. Any changes that you make to this form after you sign it must be initialed and dated by you. Under certain limited circumstances, agencies may modify your response(s) with your consent.

5. You must use the Location codes (abbreviations) listed on the back of this page when you fill out this form. Do not abbreviate the names of cities or foreign countries.

6. Whenever "City (Country)" is shown in an address block, also provide in that block the name of the country when the address is outside the U.S.

7. The 5-digit postal Zip Codes are needed to speed the processing of your investigation. Refer to an automated system approved by the U.S. Postal Service to assist you with Zip Codes.

8. For telephone numbers in the U.S., be sure to include the area code.

9. All dates provided in this form must be in Month/Day/Year or Month/Year format. Use numbers (01-12) to indicate months. For example, July 29, 1968, should be written as 07/29/1968. If you find that you cannot report an exact date, approximate or estimate the date to the best of your ability and indicate this by writing "APPROX." or "EST."

10. If you need additional space for explanation or to list your residences, employment/self-employment/unemployment, or education, you should use a continuation sheet, SF 86A. If additional space is needed to answer other items, use the Continuation Space on page 17 or a blank sheet(s) of paper. Each blank sheet of paper you use must contain your name and SSN at the top of the page.

Final Determination on Your Eligibility

Final determination on your eligibility for a national security position is the responsibility of the Federal agency that requested your investigation. You will be provided the opportunity personally to explain, refute, or clarify any information before a final decision is made.

Standard Form 86
Revised July 2008
U.S. Office of Personnel Management
5 CFR Parts 731, 732, and 736

QUESTIONNAIRE FOR
NATIONAL SECURITY POSITIONS

Form approved:
OMB No. 3206 0005
NSN 7540-00 634-4036
86-111

Penalties for Inaccurate or False Statements

The U.S. Criminal Code (title 18, section 1001) provides that knowingly falsifying or concealing a material fact is a felony which may result in fines and/or up to 5 years of imprisonment. In addition, Federal agencies generally fire, do not grant a security clearance, or disqualify individuals who have materially and deliberately falsified these forms, and this remains a part of the permanent record for future placements. Your prospects of placement or security clearance are better if you answer all questions truthfully and completely. You will have adequate opportunity to explain any information you give to us on this form and to make your comments part of the record.

DISCLOSURE INFORMATION

The information you give to us is for the purpose of investigating you for a national security position; we will protect it from unauthorized disclosure. The collection, maintenance, and disclosure of background investigative information is governed by the Privacy Act. The agency that requested the investigation and the agency that conducted the investigation have published notices in the Federal Register describing the systems of records in which your records will be maintained. The information on this form, and information collected during an investigation, may be disclosed without your consent by an agency maintaining the information in a system of records as permitted by the Privacy Act [5 U.S.C. 552a(b)], and by routine uses published by the agency in the Federal Register. The office that gave you this form will provide you a copy of its routine uses.

PRIVACY ACT ROUTINE USES

1. To the Department of Justice when: (a) the agency or any component thereof; or (b) any employee of the agency in his or her official capacity; or (c) any employee of the agency in his or her individual capacity where the Department of Justice has agreed to represent the employee; or (d) the United States Government, is a party to litigation or has interest in such litigation, and by careful review, the agency determines that the records are both relevant and necessary to the litigation and the use of such records by the Department of Justice is therefore deemed by the agency to be for a purpose that is compatible with the purpose for which the agency collected the records.

2. To a court or adjudicative body in a proceeding when: (a) the agency or any component thereof; or (b) any employee of the agency in his or her official capacity; or (c) any employee of the agency in his or her individual capacity where the Department of Justice has agreed to represent the employee; or (d) the United States Government is a party to litigation or has interest in such litigation, and by careful review, the agency determines that the records are both relevant and necessary to the litigation and the use of such records is therefore deemed by the agency to be for a purpose that is compatible with the purpose for which the agency collected the records.

3. Except as noted in Question 23 and 27, when a record on its face, or in conjunction with other records, indicates a violation or potential violation of law, whether civil, criminal, or regulatory in nature, and whether arising by general statute, particular program statute, regulation, rule, or order issued pursuant thereto, the relevant records may be disclosed to the appropriate Federal, foreign, State, local, tribal, or other public authority responsible for enforcing, investigating or prosecuting such violation or charged with enforcing or implementing the statute, rule, regulation, or order.

4. To any source or potential source from which information is requested in the course of an investigation concerning the hiring or retention of an employee or other personnel action, or the issuing or retention of a security clearance, contract, grant, license, or other benefit, to the extent necessary to identify the individual, inform the source of the nature and purpose of the investigation, and to identify the type of information requested.

5. To a Federal, State, local, foreign, tribal, or other public authority the fact that this system of records contains information relevant to the retention of an employee, or the retention of a security clearance, contract, license, grant, or other benefit. The other agency or licensing organization may then make a request supported by written consent of the individual for the entire record if it so chooses. No disclosure will be made unless the information has been determined to be sufficiently reliable to support a referral to another office within the agency or to another Federal agency for criminal, civil, administrative, personnel, or regulatory action.

6. To contractors, grantees, experts, consultants, or volunteers when necessary to perform a function or service related to this record for which they have been engaged. Such recipients shall be required to comply with the Privacy Act of 1974, as amended.

7. To the news media or the general public, factual information the disclosure of which would be in the public interest and which would not constitute an unwarranted invasion of personal privacy.

8. To a Federal, State, or local agency, or other appropriate entities or individuals, or through established liaison channels to selected foreign governments, in order to enable an intelligence agency to carry out its responsibilities under the National Security Act of 1947 as amended, the CIA Act of 1949 as amended, Executive Order 12333 or any successor order, applicable national security directives, or classified implementing procedures approved by the Attorney General and promulgated pursuant to such statutes, orders or directives.

9. To a Member of Congress or to a Congressional staff member in response to an inquiry of the Congressional office made at the written request of the constituent about whom the record is maintained.

10. To the National Archives and Records Administration for records management inspections conducted under 44 U.S.C. 2904 and 2906.

11. To the Office of Management and Budget when necessary to the review of private relief legislation.

LOCATION CODES

Alabama	AL	Hawaii	HI	Massachusetts	MA	New Mexico	NM	South Dakota	SD
Alaska	A	Idaho	ID	Michigan	MI	New York	NY	Tennessee	TN
Arizona	AZ	Illinois	IL	Minnesota	MN	North Carolina	NC	Texas	TX
Arkansas	AR	Indiana	IN	Mississippi	MS	North Dakota	ND	Utah	UT
California	CA	Iowa	IA	Missouri	MO	Ohio	OH	Vermont	VT
Colorado	CO	ansas	S	Montana	MT	Oklahoma	O	Virginia	VA
Connecticut	CT	entucky	Y	Nebraska	NE	Oregon	OR	Washington	WA
Delaware	DE	Louisiana	LA	Nevada	NV	Pennsylvania	PA	West Virginia	WV
District of Columbia	DC	Maine	ME	New Hampshire	NH	Rhode Island	RI	Wisconsin	WI
Florida	FL	Maryland	MD	New Jersey	NJ	South Carolina	SC	Wyoming	WY
Georgia	GA								

American Samoa	AS	Guam	GU	Northern Mariana Islands	MP	Palau	PW
Federated States of Micronesia	FM	Marshall Islands	MH	Puerto Rico	PR	Virgin Islands of the U.S.	VI

PUBLIC BURDEN INFORMATION

Public burden reporting for this collection of information is estimated to average 120 minutes per response, including time for reviewing instructions, searching existing data sources, gathering and maintaining the data needed, and completing and reviewing the collection of information. Send comments regarding the burden estimate or any other aspect of this collection of information, including suggestions for reducing this burden, to OPM Forms Officer, U.S. Office of Personnel Management, 1900 E Street, N.W., Washington, DC 20415. Do not send your completed form to this address; send it to the office that provided you the form. The OMB clearance number, 3206-0005, is currently valid. OPM may not collect this information, and you are not required to respond, unless this number is displayed.

Standard Form 86
Revised July 2008
U.S. Office of Personnel Management
5 CFR Parts 731, 732, and 736

**QUESTIONNAIRE FOR
NATIONAL SECURITY POSITIONS**

Form approved:
OMB No. 3206 0005
NSN 7540-00 634-4036
86-111

Investigating agency use only	Codes	Case number

AGENCY USE ONLY

A Type of investigation	**B** Extra coverage/Advance results	**C** Sensitivity level	**D** Access/Eligibility	**E** Nature of action code	**F** Date of action

G Geographic location	**H** Position code	**I** Position title	**J** SON

K Location of official personnel folder	None NPRC	At SON e-OPF	Other	Other address/Web address of e-OPF	ZIP Code

L SOI	**M** Location of security folder	None NPI	At SOI Other	Other address	ZIP Code

N IPAC	**O** TAS	**P** Obligating document number	**Q** BETC

R Accounting data and/or Agency case number	**S** Investigative requirement	Initial Reinvestigation

T Requesting official - Name	Title	Signature

Email address	Telephone number	Date

U Secondary requesting official - Name	Title

Email address	Telephone number	**V** Applicant affiliation	FED CIV MIL	CON Other

PERSONS COMPLETING THIS FORM SHOULD BEGIN WITH THE QUESTIONS BELOW AFTER CAREFULLY READING THE FOREGOING INSTRUCTIONS.

1 FULL NAME - If you have only initials in your name, use them and enter (I/O) after the initial(s). - If you have no middle name, enter "NMN." - If you are a "Jr.," "Sr.," etc. enter this in the box after your middle name.

2 DATE OF BIRTH

Last name	First name	Middle name	Jr., II, etc.

3 PLACE OF BIRTH

4 SOCIAL SECURITY NO.

City	County	State	Country (if outside the U.S.)

5 OTHER NAMES USED Have you used any other names?

NO ☐   YES ☐ → If "Yes," give other names used and the period of time you used them [for example: your maiden name, name(s) by a former marriage, former name(s), alias(es), or nickname(s)]. If the other name is your **maiden name**, put "maiden" in front of it.

Name #1	Month/Year	To	Month/Year
Name #2	Month/Year	To	Month/Year
Name #3	Month/Year	To	Month/Year
Name #4	Month/Year	To	Month/Year

6 MOTHER'S MAIDEN NAME

Last name	First name	Middle name

7 YOUR IDENTIFYING INFORMATION

Height (feet and inches)	Weight (pounds)	Hair color	Eye color	Sex	Female Male

8 YOUR CONTACT INFORMATION Check box(es) indicating when you can be reached at each phone number.

Home e-mail address	Work e-mail address

Home telephone number	Day Evening	Work telephone number	Day Evening	Mobile telephone number	Day Evening

Enter your Social Security Number before going to the next page ⟶

Page 1

Standard Form 86
Revised July 2008
U.S. Office of Personnel Management
5 CFR Parts 731, 732, and 736

QUESTIONNAIRE FOR
NATIONAL SECURITY POSITIONS

Form approved:
OMB No. 3206 0005
NSN 7540-00 634-4036
86-111

9 CITIZENSHIP Mark the box that reflects your current citizenship status and follow its instructions.

☐ I am a U.S. citizen or national by birth in the U.S. or U.S. territory/commonwealth.

☐ I am a U.S. citizen or national by birth, born outside the U.S. **Go to 9A**

☐ I am a naturalized U.S. citizen. **Go to 9B or 9C**

☐ I am not a U.S. citizen. **Go to 9D**

U.S. PASSPORT Current or most recent passport

Number	Date issued	Expired	YES / NO

ALIEN REGISTRATION NUMBER (if applicable)

Number

9A DOCUMENTATION OF U.S. CITIZENS BORN ABROAD [STATE DEPARTMENT FORM (FS) 240, DS 1350, FS 545, etc.] Report information, if applicable.

Date form was completed	Document number	Place of issuance

9B CITIZENSHIP CERTIFICATE (if applicable)

Where was this certificate issued? City/Court	State	Certificate number	Date issued

9C NATURALIZATION CERTIFICATE (if applicable)

Where was this certificate issued? City/Court	State	Certificate number	Date issued

9D IMMIGRATION STATUS   Place you entered the U.S.

City	State	Country(ies) of citizenship

Date of entry	Type of document (I-94, etc.)	Document number

10 CITIZENSHIP INFORMATION

Do you now hold or have you EVER held multiple citizenships?   ☐ YES   ☐ NO **Go to Question 11**

A If "Yes," provide the name(s) of the country(ies).   **B** During what periods of time did you hold multiple citizenships?

C Is your non-U.S. citizenship based on your birth in a foreign country or the citizenship of your parents? (If "No," explain.)
☐ YES ☐ NO, explain →

D Have you renounced or attempted to renounce your foreign citizenship(s)? (If "Yes," explain.)
☐ NO ☐ YES, explain →

11 WHERE YOU HAVE LIVED Use the Continuation Sheet(s) (SF 86A) or the Continuation Space on page 17 for additional answers.

List the places where you have lived, beginning with your present residence (#1) and working back 7 years (if an SSBI go back 10 years). **Residences for the entire 7 year period must be accounted for without breaks.** Indicate the actual physical location of your residence. Do not use a Post Office Box as an address, and do not list a permanent address when you were actually living at a school address, etc. Be sure to be as specific as possible when listing an address location: for example, do not list only your base or ship, list your barracks number or home port. You may omit temporary military duty locations (TDY) under 90 days (list your address of record instead), but you must list other part-time residences. Your actual physical location in addition to your APO/FPO address is required for overseas assignments.

For any address in the last 3 years, list a person who knew you at that address, and who preferably still lives in that area. Do not list people for residences completely outside this 3-year period, and do not list your spouse, former spouse, or other relatives. Also, for addresses in the last 3 years, if the address is "General Delivery," a Rural or State Route, or may be difficult to locate, provide directions for locating the residence on an attached continuation sheet (SF 86A). Do not list residences before your 18th birthday unless to provide a minimum of 2 years of residence history.

Residence Information and Point of Contact for that Period of Residence

#1 Month/Year To Month/Year **Present**	Status	☐ Own ☐ Rent	☐ Military housing ☐ Other (Explain)	Street address	Apt.#

APO/FPO address

City (Country)	State	ZIP Code

Name of person who knows you at this address	Current address	Apt.#

APO/FPO address (if currently applicable)

City (Country)	State	ZIP Code

Telephone number	Alternate contact number	Relationship	☐ Neighbor ☐ Friend	☐ Landlord ☐ Business associate	☐ Other (Explain)

Enter your Social Security Number before going to the next page ⟶

Page 2

Standard Form 86
Revised July 2008
U.S. Office of Personnel Management
5 CFR Parts 731, 732, and 736

**QUESTIONNAIRE FOR
NATIONAL SECURITY POSITIONS**

Form approved:
OMB No. 3206 0005
NSN 7540-00 634-4036
86-111

11 WHERE YOU HAVE LIVED (Continued)

#2 Month/Year To Month/Year Status | Own | Military housing | Street address | Apt.#
Rent | Other (Explain)

APO/FPO address

City (Country) | State | ZIP Code

Name of person who knows you at this address | Current address | Apt.#

APO/FPO address (if currently applicable)

City (Country) | State | ZIP Code

Telephone number | Alternate contact number | Relationship | Neighbor | Landlord | Other (Explain)
| | | Friend | Business associate

#3 Month/Year To Month/Year Status | Own | Military housing | Street address | Apt.#
Rent | Other (Explain)

APO/FPO address

City (Country) | State | ZIP Code

Name of person who knows you at this address | Current address | Apt.#

APO/FPO address (if currently applicable)

City (Country) | State | ZIP Code

Telephone number | Alternate contact number | Relationship | Neighbor | Landlord | Other (Explain)
| | | Friend | Business associate

#4 Month/Year To Month/Year Status | Own | Military housing | Street address | Apt.#
Rent | Other (Explain)

APO/FPO address

City (Country) | State | ZIP Code

Name of person who knows you at this address | Current address | Apt.#

APO/FPO address (if currently applicable)

City (Country) | State | ZIP Code

Telephone number | Alternate contact number | Relationship | Neighbor | Landlord | Other (Explain)
| | | Friend | Business associate

Enter your Social Security Number before going to the next page ⟶

Standard Form 86
Revised July 2008
U.S. Office of Personnel Management
5 CFR Parts 731, 732, and 736

**QUESTIONNAIRE FOR
NATIONAL SECURITY POSITIONS**

Form approved:
OMB No. 3206 0005
NSN 7540-00 634-4036
86-111

12 WHERE YOU WENT TO SCHOOL Use the Continuation Sheet(s) (SF 86A) or the Continuation Space on page 17 for additional answers.

List all schools you have attended, beginning with the most recent (#1) working back 7 years (if an SSBI go back 10 years). List college or university degrees and the dates they were received. If your most recent degree or diploma was received more than 7 years ago (10 years for an SSBI), list it below no matter when it was received.   In the Code block, show the most appropriate code to describe your school.

1 - High School	3 - Vocational/Technical/Trade School
2 - College/University/Military College	4 - Correspondence/Distance/Extension/Online School

For Correspondence/Distance/Extension/Online School, provide the address where the records are maintained.
For schools you attended in the last 3 years, list a person who knew you at school (instructor, student, etc.).
Do not list people for education periods completed more than 3 years ago.

SCHOOL INFORMATION

#1 Month/Year To Month/Year   Code   Name of school

Degree/diploma received? If "Yes," identify type of degree/diploma received and date awarded.   YES / NO

Street address and City (Country) of school   State   ZIP Code

Name of person who knows you   Current address   Apt. #

City (Country)   State   ZIP Code   Telephone number

#2 Month/Year To Month/Year   Code   Name of school

Degree/diploma received? If "Yes," identify type of degree/diploma received and date awarded.   YES / NO

Street address and City (Country) of school   State   ZIP Code

Name of person who knows you   Current address   Apt. #

City (Country)   State   ZIP Code   Telephone number

#3 Month/Year To Month/Year   Code   Name of school

Degree/diploma received? If "Yes," identify type of degree/diploma received and date awarded.   YES / NO

Street address and City (Country) of school   State   ZIP Code

Name of person who knows you   Current address   Apt. #

City (Country)   State   ZIP Code   Telephone number

#4 Month/Year To Month/Year   Code   Name of school

Degree/diploma received? If "Yes," identify type of degree/diploma received and date awarded.   YES / NO

Street address and City (Country) of school   State   ZIP Code

Name of person who knows you   Current address   Apt. #

City (Country)   State   ZIP Code   Telephone number

#5 Month/Year To Month/Year   Code   Name of school

Degree/diploma received? If "Yes," identify type of degree/diploma received and date awarded.   YES / NO

Street address and City (Country) of school   State   ZIP Code

Name of person who knows you   Current address   Apt. #

City (Country)   State   ZIP Code   Telephone number

Enter your Social Security Number before going to the next page ⟶

Standard Form 86
Revised July 2008
U.S. Office of Personnel Management
5 CFR Parts 731, 732, and 736

**QUESTIONNAIRE FOR
NATIONAL SECURITY POSITIONS**

Form approved:
OMB No. 3206 0005
NSN 7540-00 634-4036
86-111

---

13 EMPLOYMENT ACTIVITIES Use the Continuation Sheet(s) (SF 86A) or the Continuation Space on page 17 for additional answers.

List all your employment activities, beginning with the present (#1) and working back 7 years (if an SSBI go back 10 years). You should list all full-time and part-time work, paid or unpaid, consulting/contracting work, all military service duty locations, temporary military duty locations (TDY) over 90 days, self-employment, other paid work, and all periods of unemployment. **The entire period must be accounted for without breaks.** EXCEPTION: Do not list employments that occurred before your 18th birthday unless it is necessary for providing a minimum of 2 years of employment history. If you require additional space, use a continuation sheet (SF 86A).

Employer/Verifier Information. List the business name of your employer or the name of a person who can verify your self-employment or unemployment in this block. If military service is being listed, include your duty location or home port here as well as your branch of service. You should provide separate listings to reflect changes in your military duty locations or home ports. If you are a Federal Contractor, list company name, not Federal agency.

Additional Periods of Activity. Complete this block if you worked for an employer on more than one occasion at the same physical location. After entering the most recent period of employment in the initial numbered block, provide previous periods of employment at the same location on the additional lines provided. For example, if you worked at XY Plumbing in Denver, CO, during 3 separate periods of time, you would enter dates and information concerning the most recent period of employment first, and provide dates, position titles, and supervisors for the two previous periods of employment on the lines below that information.

Employment Code: Use one of the codes listed below to identify the type of employment.

1 - Active military duty stations

2 - National Guard/Reserve

3 - U.S.P.H.S. Commissioned Corps

4 - Other Federal employment

5 - State Government (Non-Federal employment)

6 - Self-employment (include business name and/or name of person who can verify)

7 - Unemployment (include name of verifier)

8 - Federal Contractor

9 - Other (explain)

13A EMPLOYMENT/UNEMPLOYMENT INFORMATION

#1 Dates of Employment	Type of Employment		
Month/Year To Month/Year **Present**	Employment code Position title/Military rank	Work hours Full-time	
		Part-time	

Employer/Verifier

Name of employer/verifier	Telephone number

Address of employer/verifier	

City (Country)	State	ZIP Code

Physical Location

Your actual work address (if different from employer address)	Telephone number

City (Country)	State	ZIP Code

Supervisor *(if different from employer)*

Name and title	Telephone number

Work address of supervisor	

City (Country)	State	ZIP Code

Additional Periods of Activity with this Employer

Month/Year To Month/Year Position title	Supervisor
Month/Year To Month/Year Position title	Supervisor
Month/Year To Month/Year Position title	Supervisor

Explanation/Reason for leaving

Enter your Social Security Number before going to the next page ⟶ [   ]

Page 5

Standard Form 86
Revised July 2008
U.S. Office of Personnel Management
5 CFR Parts 731, 732, and 736

Form approved:
OMB No. 3206 0005
NSN 7540-00 634-4036
86-111

**QUESTIONNAIRE FOR
NATIONAL SECURITY POSITIONS**

13A EMPLOYMENT/UNEMPLOYMENT INFORMATION *(Continued)*

#2 Dates of Employment | **Type of Employment**

Month/Year To Month/Year | Employment code ▼ | Position title/Military rank | Work hours Full-time / Part-time

Employer/Verifier
Name of employer/verifier | Telephone number
Address of employer/verifier
City (Country) | State | ZIP Code

Physical Location
Your actual work address (if different from employer address) | Telephone number
City (Country) | State | ZIP Code

Supervisor *(if different from employer)*
Name and title | Telephone number
Work address of supervisor
City (Country) | State | ZIP Code

Additional Periods of Activity with this Employer
Month/Year To Month/Year | Position title | Supervisor
Month/Year To Month/Year | Position title | Supervisor
Month/Year To Month/Year | Position title | Supervisor
Explanation/Reason for leaving

#3 Dates of Employment | **Type of Employment**

Month/Year To Month/Year | Employment code | Position title/Military rank | Work hours Full-time / Part-time

Employer/Verifier
Name of employer/verifier | Telephone number
Address of employer/verifier
City (Country) | State | ZIP Code

Physical Location
Your actual work address (if different from employer address) | Telephone number
City (Country) | State | ZIP Code

Enter your Social Security Number before going to the next page ⟶

Page 6

Standard Form 86
Revised July 2008
U.S. Office of Personnel Management
5 CFR Parts 731, 732, and 736

**QUESTIONNAIRE FOR
NATIONAL SECURITY POSITIONS**

Form approved:
OMB No. 3206 0005
NSN 7540-00 634-4036
86-111

13A EMPLOYMENT/UNEMPLOYMENT INFORMATION *(Continued)*

Supervisor *(if different from employer)*

Name and title	Telephone number

Work address of supervisor

City (Country)	State	ZIP Code

Additional Periods of Activity with this Employer

Month/Year To Month/Year	Position title	Supervisor
Month/Year To Month/Year	Position title	Supervisor
Month/Year To Month/Year	Position title	Supervisor

Explanation/Reason for leaving

#4 Dates of Employment | **Type of Employment**

Month/Year To Month/Year	Employment code	Position title/Military rank	Work hours	Full-time
				Part-time

Employer/Verifier

Name of employer/verifier	Telephone number

Address of employer/verifier

City (Country)	State	ZIP Code

Physical Location

Your actual work address (if different from employer address)	Telephone number

City (Country)	State	ZIP Code

Supervisor *(if different from employer)*

Name and title	Telephone number

Work address of supervisor

City (Country)	State	ZIP Code

Additional Periods of Activity with this Employer

Month/Year To Month/Year	Position title	Supervisor
Month/Year To Month/Year	Position title	Supervisor
Month/Year To Month/Year	Position title	Supervisor

Explanation/Reason for leaving

Enter your Social Security Number before going to the next page ➤

Page 7

Standard Form 86
Revised July 2008
U.S. Office of Personnel Management
5 CFR Parts 731, 732, and 736

**QUESTIONNAIRE FOR
NATIONAL SECURITY POSITIONS**

Form approved:
OMB No. 3206 0005
NSN 7540-00 634-4036
86-111

13B FORMER FEDERAL SERVICE, EXCLUDING MILITARY SERVICE, NOT INDICATED PREVIOUSLY (list below if applicable)

Dates of Federal Service Month/Year To Month/Year	Agency/City (Country)/State/ZIP Code	Position Title
#1		
#2		
#3		

13C EMPLOYMENT RECORD

	YES	NO
1. Has any of the following happened to you in the last 7 years? If "Yes," begin with the most recent occurrence and go backward, providing date fired, quit, or left, and other information requested.		

Use the following codes and explain the reason your employment was ended.

1 - Fired from a job
2 - Quit a job after being told you would be fired

3 - Left a job by mutual agreement following charges or allegations of misconduct
4 - Left a job by mutual agreement following notice of unsatisfactory performance

5 - Left a job for other reasons under unfavorable circumstances
6 - Laid off from job by employer

Month/Year	Code	Specify Reason	Employer's Name and Address (Include City/Country if outside U.S.)	State	ZIP Code

	YES	NO
2. Have you received a written warning, been officially reprimanded, suspended, or disciplined for misconduct in the workplace?		
3. Have you received a written warning, been officially reprimanded, suspended, or disciplined for violating a security rule or policy?		

If you answered "Yes," to 13C(2) and/or 13C(3), provide the name(s) of the employer(s), date(s) of incident(s), month/day/year of official action(s), location(s) or facility(ies) of incident(s), and the nature of the violation(s) in the space below. If additional space is needed, use a blank sheet(s) of paper.

14 SELECTIVE SERVICE RECORD

	YES	NO
a Are you a male born after December 31, 1959? If "No," go to Question 15. If "Yes," go to b.		
b Have you registered with the Selective Service System (SSS)? If "Yes," provide your registration number below. If "No," explain the reason for not registering below. Please consult the SSS if you are unaware of your status before signing this form.		

Registration Number	Explanation

Enter your Social Security Number before going to the next page ⟶

Standard Form 86
Revised July 2008
U.S. Office of Personnel Management
5 CFR Parts 731, 732, and 736

**QUESTIONNAIRE FOR
NATIONAL SECURITY POSITIONS**

Form approved:
OMB No. 3206 0005
NSN 7540-00 634-4036
86-111

15 MILITARY HISTORY Account for all of your military service through the questions below. If you answer "No" to both 15a and 15b, go to Question 16.	YES	NO
a Have you EVER served in the U.S. military or the U.S. Merchant Marine?		
b Have you EVER served in a foreign country's military, security forces, merchant marine, militia, or other defense forces?		
c Have you EVER received a discharge that was not honorable?		
d In the last 7 years (if an SSBI go back 10 years), have you been subject to court martial or other disciplinary proceedings under the Uniform Code of Military Justice? (Include non-judicial, Captain's mast, etc.) If "Yes," provide date(s), charge(s), military court(s) or authority(ies), and outcome(s).		

If you answered "Yes" to any question above, list all details of your military service below, starting with the most recent period of service and working back. If you had a break in service, each separate time of service should be listed.

Code (Branch of Service): Use one of the codes listed below to identify your branch of service.

1 - Air Force 3 - Navy 5 - Coast Guard 7 - Air National Guard (NG) 9 - Foreign military, defense, militia, security forces
2 - Army 4 - Marine Corps 6 - Merchant Marine 8 - Army NG

O/E: Mark "O" block for Officer or "E" block for Enlisted, if applicable.
Status: "X" the appropriate block for the status of your service during the time that you served. If your service was in the National Guard, do not use an "X": use the two-letter code for the state to mark the block.
Country: Identify the country for which you served.
Code (Type of Discharge): Use one of the codes listed below to indicate your separation status from your military service.

1 - Honorable 2 - Dishonorable 3 - Other Than Honorable 4 - General 5 - Bad Conduct 6 - Other (Explain)

Branch of Service Code	Month/Year To Month/Year	Service Number	O	E	Active Duty	Active Reserve	Inactive Reserve	Air NG State	Army NG State	Country	Type of Discharge Code

16 PEOPLE WHO KNOW YOU WELL

List three people who know you well and who preferably live in the U. S. They should be friends, peers, colleagues, college roommates, associates, etc., who are collectively aware of your activities outside of the workplace, school, or neighborhoods and whose combined association with you covers at least the last 7 years. **Do not list your spouse, former spouse(s), other relatives, or anyone listed elsewhere on this form.**

Reference name #1 | Dates known Month/Year To Month/Year | Relationship to you (Check all that apply) Neighbor / Work associate / Other (Explain) / Friend / Schoolmate | Telephone number Day / Evening
Home or work address | Apt. # | City (Country) | State | ZIP Code | Alternate telephone no.

Reference name #2 | Dates known Month/Year To Month/Year | Relationship to you (Check all that apply) Neighbor / Work associate / Other (Explain) / Friend / Schoolmate | Telephone number Day / Evening
Home or work address | Apt. # | City (Country) | State | ZIP Code | Alternate telephone no.

Reference name #3 | Dates known Month/Year To Month/Year | Relationship to you (Check all that apply) Neighbor / Work associate / Other (Explain) / Friend / Schoolmate | Telephone number Day / Evening
Home or work address | Apt. # | City (Country) | State | ZIP Code | Alternate telephone no.

Enter your Social Security Number before going to the next page ⟶

Page 9

Standard Form 86
Revised July 2008
U.S. Office of Personnel Management
5 CFR Parts 731, 732, and 736

**QUESTIONNAIRE FOR
NATIONAL SECURITY POSITIONS**

Form approved:
OMB No. 3206 0005
NSN 7540-00 634-4036
86-111

---

17 MARITAL STATUS

Mark one box to show your current marital status and provide information about your spouse(s) or cohabitant below. If there is not a middle name, enter as "NMN."

☐ 1 - Never married ☐ 3 - Separated ☐ 5 - Divorced
☐ 2 - Married (incl. Common Law) ☐ 4 - Annulled ☐ 6 - Widowed

17A CURRENT SPOUSE If applicable, complete the following about your current spouse only. If your current spouse was born outside the U.S., provide citizenship information.

Last name	First name	Middle name	Date of birth	Place of birth (include Country if outside the U.S.)

Social Security Number	Other names used (specify maiden name, names by other marriages, etc., and show dates used for each name)

Country(ies) of citizenship	Date married

Place married (City, include Country if outside the U.S.)	State

If separated, date of separation	If legally separated, where is the record located? City (Country)	State	ZIP Code

Current address of spouse, if different than your current address (Street, City, include Country if outside the U.S.)	State	ZIP Code	Telephone number

If spouse was born outside the U.S. indicate one type of documentation that he or she possesses and the document numbers.

☐ FS 240 or 545 ☐ Citizenship certificate ☐ Alien registration ☐ Other (Explain)
☐ DS 1350 ☐ U.S. Passport (current or most recent) ☐ Naturalization certificate

Document number	Explain "Other"

17B FORMER SPOUSE(S) Complete the following about your former spouse(s). Use blank sheets if needed.

Last name	First name	Middle name	Date of birth

Place of birth (include Country if outside the U.S.)	State	Country(ies) of citizenship

Date married	Place married (City, include Country if outside the U.S.)	State

Check one, then give date	☐ Divorced ☐ Annulled ☐ Widowed	Date	If divorced/annulled, where is the record located? City (Country)	State	ZIP Code

Last known address of former spouse (Street, City, include Country if outside the U.S.)	State	ZIP Code	Telephone number

17C COHABITANT [A cohabitant is a person with whom you share bonds of affection, obligation, or other commitment, as opposed to a person with whom you live for reasons of convenience (a roommate)]. If applicable, complete the following about your cohabitant. If your cohabitant was born outside the U.S., provide citizenship information.

Last name	First name	Middle name	Date of birth	Place of birth (include Country if outside the U.S.)

Social Security Number	Other names used (specifically maiden names, names by other marriages, etc., and show dates used for each name)

Country(ies) of citizenship	Date cohabitation began

If cohabitant was born outside the U.S., indicate one type of documentation that he or she possesses and the document numbers.

☐ FS 240 or 545 ☐ Citizenship certificate ☐ Alien registration ☐ Other (Explain)
☐ DS 1350 ☐ U.S. Passport (current or most recent) ☐ Naturalization certificate

Document number	Explain "Other"

Enter your Social Security Number before going to the next page ⟶ [   ]

Page 10

Standard Form 86	QUESTIONNAIRE FOR	Form approved:
Revised July 2008	NATIONAL SECURITY POSITIONS	OMB No. 3206 0005
U.S. Office of Personnel Management		NSN 7540-00 634-4036
5 CFR Parts 731, 732, and 736		86-111

18 RELATIVES

Relative Code - Use one of the following codes (1-16) listed below for each relative and give the full name and other requested information, if applicable, for each of your relatives, living or deceased, specified below.

1 - Mother	5 - Foster parent	9 - Sister	13 - Half-sister
2 - Father	6 - Child (incl. adopted and foster)	10 - Stepbrother	14 - Father-in-law
3 - Stepmother	7 - Stepchild	11 - Stepsister	15 - Mother-in-law
4 - Stepfather	8 - Brother	12 - Half-brother	16 - Guardian

Code 1	Full name	Deceased	Date of birth	Place of birth	Country(ies) of citizenship

Current address (Street, City, and State, include Country if outside the U.S.)

If relative was born outside the U.S., indicate one type of documentation that he or she possesses and provide the document number below.

FS 240 or 545 Citizenship certificate	DS 1350 Naturalization certificate	Alien registration U.S. Passport	Other (Explain below)	Document number

Code 2	Full name	Deceased	Date of birth	Place of birth	Country(ies) of citizenship

Current address (Street, City, and State, include Country if outside the U.S.)

If relative was born outside the U.S., indicate one type of documentation that he or she possesses and provide the document number below.

FS 240 or 545 Citizenship certificate	DS 1350 Naturalization certificate	Alien registration U.S. Passport	Other (Explain below)	Document number

Code	Full name	Deceased	Date of birth	Place of birth	Country(ies) of citizenship

Current address (Street, City, and State, include Country if outside the U.S.)

If relative was born outside the U.S., indicate one type of documentation that he or she possesses and provide the document number below.

FS 240 or 545 Citizenship certificate	DS 1350 Naturalization certificate	Alien registration U.S. Passport	Other (Explain below)	Document number

Code	Full name	Deceased	Date of birth	Place of birth	Country(ies) of citizenship

Current address (Street, City, and State, include Country if outside the U.S.)

If relative was born outside the U.S., indicate one type of documentation that he or she possesses and provide the document number below.

FS 240 or 545 Citizenship certificate	DS 1350 Naturalization certificate	Alien registration U.S. Passport	Other (Explain below)	Document number

Code	Full name	Deceased	Date of birth	Place of birth	Country(ies) of citizenship

Current address (Street, City, and State, include Country if outside the U.S.)

If relative was born outside the U.S., indicate one type of documentation that he or she possesses and provide the document number below.

FS 240 or 545 Citizenship certificate	DS 1350 Naturalization certificate	Alien registration U.S. Passport	Other (Explain below)	Document number

Code	Full name	Deceased	Date of birth	Place of birth	Country(ies) of citizenship

Current address (Street, City, and State, include Country if outside the U.S.)

If relative was born outside the U.S., indicate one type of documentation that he or she possesses and provide the document number below.

FS 240 or 545 Citizenship certificate	DS 1350 Naturalization certificate	Alien registration U.S. Passport	Other (Explain below)	Document number

Code	Full name	Deceased	Date of birth	Place of birth	Country(ies) of citizenship

Current address (Street, City, and State, include Country if outside the U.S.)

If relative was born outside the U.S., indicate one type of documentation that he or she possesses and provide the document number below.

FS 240 or 545 Citizenship certificate	DS 1350 Naturalization certificate	Alien registration U.S. Passport	Other (Explain below)	Document number

Enter your Social Security Number before going to the next page ⟶

Standard Form 86
Revised July 2008
U.S. Office of Personnel Management
5 CFR Parts 731, 732, and 736

**QUESTIONNAIRE FOR
NATIONAL SECURITY POSITIONS**

Form approved:
OMB No. 3206 0005
NSN 7540-00 634-4036
86-111

19 FOREIGN CONTACTS

Do you have or have you had close and/or continuing contact with foreign nationals within the last 7 years with whom you, your spouse, or your cohabitant are bound by affection, influence, and/or obligation? Include associates, as well as relatives, not already listed in Question 18. (A foreign national is defined as any person who is not a citizen or national of the U.S.)   Yes ☐   No ☐

1. Full name

Dates known Month/Year To Month/Year	Country(ies) of citizenship
	Country of residence

Nature of relationship	Type of contact (check all that apply)	Number of contacts per year
☐ Business ☐ Personal ☐ Other (Explain)	☐ Telephone ☐ Electronic correspondence ☐ Other (Explain) ☐ In person ☐ Written correspondence	☐ 1 - 2 ☐ 3 - 7 ☐ 8 - 15 ☐ More than 15

2. Full name

Dates known Month/Year To Month/Year	Country(ies) of citizenship
	Country of residence

Nature of relationship	Type of contact (check all that apply)	Number of contacts per year
☐ Business ☐ Personal ☐ Other (Explain)	☐ Telephone ☐ Electronic correspondence ☐ Other (Explain) ☐ In person ☐ Written correspondence	☐ 1 - 2 ☐ 3 - 7 ☐ 8 - 15 ☐ More than 15

3. Full name

Dates known Month/Year To Month/Year	Country(ies) of citizenship
	Country of residence

Nature of relationship	Type of contact (check all that apply)	Number of contacts per year
☐ Business ☐ Personal ☐ Other (Explain)	☐ Telephone ☐ Electronic correspondence ☐ Other (Explain) ☐ In person ☐ Written correspondence	☐ 1 - 2 ☐ 3 - 7 ☐ 8 - 15 ☐ More than 15

4. Full name

Dates known Month/Year To Month/Year	Country(ies) of citizenship
	Country of residence

Nature of relationship	Type of contact (check all that apply)	Number of contacts per year
☐ Business ☐ Personal ☐ Other (Explain)	☐ Telephone ☐ Electronic correspondence ☐ Other (Explain) ☐ In person ☐ Written correspondence	☐ 1 - 2 ☐ 3 - 7 ☐ 8 - 15 ☐ More than 15

5. Full name

Dates known Month/Year To Month/Year	Country(ies) of citizenship
	Country of residence

Nature of relationship	Type of contact (check all that apply)	Number of contacts per year
☐ Business ☐ Personal ☐ Other (Explain)	☐ Telephone ☐ Electronic correspondence ☐ Other (Explain) ☐ In person ☐ Written correspondence	☐ 1 - 2 ☐ 3 - 7 ☐ 8 - 15 ☐ More than 15

6. Full name

Dates known Month/Year To Month/Year	Country(ies) of citizenship
	Country of residence

Nature of relationship	Type of contact (check all that apply)	Number of contacts per year
☐ Business ☐ Personal ☐ Other (Explain)	☐ Telephone ☐ Electronic correspondence ☐ Other (Explain) ☐ In person ☐ Written correspondence	☐ 1 - 2 ☐ 3 - 7 ☐ 8 - 15 ☐ More than 15

20 FOREIGN ACTIVITIES   Respond for the time frame of the last 7 years.

20A Foreign Financial Interests Include stocks, personal property, company shares, investments, or ownership of corporate entities. Exclude U.S.-based fund managers and accounts managed through your employer.

		YES	NO
1.	Do you have or have you EVER had any foreign financial businesses, foreign bank accounts, or other foreign financial interests of which you have direct control or direct ownership?		

Type of financial interest	Amount of funds in U.S. dollars

2.	Do you have or have you had any foreign financial interests that someone controls on your behalf?		

Type of financial interest and name of party who controls it	Amount of funds in U.S. dollars

3.	Do you own or have you owned real estate in a foreign country?		

Type of property and date(s) owned	Location of property	Estimated value of property in U.S. dollars

4.	Do you receive or have you received any educational, medical, retirement, social welfare, or other such benefits from a foreign country?		

Type of benefit	Estimated value in U.S. dollars

Enter your Social Security Number before going to the next page ⟶

Page 12

Standard Form 86
Revised July 2008
U.S. Office of Personnel Management
5 CFR Parts 731, 732, and 736

**QUESTIONNAIRE FOR
NATIONAL SECURITY POSITIONS**

Form approved:
OMB No. 3206 0005
NSN 7540-00 634-4036
86-111

20B Foreign Business, Professional Activities, and Foreign Government Contacts Respond for the time frame of the last 7 years, unless otherwise noted. Indicate if activity was on official U.S. Government business.	YES	NO	Official Govt. Business
1. Have you provided advice or support to anyone associated with a foreign business or other foreign organization that you have not previously listed as a former employer regarding any of the following: management, strategy, financing, or technology?			
If "Yes" AND the activity was outside of official U.S. Government business, describe advice/support provided, name(s) of foreign national and/or organization(s) to which it was provided, the name(s) of foreign country(ies), timeframe(s), and if compensation was provided.			
2. Have you attended any international conferences, trade shows, seminars, or other meetings outside of the U.S.?			
If "Yes" AND the activity was outside of official U.S. Government business, provide locations, including the name(s) of foreign country(ies), date(s), sponsoring organization(s), and purpose of event(s).			
3. Have you or any of your immediate family members been asked to provide advice or serve as a consultant, even informally, by any foreign government official or agency?			
If "Yes" AND the activity was outside of official U.S. Government business, provide the date(s) of request and/or consultation(s), including the name(s) of foreign country(ies), location of consultation(s), and circumstance(s).			
4. Have you or any of your immediate family members had any contact with a foreign government, its establishment (embassies, consulates, agencies, or military services), or its representatives, whether inside or outside the U.S.?			
Answer "No" if the contact was for routine visa applications and border crossings related to either official U.S. Government travel or foreign travel listed below in Question 20C. If contact was outside of official U.S. Government business, identify the foreign government(s), establishment(s), and/or representative(s) involved and provide the circumstance(s), date(s), and location(s) of contact(s).			
5. Have you sponsored any foreign citizen to come to the U.S. as a student, for work, or for permanent residence?			
If "Yes," provide the name of the foreign citizen(s) you sponsored, the country(ies) of citizenship, the date(s) of the foreign citizen's stay in the U.S., their current address (if known), and the purpose of the foreign citizen's stay in the U.S.			
6. Have you EVER held or do you now hold a passport that was issued by a foreign government?			
If "Yes," provide the name(s), in which your foreign passport(s) was issued, the issuing country(ies), the passport number(s), the date(s) issued, the expiration date(s), and the status of each.			

20C Foreign Countries You Have Visited Respond for the time frame of the last 7 years.	YES	NO
Have you traveled outside the U.S. in the last 7 years?		

Respond for foreign countries you have visited in the last 7 years, beginning with the most current and working back. If you have lived near a border and have made short (one day or less) trips to the neighboring country (e.g. Canada or Mexico), you do not need to list each trip. Instead, provide the time period, the code, the country, and a note ("Many Short Trips"). Do not list travel under official U.S. Government business, but you must include any personal trips made in conjunction with the official U.S. Government travel.

▶ **Use these codes to indicate the purpose(s) of your visit:**   1 - Business/Professional conference   3 - Education   5 - Visit family or friends
2 - Volunteer activities   4 - Tourism   6 - Other

Code	Month/Year To Month/Year	Number of Days	Country	Code	Month/Year To Month/Year	Number of Days	Country
	#1				#4		
	#2				#5		
	#3				#6		

21 MENTAL AND EMOTIONAL HEALTH		
Mental health counseling in and of itself **is not a reason** to revoke or deny a clearance.	YES	NO
In the last 7 years, have you consulted with a health care professional regarding an emotional or mental health condition or were you hospitalized for such a condition? Answer "No" if the counseling was for any of the following reasons and was not court-ordered: 1) strictly marital, family, grief not related to violence by you; or 2) strictly related to adjustments from service in a military combat environment.		
If you answered "Yes," indicate who conducted the treatment and/or counseling, provide the following information, and sign the Authorization for Release of Medical Information Pursuant to the Health Insurance Portability and Accountability Act (HIPAA).		

Dates of Treatment and/or Counseling Month/Year To Month/Year	Name/Address of Provider	State	ZIP Code
#1			
#2			

Enter your Social Security Number before going to the next page ⟶

Page 13

Standard Form 86 Revised July 2008 U.S. Office of Personnel Management 5 CFR Parts 731, 732, and 736	**QUESTIONNAIRE FOR NATIONAL SECURITY POSITIONS**	Form approved: OMB No. 3206 0005 NSN 7540-00 634-4036 86-111

22 POLICE RECORD

For this item, report information regardless of whether the record in your case has been sealed, expunged, or otherwise stricken from the court record, or the charge was dismissed. You need not report convictions under the Federal Controlled Substances Act for which the court issued an expungement order under the authority of 21 U.S.C. 844 or 18 U.S.C. 3607. Be sure to include all incidents whether occurring in the U.S. or abroad.

	YES	NO
For questions a and b, respond for the timeframe of the last 7 years (if an SSBI go back 10 years). Exclude any fines of less than $300 for traffic offenses that do not involve alcohol or drugs.		
a. Have you been issued a summons, citation, or ticket to appear in court in a criminal proceeding against you; are you on trial or awaiting a trial on criminal charges; or are you currently awaiting sentencing for a criminal offense?		
b. Have you been arrested by any police officer, sheriff, marshal, or any other type of law enforcement officer?		
c Have you EVER been charged with any felony offense? (Include those under Uniform Code of Military Justice.)		
d Have you EVER been charged with a firearms or explosives offense?		
e Have you EVER been charged with any offense(s) related to alcohol or drugs?		

If you answered "Yes" to any question above, explain below, providing information for each and every offense.

Month/Year	Law Enforcement Authority/Court	City and Country (if outside U.S.)	State	ZIP Code	Offense	Action Taken
#1						
#2						

23 ILLEGAL USE OF DRUGS OR DRUG ACTIVITY

	YES	NO
The following questions pertain to the illegal use of drugs or drug activity. You are required to answer the questions fully and truthfully, and your failure to do so could be grounds for an adverse employment decision or action against you. Neither your truthful responses nor information derived from your responses will be used as evidence against you in any subsequent criminal proceeding.		
a In the last 7 years, have you illegally used any controlled substance, for example, cocaine, crack cocaine, THC (marijuana, hashish, etc.), narcotics (opium, morphine, codeine, heroin, etc.), stimulants (amphetamines, speed, crystal methamphetamine, Ecstacy, ketamine, etc.), depressants (barbiturates, methaqualone, tranquilizers, etc.), hallucinogenics (LSD, PCP, etc.), steroids, inhalants (toluene, amyl nitrate, etc.) or prescription drugs (including painkillers)? Use of a controlled substance includes injecting, snorting, inhaling, swallowing, experimenting with or otherwise consuming any controlled substance.		
b Have you EVER illegally used a controlled substance while possessing a security clearance; while employed as a law enforcement officer, prosecutor, or courtroom official; or while in a position directly and immediately affecting the public safety?		
c In the last 7 years, have you been involved in the illegal possession, purchase, manufacture, trafficking, production, transfer, shipping, receiving, handling, or sale of any controlled substance (see question *a above)* including prescription drugs?		
d In the last 7 years, have you received counseling or treatment or have you been ordered, advised, or asked to seek counseling or treatment as a result of your use of drugs? If you answered "Yes," provide date(s) of treatment and name(s) and address(es) of provider(s). You will be asked to sign an additional release if information is needed concerning any treatment.		

If you answered "Yes" to a - d above, provide the date(s) of use or activity, identify the controlled substance(s), and explain the use or activity.

Dates of Use/Activity Month/Year To Month/Year	Type of Controlled Substance(s)	Explain (nature of use/activity, frequency of activity and number of times used)
#1		
#2		

24 USE OF ALCOHOL Respond for the time frame of the last 7 years.

	YES	NO
a Has your use of alcohol had a negative impact on your work performance, your professional or personal relationships, your finances, or resulted in intervention by law enforcement/public safety personnel? (If "Yes," explain.)		
b Have you been ordered, advised, or asked to seek counseling or treatment as a result of your use of alcohol?		
c Have you received counseling or treatment as a result of your use of alcohol?		

If you answered "Yes" to question b or c above, provide the date(s) of treatment and the name(s) and address(es) of the counselor(s) or doctor(s) below. Do not repeat information reported in response to Question 21. You will be asked to sign an additional release if information is needed concerning any treatment.

Month/Year To Month/Year	Name/Address of Counselor or Doctor	State	ZIP Code
#1			
#2			

Enter your Social Security Number before going to the next page ⟶ [   ]

Page 14

Standard Form 86
Revised July 2008
U.S. Office of Personnel Management
5 CFR Parts 731, 732, and 736

Form approved:
OMB No. 3206 0005
NSN 7540-00 634-4036
86-111

QUESTIONNAIRE FOR
NATIONAL SECURITY POSITIONS

25 INVESTIGATIONS AND CLEARANCE RECORD

	YES	NO

a Has the U.S. Government or a foreign government EVER investigated your background and/or granted you a security clearance? If "Yes," use the codes that follow to provide the requested information below. If "Yes," but you can't recall the investigating agency and/or the security clearance received, enter the code for "Unknown." If your response is "No," or you don't know or can't recall if you were investigated and cleared, check the "No" box.

Investigating Agency Codes
1 - Defense Department
2 - State Department
3 - Office of Personnel Management
4 - Federal Bureau of Investigation
5 - Treasury Department
6 - Department of Homeland Security
7 - Foreign government (Specify country)
8 - Unknown
9 - Other (Explain below)

Security Clearance Codes
0 - Not Required
1 - Confidential
2 - Secret
3 - Top Secret
4 - Sensitive Compartmented Information
5 - Q
6 - L
7 - Issued by foreign country (specify country)
8 - Unknown
9 - Other (Explain below)

Month/Year	Agency Code	Foreign Government or Other Agency (If necessary)	Clearance Code
#1			
#2			
#3			
#4			

	YES	NO

b To your knowledge, have you EVER had a clearance or access authorization denied, suspended, or revoked; or been debarred from government employment? If "Yes," give the action(s), date(s) of action(s), agency(ies), and circumstances. Note: An administrative downgrade or termination of a security clearance is not a revocation.

Month/Year	Department or Agency Taking Action	Circumstances
#1		
#2		

26 FINANCIAL RECORD
For the following, answer for the last 7 years, unless otherwise specified in the question. Disclose all financial obligations, including those for which you are a cosigner or guarantor, on the following page.

		YES	NO
a	Have you filed a petition under any chapter of the bankruptcy code? If "Yes," indicate type.		
b	Have you had any possessions or property voluntarily or involuntarily repossessed or foreclosed?		
c	Have you failed to pay Federal, state, or other taxes, or to file a tax return, when required by law or ordinance?		
d	Have you had a lien placed against your property for failing to pay taxes or other debts?		
e	Have you had a judgment entered against you?		
f	Have you defaulted on any type of loan?		
g	Have you had bills or debts turned over to a collection agency?		
h	Have you had any account or credit card suspended, charged off, or cancelled for failing to pay as agreed?		
i	Have you been evicted for non-payment of financial obligations?		
j	Have you been delinquent on court-imposed alimony or child support payments?		
k	Have you had your wages, benefits, or assets garnished or attached for any reason?		
l	Have you been counseled, warned, or disciplined for violating terms of agreement for a travel or credit card provided by your employer?		
m	Have you been over 180 days delinquent on any debt(s)?		
n	Are you currently over 90 days delinquent on any debt(s)?		
o	Have you EVER experienced financial problems due to gambling?		
p	Are you currently delinquent on any Federal debt?		

Enter your Social Security Number before going to the next page ⟶

Page 15

302

Standard Form 86
Revised July 2008
U.S. Office of Personnel Management
5 CFR Parts 731, 732, and 736

**QUESTIONNAIRE FOR
NATIONAL SECURITY POSITIONS**

Form approved:
OMB No. 3206 0005
NSN 7540-00 634-4036
86-111

26 FINANCIAL RECORD (Continued)

For the following, answer for the last 7 years, unless otherwise specified in the question. Disclose all financial obligations, including those for which you are a cosigner or guarantor. If you answered "Yes" on the previous page (a-p), provide the information requested below. For each "Yes" answer, provide the corresponding letters.

Indicate (a-p)	Date Satisfied Month/Year	Amount of Property Value Involved	Loan/Account Number/ Bankruptcy Type	Names of Agency/Organization/Individual to Whom Debt is/was Owed		
#1 ▼						
Name/Address of Company, Court, or Agency Handling Case				Name Action/Debt is Recorded Under		Status of Action or Debt
		State	ZIP Code			
Indicate (a-p)	Date Satisfied Month/Year	Amount of Property Value Involved	Loan/Account Number/ Bankruptcy Type	Names of Agency/Organization/Individual to Whom Debt is/was Owed		
#2 ▼						
Name/Address of Company, Court, or Agency Handling Case				Name Action/Debt is Recorded Under		Status of Action or Debt
		State	ZIP Code			
Indicate (a-p)	Date Satisfied Month/Year	Amount of Property Value Involved	Loan/Account Number/ Bankruptcy Type	Names of Agency/Organization/Individual to Whom Debt is/was Owed		
#3						
Name/Address of Company, Court, or Agency Handling Case				Name Action/Debt is Recorded Under		Status of Action or Debt
		State	ZIP Code			
Indicate (a-p)	Date Satisfied Month/Year	Amount of Property Value Involved	Loan/Account Number/ Bankruptcy Type	Names of Agency/Organization/Individual to Whom Debt is/was Owed		
#4						
Name/Address of Company, Court, or Agency Handling Case				Name Action/Debt is Recorded Under		Status of Action or Debt
		State	ZIP Code			

27 USE OF INFORMATION TECHNOLOGY SYSTEMS

The following questions ask about your use of information technology systems. Information technology systems include all related computer hardware, software, firmware, and data used for the communication, transmission, processing, manipulation, storage, or protection of information. You are required to answer the questions fully and truthfully, and your failure to do so could be grounds for an adverse employment decision or action against you. Neither your truthful responses nor information derived from your responses will be used as evidence against you in any subsequent criminal proceeding.	YES	NO
a In the last 7 years, have you illegally or without proper authorization entered into any information technology system?		
b In the last 7 years, have you illegally or without authorization modified, destroyed, manipulated, or denied others access to information residing on an information technology system?		
c In the last 7 years, have you introduced, removed, or used hardware, software, or media in connection with any information technology system without authorization, when specifically prohibited by rules, procedures, guidelines, or regulations?		

Date of Incident (Month/Year)	Nature of Incident/Offense	Location Incident Took Place	Action Taken
#1			
#2			
#3			
#4			
#5			
#6			
#7			

Enter your Social Security Number before going to the next page ⟶ [   ]

Page 16

Standard Form 86
Revised July 2008
U.S. Office of Personnel Management
5 CFR Parts 731, 732, and 736

QUESTIONNAIRE FOR
NATIONAL SECURITY POSITIONS

Form approved:
OMB No. 3206 0005
NSN 7540-00 634-4036
86-111

28 INVOLVEMENT IN NON-CRIMINAL COURT ACTIONS					YES	NO
In the last 7 years (if an SSBI go back 10 years), have you been a party to any public record civil court action(s) not listed elsewhere on this form?						
If you answered "Yes," provide the information about each public record civil court action(s) requested below.						

Month/Year	Nature of Action	Result of Action	Name of Principal Parties Involved (if more space is needed, use Continuation Space on page 17)	Court Information		
#1				Court name		
				Street address		
				City	State	ZIP Code
#2				Court name		
				Street address		
				City	State	ZIP Code

29 ASSOCIATION RECORD		
The following questions pertain to your associations. You are required to answer the questions fully and truthfully, and your failure to do so could be grounds for an adverse employment decision or action against you. For the purpose of this question, terrorism is defined as any criminal acts that involve violence or are dangerous to human life and appear to be intended to intimidate or coerce a civilian population to influence the policy of a government by intimidation or coercion, or to affect the conduct of a government by mass destruction, assassination or kidnapping.		

		YES	NO
a	Have you EVER been an officer or a member of, or made a contribution to, an organization dedicated to terrorism, and which engaged in illegal activities to that end, either with an awareness of the organization's dedication to that end or with the specific intent to further such illegal activities?		
b	Have you EVER been an officer or a member of, or made a contribution to, an organization dedicated to the use of violence or force to overthrow the U.S. Government, and which engaged in illegal activities to that end, either with an awareness of the organization's dedication to that end or with the specific intent to further such illegal activities?		
c	Have you EVER been an officer or a member of, or made a contribution to, an organization that unlawfully advocates or practices the commission of acts of force or violence to discourage others from exercising their rights under the U.S. Constitution or any state of the U.S. with the specific intent to further such unlawful activities?		
d	Have you EVER advocated any acts of terrorism or activities designed to overthrow the U.S. Government by force with the specific intent to incite others to unlawful action in furtherance of such aims?		
e	Have you EVER knowingly engaged in any activities designed to overthrow the U.S. Government by force?		
f	Have you EVER knowingly engaged in any acts of terrorism? Neither your truthful response nor information derived from your response to this question will be used as evidence against you in any subsequent criminal proceeding.		
g	Have you EVER participated in militias (not including official state government militias) or paramilitary groups?		
	If you answered "Yes" to any of the questions above, explain below.		

CONTINUATION SPACE

Use the continuation sheet(s) (SF 86A) for additional answers for items 11, 12, and 13. Use the space below to continue answers to all other items and to provide any information you would like to add. If more space is needed than is provided below, use a blank sheet(s) of paper. Start each sheet with your name and SSN. Before each answer, identify the number of the item and try to maintain question format.

After completing this form and any attachments, you should review your answers to all questions to make sure the form is complete and accurate, and then sign and date the following certification and the attached release(s).

Certification

My statements on this form, and on any attachments to it, are true, complete, and correct to the best of my knowledge and belief and are made in good faith. I have carefully read the foregoing instructions to complete this form. I understand that a knowing and willful false statement on this form can be punished by fine or imprisonment or both (18 U.S.C. 1001). I understand that intentionally withholding, misrepresenting, or falsifying information may have a negative effect on my security clearance, employment prospects, or job status, up to and including denial or revocation of my security clearance, or my removal and debarment from Federal service.

Signature	Date (mm/dd/yyyy)

Enter your Social Security Number before going to the next page ⟶

Page 17

Standard Form 86-1
Revised July 2008
U.S. Office of Personnel Management
5 CFR Parts 731, 732, and 736

**QUESTIONNAIRE FOR
NATIONAL SECURITY POSITIONS**

Form approved:
OMB No. 3206 0005
NSN 7540-00 634-4036
86-111

UNITED STATES OF AMERICA

AUTHORIZATION FOR RELEASE OF INFORMATION

Carefully read this authorization to release information about you, then sign and date it in ink.

I Authorize any investigator, special agent, or other duly accredited representative of the authorized Federal agency conducting my background investigation, to obtain any information relating to my activities from individuals, schools, residential management agents, employers, criminal justice agencies, credit bureaus, consumer reporting agencies, collection agencies, retail business establishments, or other sources of information. This information may include, but is not limited to, my academic, residential, achievement, performance, attendance, disciplinary, employment history, criminal history record information, and financial and credit information. I authorize the Federal agency conducting my investigation to disclose the record of my background investigation to the requesting agency for the purpose of making a determination of suitability or eligibility for a national security position.

I Authorize the Social Security Administration (SSA) to verify my Social Security Number (to match my name, Social Security Number, and date of birth with information in SSA records and provide the results of the match) to the Office of Personnel Management (OPM) or other Federal agency requesting or conducting my investigation for the purposes outlined above. I authorize SSA to provide explanatory information to OPM, or to the other Federal agency requesting or conducting my investigation, in the event of a discrepancy.

I Understand that, for financial or lending institutions, medical institutions, hospitals, health care professionals, and other sources of information, separate specific releases may be needed, and I may be contacted for such releases at a later date.

I Authorize any investigator, special agent, or other duly accredited representative of the OPM, the Federal Bureau of Investigation, the Department of Defense, the Department of State, and any other authorized Federal agency, to request criminal record information about me from criminal justice agencies for the purpose of determining my eligibility for assignment to, or retention in, a national security position, in accordance with 5 U.S.C. 9101. I understand that I may request a copy of such records as may be available to me under the law.

I Authorize custodians of records and other sources of information pertaining to me to release such information upon request of the investigator, special agent, or other duly accredited representative of any Federal agency authorized above regardless of any previous agreement to the contrary.

I Understand that the information released by records custodians and sources of information is for official use by the Federal Government only for the purposes provided in this Standard Form 86, and that it may be disclosed by the Government only as authorized by law.

Photocopies of this authorization that show my signature are valid. This authorization is valid for five (5) years from the date signed or upon the termination of my affiliation with the Federal Government, whichever is sooner.

Signature (Sign in ink)	Full name (Type or print legibly)		Date signed (mm/dd/yyyy)
Other names used		Date of birth	Social Security Number
Current street address Apt. #	City (Country)	State	ZIP Code	Home telephone number

Enter your Social Security Number before going to the next page ⟶

Standard Form 86-2
Revised July 2008
U.S. Office of Personnel Management
5 CFR Parts 731, 732, and 736

**QUESTIONNAIRE FOR
NATIONAL SECURITY POSITIONS**

Form approved:
OMB No. 3206 0005
NSN 7540-00 634-4036
86-111

UNITED STATES OF AMERICA
AUTHORIZATION FOR RELEASE OF MEDICAL INFORMATION PURSUANT
TO THE HEALTH INSURANCE PORTABILITY AND ACCOUNTABILITY ACT (HIPAA)

If you answered "Yes" to Question 21, carefully read this authorization to release information about you, then sign and date it in ink.

Instructions for Completing this Release

This is a release for the investigator to ask your health practitioner(s) the questions below concerning your mental health consultations. Your signature will allow the practitioner(s) to answer only these questions.

Authorization

I am seeking assignment to or retention in a national security position. As part of the clearance process, I hereby authorize the investigator, special agent, or duly accredited representative of the authorized Federal agency conducting my background investigation, to obtain the following information relating to my mental health consultations.

In accordance with HIPAA, I understand that I have the right to revoke this authorization at any time by writing to the U.S. Office of Personnel Management. I understand that I may revoke this authorization except to the extent that action has already been taken based on this authorization. Further, I understand that this authorization is voluntary. My treatment, payment, enrollment in a health plan, or eligibility for benefits will not be conditioned upon my authorization of this disclosure.

I understand the information disclosed pursuant to this release is for use by the Federal Government only for purposes provided in the Standard Form 86 and that it may be disclosed by the Government only as authorized by law, but will no longer be subject to the HIPAA privacy rule.

Photocopies of this authorization with my signature are valid. This authorization is valid for one (1) year from the date signed or upon termination of my affiliation with the Federal Government, whichever is sooner.

Signature (Sign in ink)	Full name (Type or print legibly)	Date signed (mm/dd/yyyy)
Other names used		Social Security Number
Current street address Apt. #	City (Country) State ZIP Code	Home telephone number

For Use By Practitioner(s) Only

Does the person under investigation have a condition that could impair his or her judgment, reliability, or ability to properly safeguard classified national security information?

☐ Yes   ☐ No

If so, describe the nature of the condition and the extent and duration of the impairment or treatment.

What is the prognosis?

Signature (Sign in ink)	Practitioner name	Date signed (mm/dd/yyyy)

Enter your Social Security Number before going to the next page ⟶

Worldwide Mobility Agreement (FD-918)

FBI special agents and certain professional support employees must be willing to accept permanent transfers or temporary duty (TDY) assignments anywhere in the world, and all FBI employees must be available for TDY assignments away from their permanent offices. To ensure that applicants understand this policy, they are required to complete a one-page Worldwide Mobility Agreement.

In addition to special agents, those serving in several professional support positions are subject to permanent transfers. These personnel include automotive workers and mechanics, information technology specialists, data systems programmers, electronics technicians, financial analysts and accounting technicians, investigative specialists, forensic examiners, and language specialists. The FD-918 form asks applicants for these positions to certify that they are willing to accept a permanent or temporary duty assignment worldwide.

According to the Bureau's TDY policy, which is described on the form, the FBI first seeks qualified volunteers for temporary duty before making non-voluntary TDY assignments. In the certification block of this form, you must indicate whether you "...accept these terms without reservation." Any applicant who is unwilling to accept the terms of the FBI Worldwide Mobility Agreement will not be considered for FBI employment.

FD-918 (4-10-00)

WORLDWIDE MOBILITY AGREEMENT

My application is for the position of _____ in the FBI.
I am therefore responding to this agreement under section A or B accordingly.

A. I have applied for either a Special Agent position or one of the following
support positions: Automotive Worker/Mechanic, Computer Specialist, Data
Systems Programmer, Electronics Technician, Financial Analyst/Accounting
Technician, Investigative Specialist in the Special Surveillance Group Program,
Forensic Examiner, or Language Specialist; therefore:

1. As a condition of employment with the FBI, I fully understand that I will be
subject to and will remain completely available for **temporary duty (TDY)**
anywhere worldwide according to the needs of the Bureau. ☐ Yes ☐ No

2. As a condition of employment with the FBI, I fully understand that I will be subject
to and will remain completely available for **permanent transfer** anywhere
worldwide according to the needs of the Bureau. ☐ Yes ☐ No

3. I accept these terms without reservation. ☐ Yes ☐ No

B. I have applied for a support position that is not among the positions listed in
section A above; nevertheless:

1. As a condition of employment with the FBI, I fully understand that I will be subject to
and will remain available for **temporary duty (TDY)** anywhere worldwide according
to the needs of the Bureau. I am aware that the Bureau will first seek qualified
volunteers and that managers are instructed to make maximum possible use of such
volunteers for **TDY** assignments. If, however, volunteers are unavailable or
inadequate in numbers, I am willing to perform **TDY** anywhere worldwide as a
condition of employment, unless I am precluded by a disability that warrants
reasonable accommodation. ☐ Yes ☐ No

2. I accept these terms without reservation. ☐ Yes ☐ No

_____

Name (print)

_____   _____

Signature   Date

FBI\DOJ

Desirable Weight Ranges for the Special Agent Position

The FBI is committed to having a workforce that is physically fit. Strength and endurance are especially important for special agents because they are often faced with strenuous and dangerous situations. In an effort to select candidates for the special agent position who will be able to perform law enforcement responsibilities safely and effectively—and succeed during demanding physical training in the New Agent Training program—the FBI provides the Desirable Weight Ranges chart, as shown on the following pages.

These height and weight figures, as well as the body fat percentages shown at the bottom of the chart, serve as a guide for special agent candidates to follow. It is important to note that these are only desirable weight ranges for various heights, and not required weight ranges. In other words, if your height and weight are reasonably proportionate and close to the figures on the chart, you could still be considered for employment even though your numbers are outside the desirable range. The Bureau makes these determinations on a case-by-case basis. Of course, if you are significantly overweight or underweight, the FBI is not likely to hire you and hopes you will make adjustments later.

The Desirable Weight Ranges chart is only one tool used to evaluate physical fitness. Prior to appointment, special agent candidates are given a physical examination and their medical history is also reviewed. They must also complete a physical fitness test that includes push-ups, sit-ups, a 300-meter timed sprint, and 1.5-mile timed run. The final determination concerning suitability to use firearms, participate in raids, execute defensive tactics, and perform other essential functions of the job rests with the FBI's chief medical officer.

Males	
Height	**Weight in Pounds**
5' 4"	117–163
5' 5"	120–167
5' 6"	124–173
5' 7"	128–178
5' 8"	132–183
5' 9"	136–187
5' 10"	140–193
5' 11"	144–198
6' 0"	148–204
6' 1"	152–209
6' 2"	156–215
6' 3"	160–220
6' 4"	169–231
6' 5"	174–238

Females	
Height	**Weight in Pounds**
5' 0"	96–138
5' 1"	99–141
5' 2"	102–144
5' 3"	105–149
5' 4"	108–152
5' 5"	111–156
5' 6"	114–161
5' 7"	118–165
5' 8"	122–169
5' 9"	126–174
5' 10"	130–179
5' 11"	134–185
6' 0"	138–190

Body Fat Requirements
Males: 19%
Females: 22%

Language Proficiency Self-Assessment Chart

The following chart reflects proficiency standards that are generally accepted throughout the United States government community. These standards are applied by the FBI during the Applicant Self-Assessment process. Candidates for language specialist and contract linguist positions are required to assess both their English and foreign language fluency levels in speaking, listening, reading, and writing on a scale of 0 to 5. Applicants for the special agent position who want to qualify under the Language Entry Program also are required to assess their fluency using this chart.

Level	Speaking	Listening	Reading	Writing
0	**No Proficiency:** Unable to function in the spoken language.	**No Proficiency:** No practical understanding of the spoken language.	**No Proficiency:** No practical ability to read the language.	**No Proficiency:** No functional writing ability.
0+	**Memorized Proficiency:** Able to satisfy immediate needs using rehearsed utterances.	**Memorized Proficiency:** Sufficient comprehension to understand a number of memorized utterances in areas of immediate needs.	**Memorized Proficiency:** Can recognize all the letters in the printed version of an alphabetic system and high-frequency elements of a syllabary or a character system.	**Memorized Proficiency:** Writes using memorized material and set expressions.
1	**Elementary Proficiency:** Able to satisfy minimum courtesy requirements and maintain very simple face-to-face conversations on familiar topics.	**Elementary Proficiency:** Sufficient comprehension to understand utterances about basic survival needs and minimum courtesy and travel requirements.	**Elementary Proficiency:** Sufficient comprehension to read very simple connected written material in a form equivalent to usual printing or typescript.	**Elementary Proficiency:** Sufficient control of the writing system to meet limited practical needs.

(continued)

(continued)

Level	Speaking	Listening	Reading	Writing
1+	**Elementary Proficiency, Plus:** Can initiate and maintain predictable face-to-face conversations and satisfy limited social demands.	**Elementary Proficiency, Plus:** Sufficient comprehension to understand short conversations about all survival needs and limited social demands.	**Elementary Proficiency, Plus:** Sufficient comprehension to understand simple discourse in printed form for informative social purposes.	**Elementary Proficiency, Plus:** Sufficient control of the writing system to meet most survival needs and limited social demands.
2	**Limited Working Proficiency:** Able to satisfy routine social demands and limited work requirements.	**Limited Working Proficiency:** Sufficient comprehension to understand conversations on routine social demands and limited job requirements.	**Limited Working Proficiency:** Sufficient comprehension to read simple, authentic written material in a form equivalent to usual printing or typescript on subjects within a familiar context.	**Limited Working Proficiency:** Able to write routine social correspondence and prepare documentary materials required for most limited work requirements.
2+	**Limited Working Proficiency, Plus:** Able to satisfy most work requirements with language usage that is often, but not always, acceptable and effective.	**Limited Working Proficiency, Plus:** Sufficient comprehension to understand most routine social demands and most conversations on work requirements as well as some discussions on concrete topics related to particular interests and special fields of competence.	**Limited Working Proficiency, Plus:** Sufficient comprehension to understand most factual material in nontechnical prose, as well as some discussions on concrete topics related to special professional interests.	**Limited Working Proficiency, Plus:** Shows ability to write with some precision and in some detail about most common topics.

Level	Speaking	Listening	Reading	Writing
3	**General Professional Proficiency:** Able to speak the language with sufficient structural accuracy and vocabulary to participate effectively in most formal and informal conversations on practical, social, and professional topics.	**General Professional Proficiency:** Able to understand the essentials of all speech in a standard dialect, including technical discussions within a special field.	**General Professional Proficiency:** Able to read within a normal range of speed and with almost complete comprehension a variety of authentic prose material on unfamiliar subjects.	**General Professional Proficiency:** Able to use the language effectively in most formal and informal written exchanges on practical, social, and professional topics.
3+	**General Professional Proficiency, Plus:** Is often able to use the language to satisfy professional needs in a wide range of sophisticated and demanding tasks.	**General Professional Proficiency, Plus:** Comprehends most of the content and intent of a variety of forms and styles of speech pertinent to professional needs, as well as general topics and social conversations.	**General Professional Proficiency, Plus:** Can comprehend a variety of styles and forms pertinent to professional needs.	**General Professional Proficiency, Plus:** Able to write the language in a few prose styles pertinent to professional and educational needs.
4	**Advanced Professional Proficiency:** Able to use the language fluently and accurately on all levels normally pertinent to professional needs.	**Advanced Professional Proficiency:** Able to understand all forms and styles of speech pertinent to professional needs.	**Advanced Professional Proficiency:** Able to read fluently and accurately all styles and forms of the language pertinent to professional needs.	**Advanced Professional Proficiency:** Able to write the language precisely and accurately in a variety of prose styles pertinent to professional and educational needs.

(continued)

(continued)

Level	Speaking	Listening	Reading	Writing
4+	**Advanced Professional Proficiency, Plus:** Speaking proficiency is regularly superior in all respects, usually equivalent to that of a well-educated, highly articulate native speaker.	**Advanced Professional Proficiency, Plus:** Increased ability to understand extremely difficult and abstract speech as well as ability to understand all forms of speech pertinent to professional needs, including social conversations.	**Advanced Professional Proficiency, Plus:** Nearly native ability to read and understand extremely difficult or abstract prose, a very wide variety of vocabulary, idioms, colloquialisms, and slang.	**Advanced Professional Proficiency, Plus:** Able to write the language precisely and accurately in a wide variety of prose styles pertinent to professional and educational needs.
5	**Functionally Native Proficiency:** Speaking proficiency is functionally equivalent to that of a highly articulate, well-educated native speaker and reflects the cultural standards of the country where the language is natively spoken.	**Functionally Native Proficiency:** Comprehension equivalent to that of an educated native listener.	**Functionally Native Proficiency:** Reading proficiency is functionally equivalent to that of a well-educated native reader.	**Functionally Native Proficiency:** Has writing proficiency equal to that of a well-educated native.

Preliminary Application for Honors Internship Program (FD-646a)

The Honors Internship Program application form requests biographical information and basic details about your education, military service, employment history, citizenship, driver license, foreign language skills, and criminal record. In addition, there are a few questions concerning illegal drug use and your willingness to undergo urinalysis drug screening and a polygraph examination as a condition of employment. The second page of the form includes a box where you can provide additional information, if necessary. This form is one of many documents that must be submitted as part of a complete package to the FBI field office nearest your campus. The package must be delivered to the FBI no later than September 30 if you want to begin the internship in June of the following year.

FEDERAL BUREAU OF INVESTIGATION

Preliminary Application for
Honors Internship Program
(Please Type or Print in Ink)

Date: _____

FIELD OFFICE USE ONLY

HP

Div: _____ Program: _____

I. PERSONAL HISTORY

Name in Full (Last, First, Middle, Maiden)	List College(s) attended, Major, Degree (if applicable), Grade Point Average

Birth Date (Month, Day, Year)
Birth Place:

Social Security Number: (Optional)

Current Address

Street _____ Apt. No. _____

City _____ State _____ Zip Code _____

Home Phone _____

Area Code _____ Number _____

Work Phone _____

Area Code _____ Number _____

Are you: Licensed Driver ☐ Yes ☐ No   U. S. Citizen ☐ Yes ☐ No

Have you served on active duty in the Armed Forces of the United States? ☐ Yes ☐ No	Branch of military service and dates of active duty:	Type of Discharge

How did you learn or become interested in the FBI Honors Internship Program?

Do you have a foreign language background? ☐ Yes ☐ No   List proficiency for each language on reverse side.

Have you ever been arrested or charged with any violation including traffic, but excluding parking tickets? ☐ Yes ☐ No If so, list all such matters even if found not guilty, not formally charged, no court appearance, or matter settled by payment of fine or forfeiture of collateral. Include date, place, charge, disposition, details, and police agency on reverse side.

II. EMPLOYMENT HISTORY

Identify your most recent three years FULL-TIME work experience, after high school (excluding summer, part-time and temporary employment).

From	To	Description of Work	Name/Location of Employer

III. PERSONAL DECLARATIONS

Persons with a disability who require an accommodation to complete the application process are required to notify the FBI of their need for the accommodation.

Have you used marijuana during the last three years or more than 15 times? ☐ Yes ☐ No

Have you used any illegal drug(s) or combination of illegal drugs, other than marijuana, more than 5 times or during the last 10 years? ☐ Yes ☐ No

All Information provided by applicants concerning their drug history will be subject to verification by a preemployment polygraph examination.

Do you understand all prospective FBI employees will be required to submit to an urinalysis for drug abuse prior to employment? ☐ Yes ☐ No

I am aware that willfully withholding information or making false statements on this application constitutes a violation of Section 1001, Title 18, U.S. Code and if appointed, will be the basis for dismissal from the Federal Bureau of Investigation. I agree to these conditions and I hereby certify that all statements made by me on this application are true and complete, to the best of my knowledge.

_____

Signature of Applicant as usually written. (**Do Not Use Nickname**)

The Federal Bureau of Investigation is an equal opportunity employer.

CONTINUATION SPACE TO PROVIDE ADDITIONAL INFORMATION

GENERAL

This information is provided pursuant to Public Law 93-579 (Privacy Act of 1974), December 31, 1974, for individuals completing FBI employment application forms.

AUTHORITY

Title 28, Code of Federal Regulations, Section 0.137, authorizes the Director of the FBI to exercise power and authority vested in the Attorney General by law to take final action in matters pertaining to the employment, direction and general administration of personnel in the FBI. Your Social Security Account Number is requested under the authority of Executive Order 9397.

PURPOSE AND USE

The principal purpose of employment application forms is to collect information needed to determine qualifications, suitability, and availability of applicants for FBI employment and of current FBI employees for reassignment, reinstatement, transfer, or promotion. Your completed application may be used to examine, rate and/or assess your qualifications; to determine if you are entitled under certain laws and regulations such as Veterans' Preference, and restrictions based on citizenship, members of family already employed, and residence requirements; and to contact you concerning availability and/or interview. All or part of your completed FBI employment application form may be disclosed outside the FBI to:

1. Federal agencies upon request for an eligibility list of persons or individuals to consider for appointment, reassignment, reinstatement, transfer, or promotion.
2. State and local government agencies under the Intergovernment Personnel Act terms if you have expressed an interest in and availability for such employment consideration.
3. State and local government agencies under the President's Executive Program terms if you have expressed an interest in and availability for such employment consideration.
4. Federal agency investigators to determine your suitability for federal employment.
5. Federal, state, or local agencies to create other personnel records after you have been appointed.
6. To any appropriate entity responsible for investigating, prosecuting, or enforcing law, regulation, or contract, or for licensing (as to any indication of a violation of law, regulation, or contract, or of other matters bearing on licensing determinations, either on its face, or in conjunction with other information).
7. Appropriate federal, state, local, foreign or other public authority to elicit information, assistance, or cooperation in the background criminal, intelligence, or security investigation.
8. A requesting federal, state, local, foreign or other public authority to the extent the information is for employment, security, contracting, or licensing determinations by the requesting agency.
9. Federal agency selecting officials involved with internal personnel management functions.

EFFECTS OF NONDISCLOSURE

Because this employment application form requests mandatory data (qualifications and biographical information, etc.), it is in your best interest to answer all questions. Omission of an item means you might not receive full consideration for a position in which this information is needed. A false answer to a question in the employment application may be grounds for not employing you, or for dismissing you after you begin work, and may be punishable by fine or imprisonment (U.S. Code, Title 18, Section 1001). All statements are subject to investigation, including a check of your fingerprints, police records, and former employers. All information you give will be considered in reviewing your statement.

HATCH ACT REFORM PROVISION

As part of the Hatch Act Reform Amendments of 1993, codified at 5 U.S.C. 3303, the FBI is prohibited from accepting unsolicited recommendations, written or oral, from any congressional or political sources in connection with your consideration for appointment.

APPENDIX G

Applicant Background Survey (FD-804)

The Applicant Background Survey requests your name, date of birth, Social Security number, and information about your race and ethnicity, gender, and any disabilities you might have. You are required only to provide your name and date of birth and indicate the position for which you are applying. According to federal laws, listing your Social Security number and demographic data is voluntary.

The United States Code requires federal agencies to provide equal opportunities for job applicants and to carry out employment practices that are free from discrimination. The information you provide on this form is used in planning and monitoring Equal Employment Opportunity programs. The FBI uses this form to obtain demographic information in compliance with the Equal Employment Opportunity Commission's annual reporting requirements.

All applicants for internships must submit this form, while applicants for special agent and professional support positions provide this information electronically during the online application process. Information provided on the Applicant Background Survey is not used in determining basic qualifications, selecting applicants for further processing, or making appointment decisions.

FD-804

FEDERAL BUREAU OF INVESTIGATION

APPLICANT BACKGROUND SURVEY

(Please read the instructions below and read the Privacy Act
Statement on the reverse side before completing form)

Date: _____

1. Name (Last, First, MI):   Date of Birth:

---

2. Position Applied for: | 3. Social Security Number

☐☐☐ ☐☐ ☐☐☐☐

Your furnishing this information is voluntary. Please provide information on your race/ethnicity, sex, and disability status. In block 4, provide the race/ethnic code which indicates the group with which you identify yourself. Check the appropriate box in block 5, to show you sex. In block 6, enter your disability code. The codes are listed below.

---

4. Race/Ethnic Code:

☐

5. Sex:

☐ Female   ☐ Male

6. Disability Code:

☐

RACE/ETHNIC CODES

A. **American Indian or Alaskan Native** - A person having origins in any of the original peoples of North America, and who maintains cultural identification through community recognition or tribal affiliation.
B. **Asian or Pacific Islander** - A person having origins in any of the original peoples of the Far East, Southeast Asia, the Indian subcontinent, or the Pacific Islands. This area includes, for example, China, India, Japan, Korea, the Philippine Islands and Samoa.
C. **Black, Not of Hispanic Origin** - A person having origins in any of the black racial groups of Africa. Does not include persons of Mexican, Puerto Rican, Cuban, Central or South American, or other Spanish cultures or origins (See Hispanic).
D. **Hispanic** - A person having Mexican, Puerto Rican, Cuban, Central or South American, or other Spanish cultures or origins **(Regardless of Race).** Does not include persons of Portuguese culture or origin.
E. **White, Not of Hispanic Origin** - A person having origins in any of the original peoples of Europe, North Africa, or the Middle East. Does not include persons of Mexican, Puerto Rican, Cuban, Central or South American, or other Spanish cultures or origins (See Hispanic). Also includes persons not included in other categories.

DISABILITY CODES

 5 - I do not have a disability
 6 - I have a disability but it is not listed below
16 - Hearing Impairment
23 - Vision Impairment
28 - Missing Extremities
64 - Partial Paralysis

71 - Complete Paralysis
82 - Convulsive Disorder
90 - Mental Retardation
91 - Mental or Emotional Illness
92 - Severe Distortion of Limbs and/or Spine

PRIVACY ACT STATEMENT

You are requested to furnish this information under the authority of 42 U.S.C. &2000e-16, which requires that Federal employment practices be free from discrimination and provide equal employment opportunities for all. Solicitation of this information is in accordance with Department of Commerce Directive 15, "Race and Ethnic Standards for Federal Statistics and Administrative Reporting."

This information will be used in planning and monitoring equal employment opportunity programs. Your furnishing this information is voluntary. Your failure to do so will have no effect on you or on your Federal employment. If you fail to provide the information, however, then the employing agency will attempt to identify your race and national origin by visual perception.

You are requested to furnish your Social Security Number (SSN) under the authority of Executive Order 9397 (November 22, 1943). That Order requires agencies to use the SSN for the sake of economy and orderly administration in the maintenance of personnel records. Because your personnel records are identified by your SSN, your SSN is being requested on this form so that the other information you furnish on this form can be accurately included with your records. Your SSN will be used solely for that purpose. Your furnishing of your SSN is voluntary and failure to furnish it will have no effect on you; failure to provide it, however, may result in it being obtained from other agency sources.

Honors Internship Program School Certification Form (FD-956)

The Honors Internship Program School Certification Form is a simple, one-page document that is used by the FBI to verify your name; the school you are attending; your standing as a junior, senior, or graduate student; your status as a full-time student; your grade-point average; and your anticipated date of graduation. This form must be signed by the school's registrar or dean and submitted along with other application materials to the FBI by September 30.

FD-956 (9-26-02)

HONORS INTERNSHIP PROGRAM
SCHOOL CERTIFICATION FORM

Date:

This is to certify that _____ is a
(**Student's Name**)

_____ in classification and is currently attending the
(**Junior/Senior/Graduate Student**)

_____ as a full-time student.
(**Name of Institution**)

This student's **current GPA is** _____ on a 4.0 scale.

This student's **anticipated date of graduation** is _____.

School Seal

Registrar's Signature or Dean of School

1

Honors Internship Program: Program Term Acknowledgment Form

By submitting the Program Term Acknowledgment form, Honors Internship applicants provide an acknowledgment to the FBI that they are aware of the starting and ending dates of the internship and of the requirement to complete the program from start to finish. In other words, the Program Term Acknowledgment form is used by the FBI to obtain a written commitment from each applicant that they will not arrive for the internship after the first Monday in June or depart the internship prior to the second Friday in August. This form must be signed by the applicant and a representative of the FBI field office that processes the application.

HONORS INTERNSHIP PROGRAM
PROGRAM TERM ACKNOWLEDGMENT

This acknowledges that I,_____, applicant
                                                    (Printed Name)

for the Federal Bureau of Investigation Honors Internship Program (HIP),

was advised by_____,_____ , of
                                    (Printed Name)   **(Title)**

the _____ Office that the internship will begin the first
                          (Field Office Name)

Monday in June, and conclude the second Friday in August. I have also been advised

that as a condition for successful completion of the HIP, I will be required to complete

the program.

_____   _____
        (Signature of Applicant)   **(Date)**

_____   _____
      (Signature of FBI Personnel)   **(Date)**

1

APPENDIX J

FBI Field Offices and Resident Agencies

Alabama

Birmingham Field Office

FBI Birmingham Division
1000 18th Street North
Birmingham, AL 35203
(205) 326-6166
http://birmingham.fbi.gov/

Resident Agencies of the Birmingham Field Office

Florence, AL

Gadsden, AL

Huntsville, AL

Tuscaloosa, AL

Mobile Field Office

FBI Mobile Division
200 North Royal Street
Mobile, AL 36602
(251) 438-3674
http://mobile.fbi.gov/

Resident Agencies of the Mobile Field Office

Dothan, AL

Mobile, AL

Monroeville, AL

Montgomery, AL

Opelika, AL

Selma, AL

Alaska

Anchorage Field Office

FBI Anchorage Division
101 East Sixth Avenue
Anchorage, AK 99501
(907) 276-4441
http://anchorage.fbi.gov/

Resident Agencies of the Anchorage Field Office

Fairbanks, AK

Juneau, AK

Arizona
Phoenix Field Office

FBI Phoenix Division
Suite 400
201 East Indianola Avenue
Phoenix, AZ 85012
(602) 279-5511
http://phoenix.fbi.gov/

Resident Agencies of the Phoenix Field Office

Flagstaff, AZ	Gallup, NM
Lake Havasu, AZ	Lakeside, AZ
Sierra Vista, AZ	Tucson, AZ
Yuma, AZ	

Both the Phoenix and the Albuquerque field offices have agents working from the Gallup resident agency.

Arkansas
Little Rock Field Office

FBI Little Rock Division
24 Shackleford W. Blvd.
Little Rock, AR 72211
(501) 221-9100
http://littlerock.fbi.gov/

Resident Agencies of the Little Rock Field Office

El Dorado, AR	Fayetteville, AR
Fort Smith, AR	Hot Springs, AR
Jonesboro, AR	Marion, AR
Pine Bluff, AR	Texarkana, AR

California
Los Angeles Field Office

FBI Los Angeles Division
Federal Building—Suite 1700
11000 Wilshire Boulevard
Los Angeles, CA 90024
(310) 477-6565
http://losangeles.fbi.gov/

Resident Agencies of the Los Angeles Field Office

Lancaster, CA	LAX Airport
Long Beach, CA	Palm Springs, CA
Riverside, CA	Santa Ana, CA
Santa Maria, CA	Ventura, CA
Victorville, CA	West Covina, CA

Sacramento Field Office

FBI Sacramento Division
4500 Orange Grove Avenue
Sacramento, CA 95841
(916) 481-9110
http://sacramento.fbi.gov/

Resident Agencies of the Sacramento Field Office

Bakersfield, CA	Chico, CA
Fairfield, CA	Fresno, CA
Modesto, CA	Redding, CA
South Lake Tahoe, CA	Stockton, CA

San Diego Field Office

FBI San Diego Division
Federal Office Building
9797 Aero Drive
San Diego, CA 92123
(858) 565-1255
http://sandiego.fbi.gov/

Resident Agencies of the San Diego Field Office

Carlsbad, CA	Imperial, CA

San Francisco Field Office

FBI San Francisco Division
13th Floor
450 Golden Gate Avenue
San Francisco, CA 94102
(415) 553-7400
http://sanfrancisco.fbi.gov/

Resident Agencies of the San Francisco Field Office

Concord, CA	Hayward, CA
Monterey Bay, CA	Oakland, CA
Palo Alto, CA	San Jose, CA
San Rafael, CA	Santa Rosa, CA

Colorado
Denver Field Office

FBI Denver Division
Federal Building—Room 1823
1961 Stout Street—18th Floor
Denver, CO 80294
(303) 629-7171
http://denver.fbi.gov/

Colorado Resident Agencies of the Denver Field Office

Boulder, CO	Colorado Springs, CO
Durango, CO	Fort Collins, CO
Glenwood Springs, CO	Grand Junction, CO
Pueblo, CO	

Wyoming is under the jurisdiction of the Denver Field Office (except for Yellowstone National Park, which is covered by the Salt Lake City Field Office).

Connecticut
New Haven Field Office

FBI New Haven Division
600 State Street
New Haven, CT 06511
(203) 777-6311
http://newhaven.fbi.gov/

Resident Agencies of the New Haven Field Office

Bridgeport, CT	Meriden, CT

Delaware

Delaware is under the jurisdiction of the Baltimore Field Office.

Baltimore Field Office

FBI Baltimore Division
2600 Lord Baltimore
Baltimore, MD 21244
(410) 265-8080
http://baltimore.fbi.gov/

Delaware Resident Agencies of the Baltimore Field Office

Dover, DE	Wilmington, DE

District of Columbia
Washington Metro Field Office

Federal Bureau of Investigation
Washington Metro Field Office
601 Fourth Street Northwest
Washington, DC 20535
(202) 278-2000
http://washingtondc.fbi.gov/

Resident Agencies of the Washington Metro Field Office

Manassas, VA

Florida
Jacksonville Field Office

FBI Jacksonville Division
Suite 200
7820 Arlington Expressway
Jacksonville, FL 32211
(904) 721-1211
http://jacksonville.fbi.gov/

Resident Agencies of the Jacksonville Field Office

Daytona Beach, FL	Fort Walton Beach, FL
Gainesville, FL	Ocala, FL
Panama City, FL	Pensacola, FL
Tallahassee, FL	

Miami Field Office

FBI Miami Division
16320 Northwest Second Avenue
North Miami Beach, FL 33169
(305) 944-9101
http://miami.fbi.gov/

Resident Agencies of the Miami Field Office

Fort Pierce, FL	Homestead, FL
Key West, FL	West Palm Beach, FL

Tampa Field Office

FBI Tampa Division
5525 W. Gray St.
Tampa, FL 33609
(813) 253-1000
http://tampa.fbi.gov/

Resident Agencies of the Tampa Field Office

Clearwater, FL	Fort Myers, FL
Lakeland, FL	Melbourne, FL
Naples, FL	Orlando, FL
Sarasota, FL	Wesley Chapel, FL

Georgia
Atlanta Field Office

FBI Atlanta Division
Suite 400
2635 Century Parkway Northeast
Atlanta, GA 30345
(404) 679-9000
http://atlanta.fbi.gov/

Resident Agencies of the Atlanta Field Office

Albany, GA	Athens, GA
Augusta, GA	Brunswick, GA
Columbus, GA	Dublin, GA
Gainesville, GA	Macon, GA
Rome, GA	Rossville, GA
Savannah, GA	Statesboro, GA
Thomasville, GA	Valdosta, GA

Hawaii

Honolulu Field Office

FBI Honolulu Division
Room 4-230
300 Ala Moana Boulevard
Honolulu, HI 96850
(808) 566-4300
http://honolulu.fbi.gov/

Resident Agencies of the Honolulu Field Office

Kailua-Kona, HI	Maite, Guam
Pago Pago, American Samoa	Saipan, MP
Wailuku, HI	

Idaho

Idaho is under the jurisdiction of the Salt Lake City Field Office.

Salt Lake City Field Office

FBI Salt Lake City Division
257 Towers Building #1200
257 East—200 South
Salt Lake City, UT 84111
(801) 579-1400
http://saltlakecity.fbi.gov/

Idaho Resident Agencies of the Salt Lake City Field Office

Boise, ID	Coeur d'Alene, ID
Idaho Falls, ID	Lewiston, ID
Pocatello, ID	Twin Falls, ID

Illinois

The Moline Resident Agency is under the jurisdiction of the Omaha Field
Office.

Chicago Field Office

2111 W. Roosevelt Rd.
Chicago, IL 60608
(312) 421-6700
http://chicago.fbi.gov/

Resident Agencies of the Chicago Field Office

Lisle, IL   Orland Park, IL
Rockford, IL   Rolling Meadows, IL

Springfield Field Office

FBI Springfield Division
900 E. Linton Ave.
Springfield, IL 62703
(217) 522-9675
http://springfield.fbi.gov/

Resident Agencies of the Springfield Field Office

Carbondale, IL   Champaign, IL
Decatur, IL   Effingham, IL
Fairview Heights, IL   Normal, IL
Peoria, IL

Indiana

Indianapolis Field Office

FBI Indianapolis Division
Federal Building—Room 679
575 North Pennsylvania Street
Indianapolis, IN 46204
(317) 639-3301
http://indianapolis.fbi.gov/

Resident Agencies of the Indianapolis Field Office

Bloomington, IN   Evansville, IN
Fort Wayne, IN   Lafayette, IN
Merrillville, IN   Muncie, IN
New Albany, IN   South Bend, IN
Terre Haute, IN

Iowa

Iowa is under the jurisdiction of the Omaha Field Office.

Omaha Field Office

FBI Omaha Division
10755 Burt Street
Omaha, NE 68114
(402) 493-8688
http://omaha.fbi.gov/

Iowa Resident Agencies of the Omaha Field Office

Cedar Rapids, IA   Des Moines, IA

Sioux City, IA   Waterloo, IA

Kansas

Kansas is under the jurisdiction of the Kansas City (MO) Field Office.

Kansas City Field Office

FBI Kansas City Division
1300 Summit
Kansas City, MO 64105
(816) 512-8200
http://kansascity.fbi.gov/

Kansas Resident Agencies of the Kansas City Field Office

Garden City, KS   Topeka, KS

Wichita, KS

Kentucky

Louisville Field Office

FBI Louisville Division
12401 Sycamore Station Place
Louisville, KY 40299
(502) 240-5944
http://louisville.fbi.gov/

Resident Agencies of the Louisville Field Office

Ashland, KY   Bowling Green, KY

Covington, KY   Elizabethtown, KY

Frankfort, KY   Hopkinsville, KY

Lexington, KY   London, KY

Owensboro, KY   Paducah, KY

Pikeville, KY

Louisiana

New Orleans Field Office

FBI New Orleans Division
2901 Leon C. Simon Drive
New Orleans, LA 70126
(504) 816-3000
http://neworleans.fbi.gov/

Resident Agencies of the New Orleans Field Office

Alexandria, LA   Baton Rouge, LA

Lafayette, LA   Lake Charles, LA

Monroe, LA   Shreveport, LA

Maine

Maine is under the jurisdiction of the Boston Field Office.

Boston Field Office

FBI Boston Division
One Center Plaza—Suite 600
Boston, MA 02108
(617) 742-5533
http://boston.fbi.gov/

Maine Resident Agencies of the Boston Field Office

Augusta, ME   Bangor, ME
Portland, ME

Maryland

Baltimore Field Office

FBI Baltimore Division
2600 Lord Baltimore
Baltimore, MD 21244
(410) 265-8080
http://baltimore.fbi.gov/

Maryland Resident Agencies of the Baltimore Field Office

Annapolis, MD   Bel Air, MD
Calverton, MD   Frederick, MD
Salisbury, MD

Delaware is under the jurisdiction of the Baltimore Field Office.

Massachusetts

Boston Field Office

FBI Boston Division
One Center Plaza—Suite 600
Boston, MA 02108
(617) 742-5533
http://boston.fbi.gov/

Massachusetts Resident Agencies of the Boston Field Office

Hudson, MA   Lakeville, MA
Lowell, MA   Springfield, MA

New Hampshire, Maine, and Rhode Island are under the jurisdiction of the
Boston Field Office.

Michigan
Detroit Field Office

FBI Detroit Division
26th Floor
McNamara Federal Building
477 Michigan Avenue
Detroit, MI 48226
(313) 965-2323
http://detroit.fbi.gov/

Resident Agencies of the Detroit Field Office

Ann Arbor, MI	Bay City, MI
Clinton Township, MI	East Lansing, MI
Flint, MI	Grand Rapids, MI
Kalamazoo, MI	Marquette, MI
St. Joseph, MI	Traverse City, MI
Troy, MI	

Minnesota
Minneapolis Field Office

FBI Minneapolis Division
Suite 1100
111 Washington Avenue South
Minneapolis, MN 55401
(612) 376-3200
http://minneapolis.fbi.gov/

Minnesota Resident Agencies of the Minneapolis Field Office

Bemidji, MN	Duluth, MN
Mankato, MN	Rochester, MN
St. Cloud, MN	St. Paul, MN

North Dakota and South Dakota are under the jurisdiction of the Minneapolis Field Office.

Mississippi
Jackson Field Office

FBI Jackson Division
Federal Building—Room 1553
100 West Capitol Street
Jackson, MS 39269
(601) 948-5000
http://jackson.fbi.gov/

Resident Agencies of the Jackson Field Office

Columbus, MS	Greenville, MS
Gulfport, MS	Hattiesburg, MS

Meridian, MS

Oxford, MS

Pascagoula, MS

Southaven, MS

Tupelo, MS

Missouri
Kansas City Field Office

FBI Kansas City Division
1300 Summit
Kansas City, MO 64105
(816) 512-8200
http://kansascity.fbi.gov/

Missouri Resident Agencies of the Kansas City Field Office

Jefferson City, MO

Joplin, MO

St. Joseph, MO

Springfield, MO

Kansas is under the jurisdiction of the Kansas City (MO) Field Office.

St. Louis Field Office

FBI St. Louis Division
2222 Market Street
St. Louis, MO 63103
(314) 231-4324
http://stlouis.fbi.gov/

Resident Agencies of the St. Louis Field Office

Cape Girardeau, MO

Kirksville, MO

Rolla, MO

St. Peters, MO

Montana

Montana is under the jurisdiction of the Salt Lake City Field Office.

Salt Lake City Field Office

FBI Salt Lake City Division
257 Towers Building #1200
257 East—200 South
Salt Lake City, UT 84111
(801) 579-1400
http://saltlakecity.fbi.gov/

Montana Resident Agencies of the Salt Lake City Field Office

Billings, MT

Bozeman, MT

Browning, MT

Glasgow, MT

Great Falls, MT

Havre, MT

Helena, MT

Kalispell, MT

Missoula, MT

Nebraska

Omaha Field Office

FBI Omaha Division
10755 Burt Street
Omaha, NE 68114
(402) 493-8688
http://omaha.fbi.gov/

Nebraska Resident Agencies of the Omaha Field Office

Grand Island, NE   Lincoln, NE

North Platte, NE

Iowa is under the jurisdiction of the Omaha Field Office.

Nevada

Las Vegas Field Office

FBI Las Vegas Division
1787 W. Lake Mead Blvd.
Las Vegas, NV 89106
(702) 385-1281
http://lasvegas.fbi.gov/

Resident Agencies of the Las Vegas Field Office

Elko, NV   Reno, NV

New Hampshire

New Hampshire is under the jurisdiction of the Boston Field Office.

Boston Field Office

FBI Boston Division
One Center Plaza—Suite 600
Boston, MA 02108
(617) 742-5533
http://boston.fbi.gov/

New Hampshire Resident Agencies of the Boston Field Office

Bedford, NH   Portsmouth, NH

New Jersey

Newark Field Office

FBI Newark Division
11 Centre Place
Newark, NJ 07102
(973) 792-3000
http://newark.fbi.gov/

Resident Agencies of the Newark Field Office

Atlantic City, NJ

Franklin Township, NJ

Garret Mountain, NJ

Red Bank, NJ

Trenton, NJ

The Newark Field Office has jurisdiction over all counties in New Jersey except Camden, Gloucester, and Salem, which fall under the Philadelphia (PA) Field Office.

New Mexico
Albuquerque Field Office

FBI Albuquerque Division
4200 Luecking Park Avenue NE
Albuquerque, NM 87107
(505) 889-1300
http://albuquerque.fbi.gov/

Resident Agencies of the Albuquerque Field Office

Farmington, NM

Gallup, NM

Las Cruces, NM

Roswell, NM

Santa Fe, NM

Both the Phoenix and the Albuquerque Field Offices have agents working from the Gallup resident agency.

New York
Albany Field Office

FBI Albany Division
200 McCarty Avenue
Albany, NY 12209
(518) 465-7551
http://albany.fbi.gov/

New York Resident Agencies of the Albany Field Office

Binghamton, NY

Ithaca, NY

Kingston, NY

Plattsburgh, NY

Syracuse, NY

Utica, NY

Vermont is under the jurisdiction of the Albany Field Office.

Buffalo Field Office

FBI Buffalo Division
One FBI Plaza
Buffalo, NY 14202
(716) 856-7800
http://buffalo.fbi.gov/

Resident Agencies of the Buffalo Field Office

Elmira, NY   Jamestown, NY

Rochester, NY

New York Field Office

FBI New York Division
26 Federal Plaza—23rd Floor
New York, NY 10278
(212) 384-1000
http://newyork.fbi.gov/

Resident Agencies of the New York Field Office

Goshen, NY   JFK International Airport, NY

Kew Gardens, NY   Melville, NY

White Plains, NY

North Carolina

Charlotte Field Office

FBI Charlotte Division
Wachovia Building—Suite 900
400 South Tyron Street
Charlotte, NC 28285
(704) 377-9200
http://charlotte.fbi.gov/

Resident Agencies of the Charlotte Field Office

Asheville, NC   Elizabeth City, NC

Fayetteville, NC   Greensboro, NC

Greenville, NC   Hickory, NC

Raleigh, NC   Wilmington, NC

North Dakota

North Dakota is under the jurisdiction of the Minneapolis Field Office.

Minneapolis Field Office

FBI Minneapolis Division
Suite 1100
111 Washington Avenue South
Minneapolis, MN 55401
(612) 376-3200
http://minneapolis.fbi.gov/

North Dakota Resident Agencies of the Minneapolis Field Office

Bismarck, ND   Fargo, ND

Grand Forks, ND   Minot, ND

Ohio
Cincinnati Field Office

FBI Cincinnati Division
550 Main Street—Room 9000
Cincinnati, OH 45202
(513) 421-4310
http://cincinnati.fbi.gov/

Resident Agencies of the Cincinnati Field Office

Athens, OH	Cambridge, OH
Columbus, OH	Dayton, OH
Portsmouth, OH	

Cleveland Field Office

FBI Cleveland Division
Federal Office Building
1501 Lakeside Avenue
Cleveland, OH 44114
(216) 522-1400
http://cleveland.fbi.gov/

Resident Agencies of the Cleveland Field Office

Akron, OH	Canton, OH
Elyria, OH	Lima, OH
Mansfield, OH	Painesville, OH
Sandusky, OH	Toledo, OH
Youngstown, OH	

Oklahoma
Oklahoma City Field Office

FBI Oklahoma City Division
3301 West Memorial Drive
Oklahoma City, OK 73134
(405) 290-7770
http://oklahomacity.fbi.gov/

Resident Agencies of the Oklahoma City Field Office

Ardmore, OK	Durant, OK
Elk City, OK	Enid, OK
Lawton, OK	McAlester, OK
Muskogee, OK	Norman, OK
Stillwater, OK	Tulsa, OK
Vinita, OK	Woodward, OK

Oregon
Portland Field Office

FBI Portland Division
Crown Plaza Building—Suite 400
1500 Southwest 1st Avenue
Portland, OR 97201
(503) 224-4181
http://portland.fbi.gov/

Resident Agencies of the Portland Field Office

Bend, OR	Eugene, OR
Medford, OR	Pendleton, OR
Salem, OR	

Pennsylvania
Philadelphia Field Office

FBI Philadelphia Division
William Green Jr. Federal Building
600 Arch Street—8th Floor
Philadelphia, PA 19106
(215) 418-4000
http://philadelphia.fbi.gov/

Resident Agencies of the Philadelphia Field Office

Allentown, PA	Cherry Hill, NJ
Ft. Washington, PA	Harrisburg, PA
Newtown Square, PA	Scranton, PA
State College, PA	Williamsport, PA

The Philadelphia Field Office also has jurisdiction over three counties in New Jersey. These counties are covered by the Cherry Hill Resident Agency of the Philadelphia Field Office.

Pittsburgh Field Office

FBI Pittsburgh Division
3311 East Carson Street
Pittsburgh, PA 15203
(412) 432-4000
http://pittsburgh.fbi.gov/

Pennsylvania Resident Agencies of the Pittsburgh Field Office

Charleroi, PA	Cranberry TWP, PA
Elton, PA	Erie, PA
New Castle, PA	

West Virginia is under the jurisdiction of the Pittsburgh Field Office.

Puerto Rico
San Juan Field Office

FBI San Juan Division
U.S. Federal Building—Room 526
150 Carlos Chardon Avenue
Hato Rey
San Juan, PR 00918
(787) 754-6000
http://sanjuan.fbi.gov/

Resident Agencies of the San Juan Field Office

Aguadilla, PR	Fajardo, PR
Ponce, PR	St. Croix, USVI
St. Thomas, USVI	

Rhode Island

Rhode Island is under the jurisdiction of the Boston Field Office.

Boston Field Office

FBI Boston Division
One Center Plaza—Suite 600
Boston, MA 02108
(617) 742-5533
http://boston.fbi.gov/

Rhode Island Resident Agencies of the Boston Field Office

Providence, RI

South Carolina
Columbia Field Office

FBI Columbia Division
151 Westpark Boulevard
Columbia, SC 29210
(803) 551-4200
http://columbia.fbi.gov/

Resident Agencies of the Columbia Field Office

Aiken, SC	Bluffton, SC
Charleston, SC	Florence, SC
Greenville, SC	Myrtle Beach, SC
Rock Hill, SC	Spartanburg, SC

South Dakota

South Dakota is under the jurisdiction of the Minneapolis Field Office.

Minneapolis Field Office

FBI Minneapolis Division
Suite 1100
111 Washington Avenue South
Minneapolis, MN 55401
(612) 376-3200
http://minneapolis.fbi.gov/

South Dakota Resident Agencies of the Minneapolis Field Office

Aberdeen, SD   Pierre, SD

Rapid City, SD   Sioux Falls, SD

Tennessee

Knoxville Field Office

FBI Knoxville Division
Duncan Federal Building #600
710 Locust Street
Knoxville, TN 37902
(865) 544-0751
http://knoxville.fbi.gov/

Resident Agencies of the Knoxville Field Office

Chattanooga, TN   Cleveland, TN

Johnson City, TN   Oak Ridge, TN

Tullahoma, TN

Memphis Field Office

FBI Memphis Division
Eagle Crest Building #3000
225 North Humphreys Boulevard
Memphis, TN 38120
(901) 747-4300
http://memphis.fbi.gov/

Resident Agencies of the Memphis Field Office

Clarksville, TN   Columbia, TN

Cookeville, TN   Jackson, TN

Nashville, TN

Texas

Dallas Field Office

FBI Dallas Division
One Justice Way
Dallas, TX 75220
(972) 559-5000
http://dallas.fbi.gov/

Resident Agencies of the Dallas Field Office

Abilene, TX	Amarillo, TX
DFW Airport, TX	Fort Worth, TX
Frisco, TX	Lubbock, TX
Lufkin, TX	San Angelo, TX
Sherman, TX	Texarkana, TX
Tyler, TX	Wichita Falls, TX

El Paso Field Office

FBI El Paso Division
Suite 3000
660 South Mesa Hills Drive
El Paso, TX 79912
(915) 832-5000
http://elpaso.fbi.gov/

Resident Agencies of the El Paso Field Office

Midland, TX

Houston Field Office

FBI Houston Division
2500 East T.C. Jester
Houston, TX 77008
(713) 693-5000
http://houston.fbi.gov/

Resident Agencies of the Houston Field Office

Beaumont, TX	Bryan, TX
Conroe, TX	Corpus Christi, TX
Texas City, TX	Victoria, TX

San Antonio Field Office

FBI San Antonio Division
5740 University Heights Blvd.
San Antonio, TX 78249
(210) 225-6741
http://sanantonio.fbi.gov/

Resident Agencies of the San Antonio Field Office

Austin, TX	Brownsville, TX
Del Rio, TX	Laredo, TX
McAllen, TX	Waco, TX

Utah
Salt Lake City Field Office

FBI Salt Lake City Division
257 Towers Building #1200
257 East—200 South
Salt Lake City, UT 84111
(801) 579-1400
http://saltlakecity.fbi.gov/

Utah Resident Agencies of the Salt Lake City Field Office

Monticello, UT

Provo, UT

Vernal, UT

Ogden, UT

St. George, UT

Montana and Yellowstone National Park (WY) are under the jurisdiction of the Salt Lake City Field Office.

Vermont

Vermont is under the jurisdiction of the Albany Field Office.

Albany Field Office

FBI Albany Division
200 McCarty Avenue
Albany, NY 12209
(518) 465-7551
http://albany.fbi.gov/

Vermont Resident Agencies of the Albany Field Office

Burlington, VT

Rutland, VT

Virginia
Norfolk Field Office

FBI Norfolk Division
150 Corporate Boulevard
Norfolk, VA 23502
(757) 455-0100
http://norfolk.fbi.gov/

Resident Agencies of the Norfolk Field Office

Hampton, VA

Richmond Field Office

FBI Richmond Division
1970 East Parham Road
Richmond, VA 23228
(804) 261-1044
http://richmond.fbi.gov/

Resident Agencies of the Richmond Field Office

Bristol, VA	Charlottesville, VA
Fredericksburg, VA	Lynchburg, VA
Roanoke, VA	Winchester, VA

Washington
Seattle Field Office

FBI Seattle Division
1110 Third Avenue
Seattle, WA 98101
(206) 622-0460
http://seattle.fbi.gov/

Resident Agencies of the Seattle Field Office

Bellingham, WA	Everett, WA
Olympia, WA	Richland, WA
Silverdale, WA	Spokane, WA
Tacoma, WA	Vancouver, WA
Wenatchee, WA	Yakima, WA

West Virginia

West Virginia is under the jurisdiction of the Pittsburgh Field Office.

Pittsburgh Field Office

FBI Pittsburgh Division
3311 East Carson Street
Pittsburgh, PA 15203
(412) 432-4000
http://pittsburgh.fbi.gov/

West Virginia Resident Agencies of the Pittsburgh Field Office

Beckley, WV	Charleston, WV
Clarksburg, WV	Huntington, WV
Martinsburg, WV	Wheeling, WV

Wisconsin
Milwaukee Field Office

FBI Milwaukee Division
330 East Kilbourn Avenue #600
Milwaukee, WI 53202
(414) 276-4684
http://milwaukee.fbi.gov/

Resident Agencies of the Milwaukee Field Office

Eau Claire, WI	Green Bay, WI
La Crosse, WI	Madison, WI
Pleasant Prairie, WI	Wausau, WI

Wyoming

Wyoming is under the jurisdiction of the Denver Field Office (except for Yellowstone National Park, which is covered by the Salt Lake City Field Office).

Denver Field Office

FBI Denver Division
Federal Building—Room 1823
1961 Stout Street—18th Floor
Denver, CO 80294
(303) 629-7171
http://denver.fbi.gov/

Wyoming Resident Agencies of the Denver Field Office

Casper, WY	Cheyenne, WY
Jackson Hole, WY	Lander, WY

APPENDIX K

Personnel Consent to Release Information (FD-979)

Prior to the background investigation, all applicants for FBI employment and internships must submit the Personnel Consent to Release Information form. This one-page form authorizes the Bureau to obtain information from academic institutions, law enforcement agencies, courts, other government agencies, employers, credit reporting agencies, and others. The FBI uses data collected from these and other organizations to determine your suitability for employment and eligibility for access to classified information.

FD-979 (9-9-04)

FBI File Number:

_____ - ____ - _____

Personnel Consent to Release Information

To Whom It May Concern:

I hereby give consent to any authorized representative of the Federal Bureau of Investigation to obtain any information in your files pertaining to my academic, achievement, athletic, attendance, credit (including credit card and payment device numbers), disciplinary, employment, law enforcement (including, but not limited to, any record of charge, prosecution, or conviction for civil or criminal offenses), military, or professional license records (including any grievance records). I hereby direct each entity to which this form is presented to release such information upon request of the authorized recipient as described above, regardless of any other agreement or direction I may have made.

This consent is executed with full knowledge and understanding that the information is for the official use of the Federal Bureau of Investigation in connection with its determination of my suitability for employment and/or eligibility for new or continued access to classified information. Consent is granted for the Federal Bureau of Investigation to furnish such information as is described above to third parties in the course of fulfilling its official responsibilities.

Copies of this consent that show my signature are as valid as the original signed by me. This consent is valid until the termination of (i) my application for access to classified information or (ii) my affiliation with the Federal Bureau of Investigation, whichever is later.

Signature (sign in ink)	Full Name (type or print clearly)	Date Signed
Other Names Used		Social Security Account No.
Signature of Parent or Guardian (if required)	Place of Birth	Date of Birth
Signature of Witness	Name & Title of Witness	

PRIVACY ACT STATEMENT

Authority: The collection of information requested by this form is authorized under Executive Order 10450, Security Requirements for Government Employees; Executive Order 12968, Access to Classified Information; and the Fair Credit Reporting Act, 15 U.S.C. §§1681 et seq. We are requesting your Social Security Account Number (SSAN) under Executive Order 9397, Numbering System for Federal Accounts Relating to Individual Persons. Providing requested information is voluntary; however, failure to furnish the requested information and consent will likely affect your eligibility for new or continued employment and/or access to classified information.

Principal Purpose: The information will be used principally to obtain such academic, achievement, athletic, attendance, credit, disciplinary, educational, employment, law enforcement, military, and professional license records as may be necessary to determine your suitability for employment and/or eligibility for new or continued access to classified information. Your SSAN identifies you throughout your affiliation with the U.S. Government and in most of the above-listed transactions. We will use your SSAN to accurately identify your records and to process investigations, inquiries, and/or determinations related to this consent.

Routine Uses: In addition to disclosures within the Department of Justice on a need-to-know basis, information reported on this form may be disclosed in accordance with all applicable routine uses as may be published at any time in the Federal Register, including all routine uses for the FBI Central Records System. These routine uses include the following disclosures: to potential sources in order to locate, seek, and obtain information or records pertaining to you; to any appropriate governmental authorities responsible for civil or criminal law enforcement, counterintelligence, or security matters to which the information may be relevant; to non-FBI employees performing Federal assignments; to courts or adjudicative bodies when the FBI considers it has an interest in the proceedings; or as otherwise mandated by law, treaty, or Executive Order.

FBI/DOJ

APPENDIX L

Disclosure and Authorization Pertaining to Consumer Reports (DOJ-555)

As an applicant for FBI employment, you must be willing to authorize credit reporting agencies to release information about you, such as your credit history, monetary judgments, tax liens, employment held, demographic information, and other data. The FBI uses data obtained from credit reporting agencies to determine your suitability for employment and eligibility for access to classified information. You must submit this one-page form prior to the background investigation.

United States Department of Justice

Disclosure and Authorization
Pertaining to Consumer Reports
Pursuant to the Fair Credit Reporting Act
(Title 15, U.S. Code, Section 1681)

This is a release for the Department of Justice to obtain one or more consumer/credit reports

about you in connection with your application for Federal employment, during the course of your

Federal employment (including employment under contract), and/or in connection with your

security clearance or your access to classified information. One or more reports about you may

be obtained for purposes of evaluating your fitness for employment, promotion, reassignment,

retention, access to classified information, or other employment purposes.

I, _____, hereby authorize the Department of

Justice to obtain, and I further instruct any consumer/credit reporting agency to release to DOJ,

any such report(s) for the above purposes.

_____
Signature

_____
Date

_____
Social Security Number

_____
Current Organization Assigned

DOJ-555
Revised Dec. 2004
Security and Emergency Planning Staff

INDEX

I

N

O

Q

R

S